Adobe·

After Effects· CS4

STUDIO TECHNIQUES

Mark Christiansen

Adobe

Adobe® After Effects® CS4 Visual Effects and Compositing Studio Techniques

Mark Christiansen

This Adobe Press book is published by Peachpit.
For information on Adobe Press books, contact:

Peachpit
1249 Eighth Street
Berkeley, CA 94710
(510) 524-2178
Fax: (510) 524-2221

To report errors, please send a note to errata@peachpit.com

Peachpit is a division of Pearson Education
Copyright © 2009 Mark Christiansen
For the latest on Adobe Press books, go to www.adobepress.com

Project Editor: Karyn Johnson
Development and Copy Editor: Linda Laflamme
Production Editor: Becky Winter
Technical Editor: Alex Czetwertynski
Proofreader: Rebecca Rider
Composition: David Van Ness
Indexer: Karin Arrigoni
Cover design: Peachpit Press/Charlene Will
Cover illustration: Regina Cleveland

ISBN 13: 978-0-321-59201-9
ISBN 10:   0-321-59201-8

9 8 7 6 5 4 3 2 1

Printed and bound in the United States of America

Contents

Foreword   xi

Introduction   xix

Section I   Working Foundations   1

Chapter 1   Composite in After Effects   3
      Workspaces and Panels   4
      Order Reduces Effort   8
      Project, Footage, and Composition Settings   15
      Previews and View Panels   24
      Effects & Presets   33
      Output via the Render Queue   33
      Study a Shot like an Effects Artist   37

Chapter 2   The Timeline   39
      Organization   40
      Keyframes and the Graph Editor   46
      Über-duper   58
      Spatial Offsets   61
      Motion Blur   64
      Manipulate Time   68
      Conclusion   75

Chapter 3   Selections: The Key to Compositing   77
      Selection Types   79
      Compositing: Science and Nature   83
      Alpha Channels and Premultiplication   87
      Masks   91
      Combine Selections   95
      Masks in Motion   98
      Blending Modes: Compositing Beyond Selections   100
      Track Mattes   106
      Conclusion   108

Chapter 4   Optimize the Pipeline   109
      Multiple Compositions, Multiple Projects   110
      Adjustment and Guide Layers   119
      Render Pipeline   122
      Project Optimization   129
      Conclusion   132

Section II	Effects Compositing Essentials	133
Chapter 5	Color Correction	135
	Optimized Levels	137
	Color Matching	161
	Conclusion	174
Chapter 6	Color Keying	175
	Good Habits and Best Practices	176
	Linear Keyers and Hi-Con Mattes	179
	Blue and Green Screen Keys	184
	Get the Best Out of Keylight	193
	Beyond Keylight: Better Mattes	201
	Conclusion	209
Chapter 7	Rotoscoping and Paint	211
	Articulated Mattes	213
	Beyond Built-in Limitations	216
	Morph	219
	Puppet	225
	Paint and Cloning	229
	Conclusion	235
Chapter 8	Effective Motion Tracking	237
	Point Tracking Essentials	239
	Match Multiple Objects	249
	Stabilize a Moving Shot	252
	Incorporate MochaAE	255
	Use Tracking with Expressions	261
	Import 3D Tracking Data	263
	Conclusion	268
Chapter 9	The Camera and Optics	269
	Cameras: Virtual and Real	271
	Storytelling and the Camera	284
	Camera Blur	290
	The Role of Grain	295
	Film and Video Looks	301
	Conclusion	308
Chapter 10	Expressions	309
	What Expressions Are	310
	Creating Expressions	312
	The Language of Expressions	314
	Linking an Effect Parameter to a Property	314

	Using a Layer's Index	316
	Looping Keyframes	318
	Using Markers	320
	Time Remapping Expressions	324
	Layer Space Transforms	328
	Color Sampling and Conversion	337
	Extra Credit	339
	Conclusion	344
Chapter 11	**32-Bit HDR Compositing and Color Management**	**345**
	Color Management: Why Bother?	347
	Film and Dynamic Range	360
	Linear Floating Point HDR	369
	Conclusion	378
Section III	**Creative Explorations**	**379**
Chapter 12	Light	381
	Source and Direction	382
	Color Looks	386
	Source, Reflection, and Shadow	390
	Multipass 3D Compositing	399
Chapter 13	Climate and the Environment	405
	Particulate Matter	406
	Sky Replacement	410
	Fog, Smoke, and Mist	413
	Billowing Smoke	417
	Wind	422
	Precipitation	423
Chapter 14	Pyrotechnics: Heat, Fire, Explosions	429
	Firearms	430
	Energy Effects	435
	Heat Distortion	439
	Fire	442
	Explosions	446
	In a Blaze of Glory	447
Index		**448**

Scripting Appendix by Jeff Almasol and
After Effects JavaScript Guide by Dan Ebberts
available on the accompanying DVD-ROM

About the Author

Mark Christiansen is a San Francisco-based visual effects supervisor and creative director. He has worked with visual effects companies, including The Orphanage, on several Hollywood feature films such as *The Day After Tomorrow* and *Pirates of the Caribbean 3: At World's End*. As a director, producer, designer, and compositor/animator, he has worked on a diverse slate of commercial, music video, live event, and television documentary projects for clients as diverse as Sony, Interscope, HBO, and many of the world's best-known Silicon Valley companies. A little music video he directed and designed in After Effects was featured in the L.A. Shorts Fest.

Mark has used After Effects since version 2.0 and has worked directly with the After Effects development and marketing teams; he was once named the #1 After Effects beta tester (for version 6.0). A Contributing Editor at *DV Magazine*, he is also a founder of ProVideoCoalition. He has written three previous editions of this book as well as *After Effects 5.5 Magic* (with Nathan Moody), and has contributed to other published efforts including the Classroom in a Book. He has also created video training and for the last couple of years has been a professor at fxphd.com. He is a Phi Beta Kappa graduate of Pomona College. You can find him at flowseeker.com and christiansen.com, and on Twitter as Flowseeker.

About the Contributors

Jeff Almasol (Appendix: Scripting) is a quality engineer on the Adobe After Effects team by day and crafter of After Effects scripts at his redefinery.com site by night. His site provides numerous free scripts, reference material, and links to other scripting resources. Prior to Adobe, Jeff worked at Elastic Reality Inc. and Avid Technology on Elastic Reality, Marquee, AvidProNet, and other products; and at Profound Effects on Useful Things and Useful Assistants. You might find him talking in the third person on Twitter (redefinery) and other sites.

Dan Ebberts (Chapter 10: Expressions and After Effects Javascript Guide) is a freelance After Effects script author and animation consultant. His scripting services have been commissioned for a wide range of projects, including workflow automation and complex animation rigging. He is a frequent contributor to the various After Effects forums and has a special interest in expressions and complex algorithms. Dan is an electrical engineer by training, with a BSEE degree from the University of California, but has spent most of his career writing software. He can be reached through his web site at http://motionscript.com.

Stu Maschwitz (Foreword) is a cofounder and the CTO of The Orphanage, a San Francisco-based visual effects and film production company. Maschwitz spent four years as a visual effects artist at George Lucas's Industrial Light & Magic (ILM), working on such films as *Twister* and *Men in Black*, and went on to create the award-winning Magic Bullet software. At The Orphanage, Maschwitz has directed numerous commercials and supervised effects work on films including *Sin City* and *The Spirit*. Maschwitz is a guerilla filmmaker at heart and combined this spirit and his effects knowledge into a book: *The DV Rebel's Guide: An All-Digital Approach to Making Killer Action Movies on the Cheap* (Peachpit Press).

Acknowledgments

This book would never have come about had After Effects itself not been such a compelling tool that it was worth becoming an expert at using it. Thank you to the After Effects team for its integrity and willingness to hear criticism with equanimity, reshaping this tool so that it remains fully viable more than 15 years into its existence.

Had I not had the opportunity to work in the studio that was pushing After Effects beyond where anyone else thought it could go, The Orphanage, I would never have gained the clear picture of visual effects fundamentals that became the foundation of this book. And had Stu Maschwitz, CTO and co-founder of The Orphanage, not patiently traded a few hundred emails with me regarding the first edition of this book, it would not have been as strong an initial effort; had his support not remained in place for the re-edits, I would not have been so able to improve upon that first try. Ask anyone who is the most influential user of After Effects: It's Stu.

If on the other hand, you asked whom to go to for more expressions and scripting knowledge, you would get this edition's two new contributing authors, Dan Ebberts and Jeff Almasol. Having cited Dan's motionscript.com site for years as the place to learn about expressions, I was able to convince him to take on Chapter 10 and rewrite it from scratch; he put in a lot of effort to provide what I hope you will find a deep and inspirational treatment of the subject even if you are already familiar with it. Jeff Almasol took on the task of taking the topic of scripting, the most technical and nerdy corner of After Effects short of writing third-party effects, and making it accessible and friendly to the code-phobic. I really have to hand it to Jeff; he tackled the chapter, which is Appendix A on the disc, with real enthusiasm.

Thank you to Brendan Bolles who wrote such an effective Chapter 11 in the first edition of the book that I have still kept many of his figures, ideas, and even huge swaths of his writing intact. Congratulations to Brendan on having his EXR plug-ins officially licensed by Adobe for After Effects CS4.

Script coverage in this book is vastly increased thanks also to Lloyd Alvarez whose site aescripts.com has become a vital source for some truly fantastic scripts. He knows how to make them because he makes them for his own needs. Sean Kennedy and Charles Bordenave (nabscripts.com) offer TrackerViz, which really boosts the effectiveness of the After Effects tracker. Thanks also to Sean for offering examples from his own film projects.

In this edition there are more figure and footage contributors than ever to thank. Thanks for footage to John Flowers and Case Films, as well as Alex Lindsay and Pixel Corps; thanks also to Brandon Schilling at Kontent Films for shooting b-roll with me one afternoon. Thanks as always to Julie Hill and Artbeats, and my good friends and colleagues at fxphd.com, John Montgomery and Mike Seymour, along with the vast worldwide network of artists associated with that site from whom I've learned as I taught. Pete O'Connell contributed samples from his fantastic DVD *Advanced Rotoscoping Techniques for After Effects*, available at creativecow.com.

Members of the worldwide community of After Effects artists offered imagery for this book. Locally, I can thank partners in crime Kontent Films: Mark Decena for stills from his feature film Dopamine, Eric Escobar, author of the great PrepShootPost blog, and from the network of San Francisco independent filmmakers, Benjamin Morgan, director of Quality of Life, as well as Matt Ward. Further afield, thanks to Ross Webb at Mars Productions in Cape Town, South Africa and Luis Bustamente (4charros) in Mexico.

Clients gave me the firsthand experience that went into this book, and some were able to help me secure examples to share: Christina Crowley, President of The Kenwood Group; Michael Brynteson at Sony; Rama Dunayevich at The Orphanage; Coral Petretti at ABC Photography; David Donegan at Red Bull USA; Tim Fink of Tim Fink Events and Media; Gary Jaeger and Cameron Baxter at Core Studio; Jonathan Barson at The Foundry UK; Fred Lewis and Inhance Digital; Boeing and the Navy UCAV program.

I mined http://flickr.com/creativecommons/ for a few difficult-to-find source stills; a huge thank you to the gifted photographers who voluntarily chose to add the Creative Commons tag to their work: Micah Parker, Jorge L. Peschiera, Shuets Udono, Eric E. Yang, and Kevin Miller.

To the people at Adobe who've made After Effects what it is, in particular Dave Simons, Dan Wilk, Erica Schisler, and Steve Kilisky, and to some of the developers who've helped me understand it better over the years, including Michael Natkin and Chris Prosser. Huge thanks this time around to Todd Kopriva who personally delivered his marked-up copy of the previous edition to my office in San Francisco.

Thanks to the companies that contributed to the book's DVD: Peder Norrby, who *is* Trapcode, Russ Andersson of Andersson Technologies, Sean Safreed of Red Giant Software, Andrew Millin of ObviousFX LLC, Marco Paolini of SilhouetteFX, Pierre Jasmin and Pete Litwinowicz of RevisionFX, and Philipp Spoth of Frischluft. I don't include tools that I wouldn't endorse.

Other people who were helpful with technical details in earlier versions of this book include Bruno Nicoletti at the Foundry UK, Scott Squires (www. effectscorner.com), Tim Dobbert at The Orphanage, and Don Shay at *Cinefex Magazine*.

A huge thank you to Peachpit, who collectively show a strong commitment to producing the highest quality books, in particular Karyn Johnson who boldly stepped in and supplied blunt insight, humor, fun, vitamin C, archival footage, patience, whatever it took to keep the book on track. I trust Linda Laflamme to tell me when I'm not making sense. Alexandre Czetwertynski is a fellow artist I trust to give the book an honest technical read.

Thanks to all of the thoughtful folks who have dropped me a line at aestudiotechniques@gmail.com; your comments and questions matter.

Foreword

I can't see the point in the theatre. All that sex and violence. I get enough of that at home. Apart from the sex, of course.

> — Tony Robinson as Baldrick, *Blackadder*

Who Brings the Sex?

"Make it look real." That would seem to be the mandate of the visual effects artist. Spielberg called and he wants the world to believe, if only for 90 minutes, that dinosaurs are alive and breathing on an island off the coast of South America. Your job: make them look real. Right?

Wrong.

I am about to tell you, the visual effects artist, the most important thing you'll ever learn in this business: Making those Velociraptors (or vampires or alien robots or bursting dams) "look real" is absolutely *not* what you should be concerned with when creating a visual effects shot.

Movies are not reality. The reason we love them is that they present us with a heightened, idealized version of reality. Familiar ideas—say, a couple having an argument—but turned up to eleven: The argument takes place on the observation deck of the Empire State building, both he and she are perfectly backlit by the sun (even though they're facing each other), which is at the exact same just-about-to-set golden-hour position for the entire ten-minute conversation. The couple are really, really charming and impossibly good-looking—in fact, one of them is Meg Ryan. Before the surgery. Oh, and music is playing.

What's real about that? Nothing at all—and we love it.

Do you think director Alejandro Amenábar took Javier Aguirresarobe, cinematographer on *The Others*, aside and said, "Whatever you do, be sure to make Nicole Kidman look *real?*" Heck no. Directors say this kind of stuff to their DPs: "Make her look like a statue." "Make him look bulletproof." "Make her look like she's sculpted out of ice."

Did It Feel Just Like It Should?

Let's roll back to *Jurassic Park*. Remember how terrific the T-Rex looked when she stepped out of the paddock? Man, she looked good.

She looked *good*.

The realism of that moment certainly did come in part from the hard work of Industrial Light and Magic's fledgling computer graphics department, who developed groundbreaking technologies to bring that T-Rex to life. But mostly, that T-Rex *felt real* because she *looked good*. She was wet. It was dark. She had a big old Dean Cundey blue rim light on her coming from nowhere. In truth, you could barely see her.

But you sure could hear her. Do you think a T-Rex approaching on muddy earth would really sound like the first notes of a new THX trailer? Do you think Spielberg ever sat with sound designer Gary Rydstrom and said, "Let's go out of our way to make sure the footstep sounds are authentic?" No, he said, "Make that mofo sound like the *Titanic* just rear-ended the Hollywood Bowl" (may or may not be a direct quote).

It's the sound designer's job to create a soundscape for a movie that's emotionally true. They make things feel right even if they skip over the facts in the process. Move a gun half an inch and it sounds like a shotgun being cocked. Get hung up on? Instant dial tone. Modern computer displaying something on the screen? Of course there should be the sound of an IBM dot-matrix printer from 1978.

Sound designers don't bring facts. They bring the sex. So do cinematographers, makeup artists, wardrobe stylists, composers, set designers, casting directors, and even the practical effects department.

And yet somehow, we in the visual effects industry are often forbidden from bringing the sex. Our clients pigeonhole us into the role of the prop maker: Build me a T-Rex, and it better look real. But when it comes time to put that T-Rex on screen, we are also the cinematographer (with our CG lights), the makeup artist (with our "wet look" shader), and the practical effects crew (with our rain). And although he may forget to speak with us in the same flowery terms that he used with Dean on set, Steven wants us to make that T-Rex looks like a T-Rex should in a movie. Not just good—*impossibly* good. Unrealistically blue-rim-light-outa-nowhere good. Sexy good.

Have you ever argued with a client over aspects of an effects shot that were immutable facts? For example, you may have a client that inexplicably requested a little less motion blur on a shot, or that told you "just a little slower" for an object after you calculated its exact rate of fall? Do you ever get frustrated with clients who try to art-direct reality in this way?

Well, stop it.

Your client is a director, and it's their *job* to art-direct reality. It's not their job to know (or suggest) the various ways that it may or may not be possible to selectively reduce motion blur, but it is their job to feel it in their gut that somehow this particular moment should feel "crisper" than normal film reality. And you know what else? It's your job to predict that they might want this and even propose it. In fact, you'd better have this conversation early, so you can shoot the plate with a 45-degree shutter, that both the actors and the T-Rex might have a quarter the normal motion blur.

Was It Good for You?

The sad reality is that we, the visual effects industry, pigeonhole *ourselves* by being overly preoccupied with reality. We have no one to blame but ourselves. No one else on the film set does this. If you keep coming back to your client with defenses such as "That's how it would really look" or "That's how fast it would really fall," then not only are you going to get in some arguments that you will lose, but you're actually setting back our entire industry by perpetuating the image of visual effects artists as blind to the importance of the sex.

On the set, after take one of the spent brass shell falling to the ground, the DP would turn to the director and say,

"That felt a bit fast. Want me to do one at 48 frames?" And the director would say yes, and they'd shoot it, and then months later the editor would choose take three, which they shot at 72 frames per second "just in case." That's the filmmaking process, and when you take on the task of creating that same shot in CG, you need to represent, emulate, and embody that entire process. You're the DP, both lighting the shot and determining that it might look better overcranked. You're the editor, confirming that choice in the context of the cut. And until you show it to your client, you're the director, making sure this moment *feels* right in all of its glorious unreality.

The problem is that the damage is already done. The client has worked with enough effects people who have willingly resigned themselves to not bringing the sex that they now view all of us as geeks with computers rather than fellow filmmakers. So when you attempt to break our self-imposed mold and bring the sex to your client, you will face an uphill battle. But here's some advice to ease the process: Do it without asking. I once had a client who would pick apart every little detail of a matte painting, laying down accusations of "This doesn't look real!"—until we color corrected the shot cool, steely blue with warm highlights. Then all the talk of realism went away, and the shot got oohs and ahs.

Your client reacts to your work *emotionally*, but they critique *technically*. When they see your shot, they react with their gut. It's great, it's getting better, but there's still something not right. What they *should* do is stop there and let you figure out what's not right, but instead, they somehow feel the need to analyze their gut reaction and turn it into action items: "That highlight is too hot" or "The shadows under that left foot look too dark." In fact it would be better if they focused on vocalizing their gut reactions: "The shot feels a bit lifeless," or "The animation feels too heavy somehow." Leave the technical details to the pros.

You may think that those are the worst kind of comments, but they are the best. I've seen crews whine on about "vague" client comments like "give the shot more oomf." But trust me, this is exactly the comment you want.

Because clients are like customers at a restaurant, and you are the chef. The client probably wants to believe that "more oomf" translates into something really sophisticated, like volumetric renderings or level-set fluid dynamics, in the same way that a patron at a restaurant would hope that a critique like "this dish needs more flavor" would send the chef into a tailspin of exotic ingredients and techniques. Your client would never admit (or suggest on their own) that "oomf" is usually some combination of "cheap tricks" such as camera shake, a lens flare or two, and possibly some God rays—just like the diner would rather not know that their request for "more flavor" will probably be addressed with butter, salt, and possibly MSG.

The MSG analogy is the best: Deep down, you want to go to a Chinese restaurant that uses a little MSG but doesn't admit it. You want the cheap tricks because they work, but you'd rather not think about it. Your client wants you to use camera shake and lens flares, but *without telling them*. They'd never admit that those cheap tricks "make" a shot, so let them off the hook and do those things without being asked. They'll silently thank you for it. Bringing the sex is all about cheap tricks.

Lights On or Off?

There are some visual effects supervisors who pride themselves on being sticklers for detail. This is like being an architect whose specialty is nails. I have bad news for the "Pixel F*ckers," as this type are known: Every shot will always have something wrong with it. There will forever be something more you could add, some shortcoming that could be addressed. What makes a visual effects supervisor good at their job is knowing which of the infinitely possible tweaks are important. Anyone can nitpick. A good supe focuses the crew's efforts on the parts of the shot that impact the audience most. And this is always the sex. Audiences don't care about matte lines or mismatched black levels, soft elements or variations in grain. If they did, they wouldn't have been able to enjoy *Blade Runner* or *Back to the Future* or that one *Star Wars* movie—what was it called? Oh yeah: *Star Wars*. Audiences only care about the sex.

On a recent film I was struggling with a shot that was just kind of sitting there. It had been shot as a pick-up, and it needed some help fitting into the sequence that had been shot months earlier. I added a layer of smoke to technically match the surrounding shots. Still, the shot died on the screen. Finally, I asked my compositor to softly darken down the right half of the shot by a full stop, placing half the plate along with our CG element in a subtle shadow. Boom, the shot sang.

What I did was, strictly speaking, the job of the cinematographer, or perhaps the colorist. The colorist, the person who designs the color grading for a film, is the ultimate bringer of the sex. And color correction is the ultimate cheap trick. There's nothing fancy about what a Da Vinci 2K or an Autodesk Lustre does with color. But what a good colorist does with those basic controls is bring heaping, dripping loads of sex to the party. The problem is (and I mean *the* problem—the single biggest problem facing our industry today), the colorist gets their hands on a visual effects shot only *after it has already been approved.* In other words, the film industry is currently shooting itself in the foot (we, the visual effects artists, being that foot) by insisting that our work be approved in a sexless environment. This is about the stupidest thing ever, and until the industry works this out, you need to fight back by taking on some of the role of the colorist as you finalize your shots, just like we did when we made those matte paintings darker and bluer with warm highlights.

Filmmaking is a battleground between those who bring the sex and those who don't. The non-sex-bringing engineers at Panavision struggle to keep their lenses from flaring, while ever-sexy cinematographers fight over a limited stock of 30-year-old anamorphic lenses because they love the flares. I've seen DPs extol the unflinching sharpness of a priceless Panavision lens right before adding a smear of nose grease (yes, the stuff on your nose) to the rear element to soften up the image to taste. Right now this battle is being waged on every film in production between the visual effects department and the colorists of the world. I've heard effects artists lament that after all their hard work making something look real, a colorist then comes along and "wonks out the color." In truth, all that colorist did was bring the sex that the visual effects should have been starting to provide on their own. If what the colorist did to your shot surprised you, then you weren't thinking enough about what makes a movie a movie.

In Your Hands

You're holding a book on visual effects compositing in Adobe After Effects. There are those who question the validity of such a thing. Some perpetuate a stigma that After Effects is for low-end TV work and graphics only. To do "real" effects work, you should use a program such as Nuke or Shake. Those techy, powerful applications are good for getting shots to look technically correct, But they do not do much to help you sex them up. After Effects may not be on par with Nuke and Shake in the tech department, but it beats them handily in providing a creative environment to experiment, create, and reinvent a shot. In that way it's much more akin to the highly-respected Autodesk Flame and Inferno systems—it gives you a broad set of tools to *design* a shot, and has enough horsepower for you to finish it too. It's the best tool to master if you want to focus on the creative aspects of visual effects compositing. That's why this book is unique. Mark's given you the good stuff here, both the nitty-gritty details as well as the aerial view of extracting professional results from an application that's as maligned as it is loved. No other book combines real production experience with a deep understanding of the fundamentals, aimed at the most popular compositing package on the planet.

Bring It

One of the great matte painters of our day once told me that he spent only the first few years of his career struggling to make his work look *real*, but that he'll spend the rest of his life learning new ways of making his work look *good*. It's taken me years of effects supervising, commercial directing, photography, wandering the halls of museums, and waking up with hangovers after too much really good wine to fully comprehend the importance of those words. I can tell you that it was only after this particular matte painter made this conscious choice to focus on making things look *good*, instead of simply real, that he skyrocketed from a new hire at ILM to one of their top talents. Personally, it's only after I learned to bring the sex that I graduated from visual effects supervising to become a professional director.

So who brings the sex? The answer is simple: The people who care about it. Those who understand the glorious unreality of film and their place in the process of creating it. Be the effects artist who breaks the mold and thinks about the story more than the bit depth. Help turn the tide of self-inflicted prejudice that keeps us relegated to creating boring reality instead of glorious cinema. Secretly slip your client a cocktail of dirty tricks and fry it in more butter than they'd ever use at home.

Bring the sex.

Stu Maschwitz
San Francisco, October 2008

I

Introduction

If you aren't fired with enthusiasm, you will be fired—with enthusiasm.

—Vince Lombardi

Why This Book?

*A*dobe After Effects CS4 Visual Effects and Compositing Studio *Techniques* is about creating visual effects—the art and science of making disparate elements look like they were taken with a single camera, and of making an ordinary shot extraordinary yet believable. It goes deep into issues such as color correction and keying that are only touched on by books more focused on using After Effects for motion graphics, while leaving motion-graphics-only tools (Text, Shapes, and like) more or less alone.

This book does not shy away from strong opinions, even when they deviate from the official line. These opinions have been formed through actual work in production at a few of the finest visual effects facilities in the world, and they're valid not only for "high-end" productions but for any composited shot. Where applicable, the reasoning behind using one technique over another is provided. I aim to make you not a better button-pusher but a more effective artist and technician.

The visual effects industry is historically protective of trade secrets, often reflexively treating all production information as proprietary. Work on a major project, however, and you will soon discover that even the most complex shot is made up largely of repeatable techniques and practices; the art is in how these are applied, combined and customized, and what is added (or taken away).

Each shot is unique, and yet every shot relies on techniques that are tried and true. This book offers you as much of the latter as possible so that you can focus on the former. There's not much here in the way of step-by-step instructions; it's more important that you grasp how things work so that you can repurpose the technique for your individual shot.

This is emphatically not a book for beginners. Although the first section is designed to make sure you are making optimal use of the software, it's not an effective primer on After Effects in particular or digital video in general. If you're new to After Effects, first spend some time with its excellent documentation or check out one of the many books available to help beginners learn to use After Effects.

Some Key Steps

There are a few overall keys to your success as a compositor and visual effects artist, whether or not you work in After Effects:

▶ **Get reference.** You can't re-create what you can't clearly see. Too many artists skip this step.

▶ **Simplify.** This book is about helping you eliminate needless steps. To paraphrase Einstein, a good solution is as simple as possible, but no simpler.

▶ **Break it down.** As I said above, the most complicated shot consists of small, comprehensible steps—perhaps thousands of them—and each image consists of three or more channels each containing thousands of pixels.

▶ **Don't expect a perfect result on the first try.** My old colleague Paul Topolos (at this writing employed in the art department at Pixar) used to say that "recognizing flaws in your work doesn't mean you're a bad artist. It only means you have taste."

This is how it's done at the best studios, and even if you're not currently working at one of them, this is how you should do it, too.

Organization of this Book

Adobe After Effects CS4 Visual Effects and Compositing Studio Techniques is organized into three sections:

▶ Section I, "Working Foundations," is about the software. The goal is not to drag you through each menu and button and be a second manual, but instead to offer you tips and techniques that will help you into the coveted state of *flow* in After Effects, where you are focused entirely on the job at hand because you no longer have to think about the tools.

Don't assume that you're too advanced to at least skim this section; I guarantee there's information in there you don't already know.

▶ Section II, "Effects Compositing Essentials," focuses on the core techniques of effects compositing: color matching, keying, rotoscoping, motion tracking, and optics, as well as such advanced topics as expressions and HDR color. This is the heart of the book.

▶ Section III, "Creative Explorations," demonstrates actual shots you are likely to re-create, offering best practices for techniques every effects artist needs to know.

What you won't find in these sections are menu-by-menu descriptions of the interface or step-by-step tutorials that walk you through projects with little connection to real-world visual effects needs.

The Unique After Effects Workflow

Some users may be coming to this book unfamiliar with After Effects but experienced in other compositing software. Here's a brief overview of how the After Effects workflow is unique from every other compositing application out there. Each application is unique, and yet the main competitors to After Effects—Nuke, Shake, Flame, Fusion and Toxic, to name a few—are probably more similar to one another than any of them is to After Effects, which is in many ways a lot more like Photoshop.

Here are some of the features which can make After Effects easier for the beginner to use, but can constrain others:

▶ Render order is established in the Timeline and via nested compositions: layers, not nodes. After Effects has Flowchart view but you don't create your composition there the way you would with a tree/node interface.

▶ Transforms, effects, and masks are embedded in every layer and render in a fixed order.

▶ After Effects has a persistent concept of an alpha channel in addition to the three color channels. The alpha is always treated as if it is straight (not premultiplied) once an image has been imported and interpreted.

▶ An After Effects project is not a script, although version CS4 introduces a text version of the After Effects Project (.aep) file, the XML-formatted .aepx file. Most of its contents are inscrutable other than source file paths. Actions are not recordable and there is no direct equivalent to Shake macros.

▶ Temporal and spatial settings tend to be absolute in After Effects because it is composition and timeline-based. This is a boon to projects that involve complex timing and animation, but it can snare users who aren't used to it and suddenly find pre-comps that end prematurely or are cropped. Best practices to avoid this are detailed in Chapter 4.

Of these differences, some are arbitrary, most are a mixed bag of advantages and drawbacks, and a couple of them are constantly used by the competition as a metaphorical stick with which to beat After Effects. The two that come up the most are the handling of precomposing and the lack of macros.

This book attempts to shed light on these and other areas of After Effects that are not explicitly dealt with in its user interface or documentation. After Effects itself spares you details that as a casual user, you might never need to know about, but that as a professional user you should understand thoroughly. This book is here to help.

New in this Edition

After Effects CS4 is the strongest version of the software yet, but with a few exceptions, including a new user interface with a number of revamped workflows, it does not change the methodology of most of what was in the previous edition.

Where After Effects may not have evolved, however, my own thinking has continued to do so; so even techniques that would be equally valid in a previous version of the software are newly presented or revamped here. In particular, I have paid attention in this edition to the first few chapters in order to better help smart people who don't yet understand the fundamentals.

Huge changes to the book this time around are thanks to two new contributors: Dan Ebberts and Jeff Almasol.

What's on the DVD

Two of the biggest additions to this book unfortunately did not make it into print due to page constraints.

Jeff Almasol's Scripting chapter is the Appendix, found on the disc as a PDF. It is the most accessible resource available on this complicated and much feared topic, walking you through three scripts each of which builds upon the complexity of the previous. Scripting provides the ability to create incredibly useful extensions to After Effects to eliminate tedious tasks. Several of these are included in the redefinery folder as exclusives to this book.

In order to focus on more advanced and applied topics in the print edition, Dan Ebberts kicked JavaScript fundamentals to a special JavaScript addendum also included as a PDF. This is in many ways the "missing manual" for the After Effects implementation of JavaScript, omitting all of the useless web-only scripting commands found in the best available books, but extending beyond the material in After Effects help.

If you want to find out more about some of the plug-ins and software mentioned in this book, look no further than its DVD-ROM. For example, the disc includes demos of

▶ Andersson Technologies' SynthEyes (3D tracking software)

▶ Red Giant Software's Magic Bullet Looks, Knoll Light Factory Unmult, Knoll Light Factory Pro, Key Correct Pro, Magic Bullet Colorista, Trapcode Lux, Trapcode Horizon, Trapcode Form, Trapcode Particular, the brand-new Warp and more.

▶ ReelSmart Motion Blur and PV Feather from Revision FX

▶ Lenscare and ZBornToy from Frischluft

▶ Erodilation and CopyImage from ObviousFX

NOTES

To install the lesson files, footage, and software demos included on the DVD, simply copy each chapter folder in its entirety to your hard drive. Note that all .aep files are located in the Projects subfolder of each chapter folder on the disc, while .ffx files can be found in the Animation Presets subfolders.

You'll also find HD footage from Kontent Films, fxphd.com, and Pixel Corps with which you can experiment and practice your techniques. There are dozens of example files to help you deconstruct the techniques described. There are also a few useful and free third-party scripts; for more of these, see the script links listed in the aforementioned appendix on the disc.

The Bottom Line

Just like the debates about which operating system is best, debates about which compositing software is tops are largely meaningless—especially when you consider that the majority of first-rate, big-budget, movie effects extravaganzas are created with a variety of software applications on a few different platforms. Rarely is it possible to say what software was used to composite a given shot just by looking at it, because it's about the artist, not the tools.

The goal is to understand the logic of the software so that you can use it to think through your artistic and technical goals. This book will help you do that.

If you have comments or questions you'd like to share with the author, please e-mail them to AEStudioTechniques@gmail.com.

SECTION I

Working Foundations

Chapter 1   Composite in After Effects   3

Chapter 2   The Timeline   39

Chapter 3   Selections: The Key to Compositing   77

Chapter 4   Optimize the Pipeline   109

1

Composite in After Effects

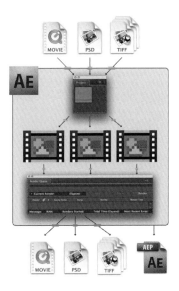

Good surfing is power, speed, and flow. The rest of it doesn't matter to me at all.

—Gary Elkerton, Australian surfer

Composite in After Effects

This is a book about visual effects compositing. If you use Adobe After Effects, the goal is to help you create believable, fantastic moving images from elements that were not shot together, and to do it with the least possible effort. This first section of the book focuses on effortlessness, offering a jump-start (if you're new) or a refresher (if you're already an After Effects artist) on the After Effects workflow.

To be an outstanding compositor, you need to employ your best skills as both an artist and an engineer. As an artist, you make creative and aesthetic decisions, but if you are not also able to understand how to put those decisions together and how the process works, the artistry of your work will suffer. Artists and engineers have much in common: both understand and respect the tools, both know that the tools themselves don't make you a great designer, and in both roles, iteration—multiple refinements—are often what separates a great effort from mediocrity.

This chapter and the rest of Section I focus on how to get things done in After Effects as effortlessly as possible. It is assumed that you already know your way around the basics of After Effects and are ready to learn to work smarter.

Workspaces and Panels

Figure 1.1 is one way of looking at the most generic of projects: it shows the Standard workspace that appears when you first open After Effects CS4, broken down into its component parts. The interface consists of

NOTES

If this book opens at too advanced a level for you, check out *Adobe After Effects CS4 Classroom in a Book* (Adobe Press), a helpful beginner's resource.

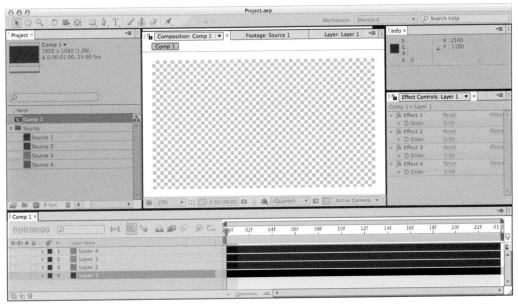

Figure 1.1 The Standard workspace layout, diagrammed in color. The top areas in red are informational only, while the purple areas contain tools and settings. The blue areas of the Timeline and Effect panel contain stacks whose order will change compositing order. Panel tabs, in yellow, can be grabbed to reorder the interface and contain menus at the upper right to adjust their appearance. The layer stack, in green, is modal and can be swapped for the Graph Editor.

▶ The main application window contains some panel groups—six of them by default (the Standard workspace), as few as two (Minimal workspace), or as many as 17 (All Panels workspace).

▶ Each group contains one or more panels each with a tab in the upper left.

▶ Separating the panel groups are dividers; panels and dividers are dragged to customize the workspace (more on that in a moment).

▶ Some panels are viewers, with a pop-up menu in the tab listing available clips.

▶ At the top is the Tools panel, which can be hidden but only appears atop the application window (and thus has no tab).

I call these out here to be done identifying them and to reassure you that this, along with a bunch of menus and a bunch more twirly arrows, is all there is to the After Effects user interface.

TIP

All available panels in After Effects are listed under the Window menu; the most common include preset keyboard shortcuts. Use these as toggles to keep your workspace clutter-free.

Are you a Zen roshi? Reveal the core essence of After Effects with the Minimal workspace (via the Workspace menu in Tools or Window > Workspace). Two of the most important three panels in After Effects are

▶ The Composition panel, a viewer where you examine a shot

▶ The Timeline panel, the true heart of After Effects, where elements are layered and timed for individual compositions (or shots). You will typically have many of these open at any given time.

For the third, choose Window > Project (**Cmd/Ctrl+0**) to add the Project panel. This is the Finder or Windows Explorer of After Effects—nothing more than files and folders representing the contents of your project.

At some point even a Zen roshi will assumedly need at least two more panels. A completed composition typically goes to the Render Queue (**Cmd/Ctrl+Alt/Option+0**) for final output (details about this important hub are found at the end of the chapter), and you are likely to add layer effects which are best adjusted in the Effect Controls (with a layer selected, **F3** or **Cmd/Ctrl+Shift+T**), although most the same controls can be found by twirling open the layer with that essential little triangle to the left of the layer name.

Other panels (found in other workspaces, or by selecting them under the Window menu) contain controls for specific tools such as paint (Paint and Brush Tips), the most significant of which are covered in detail later in the book.

Customize the Workspace

Simply by choosing the Minimal workspace and adding the Project panel, you've customized the workspace; switch to another workspace and back and you'll see that the Project panel remains until you choose Reset "Minimal" in the Workspace menu. Want to keep your new configuration? Save the Workspace under the same menu.

You can freely move any panel around the UI. To do so, click and drag its tab around the screen. As you move one panel over another, purple geometric shapes like those in **Figure 1.2** appear. These are the *drop zones*. The *docking*

Prefer your workspace customizations to the defaults? Choose New Workspace in the Workspace menu and enter an existing name to overwrite it; now After Effects will reset to your customized version.

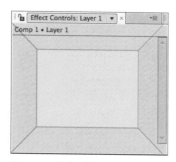

Figure 1.2 Each of the six possible drop zones is highlighted in color; drag one panel over another to reveal each of these targets. Dropping on the center or along the top has an identical result.

zones along the edges let you place a panel adjacent—for example, to the left of the Composition panel. The *grouping zones* in the center group panels together in one frame.

Drag a panel to one edge of the application window and aqua colored bands appear along the edge; when dropped the panel will occupy that entire side.

Double-arrow icons appear when you move the cursor between two or more panel groups, allowing you to resize adjacent panels. I don't do this much thanks to one of my favorite After Effects shortcuts, the Tilde key (~), which toggles the panel under the cursor to full-screen.

Which is best for After Effects, one big monitor or two smaller ones? I think the jury is somewhat out—my studio currently includes both setups, and although most artists are used to a pair of 24" screens, many prefer a single 30".

Maximize the Screen

Many After Effects artists like two HD-resolution displays side by side (**Figure 1.3**, top), although a single display can be optimal if it's large enough (**Figure 1.3**, bottom)

However, you may notice that a floating panel (**Ctrl/Cmd-drag** the tab to make it float) lacks the Zoom button along the top to send the window to full screen. The shortcut **Ctrl+\ (Cmd+\)** maximizes and centers any window. Press it again and even the top menu bar toggles off, filling the entire screen.

If you're stuck with a single small display you can press Tilde (~) to maximize a single panel and RAM Preview in full-screen mode by checking the Full Screen box in the Preview panel.

Figure 1.3 The preferred After Effects monitor setup seems to be a pair of 2K or larger displays (top) although a single 30" display at a high resolution (bottom), used with the Tilde key to zoom panels to full screen, is also quite luxuriant.

TIP

You can tear off any panel and make it float by holding down the **Ctrl/Cmd** key as you drag it away; I like to tear off the Render Queue and toggle it on and off via its shortcut (**Alt+Ctrl+0/Opt+Cmd+0**).

Order Reduces Effort

To my mind, the ideal workflow is an effortless one. Here's how to begin reducing steps you will take many, many times in a normal After Effects workday.

Figure 1.4 charts the nondestructive workflow of After Effects: from source files to comps made up of layers, which can contain settings, all of which are represented in a project file that never touches those source files.

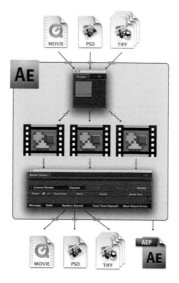

Figure 1.4 The After Effects pipeline is made up of a series of stages that are independent of one another; everywhere you see one-way arrows with hash marks, changes are pushed forward but do not affect the source, from source images to the Project to Comps to the Render Queue to final images.

Import and Organize Source

Getting a source file from a disk or server into After Effects is no big deal. You can use File > Import > File (or Multiple Files), or just drag footage directly from the Finder or Windows Explorer into the Project panel. You can also double-click in an empty area of the Project panel.

Image sequences have a couple of specific extra rules. I strongly advocate working with a sequence instead of QuickTime in production for the following reasons:

▶ An image sequence is less fragile than a QuickTime movie; if there is a bad frame in a sequence, it can be replaced, but it will corrupt an entire movie.

▶ You can interrupt and restart an image sequence render without then having to splice together multiple movies.

▶ QuickTime in particular has its own form of color management that isn't entirely compatible even with Apple's own applications, let alone the Adobe color management pipeline (explained in depth in Chapter 11).

Unfortunately, none of the Adobe applications (in particular, Bridge, which should know better) has ever become smart about recognizing sequences.

If you have a single sequence in a folder, just drag it in, but if it's the first one for this project, leave it selected for a moment in the Project panel and check its fps setting at the top; if it's not correct, see "Project, Footage, and Composition Settings" later in this chapter for how to fix this, both for that clip and for others just like it. If you really meant to bring in that folder's contents as individual files, hold down the **Option**/**Alt** key as you drag it in.

Things get more complicated if you are dealing with multiple image sequences in a single folder. If you've never run into this or can simply keep the practice of one sequence per folder, great, skip ahead. Otherwise, it's better to use the Import dialog.

With the Import dialog, it doesn't matter which specific image in a sequence you select; they are all imported provided you select only one. By holding the **Shift** or **Ctrl** (**Cmd**) key as you select more than one frame, however, you can

▶ Specify a subset of frames to be imported instead of an entire a sequence

▶ Select frames from more than one sequence in the same folder; a Multiple Sequences checkbox appears to make certain this is really what you want to do

▶ Specify sets of frames from multiple sequences (a combination of the above two modes)

This is, in many ways, a work-around for the fact that the After Effects importer doesn't group a frame sequence together the way other compositing applications do.

By default, if a sequence has missing frames (anywhere the count doesn't increment by 1), a color bar pattern is inserted with the name of the file presumed missing, which helps you track it down (see "Missing Footage," later in this chapter).

The Force Alphabetical Order checkbox in the Import dialog is for cases where the frame does not increment by 1. Say you rendered "on twos," creating every other frame from a 3D app; check this box and you avoid color bars on every other frame.

Want to be rehired repeatedly as a freelancer or be the hero on your project? Make it easy for someone to open your project cold and understand how it's organized. An ordinary project can be set up like the one shown in **Figure 1.5**; I often leave only the main composition in the root area of the project and place everything else in an appropriate subfolder.

TIP

Waiting for a long 3D render? Render the first and last 3D frames only, with their correct final sequence numbers, and import them using the Import dialog with Force Alphabetical Order unchecked. You now have a placeholder of the correct length that is fully set up as soon as the file is rendered.

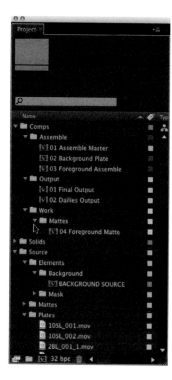

Figure 1.5 Consider how best to organize source into folders to keep things as well organized in the Project as you would want them on the source drive. Once you have a structure you like, you can reuse it. (Chapter 4 says more about how you might design it.)

On a more ambitious project, it's worth organizing a project template so that items are easy to find in predictable locations. Chapter 4 offers suggestions.

Context-Clicks (and Keyboard Shortcuts)

Stay away from the bar—the top menu bar, that is. I often refer to *context-clicking* on interface items. This is "right-clicking" unless you're on a Mac laptop or have an ancient one-button mouse, in which case you can hold down the Control key. Here's what happens:

▶ Context-click a layer in the Timeline for access to the full Layer menu, minus a few less useful items, such as the Adobe Encore submenu, and with killer additions such as Reveal Layer Source in Project and Reveal Expression Errors.

▶ Context-click on a layer in a Composition viewer for many of the same items, plus the Select option at the bottom of the menu, which gives you all of the items below your pointer (**Figure 1.6**).

▶ Context-click a panel tab to reveal the panel's menu (also found at the upper right), where a bunch of options that even advanced After Effects users hardly know exist can be found, such as the View Options for a Composition viewer.

▶ Context-click an item in the Project panel to, among other things, reveal it in the Finder or Explorer.

Having these kinds of options right under cursor keeps you focused.

Missing Footage

After Effects will link to any source footage file that can be found on your system or network, source which can easily become unlinked if anything moves or changes. To relink an item, find it in the Project panel and double-click it (or **Ctrl+H/Cmd+H**), or context-click and choose Replace Footage > File.

This is also a surreptitious way to replace a source file without any fuss or bother. If instead you need only to reload or update a source, context-click and choose

Figure 1.6 One of the biggest productivity boosts in After Effects comes from using the right mouse button of a two- (or more) button mouse, as context menus exist throughout After Effects and are always right under your cursor. This Layer context menu contains everything you'd want from the Layer menu, plus extra Timeline-specific commands.

TIP

When you context-click a Project item and choose Replace Footage, you get a couple of extra options—Placeholder and Solid—in case the footage won't be available until later.

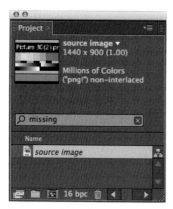

Figure 1.7 Missing footage is replaced with color bars, both in the Project thumbnail and anywhere the footage appears in the project. New in After Effects CS4, you can reveal all missing files in a Project by typing the word "missing" in the Project search field, highlighted in yellow.

Reload Footage (**Ctrl+Alt+L/Cmd+Option+L**). You can even edit a file in its source application and update it automatically in After Effects with Edit > Edit Original (**Ctrl+E/Cmd+E**), as long as you don't try anything tricky like saving it as a new file.

Sometimes it's difficult to locate a missing file or frame in your project. You may have used the Find Missing Footage checkbox in previous versions, and you may wonder where it has gone. You're not alone.

To search for particular types of footage in your project, including missing source, use search (**Ctrl+F/Cmd+F**) in the Project panel and the following commands (**Figure 1.7**):

▶ `missing` is the replacement for the Find Missing Footage checkbox

▶ `unused` gets you all of the source that isn't in any comp

▶ `used`

▶ Text strings that appear in the Project panel (say, `tif` or `Aug 26`)

Make sure to check out that last one; it's a totally new option in After Effects CS4. The date column in the Project panel may be hidden by default; context-click to reveal it, then type in yesterday's date using a three-letter month abbreviation; the Project panel now displays only the items that were introduced or updated yesterday.

Unrecognized file formats are grayed out in the After Effect Import dialog. Typically, adding a missing three-character extension solves this, although some obscure formats simply do not work cross-platform (for example, Mac-generated PICT on Windows); see the "Source Formats" section later in this chapter for the most useful and universal file types to use.

Because every project is likely to be moved or archived at some point (you *are* making backups, right?), it's best to keep all source material in one master folder; this helps After Effects automatically relink all of the related files it finds there at once, thus avoiding a lot of tedium for you.

Move, Combine, and Consolidate Projects

At some point you probably will want to know how to

▶ Move an entire After Effects project, including its source, or archive it

▶ Merge or combine two projects

▶ Clean up a project, getting rid of what's not used or extra instances of a single file

To move or archive a project with only its linked source, choose File > Collect Files. This command was designed to enable multimachine Watch Folder rendering (see Chapter 4) but is also useful for backup, as it allows you to create a new folder that contains a copy of the project and all of its source files. The source files are reorganized with a directory structure that directly replicates the one in the Project panel (**Figure 1.8**).

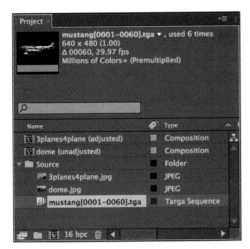

Figure 1.8 Collect Files resaves all source files from your project using the same organization and hierarchy as the Project itself.

Let the computer do what it does best and automate a clean up of your source. Choose Collect Source Files: For Selected Comps; After Effects collects only the footage needed to create that comp. If you check Reduce Project as well, the unused source is also removed from the collected project.

File > Reduce Project removes excess items from the project itself. Select the master compositions in your project and choose File > Reduce Project; After Effects eliminates project items not used in the selected comps. You even get a warning dialog telling you how many items were removed—not from the disk, only from your project.

You can instead clean out only the source footage (but keep the comps and solids) with File > Remove Unused Footage, which deletes from the project any footage that hasn't made its way into a comp. If the same clips have been imported more than once, File > Consolidate All Footage looks for the extra instances and combines them, choosing the first instance, top to bottom, in the project.

Need to combine two or more projects? Import one into the other (just drag it in), or drag several into a new project. The imported project appears in its own folder, and if the projects being combined are organized using the same set of subfolders, you can merge them with the script rd_MergeProjects.jsx, which is included on the book's disc (**Figure 1.9**).

Figure 1.9 Load the highly useful rd_MergeProjects.jsx script from the redefinery folder on the book's disc into Adobe After Effects CS4 > Scripts > ScriptUIPanels, and you can then reveal it at any time from the bottom of the Window menu. This script takes nested folders with the same name as those closer to the root and merges them, while consolidating duplicate footage. It's great for importing a project and maintaining a tidy structure.

File > Consolidate All Footage looks for two or more instances of a source file and combines them, choosing the first instance, top to bottom, in the project. File > Remove Unused Footage rids a project of footage not included in any composition (but the files do remain on your drive).

Advanced Save Options

After Effects projects are saved completely separate from the elements they contain. They tend to be small, making it easier to save a lot of them so that you don't lose your work.

File > Increment and Save attaches a version number to your saved project or increments whatever number is already there, at the end of the file name before the .aep extension.

Preferences > Auto-Save fills in the spaces between incremented versions; toggle it on and you'll never lose more than the number of minutes you specify (Save Every 20 Minutes is the default), and you'll have whatever number of most recent versions you prefer (**Figure 1.10**).

TIP

Use Increment and Save when you reach a point where you're happy with a project and ready to move on to the next step; you can then choose File > Revert to get back there in one step instead of using a series of undos.

Name	Date Modified ▼	Size
7ST001_15 auto-save 4.aep	7/16/08, 3:44 PM	8.3 MB
7ST001_15 auto-save 3.aep	7/16/08, 2:19 PM	8.4 MB
7ST001_15 auto-save 2.aep	7/16/08, 2:04 PM	8.3 MB
7ST001_15 auto-save 1.aep	7/16/08, 1:38 PM	8.4 MB
7ST001_14 auto-save 7.aep	7/16/08, 1:16 PM	8.4 MB
7ST001_14 auto-save 6.aep	7/11/08, 3:51 PM	8.3 MB
7ST001_14 auto-save 5.aep	7/11/08, 10:50 AM	8.3 MB
7ST001_14 auto-save 4.aep	7/10/08, 9:04 PM	8.3 MB
7ST001_14 auto-save 3.aep	7/10/08, 3:57 PM	8.3 MB

Figure 1.10 Auto-Save must be enabled, then at the default settings it creates 5 versions, writing a new one after each 20 minutes that you work (but not if your system sits idle). When number 5 is reached, 1 is deleted and 6 is written. When you increment the project, a new set of 5 is written. Here, each project is about 8 MB, which is large for an After Effects project but no problem compared to source file sizes.

Project, Footage, and Composition Settings

After Effects includes a bunch of settings that you need to understand or you will waste time and effort fighting them. These have to do with essentials like how time, color depth, transparency, pixel aspect, and field data are handled.

Figure 1.11 Project Settings are brought up here in Chapter 1 because they are essential, but only the biggest and most complicated section (Color Settings, in blue) doesn't get a full explanation until Chapter 11.

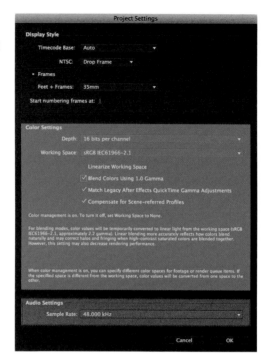

Project Settings

As shown in **Figure 1.11,** the Project Settings dialog (**Ctrl+Alt+Shift+K/Cmd+Option+Shift+K**) contains three basic sections:

▶ Display Style determines how time is displayed—predominantly whether a comp's frame count is kept in integers (frames) or in timecode. Broadly, film projects tend to work in frames, broadcast video projects in timecode. This won't effect the frame rates of your footage or comps, only how they appear.

▶ The Color Settings section includes the project-wide color depth (8, 16, or 32 bits per channel), as well as color management and blend settings. Chapter 11 covers this in ample depth.

▶ Audio Settings affects only how audio is previewed; lowering the rate can save RAM. I never touch this.

If you're displaying timecode, you'll almost never want to change the default Auto setting unless you're working with footage containing more than one frame rate and need to conform everything to a particular standard.

If you're working with frames, it's typical to start numbering them at 1, although the default is 0. This applies to imported image sequences, not comps. Numbering in a comp is determined by the Start Frame number in Composition Settings (**Ctrl+K/Cmd+K**).

Interpret Footage

This book generally eschews the practice of walking through After Effects menus, but a well-designed UI helps you think. Decisions about how footage is interpreted are both vital and somewhat tedious. This makes the Interpret Footage dialog (**Figure 1.12**), where you can specify for any source clip, even more vital as a pre-flight checklist for source footage:

► Alpha interpretation

► Frame Rate

► Fields and Pulldown

► Pixel Aspect Ratio (under Other Options)

► Color Management (under More Options with certain file types and the new Color Management tab)

NOTES

Feet+Frames in Display Style refers to actual reels of physical film, for those who still remember the 20th century.

Figure 1.12 The Interpret Footage dialog is a checklist for getting footage settings correct before you ever assemble a comp. Alpha (red) determines transparency settings, Frame Rate (yellow) is particularly essential with an image sequence, Fields and Pulldown (green) and Pixel Aspect Ratio (under Other Options, blue) convert footage optimized for playback. The Color Management tab (purple) gets a complete treatment in Chapter 11.

To bring up the Interpret Footage dialog for a given clip, select it in the Project panel and press **Ctrl+Shift+G/Cmd+Shift+G** or context-click and select Interpret Footage > Main. The Interpret Footage icon in the Project panel  is a new shortcut to open this dialog.

Alpha

To composite effectively you must thoroughly understand alpha channels. **Figure 1.13** shows the most visible symptom of a misinterpreted alpha channel: fringing.

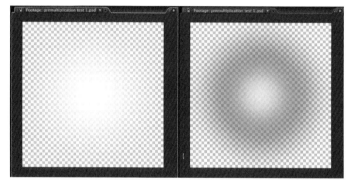

Figure 1.13 It's not hard to distinguish a properly interpreted (left) from an incorrect alpha channel (right). The giveaway is fringing, caused in this case by the failure to remove the black background color premultiplied into edge pixels. The left image is unmultiplied, the right is not.

You can easily avoid these types of problems:

▶ If the alpha channel type is unclear, click Guess in the mini Interpretation dialog that appears when importing footage with alpha. This often (not always) yields a correct setting.

▶ Preferences > Import contains a default alpha channel preference, which is fine to set on a project with consistent alpha handling. If you are in any doubt about that, set it to Ask User to avoid forgetting to set it properly.

More information on alpha channels and how they operate is in Chapter 3.

Frame Rate

I have known experienced artists to make careless errors with frame rate. Misinterpreted frame rate is typically an

TIP

After Effects does not guess an alpha unless you specifically click Guess; if you merely clear the dialog (**Esc**) it uses the previous default.

issue with image sequences only, because unlike Quick-Time, the files themselves contain no embedded frame rate. You can also override the QuickTime frame rate, which is exactly what After Effects does with footage containing any sort of pulldown (see next section).

The following two statements are both true:

▶ After Effects is more flexible than just about any video application in letting you mix clips with varying frame rates and letting you change the frame rate of a clip that's already in a comp.

▶ However, After Effects is very *precise* about how those timing settings are handled, so it is essential that your settings themselves be precise. If your true frame rate is 23.976 fps or 29.97 fps, don't round those to 24 and 30, or strange things are bound to happen: motion tracks that don't stick, steppy playback, and more.

The current frame rate and duration as well as other interpretation information is displayed at the top of the Project panel when you select a source clip (**Figure 1.14**).

Figure 1.14 Useful information about any selected item appears atop the Project panel. The carat to the right of the file name reveals specific comps in which it is used.

Fields, Pulldown, and Pixel Aspect Ratio

One surprise for the novice is that moving images are often not made up of whole frames containing square pixels like stills. A video frame, and in particular one shot for broadcast, is often interlaced into two *fields*, and its pixels are stored non-square, for the purpose of faster and more efficient capture and delivery.

TIP

You can change the default Frames Per Second setting for Sequence Footage under Preferences > Import. This should be the first thing you check when you are starting a new project so you don't have to continually change it.

CLOSE-UP

Why Sequences?

Movie formats, in particular QuickTime (.mov), are like fast food in a regular diet – bound to cause problems sooner or later when compared with the healthier image sequence option:

▶ A bad frame in a rendered sequence can typically be quickly isolated and replaced; a bad frame will sink an entire QuickTime movie, sometimes costing hours.

▶ It's easy to swap out a section of an image sequence precisely, overwriting frames instead of cutting and pasting footage.

▶ Still image formats have more predictable color management settings than QuickTime.

If QuickTime is a burger—convenient but potentially bad for the health of your project, causing bloat and slowness—then image sequences are a home cooked meal, involving more steps but offering more control over how they are made and consumed.

It's not always practical, particularly when making quick edits to video footage, to convert everything to sequences, which don't play back so easily on your system or in your nonlinear editor. Nonetheless, sequences are the best choice for larger or longer-form projects.

Fields combine two frames into one by *interlacing* them together, vertically alternating one horizontal line of pixels from the first with one from the second. The result is half the image detail but twice the motion detail. **Figure 1.15** shows this principle in action.

Figure 1.15 If a perfect ellipse traveled left to right at high speed, the interlaced result would look like this on a single frame. This contains two fields' worth of motion, alternating on vertical pixels of a single frame. If you see something like this in your comp, it hasn't been removed on import.

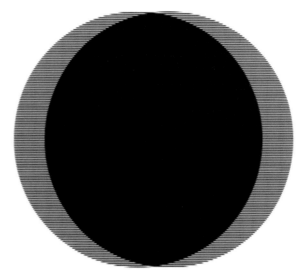

If you're doing any compositing, transformation, paint/ masking, or distortion —pretty much anything beyond basic color correction—it's best to match the Separate Fields setting to that of the footage, causing After Effects to recognize the interlace frame as two separate frames of video.

Pulldown uses fields to run 24 fps film footage smoothly at 29.97 fps by repeating one field every five frames. This creates a pattern that After Effects can accurately guess if there is sufficient motion in the first few frames of the footage. If not, the backup option (which still works) is trial-and-error, trying each initial pattern listed under Remove Pulldown until the field artifacts disappear in a 23.976 fps comp. There are two basic types of pulldown (3:2 and 24 Pa), each with five potential initial patterns.

Pixel aspect ratio (PAR) is another compromise intended to maximize image detail while minimizing frame size. The pixels in the image are displayed nonsquare on the broadcast monitor, with extra detail on one axis compensating for its lack on the other.

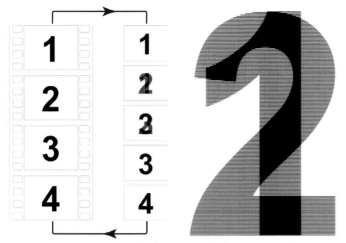

Figure 1.16 Pulldown allows 24 fps footage, the film frame rate, and allows it to play smoothly at 30 fps; without interleaving it into fields in this manner, the motion stutters, as it does if you try to go straight from 30 fps (no pulldown) to 24.

NOTES

3:2 pulldown is the traditional format designed to make footage that originated at 24 fps play smoothly at 29.97 fps; telecine conversions from film to television use this. 24P Advance Pulldown was introduced to reduce field artifacts by grouping 24 whole frames with 6 interlaced frames, which are essentially filler and can be discarded on removal (see the diagram in **Figure 1.16**).

Your computer monitor, of course, displays square pixels, so any clip with a non-square PAR will look odd if displayed without compensating for the difference. Therefore, After Effects includes a toggle below the viewer panels to stretch the footage so that its proportions look correct (**Figure 1.17**) although the footage or composition itself isn't changed.

With some digital formats such as DV, field order and pixel aspect are standardized and set automatically in After Effects. With other formats, it's best to know the correct field order and pixel aspect as specified by the camera or software that generated the image.

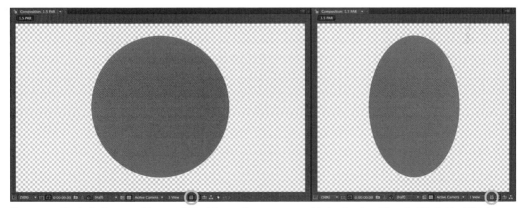

Figure 1.17 Think all of your problems with Pixel Aspect Ratio are gone with the demise of Standard Definition? Think again. DVCPRO HD footage with Pixel Aspect Ratio Correction on (left) and off (right) via the toggle (circled in green).

Source Formats

After Effects is capable of importing and exporting a wide array of footage formats, yet only a small subset of these recur regularly in production. **Table 1.1** contains a rundown of common raster image formats and some advantages and disadvantages of each.

Which formats will you use most? Probably TIFF or DPX for source, and JPEG (with a Quality setting of 7 or higher) for temporary storage when file space is at a premium.

TIFF offers lossless LZW compression, giving it an advantage over Adobe Photoshop, especially when you consider that TIFF can even store multiple layers, each with its own transparency. Other formats with lossless compression, such as TGA, don't support multiple bit-depths and layers like TIFF does. PNG is more limited and slower, but the file sizes are smaller.

One oddity of the PNG format is that it specifies that an alpha channel is saved and interpreted as Straight, with no explicit option to change the default.

TABLE 1.1 Raster Image Formats and Their Advantages

Format	Bit Depth	Lossless Compression	Lossy Compression	Alpha Channel	Output Format
TIFF	8/16/32 bit	Y	N	Y (multiple via layers)	Y
PNG	8/16	Y	N	Y (Straight only)	Y
CIN/DPX	10	N	N	N	Y (Cineon 4.5 or DPX, see Cineon Settings)
CRW	12	N	N	N	N
EXR (now native in CS4)	16/32	Y	N	Y	Y
JPG	8	N	Y	N	Y

For film and computer graphics, it is normal to pass around CIN and DPX files (essentially the same format) and EXR, designed (and open-sourced) by ILM specifically to handle HDR renders with multiple channels of data (and these can be customized to contain useful information such as Z depth and motion data). More on these formats is found in Chapters 11 and 12, which also include information on working with Camera Raw CRW images.

After Effects CS4 now includes EXR tools, which are highlighted in Chapter 12.

Photoshop Files

Although the PSD format does not offer any type of compression, it offers a few unique advantages when used with After Effects. Specifically, PSD files

▶ Can be imported directly as *identical* After Effects compositions; all of the data is preserved and most of it, including blending modes and even layer styles and text, remains editable in After Effects. In the Import File dialog, choose Composition or Composition – Cropped Layers using the Import Kind pop-up menu (**Figure 1.18**).

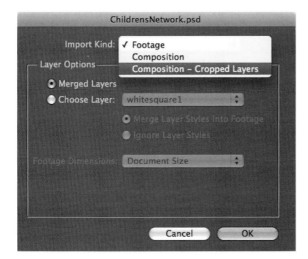

Figure 1.18 Holy Twisted Terminology, Batman! Composition Cropped Layers means "just like in Photoshop." The other option, Composition, reframes everything to the image area—and crops any pixels that fall outside frame! Choose the Cropped Layers option to ensure that each layer has its own unique Anchor Point—and is *not* cropped.

▶ Can be created from After Effects (File > New > Adobe Photoshop File or even Layer > New > Adobe Photoshop File).

▶ Can include moving footage. More about why you might want to work with video in Photoshop (for its paint tools) is included in Chapter 7.

▶ Can include Live 3D layers: 3D models with lighting, material, and surface characteristics created in Photoshop that can be manipulated in After Effects. More about this new feature is found in Chapter 9.

Once your source footage is imported and organized (Chapter 4), the next step is to place it in a composition.

The term "plate" stretches back to the earliest days of optical compositing (and indeed, of photography itself) and refers to the source footage, typically the background onto which foreground elements are composited.

Composition Settings

My advice is to begin with your *plate*: the main footage, whether a background shot or a foreground yet to be keyed. To ensure that composition settings are exactly as they should be with the least effort, try one of the following:

▶ Use a prebuilt project template that includes compositions whose settings match the intended output; you can even create and save your own.

▶ Create a new composition by dragging the plate footage (often the background plate) to the Create a New Composition icon ▦. This automatically matches pixel dimensions, Pixel Aspect Ratio, Frame Rate, and Duration, all of which are crucial.

Composition Settings also contains an Advanced tab. This pertains to temporal and spatial settings (Chapter 4) and motion blur and 3D (Chapter 9).

Previews and View Panels

How exactly does a professional work with footage in After Effects? I've noticed some good habits that experienced pros tend to share.

A 2K plate is the minimum typical horizontal film resolution: approximately 2000 pixels, or more precisely 2048 pixels in width. HD video is 1920 pixels horizontal resolution.

Resolution and Quality

First, keep in mind that you should almost never work at Full resolution, but you should almost always leave layers at Best quality. There are several effective ways to speed up previews and interactivity without ever setting a layer to Draft quality, which creates inaccurate previews by rounding off crucial values.

In rough order of preference, you can

▶ Lower viewer Resolution to Half, or in extreme cases, Quarter (see Note)

▶ Set a Region of Interest (ROI) to isolate only the area that needs to be previewed

▶ Use Shift+RAM Preview to skip frames (default setting of 1 skips every second frame—details in "Caching and Previewing," later in this chapter)

One very cool new CS4 feature is the Auto setting under the Resolution menu in the Comp viewer. This downsamples the image so that resolution is never higher than magnification; this guarantees that when you work smaller, you work faster.

Figure 1.19 Highlighted in yellow are a few easy-to-miss options (from the top): loop options let you ping-pong footage, Shift+RAM Preview is a secondary previewing option with unique settings, the default difference is a Skip setting of 1 which previews every other frame but can be raised to any number you like, and you can preview From Current Time instead of the full Work Area.

Half resolution allows four times as much data to fill a RAM preview, and Shift+RAM Preview can reduce overhead further by skipping every nth frame (according to the Skip setting in the Preview panel). The default setting of 1 plays every other frame (**Figure 1.19**).

To quickly change the display resolution in the Composition panel, use the keyboard shortcuts shown in **Table 1.2**.

TABLE 1.2 Display Resolution/Size Shortcuts

RESOLUTION/SIZE	KEYBOARD SHORTCUT
Full	Ctrl+J/Cmd+J
Half	Ctrl+Shift+J/Cmd+Shift+J
Quarter	Ctrl+Shift+Alt+J/ Cmd+Shift+Option+J
Fit in viewer	Shift+/
Fit up to 100%	Alt+/ / Option+/

Hold down the Spacebar or activate the Hand tool (H, Spacebar, or Middle Mouse Button) to move your view of a clip around. To zoom in and out, you can use

▶ **Ctrl+=/Cmd+=** and **Ctrl+-/Cmd+-**

▶ Zoom tool (**Z**); press **Alt/Option** to zoom out

▶ Comma and period keys

▶ A mouse with a scroll wheel

Figure 1.20 Region of Interest crops the active view region. Want to keep this view? Crop Comp to Region of Interest (in the Composition menu).

Ever notice yourself focusing only on a particular section of a huge image? Use the Region of Interest (ROI) tool (**Figure 1.20**), to define a rectangular preview region. Only the layer data needed to render that area is calculated and buffered, lengthening RAM previews.

Responsiveness

Has your After Effects UI slowed to crawl as you work on a big shot? Here's a quick triage you can try:

- ▶ **Deactivate Live Update (Figure 1.21a).** On by default, this toggle enables real-time update in the viewers as you adjust controls. Deactivate it and updates occur only when you release the mouse.

- ▶ **Hold Option/Alt as you make adjustments.** With Live Update on, this prevents views from updating. Deactivate Live Update and the behavior is inverted; the modifier keys instead enable real-time updates.

- ▶ **Activate Caps Lock.** If you don't mind working "blind" for periods of time, the Caps Lock key prevents updates to any viewer (**Figure 1.21b**).

TIP

With the cursor over a specific area of the frame, hold the **Option/Alt** key as you zoom to keep that point centered.

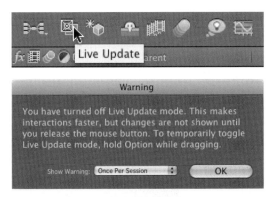

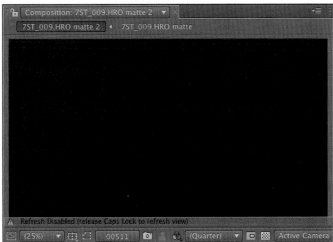

Figure 1.21 Disabling Live Update (a) and enabling Caps Lock (b) could be seen as desperation moves when interactivity becomes unacceptable, but the former is rarely necessary (you can do it temporarily with Option/Alt) and the latter can actually be a handy way to do setup as quickly as possible without worrying about previews.

> **Enable OpenGL.** Preferences > Previews includes the Enable OpenGL option, off by default (and unavailable with older graphics cards). Enable it, and OpenGL-Interactive mode in a View panel is accelerated in certain cases, for example when positioning layers in 3D space. There are two OpenGL options, Interactive and Always On; the former will help you with fast scene setup, especially in a complicated 3D scene, and the latter will give you the look of OpenGL at all times as you work.

TIP

OpenGL in After Effects can have undesirable side effects; most power users tend to leave it off most of the time.

In general, the more responsive you can make your user interface, the better will be the result because you can make more decisions in a shorter period of time. Just leave time to double-check the result if you are in the habit of disabling viewers.

Multiprocessing

Multiprocessing, which allows After Effects to use all of the processor cores on your system, is disabled by default; this does not mean that After Effects doesn't use all of your procs, just that by default it doesn't work on more than one frame at a time, and thus it doesn't maximize usage of your system.

The Preferences > Memory & Multiprocessing dialog contains dynamically updated information related to your particular system; it is designed to help you make maximum use of processing power without maxing out the system for other applications. The decision of how to balance it is yours. By default, After Effects leaves a given amount of RAM for other applications, and you can control this amount in this dialog.

Most users miss the main feature here, the Render Multiple Frame Simultaneously checkbox, which is disabled by default. Check this box and After Effects no longer waits for one frame to render before starting the next; instead it looks for available memory and CPU to render as many frames as your system can handle simultaneously.

How much multiprocessing can your system handle? Once you enable multiprocessing, you can tune how it is handled:

▶ Raise the minimum allocation per CPU to help background processes: 1.0 GB for HD footage below 32 bpc, 2.0 GB for larger than HD and 32 bpc projects (Chapter 11 tells you more about those).

▶ Weight memory more toward RAM Previews (a foreground process, so you wait for it) or faster background renders (while you continue to work).

▶ Spare whole CPUs for other applications.

The controls and descriptive text in this dialog, along with the features they describe have been enhanced for CS4 (**Figure 1.22**).

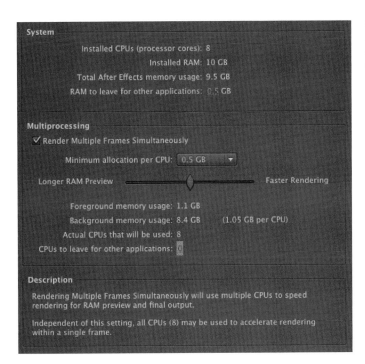

Figure 1.22 Whoa—Memory and Multiprocessing settings are not simple, although they are thoroughly described in this dynamic Preference.

Caching and Previewing

After Effects automatically caches footage as you navigate from frame to frame (**Page Up**/**Page Down**) or load a RAM preview (**0** on the numeric keypad). The green line atop the Timeline shows which frames are stored for instant playback.

Given that After Effects tops out at a bit less than 3 GB of physical memory per session (due to limitations in system memory allocation), you can do better. To extend the cache from physical memory (RAM) to physical media (ideally a high-speed local drive), enable Disk Cache in Preferences > Memory & Cache. This locks away a portion of your drive for use only by After Effects. A blue line shows frames loaded in the Disk Cache (**Figure 1.23**).

Figure 1.23 Enable Disk Cache and you may see your previews extended; the blue areas of the Timeline have been cached to disc in addition to the green areas cached into physical memory (RAM).

When you activate Enable Disk Cache, you must also specify a disk location; if in doubt just create a local folder with an intuitive name such as AE Scratch. Even the default 2 GB (2000 MB) setting greatly extends available cache without occupying permanent disk space.

TIP

The shortcut for Shift+RAM Preview is, naturally enough, **Shift+0** (on the numeric keypad). To set the Work Area to the length of any highlighted layers, use **Ctrl+Alt+B/Cmd+Option+B**.

TIP

To update an external preview device, press **/**.

TIP

To create a basic gradient background, apply the Ramp effect to a solid layer.

Disk Cache saves the time required to re-render a frame but doesn't necessarily deliver real-time playback and often is not invoked when you might think it should be. The cache is not saved between After Effects sessions.

If refined motion is not critical, use Shift+RAM Preview.

Preview Settings

Here's some cool stuff you do to customize a RAM Preview:

▶ **Loop options** (Preview panel). Hidden among the playback icons atop Preview is a toggle controlling how previews loop. Use this to disable looping, or amaze your friends with the ping-pong option.

▶ **From Current Time** (Preview panel). Tired of resetting the work area? Toggle this on and previews begin at the current time and roll through to the end of the comp.

▶ **Full Screen** (Preview panel). Self-explanatory and rarely used.

▶ **Preferences > Video Preview** lets you specify Output Device and how it is used. If you have an external video device attached with its own monitor, you can use it to preview. Third-party output devices, such as Kona and Blackmagic cards, are supported as well.

Backgrounds

You need to see what you're doing, and when you use a contrasting background it is like shining a light behind layer edges. You can customize the background color of the Composition viewer (**Ctrl+Shift+B/Cmd+Shift+B** or Composition > Background Color) or toggle the Transparency Grid icon beneath the Composition panel to evaluate edges in sharp relief.

I even insert background or reference footage or a custom gradient background that I create (**Figure 1.24**). If it's set as a Guide Layer ▦ (Layer > Guide Layer or context-click the layer), it does not show up when rendered or nested in another comp.

Composition: mustang

`100%` `00001` `Full` `Active Camera` `1 View`

Figure 1.24 If the gradient behind a matted object is made a guide layer, you can clearly see the edge details of the foreground, but the gradient doesn't show up in any subsequent comps or renders.

Several other modes and toggles are available in the viewer panels. Some are familiar from other Adobe applications:

▶ **Title/Action Safe overlays** determine the boundaries of the frame as well as its center point.

▶ **View > Show Grid** (**Ctrl+"**/**Cmd+"**) displays an overlay grid.

▶ **View > Show Rulers** (**Ctrl+R**/**Cmd+R**) displays not only pixel measurements of the viewer, but allows you to add guides as you can in Photoshop.

All of these are toggled via a single menu beneath the viewer panel (the one that looks like a crosshair). To pull out a guide, choose Show Rulers and then drag from either

TIP

Use Preferences > Grids & Guides to customize the Safe Margins in the Title/Action Safe overlay or the appearance of grids and guides.

the horizontal or vertical ruler. To change the origin point (0 on each ruler), drag the crosshair from the corner between the two rulers.

Masks, keyframes, and motion paths can get in the way. You can

▶ Hide them all using View > Hide Layer Controls (**Ctrl+Shift+H/Cmd+Shift+H**)

▶ Use the Toggle Mask and Shape Path Visibility button at the bottom of the Comp panel

▶ Customize what is shown and hidden with View > View Options (**Ctrl+Alt+U/Cmd+Option+U**)

Beginning in Chapter 5 you'll be encouraged to study images one color channel at a time. The Show Channel icon exists for this purpose (keyboard shortcuts **Alt/Option+1** through **Alt/Option+4** map to R, G, B, and A, respectively). An outline in the color of the selected channel reminds you which channel is displayed (**Figure 1.25**).

Figure 1.25 The green border indicates that only the green channel is displayed. (Image courtesy of Mark Decena, Kontent Films.)

Effects & Presets

After Effects contains about 200 effects plug-ins that ship with the application, and far more than that from third parties. Personally, I use less than 10% of these effects around 80–90% of the time, so my opinion is that you don't need to understand them all in order to use the most powerful ones.

And even cooler, once you thoroughly understand the core effects, you can use them together to do things with After Effects that you might have thought required third-party plug-ins.

To apply an effect to a layer, my advice is to avoid the Effect menu and either context-click that layer, then use the Effect context menu, or double-click it in the Effects & Presets panel.

The Effects & Presets panel is a versatile tool when problem-solving. It has options to display effects alphabetically, without their categories, as well as a search field to help you look for a specific effect by name, or for all the effects whose names include a specific word, such as "blur" or "channel" (**Figure 1.26**).

Animation Presets allow you to save specific configurations of layer properties and animations, including keyframes, effects, and expressions. They're particularly useful when working with others and sharing standardized practices. Save your own by selecting the effects and properties you want to save and choose Animation > Save Animation Preset; save it to the Presets folder (the default location) to have it show up when After Effects is started.

Figure 1.26 Type the word "blur" in the Effects & Presets search field and only effects with that text string in the name appear. You can also choose to display only effects with higher bit depths (when working at 16 or 32 bpc).

Output via the Render Queue

As you well know, the way to get completed footage out of After Effects is to render it. Here are a few things you might not already know about the process of outputting your work.

To place an item in the Render Queue, it's simplest either to use a shortcut (**Ctrl+M/Cmd+M**) or to drag items from the Project panel.

TIP

Convert raw footage by dragging it directly to the Render Queue, no comp required (one is made for you). This is a quick and easy way to convert an image sequence to a QuickTime movie, or vice versa.

There are two key sections for each Render Queue item: Render Settings and Output Module.

Render Settings: Match or Override the Comp

Render Settings breaks down to three basic sections (**Figure 1.27**):

▶ **Composition** corresponds directly to settings in the Timeline; here you choose whether to keep or override them. The more complex options, such as Proxy Use, are described in Chapter 4.

▶ **Time Sampling** gives you control over the timing of the render; not just frame rate and duration but the ability to add pulldown and fields—say when rendering a 24 fps film comp for 29.97 video—as well as motion blur and frame blending (Chapter 2).

▶ **Options** contains one super important feature: "Skip existing files," which checks for the existence of a file before rendering it. This is useful for splitting sequences between sessions (see Chapter 4 for details on how to use it).

Figure 1.27 Maybe it's helpful to see the sections of the Render Settings dialog highlighted; the real point is that the first section (in red) looks at how an individual frame is rendered, while the second (blue) section focuses on timing the whole sequence.

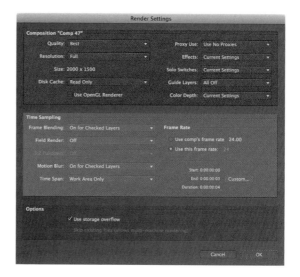

If you find that rendered output doesn't match your expectations, Render Settings is generally the place to look (unless it involves color management, compression, or audio). The Output Modules handle writing that output to a file.

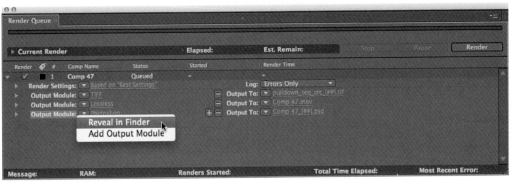

Figure 1.28 It's easy to miss that you can add multiple Output Modules to a single render queue item via Composition > Add Output Module or this context menu. This is an immense timesaver, as each frame is rendered once and written as many times as you like.

Figure 1.29 Custom-number a frame sequence here; no convoluted work-arounds needed.

Output Modules: Making Movies

Output Modules convert the rendered frame into an actual file. The main decisions here concern

▶ Format

▶ Size

▶ Audio

▶ Color management

Several elegant and easily missed problem-solving tools are embedded in Output Modules:

▶ Multiple Output Modules per Render Queue item avoid the need for multiple passes (**Figure 1.28**).

▶ Separate Output Modules can be edited together by Shift-selecting the modules themselves (not the Render Queue items that contain them).

▶ A numbered sequence can start with any number you like (**Figure 1.29**).

▶ Scaling can be nonuniform to change the pixel aspect ratio.

TIP

Want the best looking half-resolution render? Use a Stretch setting in the Output Module, instead of half resolution in Render Settings (which typically renders faster).

Naming Conventions

Part of growing a studio is devising a naming scheme that keeps projects and renders organized. It's generally considered good form to

▶ Use standard Unix naming conventions (replacing spaces with underscores, intercaps, dashes, or dots).

▶ Put the version number at the end of the project name and the output file, and have them match. To add a version number to a numbered sequence, you can name the image sequence file something like foo_bar_[####]_v01.tif for version 1.

▶ Pad sequential numbers (adding zeros at the beginning) to keep things in order as the overall number moves into multiple digits.

And remember After Effects itself doesn't like file names above 32 digits, so find a system that is concise or risk having key information, toward the end of the name, truncated in the Project panel.

Photo-JPEG is universally available, even in older versions of QuickTime. Plus, at 100%, it provides 4:4:4 chroma sampling, and at 75%, 4:2:2 (see Chapters 6 and 11 for more on chroma).

Chapter 4 tells more about how to send your project to Adobe Media Encoder for multipass encoding; this requires Adobe CS4 Production Premium.

▶ Post-Render Actions automate bringing the result back into After Effects. Chapter 4 tells all.

▶ A numbered image sequence must contain a string in the format [###] somewhere within its name. Each # sign corresponds to a digit, for padding.

▶ The Color Management tab is in effect with many still image formats. Chapter 11 tells all.

▶ Rendered files can include XMP metadata (if toggled on, as by default); this includes information that the file came from After Effects.

Save Output Modules early and often using the Make Template option at the bottom of the pop-up menu. If you intend to render with the same settings even once more, it saves time. Unfortunately these cannot be easily sent to another user.

Optimized Output

Following are some suggested output settings (Render Settings and Output Modules) for specific situations:

▶ Final output should match the delivery format; it's usually an editor who decides this. Merely choosing the default Lossless setting is not sufficient if, for example, you've been working in 16 bpc to render a 10-bit final (Lossless is only 8 bit). For sending files internally, TIFF with lossless LZW compression is solid and can handle higher bit depths and color management.

▶ Low-loss output is mostly up to you; QuickTime with Photo-JPEG at around 75% is an old standby, but all QuickTime formats may display inconsistent gamma, depending on version and platform.

▶ Online review typically should be compressed outside of After Effects; such aggressive compression formats as H.264 are most successful on multiple passes.

After Effects offers a number of output formats and can be useful for simple file conversion; you need only import source and drag it directly to the Render Queue, then add settings and press Render.

Study a Shot like an Effects Artist

Seasoned visual effects supervisors miss nothing. Fully trained eyes do not even require two takes, although in the highest end facilities, a shot loops for several minutes while the team picks it apart.

This process, though occasionally hard on the ego, makes shots look good.

You can and should scrutinize your shot just as carefully in After Effects. Specifically, throughout this book I encourage you to get in the following habits:

▸ Keep an eye on the Info palette (**Figure 1.30**).

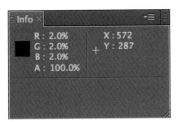

Figure 1.30 Whoops! The swatch (from the pixel under the cursor) looks black, but a glance at the Info palette shows that it is actually 2% gray. If you're uncertain about pixel values, have a glance at the Info panel.

▸ Loop or rock and roll previews.

▸ Zoom in to the pixel level, especially around edges.

▸ Examine footage channel by channel (Chapter 5).

▸ Turn the Exposure control in the comp viewer up and down to make sure everything still matches (Chapter 5).

▸ Assume there's a flaw in your shot; it's the only way around getting too attached to your intentions.

▸ Approach your project like a computer programmer and minimize the possibility of bugs (careless errors). Aspire to design in modules that anticipate what might change or be tweaked.

The Trials and Tribulations of QuickTime

QuickTime is the most ubiquitous and universal playback format among video professionals, despite that it is proprietary. There are design decisions behind QuickTime that don't change unless Apple decides to change them.

Some of these amount to a gotcha:

▸ Color management of QuickTime remains (at this writing) a moving target, with MOV files appearing differently when they are moved from one platform, software, or even monitor, to another. When I say "software" I even mean Apple applications, which don't always seem to agree on how to display the format.

▸ High Quality toggle in QuickTime Player is unchecked by default. The client is screaming about why the shot looks fuzzy and you have to direct them to Window > Show Movie Properties > Video Track > Visual Settings and the little toggle to the lower right.

▸ Many useful formats are Mac-only, such as Uncompressed 10-bit 4:2:2, an Apple format.

▸ The notorious QuickTime 7.2 caused After Effects renders to fail with a write-error.

▸ Failed or corrupted QuickTime files are typically unplayable, and the larger they are, the more susceptible they seem to be to being taken down by a spurious frame or two.

Most larger facilities rely on QuickTime only for client delivery and in the edit suite. It's inconvenient to deal with sequences when there's no free standalone player for them of the quality of FrameCycler, but sequences cause fewer of these types of problems in exchange for the overall inconvenience.

2

The Timeline

The right word may be effective, but no word was ever as effective as a rightly timed pause.

— Mark Twain

The Timeline

The Timeline can be considered After Effects' killer application. More than any other feature, it extends After Effects unique versatility to a wide range of work. With the Timeline at the center of the compositing process, you can time elements and animations precisely as you control their appearance.

The Timeline panel is also a user-friendly part of the application and full of hidden powers. By mastering its usage, you can streamline your workflow a great deal, setting the stage for more advanced work.

One major source of these hidden powers is the Timeline's set of keyboard shortcuts and context menus. These are not extras to be investigated once you're a veteran, but small productivity enhancers that you can learn gradually all the time.

Organization

The goal here isn't to keep you organized but to get rid of everything you don't need and put what you *do* need right at your fingertips.

Column Views

You can context-click on any column heading to see and toggle available columns in the Timeline, or you can start with the minimal setup shown in **Figure 2.1** and then augment or change the setup with the following tools:

Figure 2.1 This very most basic Timeline setup is close to optimal, especially if space is tight; it leaves everything you need within a single click, such as Toggle Switches/Modes. No matter how big a monitor, every artist tends to want more space for the keyframes and layers themselves.

- ▶ **Lower-left icons** 🗖 🗗 ⬍: Most (but not quite all) of the extra data you need is available via the three toggles found at the lower left of the Timeline.

- ▶ **Layer Switches** 🗖 and **Transfer Controls** 🗗 are the most-used; if you have plenty of horizontal space, leave them both on, but the F4 key has toggled them since the days when 1280 × 960 was an artist-sized display.

- ▶ **Time Stretch** ⬍ toggles the space-hogging timing columns. I'm unconvinced they're needed; the one thing I do with this huge set of controls is stretch time to either double speed or half speed (50% or 200% stretch, respectively), which I can do by context-clicking Time > Time Stretch.

- ▶ **Layer/Source (Alt/Option key toggles)**: What's in a name? Nothing until you customize it; clear labels and color (below) boost your workflow.

- ▶ **Parent**: This one is so often on when you don't need it and hidden when you do (see "Spatial Offsets" later in this chapter); use context-clicking to show/hide it.

- ▶ I can't see why you would disable **AV Features/Keys**; it takes effectively no space.

The game is to preserve horizontal space for keyframe data by keeping only the relevant controls visible.

TIP

To rename an item in After Effects, highlight it and press Return instead of clicking and hovering (as in the typical operating system).

TIP

To change the visibility (rather than the solo state) of selected layers, choose Layer > Switches > Hide Other Video.

TIP

To unlock a number of layers at once, choose Layer > Switches > Unlock All Layers (**Ctrl+Shift+L/ Cmd+Shift+L**).

NOTES

Shy layers can greatly reduce clutter in the Timeline, but if they ever trick you, study the Index numbers; if any are missing from the sequence, that's a shy layer.

Color Commentary

When dissecting something tricky, it can help to use

▸ Solo layers to see what's what

▸ Locks for layers that should not be edited further 🔒

▸ Shy layers to reduce the Timeline to only what's needed

▸ Color-coded layers and project items

▸ Tags in the comments field

Solo layers hide visible layers that are not solo'd. They are great except that other layers can stay mysteriously hidden in subsequent comps and renders. For this reason, I like to set Solo Switches to All Off in my default Render Settings.

I don't often lock layers, but it makes a heck of a lot of sense particularly for layers that you don't want "nudged" out of position, such as adjustment layers, track mattes, and background solids (but once they're locked, you can't adjust anything until you unlock them). If you're a super-organized person, you can use layer locks to check layers in and out; the locked ones are completed—for now.

Employing shy layers provides a fantastic workaround for the cluttered Timeline. Layers set to shy disappear from the Timeline (once the Timeline's own Shy toggle is enabled) but remain visible in the Composition viewer. If you've ever worked with an imported 3D track composition from such software as SynthEyes or Boujou, you know that they typically come with hundreds of null layers. I tend to make these shy immediately, leaving only the camera and background plate ready for compositing.

Colors are automagically assigned to specific types of layers (like Cameras, Lights, and Adjustment Layers) according to Preferences > Label Defaults. I often give unique colors to track matte layers so I remember not to move them. On someone else's system, the colors may change according to their preferences, although they will correspond.

Comments are generally the least used column in the Timeline, but that could change if more people start using a script called "Zorro-The Layer Tagger," which manages

Figure 2.2 Comments have become much more useful with the new Timeline search field in CS4, and the third-party script shown here, "Zorro-The Layer Tagger" (from aescripts.com), makes them even more useful. Zorro not only holds a list of keywords to apply to or remove from selected layers, it even does nifty stuff such as make layers with a given tag instantly solo or shy.

the process of adding tags to layers and using them to create selection sets (**Figure 2.2**).

Layer Markers (and, new in CS4, Comp Markers) can hold visible comments. You can add a layer marker for a given point in time with the * key on your numeric keypad, meaning you can add them while looping up a RAM Preview in real time. Comp Markers are added using **Shift** and the numbers atop your keyboard. I double-click them and make notes, both for timing and when I want to make sure a note won't get lost in the hidden Comment column.

Navigation and Shortcuts

Keyboard shortcuts make a huge difference in your ability to work speedily and effortlessly in the Timeline.

Time Navigation

Many users—particularly editors—learn time navigation shortcuts right away. Others primarily drag the current time indicator, which can quickly become tedious. See if there are any here you don't already know:

▶ **Home**, **End**, **Page Up**, and **Page Down** correspond to moving to the first or last frame of the composition, one frame backward, and one frame forward, respectively.

TIP

Laptop users in particular may prefer **Ctrl/Cmd+Left** and **Right Arrow** as an alternative to **Page Up** and **Page Down**.

▶ **Shift+Page Up** and **Shift+Page Down** skip ten frames backward or forward, respectively.

▶ **Shift+Home** and **Shift+End** navigate to the work area In and Out points respectively, and the **B** and **N** keys set these points at the current time.

▶ **I** and **O** keys navigate to the beginning and end frames of the layer.

▶ Press **Alt+Shift+J**/**Opt+Shift+J** or click on the current time status at the upper left of the Timeline to navigate to a specific frame or timecode number. In this dialog, enter +47 to increment 47 frames or –47 to decrement the same number; if you entered –47, that would navigate to a negative time position instead of offsetting by that number.

Don't bother with punctuation when entering time values into a number field in After Effects. 1000 is ten seconds (10:00) in Timecode mode.

The increment/decrement method operates in most number fields throughout After Effects (including Composition Settings).

Make Layers Behave

We were reviewing film-outs of shots in progress from *The Day After Tomorrow* at The Orphanage when my shot began to loop; it looked out a window at stragglers making their way across a snow-covered plaza and featured a beautiful matte painting by Mike Pangrazio. About two-thirds through the shot came a subtle pop. At some point, the shot had been lengthened, and a layer of noise and dirt I had included at approximately 3% transparency (for the window itself) had remained shorter in a subcomposition.

With power comes responsibility. After Effects allows you to time the entrance and exit of layers in a way that would be excruciating in other compositing applications that have no built-in sense of a layer start or end. To avoid the gotcha where a layer or comp comes up short, it is wise to make everything way longer than you ever expect you'll need— overengineer in subcomps and trim in the master comp.

To add a layer beginning at a specific time, drag the element to the layer area; a second time indicator appears that moves with your cursor (horizontally). This determines the layer's start frame. If other layers are present and visible, you can also place it in layer order by dragging it between them.

Here are some other useful tips and shortcuts:

▶ **Ctrl+/** (**Cmd+/**) adds a layer to the active composition.

▶ **Ctrl+Alt+/** (**Cmd+Opt+/**) replaces the selected layer in a composition (as does option dragging one element over another—either in the Timeline or the Project panel—this can be *hugely* useful).

▶ **J** and **K** navigate to the previous or next visible keyframe, layer marker, or work area start/end, respectively.

▶ **Ctrl+Alt+B**/**Cmd+Option+B** sets the Work Area to the length of any selected layers. To reset the Work Area to the length of the composition, double-click it.

▶ **Numeric keypad numbers** select layers with that number.

▶ **Ctrl+Up Arrow** (**Cmd+Up Arrow**) selects the next layer up; down works the same.

▶ **Ctrl+]** (**Cmd+]**) and **Ctrl+[** (**Cmd+[**) move a layer up or down one level in the stack. **Ctrl+Shift+]** and **Ctrl+Shift+[** move a layer to the top or bottom of the stack.

▶ **Context-click > Invert Selection** to invert the layers currently selected. (Locked layers are not selected, but shy layers are selected even if invisible.)

▶ **Ctrl+D** (**Cmd+D**) to duplicate any layer (or virtually any selected item).

▶ **Ctrl+Shift+D** (**Cmd+Shift+D**) splits a layer; the source ends and the duplicate continues from the current time.

▶ **[** and **]** move the In or Out points of selected layers to the current time. Add **Alt** (**Option**) to set the current frame as the In or Out point, trimming the layer.

▶ **Double-ended arrow icon** over the end of a trimmed layer lets you slide it, preserving the In and Out points while translating the timing and layer markers (but *not* keyframes).

▶ **Alt+PgUp**/**PgDn** (**Option+PgUp**/**PgDn**) nudges a layer and its keyframes forward or backward in time. **Alt**/**Option+Home** or **End** moves the layer's In point to the beginning of the comp, or the Out point to the end.

The keyboard shortcut **Ctrl+/** (**Cmd+/**) adds selected items as the top layer(s) of the active composition.

To trim a composition's Duration to the current Work Area, choose Composition > Trim Comp to Work Area.

For those who care, a preference controls whether split layers are created above or below the source layer (Preferences > General > Create Split Layers Above Original Layer).

Layer > Transform (or context-click a layer > Transform) includes three ways to fill a frame with the selected layer:

▶ **Ctrl+Alt+F** (**Cmd+Option+F**) centers a layer and fits both horizontal and vertical dimensions of the layer, whether or not this is non-uniform scaling.

▶ **Ctrl+Alt+Shift+H/Cmd+Option+Shift+H** centers but fits only the width.

▶ **Ctrl+Alt+Shift+G/Cmd+Option+Shift+G** centers but fits only the height.

Those shortcuts are a handful; context-clicking the layer for the Transform menu is nearly as easy.

Timeline Views

After Effects has a great keyframe workflow. These shortcuts will help you work with timing more quickly, accurately, and confidently:

▶ The **;** key toggles all the way in and out on the Timeline: single frame to all frames. The slider at the bottom of the Timeline zooms in and out more selectively.

▶ The scroll wheel moves you up and down the layer stack.

▶ **Shift+scroll-wheel** moves left and right in a zoomed Timeline view.

▶ **Alt/Option+scroll** zooms dynamically in and out of the Timeline, remaining focused around the cursor location.

▶ The **** key toggles between a Timeline and its Composition viewer, even if previously closed.

▶ The Comp Marker Bin contains markers you can draw out into the Timeline ruler. You can replace their sequential numbers with names.

Keyframes and the Graph Editor

Transform controls live under every layer's twirly arrow. There are keyboard shortcuts to each Transform property. For a standard 2D layer these are

▶ **A** for Anchor Point, the center pivot of the layer

▶ **P** for Position, by default the center of the comp

▶ **S** for Scale (in percent of source)

▶ **R** for Rotation (in revolutions and degrees)

▶ **T** for Opacity, or if it helps, Opaci-"T" (which is not technically spatial transform data but is grouped here anyhow because it's so essential)

Once you've revealed one of these, hold down the **Shift** key to toggle another (or to hide another one already displayed). This keeps only what you need in front of you. A 3D layer reveals four individual properties under Rotation to allow full animation on all axes.

The **Alt**/**Option** key can be used with each of these one-letter shortcuts to add the first keyframe; once there's one keyframe, any adjustments to that property at any other frame generate another keyframe automatically.

There are selection tools to correspond to Transforms:

▶ **V** activates the Selection tool, which also moves and scales in a view panel.

▶ **Y** switches to the Pan-Behind tool, which moves the anchor point.

▶ **W** stands for "wotate"—it adjusts Rotation.

Once you adjust with any of these tools, an Add Keyframe option for the corresponding Property appears under the Animation menu, so you can set the first keyframe without touching the Timeline at all.

Graph Editor

To demonstrate how best to use the Graph Editor, I devised the project 02_graphEditor.aep in the accompanying disc's Chapter02 directory. It contains a simple animation, "bouncing ball 2d," which you can create from scratch; you can also see the steps below as individual numbered compositions.

To enable the Graph Editor, click its icon in the Timeline ▨ or use the shortcut **Shift+F3**. Below the grid that appears in place of the layer stack are the Graph Editor controls (**Figure 2.3**).

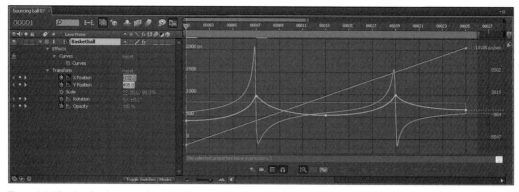

Figure 2.3 The Graph Editor is enabled in the Timeline instead of default Layer view. There is no option to see both together.

Show Properties

By default, if nothing is selected, nothing displays; what you see depends on the settings in the Show Properties menu . Three toggles in this menu control how animation curves are displayed:

▶ **Show Selected Properties** displays animation whatever property names are highlighted.

▶ **Show Animated Properties** shows everything with keyframes or expressions.

▶ **Show Graph Editor Set** displays properties with the Graph Editor Set toggle enabled.

Show Selected Properties is the easiest to use, but Show Graph Editor Set gives you the greatest control. You decide which curves need to appear, activate their Graph Editor Set toggle, and after that it no longer matters whether you keep them selected.

To begin my bouncing ball animation, I include Position in the Graph Editor Set by toggling its icon . **Alt/Option+P** sets the first Position keyframe at frame 0; after that, any changes to Position are automatically keyframed.

Basic Animation and the Graph View

Figure 2.4 shows the first step: a very basic animation blocked in using Linear keyframes, evenly spaced. It won't look like a bouncing ball yet, but it's a typical way to start when animating, for new and experienced animators alike.

TIP

To work in the Graph Editor without worrying what is selected, disable Show Selected Properties and enable the other two.

TIP

The other recommended change if you are following this section is to enable Default Spatial Interpolation to Linear in Preferences > General (**Ctrl/Command+Alt/Option+;**). You have to restart After Effects before this preference is enabled.

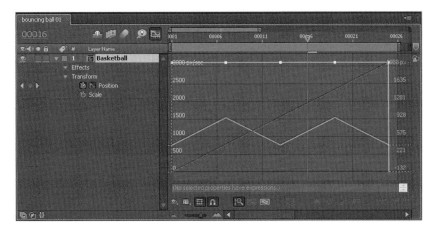

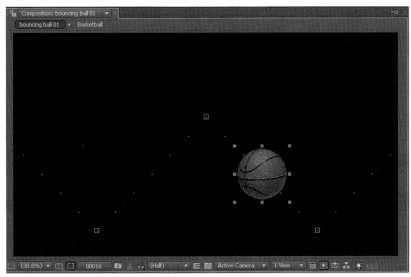

Figure 2.4 It's like a bouncing ball in that the layer travels across the frame, going up and down.

To get to this point

▶ Having set the first keyframe at frame 0, move the ball off left of frame.

▶ At frame 24, move the ball off right of frame, creating a second keyframe.

▶ Now add the bounces: At frame 6 and 18 move the ball straight downward so it touches the bottom of frame.

This leaves five Position keyframes and an extremely unconvincing looking bouncing ball animation. Great—it always helps to get something blocked in so you can clearly see what's wrong. Also, the default Graph Editor view at this point is not very helpful, because it displays the Speed Graph, and the speed of the layer is completely steady at this point—deliberately so, in fact. That's why keyframes were created in that order (although in a moment you'll see how to avoid having to do it that way with a new feature).

To get the view shown in Figure 2.4, make sure Show Reference Graph is enabled in the Graph Options menu . This is a toggle even advanced users miss, although it is now on by default; in addition to the not-very-helpful Speed Graph you now see the Value Graph in its X (red) and Y (green) values. However, the green values appear upside-down! This is the flipped After Effects Y axis in action; 0 is at the top of frame so that 0,0 is in the top left corner, as it has been since After Effects 1.0, long before 3D animation was added.

Ease Curves

The simplest way to "fix" an animation that looks too stiff like this is often to add eases. For this purpose After Effects offers the automated Easy Ease functions, although you can also create or adjust eases by hand in the Graph Editor.

Select all of the "up" keyframes—the first, third, and fifth—and click Easy Ease (**F9**). When a ball bounces, it slows at the top of each arc, and Easy Ease adds that arc to the pace; what was a flat line Speed Graph now is a series of arcing curves (**Figure 2.5**).

Technically, you could have applied Easy Ease Out (**Ctrl/Command+Shift+F9**) to the first keyframe and Easy Ease In (**Shift+F9**) to the final one, because the ease in each case only goes in one direction. The "in" and "out" versions of Easy Easy are specifically for cases where there are other adjacent keyframes and the ease should only go in one direction (you'll see one in a moment). In this case it's not really necessary.

NOTES

Auto Select Graph Type selects Speed graphs for spatial properties and Value graphs for all others.

WARNING

Mac users beware: The F9 key is used by the system for the Exposé feature, revealing all open panels in all applications. You can change or disable this feature in System Preferences > Dashboard & Exposé.

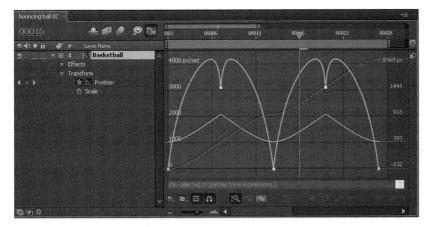

Figure 2.5 Easy Ease is applied (top) to the mid-air keyframes; Layer view (bottom) also shows the change from linear to Bézier with a changed keyframe icon.

Meanwhile, there's a clear problem here: The timing of the motion arcs, but not the motion itself, is still completely linear. Fix this in the Composition viewer by pulling Beziers out of each of the keyframes you just eased:

1. Deselect all keyframes but leave the layer selected.

2. Make sure the animation path is displayed (**Ctrl/ Command+Shift+H** toggles).

3. Click on the first keyframe in the Composition viewer to select it; it should change from hollow to solid in appearance.

4. Switches to the Pen tool with the **G** key; in the Composition viewer, drag from the highlighted keyframe to the right, creating a horizontal Bezier handle. Stop before crossing the second keyframe.

5. Do the same for the third and fifth keyframes (dragging left for the fifth).

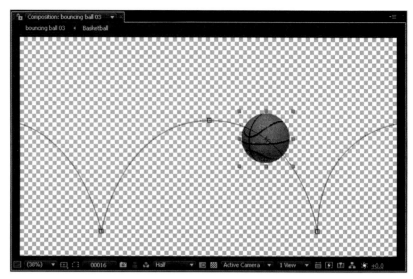

Figure 2.6 You can tell just from the graph that this is closer to how a bouncing ball would look over time. You can use Ctrl/Command+Shift+H to show and hide the animation path, or you can look in the Comp panel menu > View Options > Layer Controls.

The animation path now looks more like you'd expect a ball to bounce (**Figure 2.6**). Preview the animation, however, and you'll notice that the ball appears to be riding a pogo stick across the frame, instead of bouncing naturally. Why is that?

Separate XYX

The Graph Editor reveals the problem. The red X graph shows an unsteady horizontal motion due to the eases. The problem is that the eases should be applied only to the vertical Y dimension, whereas the X animation travels at a constant rate.

New to After Effects CS4 is the ability to animate X and Y (or, in 3D, X, Y, and Z) animation curves separately. This allows you to add keyframes for one dimension only at a given point in time, or to add keyframes in one dimension at a time.

Select Position and click Separate Dimensions . Where there was a single Position property, there are now two marked X Position and Y Position. Now try the following:

1. Disable the Graph Editor Set toggle for Y Position so that only the red X Position graph is displayed.

2. Select the middle three X Position keyframes—you can draw a selection box around them—and delete them.

3. Select the two remaining X keyframes and click the Convert Selected Keyframes to Linear button.

Now take a look in the Composition viewer—the motion is back to linear, although the temporal eases remain on the Y axis. Not only that, but you cannot redraw them as you did before; enabling Separate Dimensions removes this ability.

Instead, you can create them in the Graph Editor itself.

1. Enable the Graph Editor Set toggle for Y Position, so both dimensions are once again displayed.

2. Select the middle Y Position keyframe, and you'll notice two small handles protruding to its left and right. Drag each of these out, holding the Shift key if necessary to keep them flat, and notice the corresponding change in the Composition viewer (**Figure 2.7**).

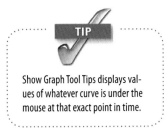

TIP

Show Graph Tool Tips displays values of whatever curve is under the mouse at that exact point in time.

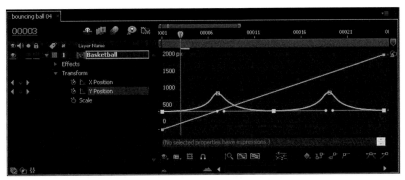

Figure 2.7 If Separate Dimensions is activated, pull out the handles to create the motion arcs right in the Graph Editor; the handles are no longer adjustable in Comp view.

3. Select the first and last Y Position keyframes and click Easy Ease; the handles move outward from each keyframe without affecting the X Position keyframes.

4. Drag the handles of the first and last Y Position keyframes as far as they will go (right up to the succeeding and preceding keyframes, respectively).

Preview the result and you'll see that you now have the beginnings of an actual bouncing ball animation; it's just a little bit too regular and even, so from here you will give it your own organic touch.

The Transform Box

The Transform Box lets you edit keyframe values in all kinds of wacky ways. Toggle on Show Transform Box and select more than one keyframe, and a white box with vertices surrounds the selected frames. Drag the handle at the right side left or right to change overall timing; the keyframes remain proportionally arranged.

So, does the Transform Box help in this case? Well, it could, if you needed to

NOTES

There is a whole menu of options to show items that you might think are only in Layer view: layer In/Out points, audio waveforms, layer markers, and expressions.

▶ Scale the animation timing around a particular keyframe: drag the anchor to that frame, then **Ctrl**-drag/ **Cmd**-drag.

▶ Reverse the animation: **Ctrl**-drag/**Cmd**-drag from one edge of the box to the other (or for a straight reversal, simply context-click and choose Keyframe Assistant > Time-Reverse Keyframes).

▶ Add a decay to the animation so that the ball bounces lower each time: **Alt**-drag (**Option**-drag) on the lower right corner handle (**Figure 2.8**).

NOTES

The Snap button snaps to virtually every visible marker, but not—snap!—to whole frame values if Allow Keyframes Between Frames is on .

If you **Ctrl+Alt**-drag (**Cmd+Option**-drag) on a corner that will taper values at one end, and if you **Ctrl+Alt+ Shift**-drag (**Cmd+Option+Shift**-drag) on a corner, it will skew that end of the box up or down. I don't do this stuff much, but with a lot of keyframes to scale proportionally, it's a good one to keep in your back pocket.

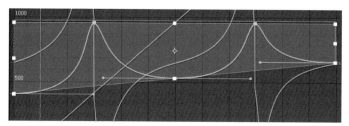

Figure 2.8 How do you do that? Add the Alt/Option key when dragging a corner of the Transform Box; this adjustment diminishes the height of the ball bounces proportionally over time.

Holds

At this point you may have a fairly realistic looking bouncing ball; maybe you added a little Rotation animation so the ball spins forward as it bounces, or maybe you hand-adjusted the timing or position keys to give them that extra little organic unevenness.

Hold keyframes won't help improve this animation, but you could make the ball disappear each time it hits the ground, and reappear at the top of the arc, with no eases. A Hold keyframe  (**Ctrl+Alt+H/Cmd+Shift+H**) prevents any change to a value until the next keyframe.

Add keyframes alternating between 100% and 0% Opacity at the same time as the existing Y Position keyframes. If you leave them as linear keyframes, the ball oscillates between opaque and transparent, but if you toggle them to Hold keyframes, it snaps on and off (**Figure 2.9**).

Figure 2.9 Linear keyframes hold a value across time, until the next keyframe value appears.

Beyond Bouncing Balls

In the (possibly likely) case that the need for a bouncing ball animation never comes up, what does this example show you? Let's recap:

▶ You can control a motion path in the Composition viewer using Bézier tools and the Pen tool (usage detailed in the next chapter).

▶ Realistic motion often requires that you shape the motion path Béziers and add temporal eases; the two actions are performed independently on any given keyframe, and in two different places (in the viewer and Timeline).

Animation can get a little trickier in 3D, but the same basic rules apply (see Chapter 9 for more).

Three preset keyframe transition types are available, each with a shortcut at the bottom of the Graph Editor: Hold , Linear, and Automatic Bezier. Adjust the handles or apply Easy Ease and the preset becomes a custom Bezier Shape.

CLOSE-UP

Roving Keyframes

Sometimes an animation must follow an exact path, hitting precise points, but progress steadily, with no variation in the rate of travel. This is the situation for which Roving keyframes were devised. **Figure 2.10** shows a before and after view of a roving keyframe; the path of the animation is identical, but the keyframes proceed at a steady rate.

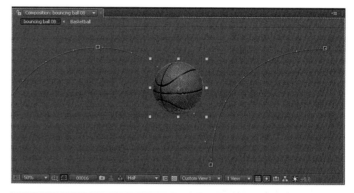

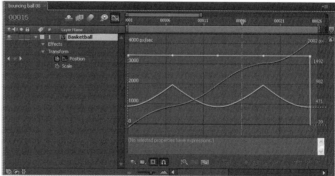

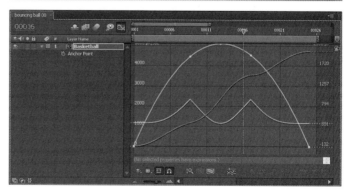

Figure 2.10 Compare this graph with the one in Figure 2.5 (top); the Speed Graph is back to a flat-line because the animation runs at a uniform pace. It's not helpful to bounce a ball, but it works with any complex animation, and it maintains eases on the start and end frame.

Copy and Paste Animations

Yes, copy and paste; everyone knows how to do it. Here are some things that aren't necessarily obvious about copying and pasting keyframe data:

▶ Got Excel or another spreadsheet application? Copy a set of keyframes from After Effects and paste them into a spreadsheet, and the After Effects keyframe format is laid bare.

▶ You can paste from one property to another, so long as the format matches (the units and number of parameters). Copy the source, highlight the target, and paste.

▶ Keyframes respect the position of the current time indicator; the first frame is always pasted at the current time (useful for relocating timing, occasionally a surprise).

▶ There's a lock on the Effect Controls tab to keep a panel forward even when you select another layer to paste to it.

▶ Copy and paste keyframes from an effect that isn't applied to the target, and it is added along with the animation, natch; you don't get any properties you didn't select and copy, however.

Therefore, pay attention to the current time and what is selected when copying, but in particular, when pasting animation data.

Layer vs. Graph

To summarize the distinction between Layer and Graph Editor views, in Layer view you can

▶ Block in keyframes with respect to the overall composition

▶ Establish broad timing (where Linear, Easy Ease, and Auto-Bezier keyframes are sufficient)

The Graph Editor is essential to

▶ Refine an individual animation curve

▶ Compare spatial and temporal data

▶ Scale animation data, especially around a specific pivot point

TIP

You can use an Excel spreadsheet to reformat keyframe data from other applications; just paste in After Effects data to see how it's formatted, and then massage the other data to match that format. Once done, copy and paste back into After Effects.

▶ Perform extremely specific timing (adding a keyframe is between frames, hit a specific tween point with an ease curve)

With either view you can

▶ Edit expressions

▶ Change keyframe type (Linear, Hold, Ease In, and so on)

▶ Make editorial/compositing decisions regarding layers (start/stop/duration, split layers, order—possible in both, easier in Layer view)

By no means, then, does the Graph Editor make Layer view obsolete; it is still where the majority of compositing and simple animation is accomplished.

Über-duper

The following keyboard shortcuts have broad usage when applied with layers selected in the Timeline:

▶ **U** toggles all properties with keyframes or expressions applied.

▶ **UU** (U twice in quick succession) toggles all properties set to any value besides the default; or every Property in the Timeline that has been edited.

▶ **E** toggles all applied effects.

▶ **EE** toggles all applied expressions.

When I use the term "toggle" in the above list, I mean that not only do these shortcuts reveal the listed properties, they can also conceal them, or with the **Shift** key, they can be used in combination with one another and with many of the shortcuts detailed earlier (such as the Transform shortcuts **A**, **P**, **R**, **S**, and **T** or the Mask shortcuts **M**, **MM**, and **F**). You want all the changes applied to Masks and Transforms, not Effects? **UU**, then **Shift+E**. Lose the Masks? **Shift+M**.

The **U** shortcut is a quick way to find keyframes to edit or to locate a keyframe that you suspect is hiding somewhere. But **UU**—now *that* is a full-on problem-solving tool all to itself. It allows you to quickly investigate what has been edited on a given layer, is helpful when troubleshooting

You must enable Allow Keyframes Between Frames in the Graph Editor if you want that feature. However, when you scale a set of keyframes using the Transform Box, keyframes will often fall in between frames whether or not this option is enabled.

The term "überkey" seems to play on Friedrich Nietzsche's concept of the "übermensch"—it is a shortcut more powerful and important than others.

your own layer settings, and is nearly priceless when investigating an unfamiliar project.

Highlight all the layers of a Comp and press **UU** to reveal all edits, enable Switches, Modes, Parent, and Stretch columns, and you see everything in a Comp, with the exception of

▶ Contents of nested compositions, which must be opened (**Alt/Option**-double-click) and analyzed individually

▶ Locked layers

▶ Shy layers (disable them atop the Timeline to show all)

▶ Comp settings themselves, such as motion blur and frame rate

In other words, this is an effective method to use to understand or troubleshoot a shot.

Dissect a Project

If you've been handed an unfamiliar project and need to make sense of it quickly, there are a couple of other tools that may help.

The new one of these is probably my favorite new feature in After Effects CS4: Miniflow (**Shift** key toggles with the Timeline, Comp, or Layer view active, **Figure 2.11b**). It quickly maps any upstream or downstream comps and allows you to open any of them simply by clicking on it.

If you're looking for a whole visual map of the project instead, try Flowchart view (**Ctrl+F11/Cmd+F11** or the tree/node icon in the Composition viewer). You have to see it to believe it: a nodal interface in After Effects (**Figure 2.11a**), perhaps the least nodal of any of the major compositing applications.

This view shows how objects (layers, compositions, and effects) are used, and in what relationship to one another. The + button above a composition reveals its components; for the cleanest view, toggle layers and effects off at the lower left.

You can't make any edits here, but you can double-click any item to reveal it where you can edit it—back in the Timeline, of course.

Nerd-Based Compositing

Flowchart, the After Effects nodal view, reveals the truth that all compositing applications are, at their core, nodal in their logic and organization. However, this particular tree/node view is diagnostic and high-level only; you can delete a layer but you can't create one here.

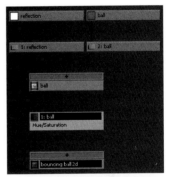

Figure 2.11 The tree/node interface in Flowchart (a, top) is a diagnostic rather than a creative tool. Click the ■ icon to switch the view to flow left to right, which fits well on a monitor, or Option-click it to clean up the view. Its usage has largely been superceded by the new Miniflow (b, bottom), which focuses interactively on the current comp.

Keyframe Navigation and Selection

Although no shortcut can hold a candle to the überkey, there are several other useful Timeline shortcuts:

▶ **J** and **K** keys navigate backward and forward, respectively, through all *visible* keyframes, layer markers, and Work Area boundaries; hide the properties you don't want to navigate.

▶ Click *Property name* to select all keyframes for a property.

▶ Context-click keyframe > Select Previous Keyframes or Select Following Keyframes to avoid difficult drag selections.

▶ Context-click keyframe > Select Equal Keyframes to hit all keyframes with the same setting.

▶ **Alt/Option+Shift+**Transform shortcut (**P**, **A**, **S**, **R**, or **T**) sets a keyframe; no need to click anywhere.

▶ Click a property Stopwatch to set the first keyframe at the current frame (if no keyframe exists), or delete all existing keyframes.

▶ **Cntl/Command-click** an Effect stopwatch to set a keyframe.

▶ **Ctrl+Alt+A/Cmd+Option+A** selects all visible keyframes while leaving the source layers, making it easy to delete them when, say, duplicating a layer but changing its animation.

▶ **Shift+F2** deselects keyframes only.

Read on; you are not a keyframe Jedi—yet.

Keyframe Offsets

To offset the values of multiple keyframes by the same amount in Layer view, select them all, *place the current time indicator over a selected keyframe,* and drag the setting; all change by the same increment. If instead you type in a new value, or enter an offset, such as +20 or +-47, with a numerical value, all keyframes take on the (identical) new value.

With multiple keyframes selected you can also

▶ **Alt+Right/Left Arrow** (**Option+Right/Left Arrow**) to nudge keyframes forward or backward in time

- ▶ Context-click > Keyframe Assistant > Time-Reverse Key-frames to run the animation in reverse without changing the duration and start/end point of the selected keyframe sequence

- ▶ **Option**-drag the first or last selected keyframe to scale timing proportionally in Layer view (or use the transform box in the Graph Editor)

Spatial Offsets

3D animators will be familiar with the idea that every object (or layer) has a pivot point. In After Effects, there are two fundamental ways to make a layer pivot around a different location: change the layer's own Anchor Point setting, or parent it to another layer.

After Effects is generally designed to preserve the appearance of the composition when you are merely setting up animation, toggling 3D on, and so forth. Therefore editing an anchor point position with the Pan Behind tool triggers the inverse offset to the Position property. Parent a layer to another layer and the child layer maintains its relative position until you further animate either of them.

It's typically best to set up your offsets and hierarchy before animating, although this section shows how to go about changing your mind once keyframes are in place. The Option key is key to all options.

Anchor Point

The Pan Behind tool (**Y**) repositions an anchor point in the Composition panel and offsets the Position value to compensate. This prevents the layer from appearing in a different location on the frame in which you're working.

The Position offset is for that frame only, however, so if there are Position keyframes, the layer may appear offset on other frames if you drag the anchor point this way. To reposition the anchor point without changing Position

- ▶ Change the Anchor Point value in the Timeline

- ▶ Use the Pan Behind tool in Layer view instead

- ▶ Hold the **Option** key as you drag with the Pan Behind tool

Any of these options lets you reposition the anchor point without messing up an animation by changing one of the Position keyframes.

You can also animate the anchor point, of course; this allows you to rotate as you pan around an image while keeping the view centered. If you're having trouble seeing the anchor point path as you work, open Layer view and choose Anchor Point Path in the View pop-up menu (**Figure 2.12**).

Figure 2.12 Switch default Masks to Anchor Point Path for easy viewing and manipulation of the layer anchor point. For the bouncing ball, you could move the anchor point to the base of the layer to add a little cartoonish squash and stretch, scaling Y down at the impact points.

Parent Hierarchy

Layer parenting, in which all of the Transform settings (except Opacity, which isn't really a Transform setting) are passed from parent to child, can be set up by revealing the Parent column in the Timeline. There, you can choose a layer's parent either by selecting it from the list, or by dragging the Pickwhip to the parent layer, and use the setup as follows:

▶ Parenting remains valid even if the parent layer moves, is duplicated, or changes its name.

▶ A parent and all of its children can be selected by context-clicking the parent layer and choosing Select Children.

▶ Parenting can be removed by choosing None from the Parent menu.

▶ Null Objects (**Ctrl+Alt/Command+Option+Shift+Y**) exist only to be parents; they are actually 100 × 100 pixel layers that do not render.

You probably knew all of that. You might *not* know what happens when you add the **Option** key to Parent settings:

▶ Hold **Option** as you select the None option and the layer reverts to the Transform values it had before being parented (otherwise the offset at the time None is selected remains).

▶ Hold **Option** as you select a Parent layer and its Transform data at the current frame applied to the child layer prior to parenting.

This last point is a very cool and easily missed method for arraying layers automatically. You duplicate, offset, and parent to create the first layer in a pattern, then duplicate that layer and Option+Parent it to the previous duplicate. It behaves like the Duplicate and Offset option in Illustrator (**Figure 2.13**).

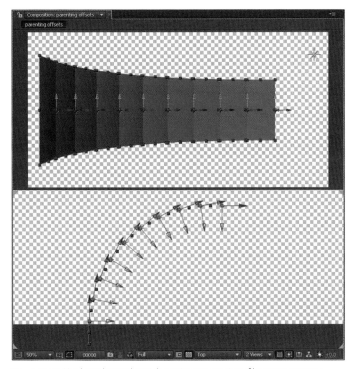

Figure 2.13 Until you know the trick, setting up a series of layers as an array seems like a big pain. The trick is to create the first layer, duplicate, and offset; now you have two. Duplicate the offset layer and—this is the key—Alt/Option+Parent the duplicate to the offset. Repeat this last step with as many layers as you need; each one repeats the offset. (Tip of the hat to Danny Princz!)

Motion Blur

Motion blur is obviously essential to a realistic shot with a good amount of motion. It is the natural result of movement that occurs while a camera shutter is open, causing objects in the image to be recorded at every point from the shutter opening to closing. The movement can be individual objects or the camera itself.

Although it essentially smears layers in a composition, motion blur is generally desirable; it adds to persistence of vision, relaxes the eye, and is a natural phenomenon. Aesthetically, it can be quite beautiful.

The typical idea with motion blur in a realistic visual effects shot is to match the amount of blur in the source shot, assuming you have reference; if you lack visual reference, a camera report can also help you set this correctly.

A moving picture camera has a *shutter speed* setting that controls the amount of motion blur. This is not the camera's frame rate, although the shutter does obviously have to be fast enough to accommodate the frame rate. A typical film camera shooting 24 frames per second has a shutter that is open half the time, or $\frac{1}{48}$ of a second.

Motion blur occurs in your natural vision, although you might not realize it—stare at a ceiling fan in motion, and then try following an individual blade around instead and you will notice a dramatic difference. There is a trend in recent years to use extremely high-speed electronic shutters, which drastically reduces motion blur and gives the psychological effect of heightened awareness by making your eye feel as if it's tracking motion in this manner. This seems to have started with live television sports coverage and the use of extremely fast shutters for slow motion replay cameras.

Decoding After Effects Motion Blur

The Advanced tab of Composition Settings (**Ctrl/Command+K**) contains Motion Blur settings (**Figure 2.14**):

▶ **Shutter Angle** controls shutter speed, and thus the amount of blur.

Motion Blur

Shutter Angle: 180°   Shutter Phase: -90°

Samples Per Frame: 16   Adaptive Sample Limit: 128

Samples Per Frame controls the number of motion blur samples for 3D layers, shape layers, and certain effects. 2D layer motion automatically uses more samples per frame when needed, up to the Adaptive Sample Limit.

Figure 2.14 These are the default settings; 16 is really too low for good looking blur at high speed but a 180 degree shutter and –90 Shutter Angle match the look of a film camera. Any changes you make here stick and are passed along to the next composition, or even the next project, until you change them.

▶ **Shutter Phase** determines at what point the shutter opens.

▶ **Samples Per Frame** applies only to 3D motion blur; it sets the number of slices in time (samples), and thus, smoothness.

▶ **Adaptive Sample Limit** applies only to 2D motion blur, which automatically uses as many samples as are needed up to this limit (**Figure 2.15**).

Here's a bit of a gotcha: the default settings that you see in this panel are simply whatever was set the last time it was adjusted (unless never, in which case there are defaults). It's theoretically great to reuse settings that work across several projects, but I've seen artists faked out by vestigial extreme settings like 2 Samples Per Frame or a 720 degree blur that may have matched perfectly in some unique case.

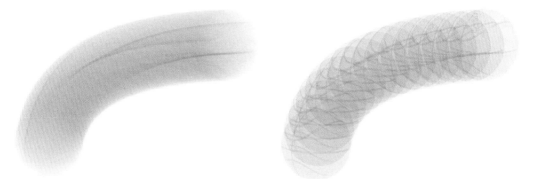

Figure 2.15 The low default 16 Samples Per Frame setting creates steppy looking blur on a 3D layer only; the same animation and default settings in 2D uses the higher default Adaptive Sample Limit of 128. The reason for the difference is simply performance; 3D blur is costlier, but like many settings it is conservative. Unless your machine is ancient, boost the number; the boosted setting will stay as a preference.

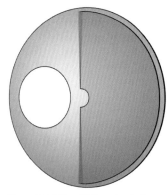

Figure 2.16 The 180° mechanical shutter of a film camera prevents light from exposing film half the time, for an effective exposure of 1/48th of a second. This is the look of film; electronic shutters can have a higher equivalent radius, blurring nearly continuously from one frame to the next, or a very fast shutter, which permits little or no blur.

Shutter Angle refers to an angled mechanical shutter present in some cameras; it is a hemisphere of a given angle that rotates on each frame. The angle is its radius (**Figure 2.16**). A typical film shutter is 180 degrees—open half the time, or $\frac{1}{48}$ of a second at 24 frames per second.

Electronic shutters are variable but refer to Shutter Angle as a benchmark; they can operate down in the single digits or close to a full 360 degrees. After Effects motion blur goes to 720 degrees simply because sometimes mathematical accuracy is not the name of the game, and you simply want more than 360 degrees.

If you don't know this setting, you can typically nail it by zooming in and matching background and foreground elements by eye (**Figure 2.17**). If your camera report includes shutter speed, you can calculate the Shutter Angle setting using the following formula:

shutter speed = 1 / frame rate * (360 / shutter angle)

This isn't as gnarly as it looks, but if you dislike formulas, think of it like this: If your camera takes 24 frames per second, but Shutter Angle is set at 180 degrees, then the

Figure 2.17 The white solid tracked to the side of the streetcar has been eye matched to have an equivalent blur by adjusting Shutter Angle; care is also taken to set the Shutter Phase to –50% of the Shutter Angle so that the layer stays centered on the track.

frame is exposed half the time ($180/360 = \frac{1}{2}$) or $\frac{1}{48}$ of a second. However, if the shutter speed is $\frac{1}{96}$ per second with this frame rate, Shutter Angle should be 90 degrees. A $\frac{1}{1000}$ per second shutter would have a 9 degree Shutter Angle.

Shutter Phase determines how the shutter opens relative to the frame, which covers a given fraction of a second beginning at a given point in time. If the shutter is set to 0, it opens at that point in time, and the blur appears to extend forward through the frame, which makes it appear offset.

The default −90 Shutter Phase setting (with a 180° Shutter Angle) causes half the blur to occur before the frame so that blur extends in both directions from the current position. This is how blur appears when taken with a camera, so a setting that is −50% of Shutter Angle is essential when you're adding motion blur to a motion tracked shot. Otherwise, the track itself appears offset.

Add, Do Not Subtract

Although software may one day be developed to resolve a blurred image, it is much, much harder to sharpen a blurred image elegantly than it is to add blur to a sharp image. Motion Blur comes for free when you keyframe motion in After Effects; what about when there is motion but no blur and no keyframes, as can be the case in pre-exising footage?

If you have imported a 3D element with insufficient blur, or footage shot with too high a shutter speed, you have the options to add the effect of motion blur using

▶ Directional Blur, which can mimic the blur of layers moving in some uniform X and Y direction

▶ Zoom Blur, which can mimic motion in Z depth (or spin)

▶ Timewarp, which can add motion blur without retiming footage

Yes, you read that last one correctly. There's a full section on Timewarp later in this chapter, but to use it to add procedural motion blur, just set Speed to 100 and toggle Enable Motion Blur, then raise Shutter Angle and Shutter Samples (being aware that the higher you raise them, the longer the render time). The methodology is similar to that of Reel Smart Motion Blur (RE:Vision Effects); try the demo on the book's disc and compare quality and render time.

Don't forget motion blur when matching foreground and background elements (Chapter 5). An element perfectly matched for color and lighting will look wrong until its motion blur also matches that of the surrounding scene.

Manipulate Time

After Effects is more flexible when working with time than most video applications. You can retime footage or mix and match speeds and timing using a variety of methods.

Absolute (Not Relative) Time

After Effects measures time in absolute seconds, rather than frames, whose timing and number are relative to the number per second. If frames instead of seconds were the measure of time, changing the frame rate on the fly would pose a much greater problem than it does.

Change the frame rate of a comp and the keyframes maintain their position in actual time, so the actual timing of an animation doesn't change (**Figure 2.18**), only the position of the keyframes relative to frames. Here's a haiku:

keyframes reposition
falling between retimed frames
time remains unchanged

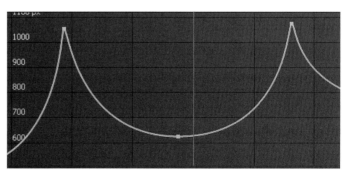

Figure 2.18 The bounce animation remains the same as the comp frame rate changes; keyframes now fall in between whole frames, the vertical lines on the grid.

Likewise, footage (or a nested composition) with a mismatched frame rate syncs up at least once a second, but the intervening source frames may fall in between comp frames. Think of a musician playing 3 against 4; one second in After Effects is the down beat of each rhythm.

Time Stretch

Time Stretch lets you alter the duration (and thus the speed) of a source clip—but it doesn't let you animate the retiming itself (that requires Time Remap or Timewarp). The third of the three icons at the lower left of the Timeline reveals the In/Out/Duration/Stretch columns.

I mostly change the Stretch value and find the four-column approach redundant. I also never use a Time Stretch setting that is anything but an integer multiple or division by halves: 200%, 300%, 50% or 25%. You can do without the columns altogether using the Time Stretch dialog (context-click > Time > Time Stretch).

Ctrl+Alt+R (Cmd+Option+R) or Layer > Time > Time-Reverse Layer sets the Stretch value to –100%. The layer's appearance alters to remind you that it is reversed (**Figure 2.19**).

Figure 2.19 The candy striping along the bottom of the layer indicates that the Stretch value is negative and the footage will run in reverse.

Layer > Time > Freeze Frame applies the Time Remap effect with a single Hold keyframe at the current time.

Frame Blending

Suppose you don't use a stretch value that factors evenly into 100% (such as 50% or 200%); footage is likely to lurch in a distracting, inelegant fashion. Enable Frame Blending for the layer and the composition, and After Effects averages the adjacent frames together to create a new image on frames that fall in between the source frames. This also works when you're adding footage to a comp with a mismatched frame rate. There are two modes:

▶ Frame Mix mode overlays adjoining frames, essentially blurring them together.

▶ Pixel Motion mode uses optical flow techniques to track the motion of actual pixels from frame to frame, creating new frames that are something like a morph of the adjoining frames.

Confusingly, the icons for these modes are the same as Draft and Best layer quality, respectively (**Figure 2.20**), yet there are cases where Frame Mix may be preferable instead of merely quicker to render. Pixel Motion can often appear too blurry, too distorted, or contain too many noticeable frame artifacts, in which case you can move back to Frame Mix, or move up to the Timewarp effect, with greater control of the same technology (later in this chapter).

The optical flow in Pixel Motion and the Timewarp effect was licensed from The Foundry. The same underlying technology is also used in Furnace plug-ins for Shake, Flame, and Nuke.

Figure 2.20 The Frame Blending switches for the Comp and Layer are highlighted. Just because Pixel Motion mode uses the same icon as Best in the Quality switch, to the left, doesn't mean it's guaranteed to be the best choice.

Nested Compositions

Time Stretch (or Time Remap) applies the main composition's frame rate to a nested composition; animations are not frame-blended, instead the keyframe interpolation is resliced to the new frame rate.

Effect > Time > Posterize Time can force any layer to take on the specified frame rate, but effects in the Time category should be applied before all other effects in a given layer. Posterize Time often breaks preceding effects.

Most of the time, if you put a comp with a lower frame rate into a master comp, you intended to keep the frame rate of the embedded composition. In such a case, go to the *nested* comp's Composition Settings > Advanced panel and toggle Preserve Frame Rate When Nested or in Render Queue (**Figure 2.21**). This forces After Effects to use only whole frame increments in the underlying composition, just as if the comp were pre-rendered with that frame rate.

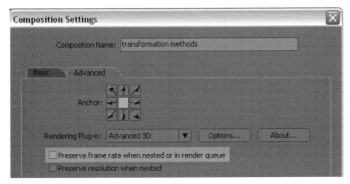

Figure 2.21 The subcomposition will run at its own frame rate when placed in the master composition instead of resampling, if they are different from one another.

Time Remap

Time Remap definitely trumps Time Stretch. The philosophy is elusively simple: Time has a value, just like any other property, so you can keyframe it, ease in and out of it, loop and ping-pong it—basically treat it like any other animation data. All true, but the concept of animating and bending time can become complex.

Ctrl+Alt+T/**Cmd+Option+T** or Layer > Time > Enable Time Remapping sets two Time Remap keyframes: at the beginning and one frame beyond the end of the layer. Time remapped layers have a theoretically infinite duration, so the final Time Remap frame effectively becomes a Hold keyframe; you can then freely scale the layer length beyond that last frame.

Beware when applying Time Remap to a layer whose first or last frame extends beyond Comp duration; you may not be able to see those keyframes. In such a case, I tend to add keyframes at the comp start and end points, click Time Remap to select all keyframes, Shift-deselect the ones I can see in the Timeline, and delete to get rid of the ones I can't see.

There is also a Freeze Frame option in After Effects; context-click a layer, or from the Layer menu choose Time > Freeze Frame, which sets Time Remap (if not already set) with a single hold keyframe.

TIP

The final Time Remap keyframe is one greater than the total timing of the layer (in most cases a nonexistent frame) to guarantee that the final source frame is reached, even when frame rates don't match.

Timewarp

Although The Foundry's amazing Furnace plug-ins are not, at this writing, available for After Effects, Adobe licensed one component of Furnace, the retiming tool known as Kronos, to provide the technology used in Pixel Motion and Timewarp. Pixel Motion is an automated setting described earlier, and Timewarp adds a set of controls to allow you to improve on its result using the same basic technology.

Timewarp works by calculating the motion in the footage in order to generation motion vectors; these describe how each pixel moves from frame to frame. With an accurate analysis it is then possible to generate an image made up of those same pixels, interpolated along those vectors, with different timing.

Timewarp is just like Time Remap in the following ways:

▶ It can be used to speed up, slow down, or dynamically animate the timing of a clip.

▶ It incorporates the same three Frame Blending modes (Whole Frames, Frame Mix, and Pixel Motion) as are available to Time Remap in the Timeline settings; these live in Timewarp's Method menu.

▶ Time Remap keyframes can even be transferred directly to Timewarp, but it requires an expression (see note) because one uses frames and the other seconds to measure time.

However, used with the default Pixel Motion Method setting, Timewarp goes beyond Time Remap plus Frame Blending with the same setting in a couple of ways:

▶ Enable Motion Blur toggle kicks in when footage is sped up to add motion blur.

▶ Tuning section lets you refine the automated results of Pixel Motion.

Timewarp is most typically used to slow footage down, which requires one extra bit of setup or the layer ends short. Enable Time Remapping and extend the layer across your Comp; the Time Remap settings don't even matter as Timewarp will override them.

NOTES

To transfer Time Remap keyframes to Source Frame mode in Timewarp, enable an expression (Chapter 10) for Source Frame and enter the following:
```
d = thisComp.
➥frameDuration
timeRemap * 1/d
```

Figure 2.22 This sequence was taken Matrix-style, with an array of still cameras firing in sequence around the subject. To transform this into a slow-motion visual effect requires optical-flow retiming, and because the foreground travels in one direction and the background the other, it helps Timewarp to add a matte. (Sequence courtesy of fxphd.com)

Here are some tips to improve on the default Pixel Motion result with Timewarp:

▶ Matte Layer and Matte Channel menus can point to a matte channel used to isolate foreground and background motion, as in **Figure 2.22**. This can be the source alpha channel, or a matte channel from a separate layer.

▶ Warp Layer control analyzes a separate layer (as specified in the menu) and applies the result. Sometimes you need to adjust footage (contrast, luminance, key) in order to get a better result, but you don't want those adjustments in your shot; apply them to a duplicate layer instead and set that.

The Tuning section is where you trade render time and accuracy, but don't assume that greater accuracy always yields a better result—it's just not so. These tools make use of Local Motion Estimation (LME) technology, which is thoroughly documented in the Furnace User Guide.

The following settings control how Timewarp analyzes footage:

▶ Raising Vector Detail certainly increases accuracy; a setting of 100 assigns one vector per pixel. Not only does this drastically increase render time, it will in some cases simply increase artifacts with fast motion. This is because it is analyzing too much detail, similar to setting a motion track to too small (and noisy) a search region.

▶ Smoothing relates directly to Vector Detail; vectors must join similar pixels of adjacent frames but not be noisy. You can raise Global Smoothness (all vectors), Local Smoothness (individual vectors) and Smoothing Iterations in order to combat the noise, but go very far and lots of detail will be missed. The Foundry claims that the defaults, which are balanced, work best for most sequences.

▶ It typically takes two adjacent images—before and after—to make a vector, but you can choose Build From One Image to use only one if that helps.

▶ LME depends on object brightness remaining consistent throughout the shot. Toggling Correct Luminance Changes on warns Timewarp that there will be fluctuations, whether sudden (image flicker) or gradual (moving highlights).

▶ Error Threshold evaluates each vector before letting it contribute; raise this value and more vectors are eliminated for having too much perceived error.

▶ Block Size determines the width and height of the area each vector tracks; like Smoothing, lower values generate more noise, higher values less detail. The Foundry documentation indicates that this value should "rarely need editing."

▶ Weighting lets you control how much a given color channel is factored. The defaults may seem odd, but as you'll learn in Chapter 5 they correspond to how the eye weights each color and so they produce a perfectly monochrome image. If one channel is particularly noisy—usually blue—you might consider lowering its setting.

▶ Filtering applies to the render, not the analysis; it increases the sharpness of the result. It will cost you render time, so if you do enable it, wait until you're done with your other changes and are ready to render.

Despite that Timewarp is included free, many knowledgeable After Effects artists still depend on Twixtor (RE:Vision Effects); like 3D trackers, keyers, and other automated solutions, this is more a question of what works for you than of one being better than another. A demo of Twixtor can be found on the book's disc.

TIP

Did you notice back in the Motion Blur section that Timewarp can be used to generate procedural motion blur without retiming footage (**Figure 2.23**)?

Figure 2.23 Footage that is shot overcranked (at high speed, a) typically lacks sufficient motion blur when retimed. Timewarp can add motion blur to speed up footage; it can even add motion blur to footage with no speed-up at all, in either case using the same optical flow technology that tracks individual pixels. It looks fantastic.

Conclusion

The elegance and logic of the After Effects Timeline is not always evident to the new user, but this chapter taught you that shortcuts and other workflow enhancements help streamline what might otherwise be tedious or exacting edits. The Timeline and Graph Editor, once mastered, give you the control you need over the timing and placement of elements.

If this chapter's information seems overwhelming on first read, keep coming back to it so that specific tips can sink in once you've encountered the right context in which to use them.

3

Selections:
The Key to Compositing

I'm fixing a hole where the rain gets in
And stops my mind from wandering
Where it will go.

—John Lennon and Paul McCartney

Selections:
The Key to Compositing

A particle physicist works with atoms, bakers and bankers each work with types of dough, and compositors work with selections—many different types of selections, potentially thousands, each derived uniquely.

If compositing were simply a question of taking pristine, perfect foreground source A and overlaying it onto perfectly matching background plate B, there would be no compositor in the effects process; an editor could accomplish the job before lunchtime.

Instead, compositors break sequences of images apart and reassemble them, sometimes painstakingly, first as a still frame and then in motion. Often, it is one element, one frame, or one area of a shot that needs special attention. By the clever use of selections, a compositor can save the shot by taking control of it.

This chapter focuses on how a layer merges with those behind it. Then Section II, "Effects Compositing Essentials," and in particular in Chapters 6 and 7, examines particular ways to refine selections, create high-contrast mattes, and pull keys.

Selection Types

You may already be familiar with all of the ways to create layer transparency; here's a review just in case.

Matte

Mattes do not only apply when keying out the blue or green from a visual effects shoot (**Figure 3.1**); *high-contrast (hi-con) mattes* are created by maximizing the contrast of a particular channel or area of the image. You can effectively matte an image with itself—with its own highlights or color areas.

Chapter 6 goes into depth about using mattes—the process involves using pixel values to create transparency.

Figure 3.1 This split-screen image shows a blue-screen shoot (left) and the resulting matte.

The built-in assumption of unmultiplied edge pixels can, in some cases, make life more difficult should things not go as planned. The "Alpha Channels and Premultiplication" section later in this chapter offers the lowdown on changing edge multiplication midstream.

Alpha Channel

An alpha or transparency channel is just a matte that has already been created outside of After Effects and embedded in an imported image. After Effects itself can, of course, also create alpha and transparency channels in rendered images (**Figure 3.2**).

After Effects is unique among compositing applications in that alpha channel information persists everywhere. Every image (and viewer) contains three channels of color and a fourth transparency channel.

After Effects is also unique in that, internally, it assumes that any edge premultiplication has been removed. Internally, all alphas in After Effects are straight (see Chapter 1 for a review of how this is determined on import).

Figure 3.2 A computer-generated baseball's color and alpha channels.

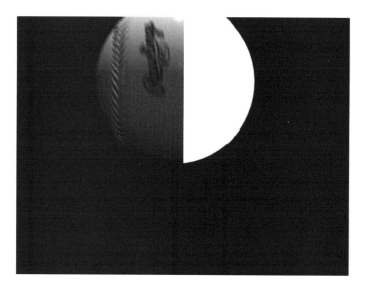

Mask

A mask is a vector shape, drawn by hand (**Figure 3.3**). As a vector shape, it can be infinitely scaled without losing any definition, but because it is drawn by hand, an animated mask has to be considered costlier than procedural options. The process of hand-animated selection is known as *rotoscoping* and is detailed in Chapter 7.

Figure 3.3 This split-screen view shows the garbage matte mask that was added to remove areas of the stage not covered by the blue screen.

There is also a procedural option to create animated vector masks by tracking raster data (pixel values): Layer > Auto-trace. While technically impressive, Auto-trace is problematic as a selection tool because it typically creates dozens of masks on any but the simplest live-action shot; you have less control than with the other methods, with extra benefits only if you want to do something stylized with those masks (**Figure 3.4**).

Figure 3.4 Apply Auto-trace to a complex image like this, where you would hope it would help with automatic rotoscoping, and you get dozens or even hundreds of individual colored mask shapes; a hi-con matte would give you more control.

Blending Mode

Blending modes apply a specific mathematical formula to the operation of compositing a layer with those behind it. These are essential because they mimic real-world optics (**Figure 3.5**).

Figure 3.5 Blending modes are the preferred way to composite elements that are composed predominantly of light rather than matter. Fire and smoke are added and multiplied into this scene detailed in Chapter 14, respectively.

When compositing an element that is made up more of light or shadows than reflective surfaces, for example footage of fire shot on black, it is essential to use blending modes instead of a luminance matte—don't try keying out the black (see Chapter 14 for more details). You can of course use selections combined with blending modes to get the best of both worlds.

The primary useful blending modes are detailed later in this chapter.

Effect

Many effects generate transparency: some (such as Levels and Curves) by offering direct adjustment of the alpha channel, others (in the Channel folder) by creating or replacing the alpha channel, and still others that generate images from scratch that can optionally include an alpha channel.

Combined Techniques

Even an ordinary effects shot will typically combine more than one of the above techniques. You will typically apply a garbage matte prior to a color key, or enhance the effect of a blending mode with a matte.

The art is in knowing which approach to apply for a given situation, and for this, there is no substitute for a deep understanding of how they work.

Compositing: Science and Nature

What exactly is happening in a simple A over B composite? In After Effects, it seems nearly as natural as laying one object on top of another does in the real world. In most other compositing applications even A over B is a compositing *operation* and that is closer to the truth—a truth that After Effects obscures in order to make the process more natural to an artist (particularly one who understands Photoshop).

Not only that, but there is more to what is going on in the real world than might be obvious, because of the phenomena of optics. The three realms of virtual images—the physical world, human vision, and optics—are interdependent; if you're shaky in your understanding of one of them, it will probably affect all three.

You as a compositor are not supposed to re-create reality on your computer screen, but rather re-create the way the camera (and the eye) sees the world. This affects something even so fundamental as how the edges of things should look in order for the eye to accept them.

Close-Up: The Compositing Formula

Do you really want to know what happens when you combine one layer with transparency data (an alpha channel) over another layer?

The foreground pixel values are first multiplied by the percentage of transparency, which, if not fully opaque, reduces their value. The background pixels are multiplied by the percentage of opacity (the inverse of the foreground layer's transparency), and the two values are added together to produce the composite. Expressed as a formula, it looks like $(Fg * A) + ((1-A)*Bg) = Comp$

With real RGB pixel data of R: 185, G: 144, B: 207 in the foreground and R: 80, G: 94, B: 47 in the background, calculating one edge pixel only might look like
$[(185, 144, 207) 3 .6] + [.4 3 ➥(80, 94, 47)] = (143, 124, 143)$

The result is a weighted blend between the brightness of the foreground and the darker background.

Other effects compositing programs, such as Shake, do not take this operation for granted the way that After Effects and Photoshop do. You can't simply drag one image over another in a layer stack—you must apply an Over function to create this interaction.

This is not a disadvantage of After Effects—it actually makes basic compositing simpler and faster—but it can obscure important related details such as edge pixel premultiplication (detailed later in this chapter).

Bitmap Alpha

A *bitmap selection channel* is one in which each pixel is either fully opaque or fully transparent. This is the type of selection generated by the Magic Wand tool in Photoshop. You can feather or blur the resulting edge, but the initial selection contains no semitransparent pixels.

This type of selection may have an occasional use, but it belongs to the world of computers, not nature (or optics). An edge made up of pixels that are either fully opaque or invisible cannot describe a curve or angle smoothly, and even a straight line looks unnatural in a natural image if it completely lacks edge thresholding (**Figure 3.6**).

Figure 3.6 This bitmap image contains no threshold pixels. Compare this result with that of Figure 3.7 to see how your monitor displays a curved shape.

Feathered Alpha

Although it's easy enough to see that a bitmap edge does not occur in nature, it's hard to imagine that hard objects should have transparent, feathered edges. Examine the edge of this book. It appears sharp.

But now study an image of the same thing, and you'll find some degree of edge softness. Adding softness, threshold, or "feather" to an edge approximates this softness in the hard digital world of single pixels, which are square and fundamentally either on or off. Properly feathered edges can

Figure 3.7 Zoom in far enough on a diagonal or curve and you see square pixels, yet further away your eye accepts the illusion.

▶ Approximate organic curves (**Figure 3.7**)

▶ Mimic optics behavior

The first point is intuitive enough once you've gained some experience working with *raster images*, which are digital images made up of pixels.

Optics can be observed in any photo with no compositing whatsoever (**Figure 3.8**). Viewed close-up, areas at the edge of objects become a fine wash of color combining the foreground and background. This is not due to inaccuracy in the camera; it is what happens to light as it travels around objects in the physical world and then through the lens of the camera (or your eye).

Figure 3.8 This image is not composited. Natural softness is apparent along the hard edges of the sign despite that they are in focus.

Opacity

Take two identical layers, no alpha/transparency information for either layer. Set each layer to 50% Opacity, and the result does not add up to 100%. Here's why.

Ctrl+Alt (Command+Option) and the **+** or **−** key raises or lowers layer Opacity by 1%. As everywhere in After Effects, add the **Shift** key and the increment is 10× or 10%.

Figure 3.9 shows light filtering through two overlapping sheets of paper. Yes, no expense is spared bringing you these real-world simulations. Let's suppose that each sheet is 75% opaque; 25% of the background light passes through. Add a second sheet and 25% of 25%—roughly 6%—passes through both layers. It's not a lot of light, but it's not zero; it would take a few more layers of paper to block out the light completely.

Figure 3.9 Although a single sheet of paper is more than 50% opaque, two sheets of paper layered one on top of another are not 100% opaque. This is how overlapping Opacity is calculated in After Effects.

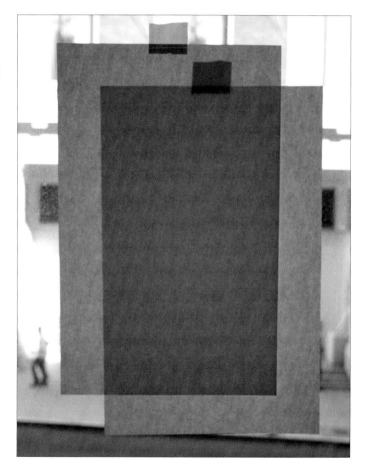

After Effects mimics this behavior, adding fractional and not whole Opacity values of two or more layers. This is *not* how it's handled in most other compositing applications, such as Shake, and so it takes some veterans by surprise.

Alpha Channels and Premultiplication

One major source of confusion and even derision for After Effects has to do with its handling of alpha channels and premultiplication. After Effects has a persistent concept of the alpha channel as part of every image, and this channel is expected always to be unmultiplied within After Effects, whether it originated that way or not.

Any color multiplied into edge pixels is to be removed upon import (in the Alpha section of the Interpret Footage dialog), and reintroduced only on output. Provided those Alpha settings are correct, this works surprisingly well, but at some point you may need to better understand how to take control of edge multiplication within After Effects.

Premultiplication Illustrated

Premultiplication exists for one reason only: so that rendered images have realistic, anti-aliased edges *before they are composited*. Without it, a 3D rendering of a silver spaceship against a plain black background would appear to have a crude, blocky outline because the edge pixels would not contain any of that black background. It's as if the ship has already been composited against a solid color and needs to be uncomposited before it can be composited again.

When you ask After Effects to "guess" how to interpret the footage (on import, by choosing Guess in the Interpret Footage dialog, or pressing **Ctrl+Alt+G**/**Cmd+Option+G**), it looks for indications of a solid color background multiplied into edge pixels, indicating that the setting should be Premultiplied.

Imagine the background value to be 0,0,0 or solid black; an edge pixel is multiplied by 0 (making it pure black) and then added back to the source, in proportion to the amount of transparency in the alpha channel pixel.

Removing edge multiplication with the Premultiplied setting subtracts this extra black from those edge pixels.

The close-ups in **Figure 3.10** show a section of the same foreground image with two alpha interpretations, one interpreted correctly, the other not. A misinterpreted alpha either fails to remove the background color from the edge pixels or removes color that should actually be present.

Figure 3.10 Motion blur and a white background clearly reveal improper edge multiplication, especially when compared with the correct version (top). There is dark matting all around the edges, including areas of the canopy meant to be translucent, and around the blur of the propeller (bottom).

NOTES

Most computer-generated images are premultiplied, unless specific steps are taken to counteract the process. The Video Output section of the Output Module Settings for items in the Render Queue includes a menu to specify whether you render with Straight or Premultiplied alpha; by default, it is set to Premultiplied.

You may find that fringing appears in your comps despite your careful managing of the alpha channel interpretation on import. This does not indicate some bug in After Effects, but rather a mystery you must solve. There are two basic ways it can occur:

▶ An alpha channel is misinterpreted in Interpret Footage.

▶ Edge multiplication is added within After Effects, probably unintentionally, by applying a matte to a layer that has already been matted.

Unfortunately, artists who misunderstand the underlying problem will resort to all sorts of strange machinations to fix the black edge, ruining what may be a perfectly accurate edge matte.

Get It Right on Import

Preferences > Import > Interpret Unlabeled Alpha As determines what happens when footage with an unlabeled alpha channel is imported; the default is to Ask User.

The Ask User dialog has three choices, one of which is checked, and a Guess button (**Figure 3.11**). This is confusing to most users, as it seems as if After Effects has already guessed, when it has not: *It is merely using whatever was the setting the previous time.*

The Guess option is not accurate 100% of the time; if the foreground and background are similar, it can be fooled.

After Effects attempts to guess not only the setting but the background color of a premultiplied image; generally this is black or white, but watch out for situations where a 3D artist has become creative and rendered against canary yellow or powder blue. For that reason, there is an eyedropper adjacent to the Matted With Color setting (Figure 3.11).

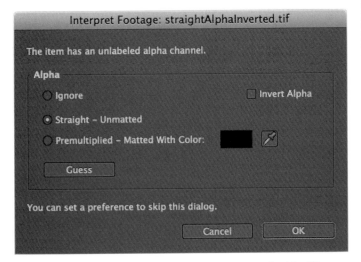

Figure 3.11 Be careful here: Many experienced artists assume that After Effects has already made a guess (here, "Straight") when it is merely using whatever was set the last time. If you want it to guess, you have to click that button; ideally you should avoid the need to do so, of course, but you didn't need me to tell you that.

Ideally you will work on a project whose images are consistent (in terms of edge multiplication and background color); in that case, you can set an Import preference. Typically, however, it's best to be able to find out from whomever created it whether your source contains edge multiplication, and what settings to use.

When that's not possible, you need to be able to examine your images and spot the symptoms of a misinterpreted alpha: dark or bright fringing in the semi-opaque edges of your foreground.

RGB Straight (**Alt+Shift+4/ Option+Shift+4** or use the Show Channel menu at the bottom of a viewer panel) displays the image in straight alpha mode, as After Effects views it internally.

Solve the Problem Internally

The really gnarly fact is that premultiplication errors can be introduced within a composition, typically by applying a matte to footage that is already somehow blended—multiplied—with a background.

If you see fringing in your edges, you can try the Remove Color Matting effect (**Figure 3.12**). This effect has one setting only, for background color, because all it does is apply the unpremultiply calculation (the antidote to premultiplication) in the same manner that it would be applied in Interpret Footage.

An even better option in cases where you have an element against black and no alpha channel is UnMult, originally created by John Knoll and included on the book's disc in the Red Giant Software folder. This effect uses black areas of the image to create transparency and removes the multiplied black from the resulting transparent pixels.

TIP

The Remove Color Matting effect will not work properly on a layer with a track matte; be sure to precompose the layer and its track matte prior to applying Channel > Remove Color Matting.

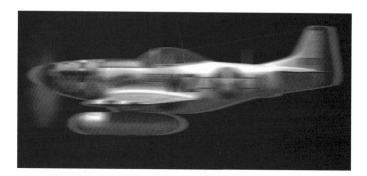

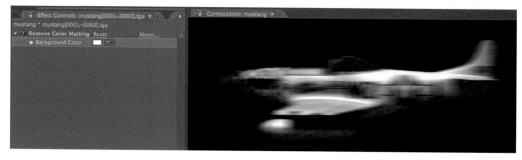

Figure 3.12 The plane was matted against a white background, but transparency has been applied via a track matte (the equivalent of a straight alpha), so white fringing appears against black (top). Remove Color Matting with Color set to pure white corrects the problem (bottom), but only when applied to a precomp of the image and matte.

Masks

Masks are the principal non-procedural method to define transparency in a layer; they are vector shapes that you draw by hand. There are five basic shapes (the **Q** key cycles through them) and the Pen tool (**G**) for drawing free-form.

A mask can be drawn in either the Composition or Layer viewer. In Layer view the source image persists in its default view; there is a Render toggle next to the Masks selection in the View menu to disable all mask selections. Artists may want to see a masked layer in the context of the comp but find it difficult to adjust the mask in that view—in such a case, the Layer and Composition views can be arranged side-by-side (**Figure 3.13**).

NOTES

Shape layers are directly related to masks; they are drawn with the same tools. If a layer that can receive a mask is selected, then After Effects draws a mask; otherwise, it creates a new Shape layer.

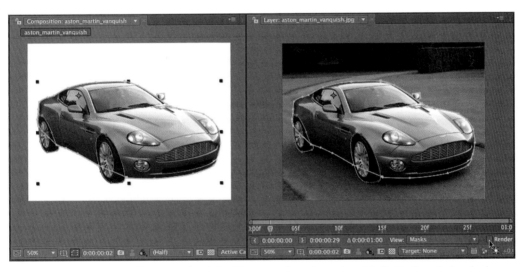

Figure 3.13 With the Comp and Layer panels side-by-side, you can leave the mask enabled in the Comp but uncheck Render in the Layer.

When using a Mask Shape tool

▶ Double-click the tool (in the Tools palette) to set the boundaries of the mask shape to match those of the layer.

▶ Press **Shift** to constrain proportions when drawing or scaling.

▶ Use **Ctrl/Cmd** to draw from the center (with the Rectangle, Rounded Rectangle, and Ellipse tools).

TIP

Look for situations where starting with a Mask Shape and editing it can help you; for example, you can make a half-circle by deleting one vertex and adjusting two others of an ellipse.

▶ Click Shape under Mask Path (**M**) in the Layer Switches column to open the Mask Shape dialog; here you can enter exact mask dimensions.

▶ Double-click the shape with the Selection tool to activate Free Transform mode, then

   ▶ Shift-drag on corner to scale the mask proportionally.

   ▶ Shift-drag outside corner to snap rotation to 45-degree increments.

   ▶ Shift-drag anywhere else to transform on one axis only.

▶ Press the **M** key twice, rapidly, to reveal all Mask options for the selected layer.

▶ Press the **F** key to solo the Mask Feather property. Feather is applied everywhere equally on the mask, equidistant inward and outward from the mask shape.

▶ Use Mask Expansion to expand or (given a negative value) contract the mask area. Two masks can be used together, one contracted, one expanded, to create an edge selection.

Chapter 7 has more information about drawing precise masks; big, soft masks are referenced throughout the book for all kinds of lighting, smoke, and glow effects (**Figure 3.14**).

Ctrl+Alt+Shift- (**Cmd+Opt+Shift-**) click on Mask Expansion. The property disappears. Click **MM** twice to reveal it as "Mask Embiggen"—an easter egg referencing Season 3 Episode 13 of The Simpsons.

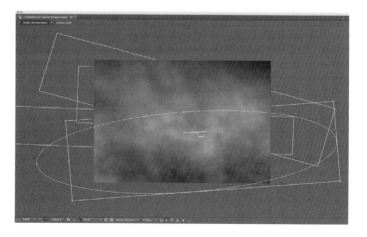

Figure 3.14 You can build up a series of layers with soft masks to create depth in cloud cover, these clouds are made up of a series of overlapping masked layers, and each mask has a Feather value of 200–500 pixels.

Bézier Masks

By default, the Pen tool creates Bézier shapes; learn the keyboard shortcuts and you can fully edit a mask without ever clicking anywhere except right on the mask.

I like to start by placing points at key transitions and corners, without worrying about fine tuning the Béziers. Or, as I draw a point, I can

▸ **Shift**-hold and drag to move the vertex

▸ Hold and drag out a Bézier tangent

before drawing the next point. Once I've completed a basic shape, I can activate the Pen Tool (**G**) ♌ and

♌ Click a point to delete it.

♌ Click a segment between points to add a point.

⌐ **Alt/Option**-click on a point to enable the Convert Vertex tool, which toggles Bézier handles; drag a point with no handles to create them, or click a point with handles to kill them.

⌐ Click a Bézier handle to break the handles and adjust them independently.

▶ Press the **Shift** key with the mouse still down to pull out Bézier handles.

▶ **Ctrl/Cmd**-click to toggle the Selection tool temporarily (to move a point).

▸ Press the **V** key to activate the Selection tool. Pressing the **G** key switches back to the Pen.

▸ Press **F2** or **Ctrl+Shift+A** (**Cmd+Shift+A**) to deselect the current mask and start a new one without switching tools, leaving the Pen tool active.

Context-click on a mask path to change settings in the Mask submenu. This includes all settings from the Timeline as well as Motion Blur settings just for the mask (optionally separate from the Layer). The Mask and Shape Path submenu contains special options to close an open shape, set the First Vertex (see later in this chapter) and toggle Rotobeziers (Chapter 7).

Shape Layers

Shape layers add functionality from Adobe Illustrator directly into After Effects. The same tools can be used to draw either a mask or a Shape layer. Here's how they differ:

▶ Create a Star, Polygon, or Rounded Rectangle as a mask and its vertices can be edited as normal Béziers. Shapes offer a different type of control in the Timeline of properties such as number of points and inner and outer roundness.

▶ Shapes can contain Shape Effects such as Pucker & Bloat, Twist, and Zig Zag that procedurally deform the entire shape.

▶ Shapes display with two optional characteristics: Fill and Stroke. With a Shape active, Alt/Option-click on Fill and Stroke in the toolbar to cycle through the options (also available in the Timeline).

▶ Shapes can be instanced and repeated in 2D space; Option-drag to duplicate (as in Illustrator) or use a Repeater effect to instance and array a shape.

Definitely consider shapes when you need a repeatable pattern of some type, as in **Figure 3.15**. Using the Repeater, you only have to adjust a single shape to edit all instances of it and how it is arrayed. For the time being, there is no option to array shapes in 3D.

Figure 3.15 Shapes are not mere eye candy fodder, are they? The sprocket holes in this film were made with a Rounded Corner shape and a Repeater (I even added an Inner Shadow Layer Style to give a little feeling of depth and dimension).

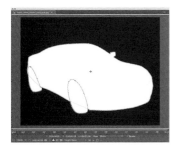

Figure 3.16 Add mode combines the luminance values of overlapping masks.

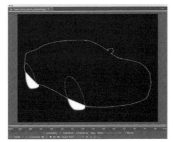

Figure 3.17 Subtract mode is the inverse of Add mode.

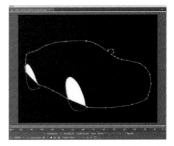

Figure 3.18 Intersect mode adds only the overlapping areas of opacity.

Combine Selections

By default, all masks are drawn in Add mode, meaning that the contents of the mask are added to the layer selection, and the area outside all of the masks is excluded. You can set the mask mode to

▶ Add to mask contents to the image as a whole (**Figure 3.16**)

▶ Subtract to mask contents from displayed areas of the image (**Figure 3.17**)

▶ Intersect to mask contents to show only areas overlapping with masks higher in the stack (**Figure 3.18**)

▶ Difference to mask contents to hide areas overlapping with masks higher in the stack (**Figure 3.19**)

▶ None to disable the mask (**Figure 3.20**)

The Inverted toggle next to Mask Mode menu combined with Add causes the areas outside the mask to be added; combined with Subtract causes the areas outside the mask to be subtracted, and so on.

The Mask Opacity property (**M**) attenuates the strength of a mask; setting any mask other than the first one to 0% is like disabling it. This control works differently for the first (top) mask. A single Add mask set to 0% Mask Opacity causes the entire layer to disappear, inside or outside the mask.

However, if you set the first mask to Subtract, and Mask Opacity to 50%, it does just that—instead of the area inside the mask reappearing, the rest of the scene becomes 50%

Figure 3.19 The inverse of Intersect, Difference mode subtracts overlapping areas.

Figure 3.20 With None mode, the mask is effectively deactivated.

TIP

Preferences > User Interface Color > Cycle Mask Colors assigns a unique color to each new mask. Enable it.

NOTES

Chapter 7 demonstrates how effective rotoscoping ideally involves many simple masks working together instead of one big complex mask.

transparent, just as with Add > Inverted. If you want this to behave as it should, set the first mask full-frame to Add mode (just double-click the rectangle mask), *then* add the Subtract mask as the second (or later).

To keep multiple masks organized

▸ Enable Preferences > User Interface Color > Cycle Mask Colors to assign a unique color to each new mask

▸ Press the Return key with mask selected, then type in a unique name

▸ Click Mask Color swatch (to the left of the name) to make it more visible or unique

▸ Context-click > Mask > Locked, Mask > Lock Other Masks, or Mask > Hide Locked Masks to keep masks you no longer wish to edit out of your way

Overlapping Transparency

"Density" is traditionally a film term describing how dark (opaque) the frame of film is at a given area of the image: the higher the density, the less light is transmitted. Masks and alpha channels are also referred to in terms of "density," and when two masks or mattes overlap, density can build up when it should not (with masks) or fail to build up when it should (with mattes).

Figures 3.21 and **3.22** show the simple solution to a common problem; the Darken and Lighten mask modes prevent any pixel from becoming more dense than it is in the semi-transparent areas of either matte. These modes should be applied to the masks that are below overlapping masks in the stack in order to work.

Overlap Inverted Layers Seamlessly

Suppose you want to slice a layer into segments and adjust each segment individually but let them appear combined in the final result. A gap will appear along the threshold areas of the matte for the reasons explained in the Opacity section earlier; two overlapping 50% opaque pixels do not make a 100% opaque combined pixel.

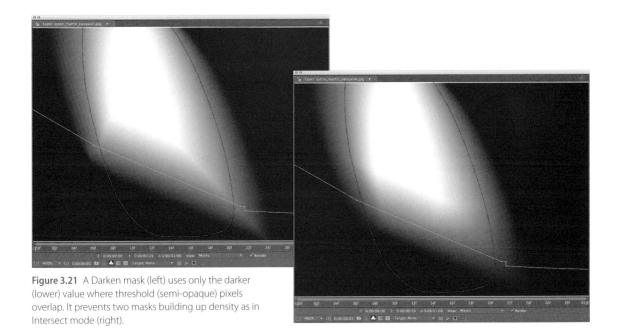

Figure 3.21 A Darken mask (left) uses only the darker (lower) value where threshold (semi-opaque) pixels overlap. It prevents two masks building up density as in Intersect mode (right).

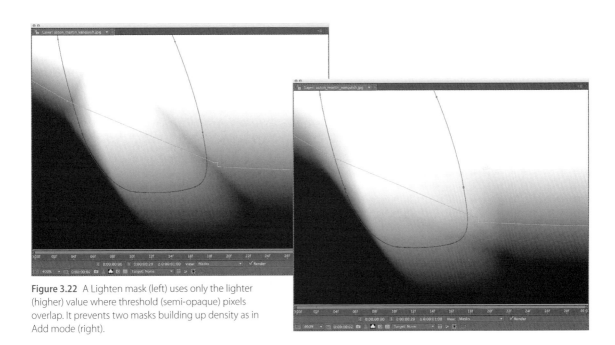

Figure 3.22 A Lighten mask (left) uses only the lighter (higher) value where threshold (semi-opaque) pixels overlap. It prevents two masks building up density as in Add mode (right).

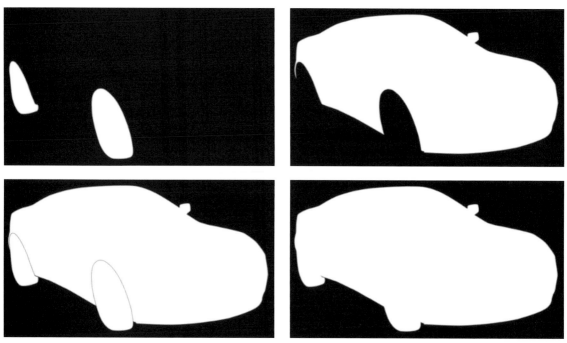

Figure 3.23 Comp a layer with matte A (upper left) over one with matte B (upper right) and you get a halo along the overlapping, inverted threshold edge pixels—around the wheels (bottom left). Alpha Add does just what the title implies, adding the alpha values together directly (bottom right).

Just as the name implies, the Alpha Add blending mode directly adds transparent pixels, instead of scaling them proportionally (**Figure 3.23**). You can cut out a piece of a layer, feather the matte, apply the inverted feathered matte to the rest of the layer, and recombine them with Alpha Add applied to the top layer. The seam disappears.

Masks in Motion

Ahead of Chapter 7's more detailed discussion of rotoscoping, here are the basics to put a mask in motion.

Alt/Option+M sets a mask keyframe to all unlocked layer masks. Mask movement can be eased temporally, but there are no spatial curves; each mask point travels in a completely linear fashion from one keyframe to the next. An arced motion requires many more keyframes.

You can only adjust a mask point on one keyframe at a time, even if you select multiple Mask Path keyframes before adjusting.

To arc or offset the movement of a mask animation, you can duplicate the masked layer and use it as an alpha track matte for an unmasked source of the same layer (see Chapter 7 for more); you can then keyframe and transform its position and anchor point like any animated layer, with curved paths and offsets.

Move, Copy, and Paste Masks

Copy a mask path from any compatible source

▶ A Mask Path property from a separate Mask or Layer

▶ A Mask Path keyframe from the same or a separate Mask

▶ A Mask Path from a separate Adobe application such as Illustrator or Photoshop

and paste it into an existing Mask Path channel, or paste it to the layer to create a new Mask. If there are any keyframes, they are pasted in as well, beginning at the current time; make sure they don't conflict with existing keyframes in the Mask Shape.

To draw an entirely new shape for an existing, keyframed Mask Path, use the Target menu along the bottom of the Layer panel to choose the existing mask as a target, and start drawing. This replaces the existing shape (**Figure 3.24**).

NOTES

If the target layer has unique dimensions, the mask stretches proportionally.

Figure 3.24 This pop-up menu along the bottom of the Layer panel makes it easy to create a new mask path that replaces the shape in the target mask. If the target mask has keyframes, After Effects creates a new keyframe wherever the new shape is drawn.

First Vertex

When pasting in shapes or radically changing the existing mask by adding and deleting points, you may run into difficulty lining up the points. Hidden away in the Layer > Mask (or Mask context) menu, and available *only with a single vertex of the mask selected*, is the Set First Vertex command.

If your mask points twist around to the wrong point during an interpolation, setting the First Vertex to two points that definitely correspond should help straighten things out. This also can be imperative for effects that rely on mask shapes, such as the Reshape tool (described in Chapter 7).

Blending Modes: Compositing Beyond Selections

After Effects includes 36 blending modes, each created with a specific purpose—except maybe Dancing Dissolve, was that one ever useful? For effects work, moreover, the majority of them are not particularly recommended.

So how do you tell which are the useful ones? Once you understand how your options work, you can make informed compositing decisions instead of relying on trial and error.

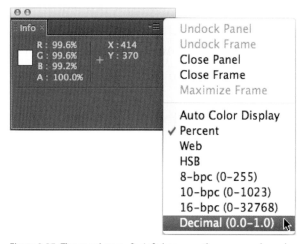

Figure 3.25 The panel menu for Info has more than one mode, and you can choose whichever you like. Whichever mode you select also carries over to the Adobe Color Picker.

To help you understand what the various blending modes are doing, **Figures 3.26** through **3.33** blend a grayscale gradient over a fully saturated background. Contextual examples using these blending modes follow in the next section.

Figure 3.26 Blending in this figure is set to Normal for purposes of comparison with those that follow.

Add and Screen

Add and Screen modes both brighten the foreground image while making darker pixels transparent. Screen yields a subtler blend than Add in normal video color space but does not work correctly with linear color (details in Chapter 11).

Add mode is every bit as simple as it sounds; the formula is

```
newPixel = A + B
```

where A is a pixel from the foreground layer and B is a background pixel. The result is clipped at 1 for 8- and 16-bit pixels.

Add is incredibly useful with what After Effects calls a Linearized Working Space, where it perfectly re-creates the optical effect of combining light values from two images. It is useful for laying fire and explosion elements shot in negative space (against black) into a scene, adding noise or grain to an element, or any other element that is made up of light and texture (**Figure 3.27**).

NOTES

Linear Dodge and Add are identical blending modes; the former is merely Photoshop's term for the latter.

Figure 3.27 Add mode (top left) takes the source foreground element, the fire shot against a black background (top right), and adds its pixel values channel by channel to the background (bottom left), causing the pure black pixels to disappear completely (bottom right).

NOTES

In Screen mode, fully white pixels stay white, fully black pixels stay black, but a midrange pixel (0.5) takes on a brighter value (0.75), just not as bright as it would be with Add (1).

Screen mode has an influence similar to Add mode's, but via a slightly different formula. The pixel values are inverted, multiplied together, and the result is inverted:

```
newPixel = 1-((1-A) * (1-B))
```

Once you discover the truth about working linearized with a 1.0 gamma, you understand that Screen is a workaround, a compromise for how colors blend in normal video space. Screen is most useful in situations where Add would blow out the highlights too much—glints, flares, glow passes, and so on (**Figure 3.28**).

Figure 3.28 The difference between Screen and Add (Figure 3.27) may be subtle in printed figures until you look closely; notice there's less brightness in the "hottest" areas of the fire.

Multiply

Multiply is another mode whose math is as elementary as it sounds; it uses the formula

```
newPixel = A * B
```

Keep in mind that this formula uses color values between 0 and 1 to correspond to the colors on your monitor. Multiplying two images together, therefore, actually has the effect of reducing midrange pixels and darkening an image overall, although pixels that are full white in both images remain full white.

Multiply or Add has the inverse effect of Screen mode, darkening the midrange values of one image with another. It emphasizes dark tones in the foreground without replacing the lighter tones in the background, useful for creating texture, shadow, or dark fog (**Figure 3.29**).

NOTES

To fully comprehend the difference between Add and Screen requires an understanding of a linearized working space, which is offered in Chapter 11.

Figure 3.29 Dark smoke (actually a grayscale fractal noise pattern) is multiplied over the background, darkening the areas that are dark in either the foreground or background further.

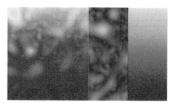

Figure 3.30 Overlay and its inverse, Hard Light, are useful for combining color and texture. Here, an instant lava lamp texture was created using the components shown at the right: a solid with Fractal Noise applied set to Overlay mode on top of a red-to-yellow gradient.

Overlay and the various Light modes do not work properly with values above 1.0, as can occur in 32 bpc linearized working spaces (see Chapter 11).

Overlay and the Light Modes

Overlay uses Screen or Multiply, depending on the background pixel value. Above a threshold of 50% gray (or .5 in normalized terms), Screen occurs, and below the threshold, Multiply. Hard Light operates similarly, instead using the top layer to determine whether to screen or multiply, so the two are inverse effects.

These modes, along with Linear and Vivid Light, can be most useful for combining a layer that is predominantly color with another layer that is predominantly luminance, or contrast detail (**Figure 3.30**). Much of the lava texturing in the Level 4 sequence of *Spy Kids 3-D* was created by using Hard Light to combine a hand-painted color heat map with moving fractal noise patterns.

Reversing layer order and swapping Overlay for Hard Light yields an identical result.

Difference

Difference inverts a background pixel in proportion to the foreground pixel. It can help you line up two identical layers, which is handy while working even if you rarely use it for final output (**Figure 3.31**).

Figure 3.31 The selection area in the foreground is identical to the background; when they are perfectly aligned, all pixels cancel out to black.

HSB and Color Modes

The Hue, Saturation, and Brightness modes each combine one of these values (H, S, or B) from the foreground layer with the other two from the background layer. Color takes both the hue and saturation from the top layer, using only the luminance (or brightness) from the underlying background (**Figure 3.32**).

Figure 3.32 Setting a deep-blue-colored solid to Color mode and overlaying it on the plate footage has the effect of tinting the colors in the image blue. Artistic uses of this mode are explored in Chapter 12.

These modes are often useful at an Opacity setting below 100%, to combine source HSB values with ones that you choose.

Stencil, Silhouette, and Preserve Transparency

Commonly overlooked, Stencil and Silhouette blending modes operate only on the alpha channel of the composition. The layer's alpha or luminance values become a matte for all layers below it in the stack. Stencil makes the brightest pixels opaque, and Silhouette the darkest.

Suppose instead you have a foreground layer that is meant to be opaque only where the underlying layers are opaque, as in **Figure 3.33**. The small highlighted checkbox, labeled Preserve Underlying Transparency, makes this happen, much to the amazement of many who've wished for this feature and not realized it was already there.

NOTES

Stencil Alpha and Silhouette Alpha are useful to create custom edge mattes as well as a light wrap effect, demonstrated in Chapter 12.

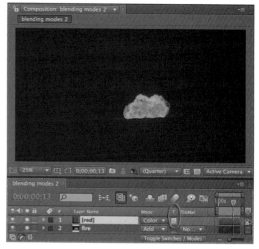

Figure 3.33 Among the hardest-to-find and most-easily-forgotten features in the Timeline is the Preserve Underlying Transparency toggle, circled. This re-creates behavior familiar to Photoshop users, where a layer's own transparency only applies where it intersects with that of the underlying layer, one more way to avoid track mattes or precomping.

Luminescent Premultiply

Luminescent Premultiply is one method you can use to remove premultiplication on the fly from source footage, retaining bright values in edge pixels that are otherwise clipped. Premultiplication over black causes all semitransparent pixels to become darker; removing it can cause them to appear dimmer than they should.

Luminescent Premultiply can be useful in cases where an element with transparency has been created against a black background within After Effects, bypassing the opportunity to remove premultiplication on import.

Track Mattes

Track mattes allow you to use the alpha or luminance information of one layer as the transparency of another layer (**Figure 3.34**). It's a simple enough concept, yet one that is absolutely fundamental as a problem-solving tool for complex composites.

The perceptual difference between an alpha channel and a track matte isn't, for the most part, too difficult to grasp. In both cases, you have pixels with a value (in 8-bit color

space) between 0 and 255, whether a grayscale alpha channel or three channels of color. With color, the three channels are simply averaged together to make up a single grayscale alpha. With 16 and even 32 bpc, it's finer increments in the same range.

To set a track matte, place the layer that contains the transparency data directly above its target layer in the Timeline and choose one of the four options from the Track Matte pop-up menu:

▶ Alpha Matte: The alpha channel of the track matte layer is the alpha

▶ Alpha Inverted Matte: Same but the black areas are opaque

▶ Luma Matte: Uses the average brightness of red, green, and blue as the alpha

▶ Luma Inverted Matte: Same but the black areas are opaque

By default, visibility of the track matte layer is disabled when you activate it from the layer below by choosing one of these four modes, which is generally desirable. Some clever uses of track mattes leave them on; for example, by matting out the bright areas of the image and turning on the matte, setting it to Add mode, you could naturally brighten those areas even more.

Track mattes solve a lot of compositing problems. They also help overcome limitations of After Effects. Chapter 7 describes how you can keep an entire sequence buffered in RAM for fast access while rotoscoping on a track matte layer, and how you can add tracking capabilities to masks in this manner.

Gotchas

Even an advanced user has to pay attention when working in a composition with track mattes. Unlike parented

Share a Matte

Node-based compositing programs make it easy for a single node to provide transparency to as many others as is needed. The one-to-many capacity in After Effects involves precomping the track matte and making all changes in the nested comp. This can be a pain, but check Chapter 4 for more tips to smooth the process, such as the ability to display more than one Timeline simultaneously.

layers, track mattes do not stay connected with their target if moved around; they must occupy the layer directly above in order to work.

After Effects does at least help you in certain ways. Duplicate a layer (**Ctrl+D/Cmd+D**) with a track matte activated and it moves up two layers, above the track matte layer. Include the track matte when you duplicate and it also moves up two layers, so layer order is preserved (**Figure 3.35**).

Figure 3.35 Select and duplicate the layers from Figure 3.34, and the two new layers leapfrog above to maintain the proper image/matte relationship.

NOTES

Combine a track matte and an image with an alpha channel, and the selection uses an intersection of the two.

There is a work-around that allows a matte layer to be anywhere in the Timeline, but it contains its own perils. Effect > Channel > Set Matte not only lets you choose any layer in the comp as a matte, it keeps track if that layer moves to a different position. It also offers a few custom matte handling options regarding how the matte is scaled and combined. However, nothing you add to the other layer, including Transform keyframes, is passed through.

Render Order

NOTES

If you're not certain whether your edits to the matte are being passed through, save the project and try cranking them up so it's obvious. Then undo/revert. If it's not working, precomp the matte layer.

This brings us to render order with track mattes. In most cases, adjustments and effects that you apply to the matte layer are calculated prior to creating the target matte. To see how this can break, however, try applying a track matte to another track matte? It works… sometimes, but not often enough that it should become something you try unless you're willing to troubleshoot it.

Conclusion

Now that we've examined selections in detail, the next chapter looks in depth at solving issues such as those described above for render order; you'll begin to see how to use the Timeline as a visual problem-solving tool for such situations.

4

Optimize the Pipeline

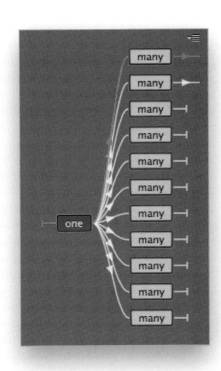

Build a system that even a fool can use and only a fool will want to use it.

—George Bernard Shaw

Optimize the Pipeline

This chapter examines how image data flows through an After Effects project in detail. That may not sound gripping until you realize how much your creativity is hampered by remaining ignorant of this stuff.

Sometimes you take the attitude of a master chef—you know what can be prepped and considered "done" before the guests are in the restaurant and it's time to assemble the piece de resistance. At other times, you're more like a programmer, isolating and debugging elements of a project, even creating controlled tests to figure out how things are working. This chapter helps you artistically and technically, as if the two can be separated.

Once you

- ▶ Understand how to use multiple compositions
- ▶ Know when to precompose
- ▶ Know how to optimize rendering time

you may find the After Effects experience closer to what you might call "real-time." Efficient rendering, however, depends on well-organized compositions and the ability to plan for bottlenecks and other complications.

Multiple Compositions, Multiple Projects

It's easy to lose track of stuff when projects get complicated. This section demonstrates

- ▶ How and why to create a project template
- ▶ How to keep a complex, multiple-composition pipeline organized
- ▶ Shortcuts to help orient you quickly

These tips are especially useful if you're someone who knows compositing well but find After Effects disorienting at times.

Project Templates

I'm always happiest with a project that is well organized, even if I'm the only one likely ever to work on it. Keeping the Project panel well organized and tidy can clarify your ability to think about the project itself.

Figure 4.1 shows a couple of typical project templates containing multiple compositions to create one final shot, although these could certainly be adapted for a group of similar shots or a sequence. When you need to return to a project over the course of days or weeks, this level of organization can be a lifesaver.

Figure 4.1 The template on the left is based on how a film shot might be generically organized, including numbering that reflects pipeline order and Output comps in two formats. The template on the right is the minimum I would use on any project; you need a folder for Source and one for Precomps to keep things tidy even if the main comp stays at the root level.

Here are some criteria to use when creating your own:

▶ **Create folders to group specific types of elements,** such as Source, Precomps, and Reference.

▶ **Use numbering to reflect comp and sequence order** so that it's easy to see that order in the Project panel.

▶ **Create a unique Final Output comp** that has the format and length of the final shot, particularly if the format is at all different from what you're using to work (because it's scaled, cropped, or uses a different frame rate or color profile).

▶ **Use guide layers and comments** as needed to help artists set up the comp (**Figure 4.2**).

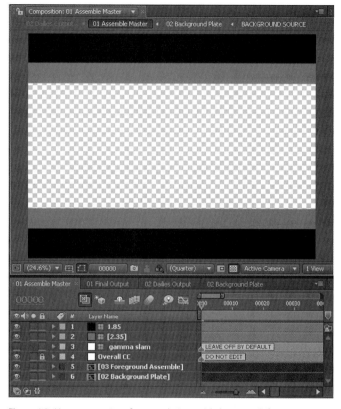

Figure 4.2 Here are a series of nonrendering guide layers to define action areas and color. Notice the new feature in CS4 that shows where this comp fits in a series of precomps; each of those buttons opens the corresponding comp.

▶ **Organize Source folders** for all footage, broken down as is most logical for your project.

The basic elements of a Master comp, source comps, and a render comp seem useful on a shot of just about any complexity, but the template can include a lot more than that: custom expressions, camera rigs, Color Management settings, and recurring effects setups.

Mini-Flowchart View

The Timeline is great for timing, but the bane of the Timeline is precomping. There are many times where there is no way around sending a set of layers into their own Timeline, yet most artists will do anything to avoid this step because it locks those layers and controls out of the main Timeline. In the past, precomping also made it harder simply to find where everything was; it is standard for an After Effects artist working on a complex comp to be left with the "where did I do that" feeling at one time or another.

That's now less the case, thanks to CS4's Mini-Flowchart, or Miniflow. You can access it via a button in the Timeline , but you may have already discovered that simply tapping the **Shift** key with the Timeline forward enables it.

By default, the comp order is shown flowing right to left. The reason for this is probably that if you open subcomps from a master comp, the tabs open to the right; however, a convincing argument can and has been made to choose Flow Left to Right in the panel menu of the Mini Flowchart. Try it and see if you breathe a little sigh of relief.

Either direction, Miniflow is the best workflow addition to After Effects CS4. It shows only the nearest neighbor comps (**Figure 4.3**) but click on the flow arrows at either end and you navigate up or down one level in the hierarchy. Click on any arrows or items in between the ends and that level is brought forward.

Figure 4.3 Miniflow is a quietly revolutionary small new feature in After Effects CS4. It makes the process of navigating subcomps nearly effortless.

Miniflow does not display the entire compositing tree like Flowchart view does, but it's much more useful. The most complicated it gets is in multiple one-to-many relationships, because you can only trace your way down one flow at a time, but that turns out not to be such a big deal. It's much simpler to open a comp and see where it's used than the previously existing alternatives.

TIP

Miniflow makes Comp naming more important than ever. On a big project, pick a system and stick with it.

More Ways to Manage Many Comps

Miniflow makes it even more possible to close all the Timelines when you're done with a set of changes (**Ctrl+Alt+W/ Command+Option+W**) and reopen only the ones you need, starting with the master comp.

The Lock icon 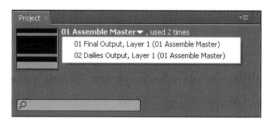 at the upper left of the Composition viewer lets you keep that Composition viewer forward while you open another Timeline. Typically, you would lock the master comp and double-click a nested comp to open its Timeline; as you make adjustments in that Timeline, you see their effect on the overall comp.

The Always Preview this View toggle ▣ lets you instead work entirely in a precomp, but preview the result automatically in the master comp (if this is toggled in that comp) without having to switch to it. Use it if you're only interested in how changes look in your final.

Ctrl+Alt+Shift+N (**Cmd+Option+Shift+N**) creates two Composition viewers side-by-side, and locks one of them, for any artist with ample screen real estate who wants the best of both worlds.

To locate comps in the Project panel, you can

▶ Select an item in the Project panel; adjacent to its name by the thumbnail at the top of the panel is a small pull-down caret, along with the number of times, if any, the item is used in a comp (**Figure 4.4**).

Figure 4.4 Click the caret next to the total number of times an item is used to see a list of where it is used.

▶ Context-click an item in the Project panel and choose Reveal in Composition; choose a composition and that comp is opened with the item selected (**Figure 4.5**).

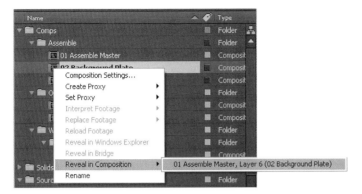

Figure 4.5 Context-click any item, and under Reveal in Composition, choose from a list, if applicable; that Timeline opens with the item selected.

▶ Context-click a layer in the Timeline and choose Reveal Layer Source in Project to highlight the item in the Project panel (**Figure 4.6**).

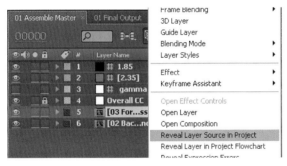

Figure 4.6 Context-click any footage item in the Timeline and you can choose to reveal it either in the Project panel or in Flowchart view.

▶ Context-click in the empty area of a Timeline and choose Reveal Composition in Project to highlight the comp in the Project panel (**Figure 4.7**).

Figure 4.7 Find the empty area below the layers in the Timeline and context-click; you can reveal the current comp in the Project panel.

TIP

You've no doubt already discovered the reversed functionality to open nested comps; double-click opens a nested comp, and Alt/Option-double-click reveals it in the Layer viewer. It's friendlier for new users but requires the rest of us to adjust.

Precomping and Composition Nesting

Precomping is often regarded as the major downside of compositing in After Effects, because it obscures vital information from view. Artists will let a composition become completely unwieldy, with dozens of layers, rather than bite the bullet and precomp. Yet precomping is an effective way to solve problems and optimize a project, provided you plan things out a little.

Just to get our terms straight, *precomping* is the action of selecting a set of layers in a composition and assigning them to a new subcomp. Closely related to this is *composition nesting*, the action of placing one already created composition inside of another.

Typically, you precomp by selecting the layers of a composition that can and should be grouped together and choosing Precompose from the Layer menu (keyboard shortcut **Ctrl+Shift+C**/**Cmd+Shift+C**).

Two options are presented, the second one unavailable if multiple layers are selected: to leave attributes (effects, transforms, masks, paint, blending modes) in place or transfer them into the new composition.

Why Precomp?

Precomping prevents a composition from containing too many layers to be seen and managed in one Timeline, but it also allows you to do the following:

▶ Reuse a set of elements and manage them from one place.

▶ Fix render order problems, for example apply an effect first, then a mask.

▶ Organize your project; grouping elements that are interrelated is a good idea in a nodal application such as Nuke or Shake too, because it influences how you think about the composite.

▶ Consider an element or set of layers "done" (and even prerender them as proxies, as discussed later in this chapter).

If you're already comfortable with the idea of precomping, focus on the last point. This chapter describes the advantages to finishing an element, if only for the time being, instead of always keeping options open. It's a secret of most "real-time" compositing systems that they rely heavily on the equivalent of prerendered subcomps (they just don't call them that).

Gotchas

Precomping several layers together can solve problems, but it can also create new ones. Common gotchas include

- You want some but not all properties to be precomped.
- It can be a pain to undo in order to restore precomped layers to the master composition.
- You must deal with the all-or-nothing behavior of blending modes and 3D layers, depending on the Collapse Transformations setting.
- It can be unclear how motion blur, frame blending, and collapsed transformation switches in the master composition affect nested comps.
- Layer timing (duration, In and Out points) and dimensions can become constraints.

If you recognize any of these problems and haven't solved them, check out the following useful strategies.

Boundaries of Time and Space

Each composition in After Effects contains its own fixed timing and pixel dimensions, which a couple of strategies help navigate:

- Make source compositions longer than the shot is ever anticipated to be to avoid truncating timing.
- Enable Collapse Transformations for the nested composition to ignore its boundaries (**Figure 4.8**).

These two simple rules will cover many situations, but Collapse Transformations has extra benefits and limitations of its own.

> **TIP**
>
> The script preCompToLayerDur.jsx from Dan Ebberts is included on the disk; even if a layer to be precomped doesn't start at frame 0, the precomp does.

Figure 4.8 The nested comp has a blue background and the leg of the letter "p" extends outside its boundaries (top); a simple quick-fix is to enable Collapse Transformations, and the boundaries of the nested comp are ignored (bottom).

Collapse Transformations

Switches Affect Nested Comps is enabled by default in General Preferences. Enable frame blending or motion blur in a master composition and those switches are passed through to any nested composition. 3D position data and blending modes, on the other hand, are ignored if Collapse Transformations is not enabled (**Figure 4.9**). Enable it and it is as if the precomposed layers resided in the Master comp.

Figure 4.9 The highlighted switch has two roles (and two names): Collapse Transformations passes through blending modes and 3D positions from nested comps as if not precomped; Continuous Rasterization maintains vector source without rasterizing until final render and applies to source in formats such as Adobe Illustrator.

Collapse Transformations prevents the application of a blending mode on the collapsed layer. Apply any effect to the layer (even disable it) and After Effects must render the collapsed layer (making it what the Adobe developers call a *parenthesized* comp, one that has qualities of being both rendered and live). You can then apply a Blending mode, but 3D data is not passed through.

Thus if you want to collapse transformations but not 3D data, applying any effect—even one of the Expression Controls effects that don't by themselves do anything—will parenthesize the comp. It's a good trick to keep in your pocket.

Nested Time

After Effects is less rigid than most digital video applications when working with time. All compositions in a given project need not use the same frame rate, and as has been shown, you can change the frame rate of an existing composition on the fly, and keyframes retain placement relative to overall time.

CLOSE-UP

Grow Bounds

Sometimes enabling Collapse Transformations is not desirable—for example, if you set up 3D layers in a subcomp and don't want their position to be changed by a camera in the Master comp. The Grow Bounds effect overcomes one specific (and fairly rare) problem, where layers in a nested comp are cut off by the comp boundary.

With power comes responsibility, of course, so pay particular attention when you

▶ Import an image sequence.

▶ Create a new composition from scratch.

▶ Embed a composition with a given frame rate into another with a different frame rate.

In the first two cases you're just watching out for careless errors, but in the third, you might have reason to maintain different frame rates in subcomps, in which case you must set it deliberately on the Advanced tab of the Composition Settings dialog, or apply the Posterize Time effect set to the desired rate.

Advanced Composition Settings

In addition to the Motion Blur settings introduced in Chapter 2 and detailed in Chapter 8, Composition Settings: Advanced contains two Preserve toggles that influence how time and space are handled when the composition is nested into another.

Preserve Frame Rate maintains the frame rate of the composition wherever it goes—into another composition with a different frame rate or into the Render Queue with different frame rate settings. So if a simple animation cycle looks right at 4 frames per second (fps), it won't be expanded across the higher frame rate but will preserve the look of 4 fps.

Preserve Resolution When Nested controls what is called *concatenation*. Typically, if an element is scaled down in a precomp and the entire composition is nested into another comp and scaled up, the two operations are treated as one, so that no data loss occurs via quantization. This is concatenation, and it's usually a good thing. If the data in the subcomp is to appear pixilated, as if it were scaled up from a lower-resolution element, this toggle preserves the big pixel look.

TIP

Annoyed to find sequences importing at the wrong frame rate for your project? Change the default Sequence Footage Frames per Second under Preferences > Import.

Adjustment and Guide Layers

Two special types of layers that don't render, adjustment and guide layers, offer extra benefits that might not be immediately apparent.

Adjustment Layers

An *adjustment layer* is itself invisible, but its effects are applied to all layers below it. It is a fundamentally simple feature with many uses. To create one, context-click in an empty area of the Timeline, and choose New > Adjustment Layer (**Ctrl+Alt+Y/Command+Option+Y**) (**Figure 4.10**).

Figure 4.10 Any pixel layer becomes an adjustment layer by toggling this switch. An adjustment layer created by After Effects is a white, comp-sized solid with this switch toggled on.

Adjustment layers allow you to apply effects to an entire composition without precomping it. That by itself is pretty cool, but there's more:

▶ Move the adjustment layer down the stack and layers above it are unaffected.

▶ Change its timing and the effects appear only on frames within the adjustment layer's In/Out points.

▶ Time any effect in an adjustment layer by setting layer In/Out points.

▶ Use Opacity to attenuate the amount effects are applied. Many effects do not themselves include so direct a control, even when it makes perfect sense to "dial it back 50%," which you can do by setting Opacity to 50%.

▶ Apply a matte to an adjustment layer to apply an effect to one area of the image.

▶ Add a blending mode and the adjustment layer is first applied and then blended back into the result (**Figure 4.11**).

It's a good idea 99% of the time to make sure that an adjustment layer remains 2D and at the size and length of the comp, as when applied; it's rare that you would ever want to transform an adjustment layer in 2D or 3D, but it is possible, so don't let it happen by accident. If you enlarge the composition, you must resize the adjustment layers as well.

NOTES

Alpha channel effects change the alphas of the layers below, not of the adjustment layer itself.

Figure 4.11 The ball on the top left was created with a Shape layer. To the right is the ball with a Glow effect applied (default settings), and with the Blending mode set to Normal. The bottom image shows what occurs when the Blending mode is changed to Add: The result of the second ball has been added to the first.

Guide Layers

Like adjustment layers, *guide layers* are normal layers with special status. A guide layer appears in the current composition but not in any subsequent compositions or the final render (unless you specifically override this functionality in Render Settings, which kind of defeats the purpose). Common uses include

▶ Foreground reference clips

▶ Temporary backgrounds to check edge transparency

▶ Text reminders (Specific render instructions? Add a text layer with a bullet-pointed list in the render comp and set it as a guide layer.)

▶ Adjustment layers that are used only to check images (described further in the next chapter); a layer can be both an adjustment and a guide layer

Any image layer can be made a guide layer either by context-clicking it or by choosing Guide Layer from the Layer menu. Within the current comp, you'll notice no difference (**Figure 4.12**). You can still apply effects to this layer or have other layers refer to it, and it is fully visible. Nest this composition in another composition, however, and the guide layer disappears.

Figure 4.12 A gradient can clarify matte problems; to ensure that it doesn't render, make the background a guide layer.

Render Pipeline

To become an expert compositor is to precisely understand the order in which actions are performed on an image, also known as the *render pipeline*. For the most part render order is plainly displayed in the Timeline and follows consistent rules:

▶ 2D layers are calculated from bottom to top of the layer stack.

▶ Layer properties (masks, effects, transforms, paint, and type) are calculated from top to bottom (twirl down to see the order).

▶ 3D layers are of course calculated based on distance from the camera; coplanar 3D layers respect stacking order and behave—relative to one another—like 2D layers.

TIP

3D calculations are precise well below the decimal level, but do round at some point. Coplanar 3D layers can thus introduce rendering errors and should generally be avoided by precomping them in 2D.

In a 2D composition, After Effects starts at the bottom layer and calculates any adjustments to it in the order that properties are shown, top to bottom. Then, it calculates adjustments to the layer above it, composites the two of them together, and continues up to the top layer of the stack, while the properties of an individual layer render top to bottom (**Figure 4.13**).

Figure 4.13 2D layers render starting with the bottom layer, rendering and compositing each layer above in order. Layer properties render in the order shown when twirled down; there is no direct way to change the order of these categories.

So, although effects within layers always calculate prior to transforms, by applying an effect to an adjustment layer above, you guarantee that it is rendered after the transforms of all layers below it.

Track mattes (and blending modes) are applied last, after all other layer properties (masks, effects, and transforms) have been calculated, *and* after their own mask, effect, and transform data are applied. Therefore, you don't generally need to pre-render a track matte just because you've edited it.

Optimize Previews and Renders

As I work, I organize portions of my master comp that I consider finished into their own subcomps, and if they require any render cycles at all, I prerender them. Failure to commit to decisions—keeping options open—costs time and efficiency. It's as true in After Effects as it is in life as a whole.

Pre-rendering a subcomp does, however, lead to a decision about what happens after you render it.

Post-Render Options

Tucked away in the Render Queue panel, but easily visible if you twirl down the arrow next to Output Module, is a

TIP

The Transform effect allows you to transform before other effects are applied to avoid precomping for this purpose.

TIP

Although the UI doesn't prohibit you from doing so, don't apply a track matte to another track matte and expect consistent results. Sometimes it works, sometimes it doesn't.

TIP

Preferences > Display > Show Rendering in Process in Info Panel and Flowchart shows what is happening on your system. It is disabled by default because it requires extra processing power; I leave it on because it costs more time not to know.

menu of three post-render actions. After the render is complete, you can choose

▶ **Import:** Simply imports the result

▶ **Import & Replace Usage:** Keeps the source comp but replaces its use—or that of any other element you choose instead—in the project

▶ **Set Proxy:** Adds a proxy to the source comp (or any other item you specify)

With either of the latter two, the Pickwhip icon adjacent to the menu can be clicked and dragged to whatever item in the Project panel needs replacement so that if you've already created a pre-render or proxy, you can replace it (**Figure 4.14**).

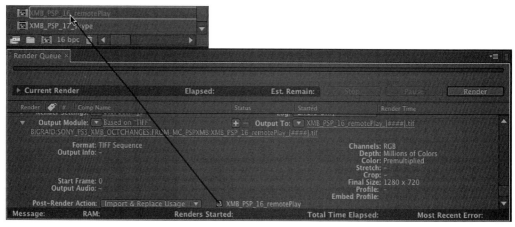

Figure 4.14 Virtually any Project item can be the target for replacement or a proxy; click and drag the Pickwhip icon to choose the item to be replaced by the render.

TIP

If you choose Import & Replace Usage and then need to change back, Alt/Option-drag the source comp over the replacement clip in the Project to globally replace its usage.

Proxies have the best potential to speed up your work on a heavy project, but not everyone likes them because their implementation complicates the rendering process.

Proxies and Pre-Renders

Any visual item in your Project panel can be set with a *proxy*, which is an imported image or sequence that stands in for that item. Its pixel dimensions, color space, compression, and even its length can differ from the item it replaces; for example, you can use a low-resolution, JPEG-compressed still image to stand in for a full-resolution, moving image background.

To create a proxy, context-click an item in the Project panel and choose Create Proxy > Movie (or Still). A render queue item is created and automatically renders at Draft quality and half-resolution; the Output Module settings create a video file with alpha, so that transparency is preserved, and the Post-Render Action uses the Set Proxy setting.

Figure 4.15 shows how a proxy appears in the Project panel. Although the scale of the proxy differs from that of the source item, transform settings within the comps that use this item remain consistent with those of the source item so that it can be swapped in for final at any time. This is what proxies were designed to do, to allow a low-resolution file to stand in, temporarily and nondestructively, for the high-resolution final.

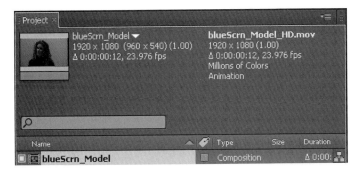

Figure 4.15 The black square icon to the left of an item in the Project panel indicates that a proxy is enabled; a hollow square indicates that a proxy is assigned but not currently active. Both items are listed atop the Project panel, the active one in bold.

By default, the source file or composition is used to render unless specifically set otherwise in Render Settings > Proxy Use. Choosing Use Comp Proxies Only, Use All Proxies, or Current Settings options (**Figure 4.16**) allows proxies to be used in the final render. To remove them from a project, select items with proxies, context-click (or go to the File menu), and choose Set Proxy > None.

Figure 4.16 I typically set Proxy Use to Current Settings, but Use Comp Proxies Only lets you set low-res stand-ins for footage and full-res pre-renders for comps, saving gobs of time.

Similar to proxies, but with a different intended use, are pre-rendered elements. With a composition selected, choose Composition > Pre-render and a moving image file is set to render at Best quality, full resolution; the Import and Replace Usage is set for the Output Module.

See Chapter 1 for specifics on multiprocessing, caching, and previewing.

You don't have to follow this usage; I have made proxies behave as pre-rendered elements and set my Render Settings to Current so I can choose whether to use the proxy or re-render. Managing that process, however, adds an extra set of steps.

Background Renders

One way to get a lot more power out of After Effects is to improve upon the standard method of rendering, which ties up the application itself, and most of the machine's processing power, for as long as is needed to output footage.

aerender

Almost any production system these days has multiple processors and cores, and this has opened the possibility of *background rendering*, which allows a render to occur in the background while you continue to work in the foreground.

The last edition of this book mentioned using the command line (in Terminal Unix shell on Mac or the DOS shell in Windows) to run aerender; to do this, you can locate it in your After Effects CS4 folder and drag it into the shell window; then press Enter to get the manual. Arguments in quotes can be added to the command aerender and the location string of the project file.

However, that's a little complicated and involves typing in commands, not the favorite activity of most visual artist types. For that reason I highly recommend loading a free script from aescripts.com called BG Renderer into the Script UI Panels folder, also in the After Effects CS4 folder. This script automatically sets up the command line not only to render in the background, freeing the open application to be used for more work, but using extra commands such as nice to set the priority and number of processors that you specify.

Network Rendering

The aerender command is also key to third-party rendering solutions such as Rush Render Queue (http://seriss. com/rush/). These programs run scripts that manage the process of running aerender on multiple machines (**Figure 4.17**). The better applications among them, Rush included, are capable of far more than just straight-ahead renders; you can, for example, have one render wait until a certain time or for another one to complete before commencing, and you can automatically requeue renders that fail for any reason.

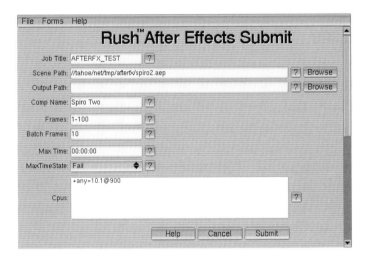

Figure 4.17 One look at Rush Render Queue's UI will tell you you're not in After Effects land anymore, but it's plenty sophisticated at managing network renders from After Effects and the many other applications, 2D and 3D, that enable command line render management.

This type of software is not generally even implemented via a standard installer; required instead are the implementation skills of a system administrator or equivalent technical expert. Most larger facilities have just such a "geek" on staff, and many advanced After Effects users are themselves capable of setting this up in smaller studios.

Multiple After Effects Versions

Alternatively, you can open multiple versions of After Effects including the UI. Although memory intensive, this allows you to actually investigate, compare, and edit two projects at once, which is occasionally handy.

On a Mac, all you need to do is locate Adobe After Effects CS4.app in the Finder (most likely in Applications/Adobe

After Effects CS4) and duplicate it (**Cmd+D**). You now have two versions of the application that will open separately, and you are free to render a project in one version while continuing to work in the other. Give one of them a unique name so you can tell them apart.

On Windows, you can open a second version of After Effects from the command line. From the Start menu, choose Run, type cmd, and click OK. In the DOS shell that opens, drag in AfterFX.exe from your Programs folder and then add " –m" (that's a space, a dash, and m as in multiple). Voilà, a second version initializes. Write a .bat file and you can do all of this with a double-click. The same basic trick even works in the Mac Terminal.

Watch Folder

The slightly senile grandaddy of network rendering on After Effects is Watch Folder. File > Watch Folder looks in a given folder for projects ready to be rendered; these are set up using the Collect Files option. The help topic "Rendering on the Network: Using a Watch Folder" page includes everything you need to know, so there's no reason to reiterate setup here.

Watch Folder is okay on small, intimate networks, but it has to be set up manually on each machine, and if anything goes wrong, it has to be re-queued. A single machine has so much rendering power these days, it is years since I've bothered using it even though my studio is about the right size for it: big enough to have several systems, small enough to have them all in the same physical space.

Adobe Media Encoder

Adobe Media Encoder is a dedicated render application for certain video formats, including Flash Video, H.264, MPEG-2, and Adobe Clip Notes. Choose one of these in Output Module settings and the Encoder reveals many specialized options having to do with that particular format.

Owners of Adobe Production Premium or Master Collection can also access Media Encoder from Premiere Pro, where it can perform multipass encoding (essential for the best quality compression) and Speech Search, this new ability to convert spoken words on the soundtrack to timed text. Each word shows up as a layer marker, theoretically making it easy to time footage that includes speech, a very cool concept.

Project Optimization

Finally, to finish Section I of this book, here's a clean sweep of preferences, memory management settings, and what do to if After Effects crashes.

Setting Preferences and Project Settings

The preference defaults have changed in version CS4 and you may be happy with most of them. Here, however, are a few you might want to adjust that haven't been mentioned yet:

- ▶ **Preferences > General > Levels of Undo:** The default is 32, which may be geared toward a system with less RAM than yours. Setting it to the maximum value of 99 won't bring the application to a grinding halt, but it may shorten the amount of time available in RAM Previews.

- ▶ **Preferences General:** Check the options Allow Scripts to Write Files and Access Network to use some of the scripts included with this book. Most advanced users also prefer Default Spatial Interpolation to Linear (Chapter 2).

- ▶ **Preferences > Display:** I tend to check all three boxes; I don't need to wait for thumbnails to update from some network location each time I select a source file, I like to see rendering progress even though it costs processing time (as I said earlier), and I have a good OpenGL card so I hardware accelerate the UI.

- ▶ **Preferences > User Interface Colors:** The default UI is darker than it used to be, so I am often fine with its shade. If you like it darker, consider enabling Affects Label Colors so they darken too. Either way, Cycle Mask Colors so that multiple masks applied to a layer automatically have different colors (I have no idea why that's disabled by default).

TIP

Alt+Ctrl+Shift/Option+Cmd+ Shift immediately after launching After Effects resets Preferences. Hold **Alt/Option** while clicking OK to delete the shortcuts file as well.

Hack Shortcuts, Text Preferences, or Projects

After Effects Shortcuts and Preferences are saved as text files that are fully editable and relatively easy to understand, although if you're not comfortable with basic hacking (learning how code works by looking at other bits of code) I don't recommend it. The files are located as follows:

Windows: Documents and Settings\[user profile]\Application Data\Adobe\After Effects\8.0\

Mac OS: Users/[user profile]/Library/Preferences/Adobe/Adobe After Effects/8.0/

The names of the files are

Adobe After Effects 8.0 Prefs

Adobe After Effects 8.0 Shortcuts

These can be opened with any text editor that doesn't add its own formatting and works with Unicode. The default applications, TextEdit on the Mac and Notepad on Windows, are acceptable, although there are more full-featured alternatives. Make a safety copy before editing by simply duplicating the file (any variation in the file name causes it not to be recognized by After Effects). Revert to the safety by giving it the original file name should anything start to go haywire after the edit.

The Shortcuts file includes a bunch of comments at the top (each line begins with a # sign). The Shortcuts themselves are arranged in a very specific order that must be preserved, and if you add anything, it must be added in the right place. You can add the line

```
"NewEffectsLayer" = "(Cmd+Option+Y)"
```

or on Windows

```
"NewEffectsLayer" = "(Ctrl+Alt+Y)"
```

between `NewDebugComp` and `NewLight`—this gives you a shortcut to create a new adjustment layer. If you understand this basic format, you can change other shortcuts to be what you like. For example, if you don't like the fact that Go To Time was changed in CS3 (apparently to align it with other Adobe applications), search for `GoToTime` and make your changes to the shortcut in quotes after the = sign; "(Alt+Shift+J)" becomes "(Ctrl+G)" on Windows, "(Opt+Shift+J)" becomes "(Cmd+G)" on Mac (but make sure to change the Group shortcut to something else).

Be extra careful when editing Preferences—a stray character in this file can make After Effects unstable. Most of the contents should not be touched, but here's one example of a simple and useful edit (for studios where a dot is preferred before the number prefix instead of the underscore): change

```
"Sequence number prefix" = "_"
```

to

```
"Sequence number prefix" = "."
```

In other cases, a simple and easily comprehensible numerical value can be changed:

```
"Eye Dropper Sample Size No Modifier" = "1"
"Eye Dropper Sample Size With Modifier" = "5"
```

In many cases the value after the = is a binary yes/no value, expressed as 0 for no or 1 for yes, so if you're nostalgic for how the After Effects render chime sounded in its first several versions, find

```
"Play classic render chime" = "0"
```

and change the 0 to a 1. Save the file, restart After Effects, and invoke nostalgic memories of past renders.

XML

After Effects CS4 projects can be saved as .aepx files. These are identical to use, but are written in plain Unicode text; you can edit them with an ordinary text editor. Most of what is in these files is untouchable, but a few strings, such as source file locations, are easily recognizable.

This feature was added for one reason only: scriptability. Anyone capable of writing scripts to, say, swap source files procedurally (and you know who you are) now has a way to get at this data without having to open After Effects in order to do it.

TIP

A fantastic script for specifying your own modifier keys called KeyEd Up was developed specifically for After Effects by Jeff Almasol, author of other scripts included with this book.

On the Mac: Force a Crash

One benefit of After Effects has historically been that it is among the most stable applications in its category, and when it does crash, it attempts to do so gracefully, offering the option to save before it exits. The new auto-save options, if used properly, further diminish the likelihood that you are ever likely in danger of losing project data.

For OS X users, there is an extra feature that may come in handy if the application becomes unresponsive but does not actually crash.

Open Terminal, and enter ps −x (then press Return) to list all processes. Scan the resulting list for After Effects and note its PID (Process ID) value.

Now enter kill −SEGV ### where "###" is replaced by the After Effects PID value. This causes the application to crash with a save opportunity.

This feature may open the door to more easily editable properties appearing in an .aepx file in future versions of After Effects, but these files are far from the equivalent of, say, a Shake script, in which every virtually line is easily understood and potentially editable.

Memory Management

In OS X, After Effects can see and use up to 3.5 GB of physical memory. Your machine may have more total RAM than this, but most applications on a Mac are still limited to 32-bit 4 GB address spaces.

On Windows XP, the maximum amount of memory supported for a single application is 4 GB (again, using 32-bit 4 GB address spaces). According to Microsoft, however, "The virtual address space of processes and applications is still limited to 2 GB unless the /3GB switch is used in the Boot.ini file." Editing this file is out of the scope for this book, so check out microsoft.com for specific information.

Extra memory is most helpful for multiprocessing, because each process has the just described memory potential. With multiprocessing, you could use the maximum memory on an 8 core (or more—only rumored at this writing) system.

Conclusion

You've reached the end of Section I (assuming you're reading this book linearly, that is) and should now have a firm grasp on getting the most out of the After Effects workflow. Now it's time to focus more specifically on the art of visual effects. Section II, "Effects Compositing Essentials," will teach you the techniques, and Section III, "Creative Explorations," will show you how they work in specific effects situations.

Now comes the fun part.

SECTION II

Effects Compositing Essentials

Chapter 5   Color Correction   135

Chapter 6   Color Keying   175

Chapter 7   Rotoscoping and Paint   211

Chapter 8   Effective Motion Tracking   237

Chapter 9   The Camera and Optics   269

Chapter 10 Expressions   309

Chapter 11 32-Bit HDR Compositing
              and Color Management   345

5

Color Correction

Color is my obsession, joy and torment... one day, at the deathbed of a dear friend, I caught myself in the act of focusing on her temples, analyzing the succession of appropriately graded colors which death imposed on her motionless face.

—Claude Monet

Color Correction

No skill is as essential for a compositor as the ability to authoritatively and conclusively take control of color, such that foreground and background elements seem to inhabit the same world, shots from a sequence are consistent with one another, and their overall look matches the artistic direction of the project.

The compositor, after all, is typically the last one to touch a shot before it goes into the edit. Inspired, artistic color work injects life, clarity, and drama into standard (or even substandard) 3D output, adequately (or even poorly) shot footage, and flat, monochromatic stills. It draws the audience's attention where it belongs, never causing them to think about the compositing at all.

Good compositors are credited with possessing a "good eye," but color matching is a skill that you can practice and refine even if you have no feel for adjusting images—indeed, even if you consider yourself color blind.

And despite the new color tools that appear each year to refine your ability to dial in color, for color matching in After Effects, three color correction tools allow you to do most of the heavy lifting: Levels, Curves, and Hue/Saturation (and because Levels and Curves overlap in their functionality, in many cases you're just choosing one or two of the three). These endure (from the earliest days of Photoshop) because they are stable and fast, and they will get the job done every time—just learn how to use them, and keep practicing.

A skeptic might ask

▶ Why these old tools with so many cool newer ones?

▶ Why not use Brightness & Contrast to adjust, you know, brightness and contrast, or Shadow and Highlight if that's what needs adjustment?

▶ What do you mean I can adjust Levels even if I'm color blind?

This chapter holds the answers to these questions and many more. First, we'll look at optimizing a given image using these tools, and then we'll move into matching a foreground layer to the optimized background, balancing the colors. The goal is to eliminate the need to hack at color work and to build skills that eliminate a lot of the guesswork.

This chapter introduces topics that resound throughout the rest of the book. Chapter 11 deals specifically with HDR color, and then Chapter 12 focuses on specific light and color scenarios, while the rest of Section III describes how to create specific types of effects shots.

Optimized Levels

What constitutes an "optimized" clip? What makes a color corrected image correct? Let's look at what is typically "wrong" with source footage levels and the usual methods for correcting them, laying the groundwork for color matching. As an example, we'll balance brightness and contrast of a *plate* image, with no foreground layers to match.

Levels

Levels may be the most-used tool in After Effects, and yet it's rare to find detailed descriptions of how best to use it. It consists of five basic controls—Input Black, Input White, Output Black, Output White, and Gamma—each of which can be adjusted in five separate contexts (the four individual image channels R, G, B, and A, as well as all three color channels, RGB, at once). There are two different ways to adjust these controls: via their numerical sliders or by dragging their respective carat sliders on the histogram. The latter is the more typical method for experienced users.

NOTES

The term *"plate"* stretches back to the earliest days of optical compositing (and indeed, of photography itself) and refers to the source footage, typically the background onto which foreground elements will be composited. A related term, *"clean plate,"* refers to the background with any moving foreground elements removed; its usage is covered in the following chapter.

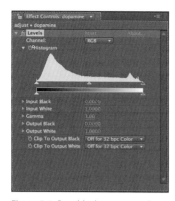

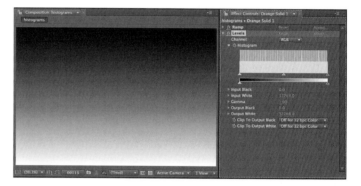

Contrast: Input and Output Levels

Four of the five controls—Input Black, Input White, Output Black, and Output White (**Figure 5.1**)—determine brightness and contrast, and combined with the fifth, Gamma, they offer more precision than is possible with the effect called Brightness & Contrast.

Figure 5.2 shows a Ramp effect applied to a solid using the default settings, followed by the Levels effect. Move the black caret at the lower left of the histogram—the Input Black level—to the right, and values below its threshold (the numerical Input Black setting, which changes as you move the caret) are pushed to black. The further you move the caret, the more values are "crushed" to pure black.

Figure 5.1 Possibly the most used "effect" in After Effects, Levels consists of a histogram and five basic controls per channel; the controls are typically adjusted using the triangles on the histogram, although the corresponding numerical/slider controls appear below.

NOTES

Two check boxes at the bottom of the Levels effect controls specify whether black and white levels "clip" on output. These are checked on by default, and until you work in HDR (Chapter 11), you might as well ignore their very existence; they handle values beyond the range that your monitor can display.

Figure 5.2 Levels is applied to a layer containing a Ramp effect at the default settings, which creates a smooth gradient from black to white. The spikes occur simply because the gradient height does not have an exact multiple of 256 pixels. The histogram in Figure 5.1 corresponds to the image shown here, unadjusted. (Image from the film "Dopamine," courtesy of Mark Decena, Kontent Films.)

Move the Input White carat at the right end of the histogram to the left, toward the Input Black caret. The effect is similar to Input Black's but inverted: more and more white values are "blown out" to pure white (**Figure 5.3**).

Either adjustment effectively increases contrast, but note that the midpoint of the gradient also changes if one is adjusted further than the other. In Figure 5.3 Input Black has been adjusted more heavily than Input White, causing the horizon of the gradient to move closer to white and more of the image to turn black. You can re-create this adjustment with Brightness & Contrast (**Figure 5.4** on the next page), but to do so you must adjust both contrast

TIP

Compositing is science as well as art, and so this section employs a useful scientific tool: the control, which is a study subject that eliminates random or hidden variables. This control for the Levels effect is a grayscale gradient I generated with the Ramp effect. You can often set up similar experiments to clarify your understanding of computer graphics applications.

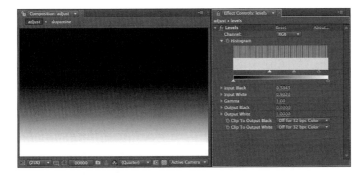

Figure 5.3 Raising Input Black and lowering Input White has the effect of increasing contrast at either end of the scale; at an extreme adjustment like this, many pixels in an 8 bpc or 16 bpc project are pushed to full white or black or "crushed."

Figure 5.4 You can use Brightness & Contrast to match the look of Figure 5.3's gradient, but if you need to shift the gamma (midpoint) you need a different tool.

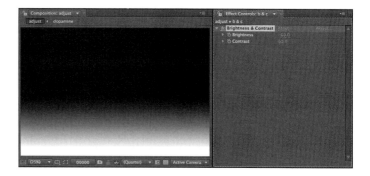

Figure 5.5 The source (left) was balanced for the sky, leaving foreground detail too dark to make out. Raising Brightness to bring detail out of the shadows makes the entire image washed out (middle); raising Contrast to compensate completely blows out the sky (right). Madness.

TIP

You can reset any individual effect control by context-clicking it and choosing Reset. You know it's individual if it has its own stopwatch.

NOTES

Note that you can even cross the two carets; if you drag Output White all the way down and Output Black all the way up, you have inverted your image (although the more straightforward way to do this typically is to use the Channel: Invert effect).

and brightness, with no direct control of the midpoint (gamma) of the image (**Figure 5.5**).

Reset Levels (click Reset at the top of the Levels effect controls) and try the same experiment with Output Black and Output White, whose controls sit below the little gradient. Output Black specifies the darkest black that can appear in the image; adjust it upwards and the minimum value is raised.

Similarly, lowering Input White is something like dimming the image, cutting off the maximum possible white value at the given threshold. Adjust both and you effectively reduce contrast in the image; with them close together, the gradient becomes a solid gray (**Figure 5.6**).

Evidently the Input and Output controls have the opposite effect on their respective black and white values, when examined in this straightforward fashion. However, there are even situations where you would use them together.

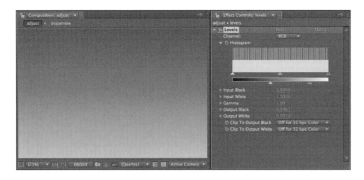

Figure 5.6 Raising Output Black and lowering Output White reduces contrast in the dark and light areas of the image, respectively; this doesn't produce such a beautiful image but comes into play in the Matching section.

As is the case throughout After Effects, the controls are operating in the order listed in the interface. In other words, raising the Input Black level first crushes the blacks, and then a higher Output Black level raises all of those pure black levels as one (**Figure 5.7** on the next page). It does not restore the black detail in the original pixels; the blacks remain crushed, they all just become lighter.

If you're thinking, "So what?" at this point, just stay with this—the controls are being broken down to build up an understanding.

Figure 5.7 Black and white levels crushed by adjusting the Input controls aren't then brought back by the Output controls, which instead simply limit the overall dynamic range of the image, raising the darkest possible black level and lowering the brightest possible white.

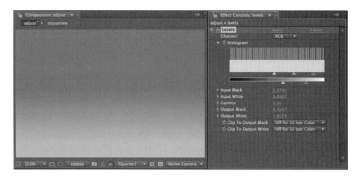

Brightness: Gamma

As you adjust the Input Black and White values, you may have noticed the third caret that maintains its place between them. This is the Gamma control, affecting midtones (the middle gray point in the gradient) at the highest proportion and black and white, not at all. Adjust it over the gradient and notice that you can push the grays in the image brighter (by moving it to the left) or darker (to the right) without changing the black and white levels.

Many images have healthy contrast, but a gamma boost gives them extra punch. Similarly, an image that looks a bit too "hot" may be instantly adjusted simply by lowering gamma. As you progress through the book, you will see that it plays a crucial role not only in color adjustment but also in the inner workings of the image pipeline itself (more on that in Chapter 11).

In most cases, the histogram won't itself offer much of a clue as to whether the gamma needs adjusting, or by how much (see "Problem Solving using the Histogram," later in this chapter for more on the topic). The image itself provides a better guide for how to adjust gamma (**Figure 5.8**).

So what is your guideline for how much you should adjust gamma, if at all? I first learned to adjust too far before dialing back, which is especially helpful when learning. An even more powerful gamma adjustment tool that scares most novice artists away is Curves (more on this later).

By mixing these five controls together, have we covered everything there is to know about using Levels? No—because there are not, in fact, five basic controls in Levels (Input and Output White and Black plus Gamma), but instead, five times five (RGB, Red, Green, Blue, and Alpha).

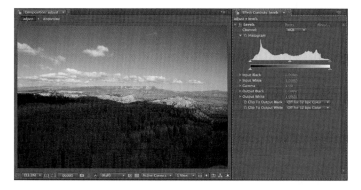
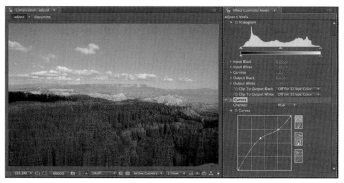

Figure 5.8 The top image is improved with a boost to gamma using Curves (explained later on); the indication that this is a good idea comes not from the histogram, which looks fine, but from the image itself, which visibly lacks foreground detail.

Geek Alert: What Is Gamma, Anyway?

It would be so nice simply to say, "gamma is the midpoint of your color range" and leave it at that. The more accurate the discussion of gamma becomes, the more obscure and mathematical it gets. There are plenty of artists out there who understand gamma intuitively and are able to work with it without knowing the math behind it—but here it is anyhow, just in case.

Gamma adjustment shifts the midpoint of a color range without affecting the black or white points. This is done by taking a pixel value and raising it to the inverse power of the gamma value:

`newPixel = pixel (1/gamma)`

You're probably used to thinking of pixel values as fitting into the range 0 to 255, but this formula works with values *normalized* to 1. In other words, all 255 8-bit values occur between 0 and 1, so 0 is 0, 255 is 1, and 128 is .5—which is how the math "normally" operates behind the scenes.

Why does it work this way? Because of the magic of logarithms: Any number to the power of 0 is 1, any number to the power of 1 is itself, and any fractional value (less than 1) raised to a higher power approaches 0 without ever reaching it. Lower the power closer to 0 and the value approaches 1, again without ever reaching it. Not only that, but the values distribute proportionally, along a curve, so the closer an initial value is to pure black (0) or pure white (1) the less it is affected by a gamma adjustment.

Individual Channels for Color Matching

Many After Effects artists completely ignore that pop-up menu at the top of the Levels control that isolates red, green, blue, and alpha adjustments, and even those who do use it once in a while may do so with trepidation; how can you predictably understand what will happen when you adjust the five basic Levels controls on an individual channel? The gradient again serves as an effective learning tool to reveal what exactly is going on.

Reset the Levels effect applied to the Ramp gradient once more. Pick Red, Green, or Blue in the Channel pop-up menu under Levels and adjust the Input and Output carets. Color is introduced into what was a purely gray-scale image. With the Red channel selected, by moving Red Output Black inward, you tint the darker areas of the image red. If you adjust Input White inward, the midtones and highlights turn pink (light red). If, instead, you adjust Input Black or Output White inward, the tinting goes in the opposite direction—toward cyan—in the corresponding shadows and highlights. As you probably know, on the digital wheel of color, cyan is the opposite of red, just as magenta is the opposite of green and yellow is the opposite of blue (a sample digital color wheel and a visual guide to how levels adjustments operate on individual channels are included on the book's disc).

Gradients are one thing, but the best way to make sense of this with a real image is to develop the habit of studying footage on individual color channels as you work. This is the key to effective color matching, detailed ahead.

Along the bottom of the Composition panel, all of the icons are monochrome by default save one: the Show Channel menu. It contains five selections: the three color channels as well as two alpha modes. Each one has a shortcut that, unfortunately, is not shown in the menu: **Alt+1** through **Alt+4** (**Option+1** through **Option+4**) reveal each color channel in order. These shortcuts are toggles, so reselecting the active channel toggles RGB. A colored outline around the edge of the composition palette reminds you which channel is displayed (**Figure 5.9**).

CLOSE-UP

Same Difference: Levels (Individual Controls)

Both Levels and Levels (Individual Controls) accomplish the exact same task. The sole difference is that Levels lumps all adjustments into a single keyframe property, which expressions cannot use. Levels (Individual Controls) is particularly useful to

▶ Animate and time Levels settings individually

▶ Link an expression to a Levels setting

▶ Reset a single Levels property (instead of the entire effect)

Levels is more commonly used, but Levels (Individual Controls) is sometimes more useful.

Figure 5.9 Four Views mode is generally intended for 3D use, but it can also be used to show RGB and individual red, green, and blue channels. This becomes extremely useful for color matching; for now, observe how radically different the three channels appear, and the colored outline showing which is which.

Try adjusting a single channel of the gradient in Levels while displaying only that channel. You are back on familiar territory, adjusting brightness and contrast of a grayscale image. This is the way to work with individual channel adjustments, especially when you're just beginning or if you are at all color-blind. As you work with actual images instead of gradients, the histogram can show you what is happening in your image.

The Levels Histogram

You might have noticed the odd appearance of the histogram for an unadjusted gradient. If you were to try this setup on your own, depending on the size of the layer to which you applied Ramp, you might see a histogram that is flat along the top with spikes protruding at regular intervals (**Figure 5.10**).

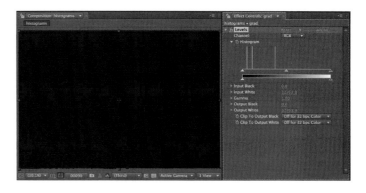

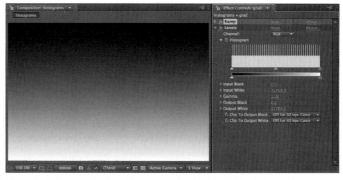

Figure 5.10 Strange-looking histograms. A colored solid (top) shows three spikes, one each for the red, green, and blue values, and nothing else. With Ramp (bottom) the distribution is even, but the spikes at the top are the result of the ramp not being an exact multiple of 255 pixels, causing certain pixels to recur more often than others.

TIP

An often overlooked feature of Levels is that it allows direct adjustment of brightness, contrast, and gamma of the grayscale transparency channel (Alpha Channel). More on this in Chapter 6.

The histogram is exactly 256 pixels wide; it is effectively a bar chart made up of 256 single pixel bars, each corresponding to one of the 256 possible levels of luminance in an 8 bpc image (these levels are displayed below the histogram, above the Output controls). In the case of a pure gradient, the histogram is flat because luminance is evenly distributed from black to white; if spikes occur in that case, it's merely an indication that the image height in pixels is not an exact multiple of 256.

In any case, it's more useful to look at real-world examples, because the histogram is useful for mapping image data that isn't plainly evident on its own. Its basic function is to help you assess whether any color changes are liable to help or harm the image. There is in fact no one typical or ideal histogram—they can vary as much as the images themselves, as seen back in Figure 5.8.

Despite that fact, there's a simple rule of thumb for a basic contrast adjustment. Find the top and bottom end of the RGB histogram—the highest and lowest points where there is any data whatsoever—and bracket them with the Input Black and Input White carets. To "bracket" them means to adjust these controls inward so each sits just outside its corresponding end of the histogram (**Figure 5.11**). The result stretches values closer to the top or bottom of the dynamic range, as you can easily see by applying a second Levels effect and studying its histogram.

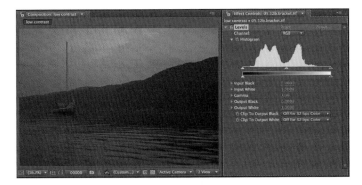

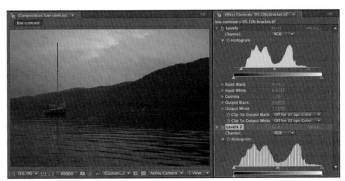

Figure 5.11 Here is a perfect case for bringing the triangle controls corresponding to Input Black and Input White in to bracket the edges of the histogram, increasing contrast and bringing out vibrant colors without losing detail.

Try applying Levels to any image or footage from the disc and see for yourself how this works in practice. First crush the blacks (by moving Input Black well above the lowest

TIP

Footage is by its very nature dynamic, so it is a good idea to leave headroom for the whites and foot room for the blacks until you start working in 32 bits per channel. Headroom is particularly important when anything exceptionally bright—such as a sun glint, flare, or fire—enters frame.

NOTES

Many current displays, and in particular flat-panels and projectors, lack the black detail that can be produced on a good CRT monitor or captured on film. The next time you see a projected film, notice how much detail you can see in the shadows and compare.

black level in the histogram) and then blow out the whites (moving Input White below the highest white value). Don't go too far, or subsequent adjustments will not bring back that detail—unless you work in 32 bpc HDR mode (Chapter 11). Occasionally a stylized look will call for crushed contrast, but generally speaking, this is bad form.

Black and white are not at all equivalent in terms of how your eye sees them. Blown-out whites are ugly and can be a dead giveaway of an overexposed digital scene, but your eye is much more sensitive to subtle gradations of low black levels. These low, rich blacks account for much of what makes film look like film, and they can contain a surprising amount of detail, none of which, unfortunately, would be apparent on the printed page.

The occasions on which you would optimize an image by raising Output Black or lowering Output White controls are rare, as this lowers dynamic range and the overall contrast. However, there are many uses in compositing for lowered contrast, to soften overlay effects (say, fog and clouds), high-contrast mattes, and so on. More on that later in this chapter and throughout the rest of the book.

Problem Solving Using the Histogram

As you've no doubt noticed, the Levels histogram does not update as you make adjustments. After Effects lacks a panel equivalent to Photoshop's Histogram palette, but you can, of course, apply a Levels effect just for the histogram, if only for the purposes of learning (as was done in Figure 5.11).

The histogram reveals a couple of new wrinkles in the backlit shot from Figure 5.5, now adjusted with Levels to bring out foreground highlights (**Figure 5.12**). At the top end of the histogram the levels peak into a spike. This may indicate clipping and a loss of image detail.

At the other end of the scale is the common result of a Gamma adjustment: a series of spikes rising out of the lower values like protruding hash marks, even though a 16 bpc project prevents quantization. Raising Gamma stretches the levels below the midpoint, causing them to clump up at regular intervals. As with crushing blacks and

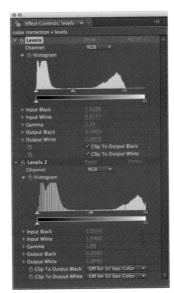

Figure 5.12 In the first instance of Levels, Gamma is raised and the Input White is brought in to enhance detail in the dark areas of the foreground. The second instance is applied only to show its histogram.

blowing out highlights—the net effect is a loss of detail, although in this case, the spikes are not a worry because they occur among a healthy amount of surrounding data. In more extreme cases, in which there is no data in between the spikes whatsoever, you may see a prime symptom of overadjustment, *banding* (**Figure 5.13**).

Figure 5.13 Push an adjustment far enough and you may see quantization, otherwise known as banding in the image. Those big gaps in the histogram are expressed as visible bands on a gradient. Switching to 16 bpc from 8 bpc is an instant fix for this problem in most cases.

Banding is typically the result of limitations of 8-bit color, and 16-bit color mode was added to After Effects 5.0 specifically to address that problem. You can switch to 16 bpc by **Alt**-clicking (**Option**-clicking) on the bit-depth identifier along the bottom of the Project panel (**Figure 5.14**) or by changing it in File > Project Settings. Chapter 11 explains more.

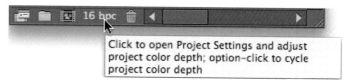

Click to open Project Settings and adjust project color depth; option-click to cycle project color depth

Figure 5.14 An entire project can be toggled from the default 8-bit color mode to 16-bit mode by Alt-clicking (Option-clicking) the project color depth toggle in the Project panel; this prevents the banding seen in Figure 5.13.

Perfecting Brightness with Curves

Curves rocks. I heart Curves. The Curves control is particularly useful for gamma correction, because

▶ Curves lets you fully (and visually) control how adjustments are weighted and roll off.

▶ You can introduce multiple gamma adjustments to a single image or restrict the gamma adjustment to just one part of the image's dynamic range.

▶ Some adjustments can be nailed with a single well-placed point in Curves, in cases where the equivalent adjustment with Levels might require coordination of three separate controls.

It's also worth understanding Curves controls because they are a common shorthand for how digital color adjustments are depicted; the Curves interface recurs in many—most—color correction toolsets.

Curves does, however, have drawbacks, compared with Levels:

▶ It's not immediately intuitive, it can easily yield hideous results if you don't know what you're doing, and there are plenty of artists who aren't comfortable with it.

▶ Unlike Photoshop, After Effects doesn't offer numerical values corresponding to curve points, making it a purely visual control that can be hard to standardize.

▶ Without a histogram, you may miss obvious clues about the image (making Levels more suitable for learners).

The most daunting thing about Curves is clearly its interface, a simple grid with a diagonal line extending from lower left to upper right. There is a Channel selector at the top, set by default to RGB as in Levels, and there are some optional extra controls on the right to help you draw, save, and retrieve custom curves. To the novice, the arbitrary map is an unintuitive abstraction that you can easily use to make a complete mess of your image. Once you understand it, however, you can see it as an elegantly simple description of how image adjustment works. You'll find the equivalent Curves graph to the Levels corrections on the book's disc.

Figure 5.15 shows the more fully featured Photoshop Curves, which better illustrates how the controls work.

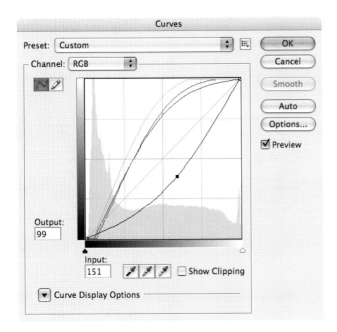

Figure 5.15 Photoshop's more deluxe Curves includes a histogram, built-in presets, displays of all channels together, and fields for input and output values for a given point on the curve.

Figures **5.16a** through **d** show some basic Curves adjustments and their effect on an image. **Figures 5.17a** through **f** use linear gradients to illustrate what some common Curves settings do. I encourage you to try these on your own.

Figure 5.16a The source image.

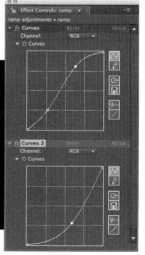

Figure 5.16b An increase in gamma above the shadows.

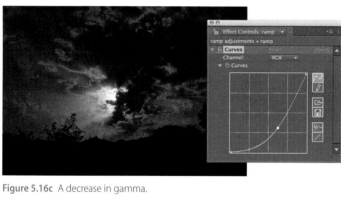

Figure 5.16c A decrease in gamma.

Figure 5.16d Both corrections combined.

Figures 5.16a through d What you see in an image can be heavily influenced by gamma and contrast.

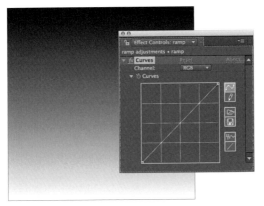

Figure 5.17a The default gradient and Curves setting.

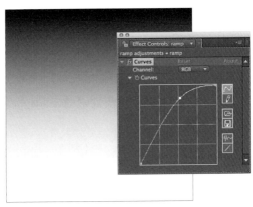

Figure 5.17b An increase in gamma.

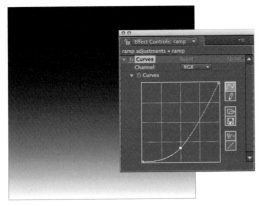

Figure 5.17c A decrease in gamma.

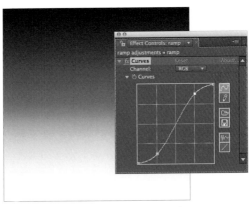

Figure 5.17d An increase in brightness and contrast.

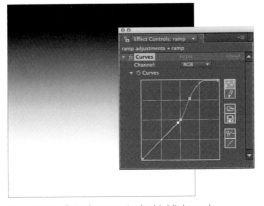

Figure 5.17e Raised gamma in the highlights only.

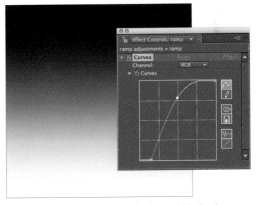

Figure 5.17f Raised gamma with clamped black values.

Figures 5.17a through f This array of Curves adjustments applied to a gradient shows the results of some typical settings.

More interesting are the types of adjustments that only Curves allows you to do—or at least do easily. I came to realize that most of the adjustments I make with Curves fall into a few distinct types that I use over and over, and so those are summarized here.

The most common adjustment is to simply raise or lower the gamma with Curves, by adding a point at or near the middle of the RGB curve and then moving it upward or downward. **Figure 5.18** shows the result of each. This produces a subtly different result from raising or lowering the Gamma control in Levels because of how you control the roll-off (**Figure 5.19**).

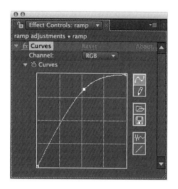

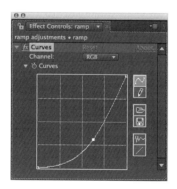

Figure 5.18 Two equally valid gamma adjustments employ a single point adjustment in the Curves control. Dramatically lit footage particularly benefits from the roll-off possible in the highlights and shadows.

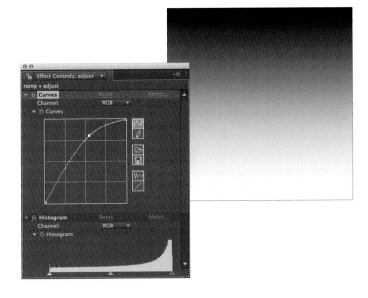

Figure 5.19 Both the gradient itself and the histogram demonstrate that you can push the gamma harder, still preserving the full range of contrast, with Curves rather than with Levels, where you face a choice between losing highlights and shadows somewhat or crushing them.

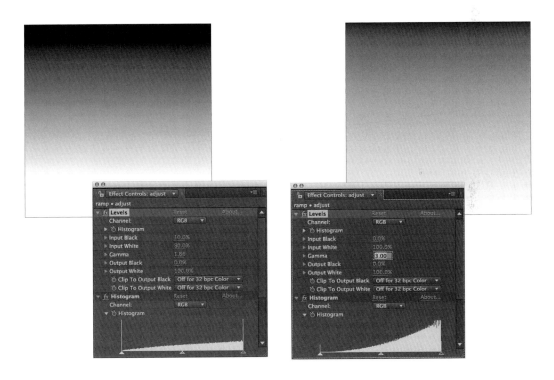

The classic S-curve adjustment, which enhances brightness and contrast and introduces roll-offs into the highlights and shadows (**Figure 5.20**), is an alternative method to get the result of the double curves in Figure 5.16d.

Figure 5.20 The classic S-curve adjustment: The midpoint gamma in this case remains the same, directly crossing the midpoint, but contrast is boosted.

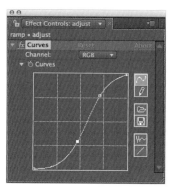

Some images need a gamma adjustment only to one end of the range—for example, a boost to the darker pixels, below the midpoint, that doesn't alter the black point and doesn't brighten the white values. Such an adjustment requires three points (**Figure 5.21**):

▶ One to hold the midpoint

▶ One to boost the low values

▶ One to flatten the curve above the midpoint

Figure 5.21 The ultimate solution to the backlighting problem presented back in Figure 5.5: Adding a mini-boost to the darker levels while leaving the lighter levels flat preserves the detail in the sky and brings out detail in the foreground that was previously missing.

A typical method for working in Curves is to begin with a single point adjustment to adjust gamma or contrast, then to modulate it with one or two added points. More points quickly become unmanageable, as each adjustment changes the weighting of the surrounding points. Typically, I will add a single point, then a second one to restrict its range, and a third as needed to bring the shape of one section back where I want it. The images used for the figures in this section are included as single stills on the book's disc for your own experimentation; open 05_colorCorrection.aep to find them.

Just for Color: Hue/Saturation

The third of three essential color correction tools in After Effects is Hue/Saturation. This one has many individualized uses:

▶ Desaturating an image or adding saturation (the tool's most common use)

▶ Colorizing images that were created as grayscale or monochrome

▶ Shifting the overall hue of an image

▶ De-emphasizing, or knocking out completely, an individual color channel

All of these uses recur in Chapters 12 through 14 to create monochrome elements, such as smoke, from scratch.

The Hue/Saturation control allows you to do something you can't do with Levels or Curves, which is to directly control the hue, saturation, and brightness of an image. The HSB color model is merely an alternate slice of RGB color data. All real color pickers, including the Apple and Adobe pickers, handle RGB and HSB as two separate but interrelated modes that use three values to describe any given color.

In other words, you could arrive at the same color adjustments using Levels and Curves, but Hue/Saturation gives you direct access to a couple of key color attributes that are otherwise difficult to get at. To desaturate an image is essentially to bring the red, green, and blue values closer together, reducing the relative intensity of the strongest of them; a saturation control lets you do this in one step, without guessing.

NOTES

Chapter 12 details why Tint, not Hue/Saturation, is the right tool to convert an entire image to grayscale.

Often is the case where colors are balanced but merely too "juicy" (not a strictly technical term, but one that may make sense in this context), and lowering the Saturation value somewhere between 5 and 20 can be a direct and effective way to pull an image adjustment together (**Figure 5.22**). It's essential to understand the delivery medium as well, because film is more tolerant and friendly to saturated images than television.

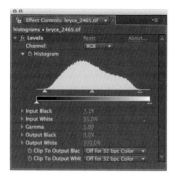

Figure 5.22 Boosting a saturated image's contrast can make its saturation a bit too juiced up with color; if you recognize this, a simple and modest pull-back in overall Saturation is a quick solution.

The other quick fix that Hue/Saturation affords you is a shift to the hue of the overall image or of one or more of its individual channels. The Channel Control menu for Hue/Saturation includes not only the red, green, and blue channels but also their chromatic opposites of cyan, magenta, and yellow. When you're working in RGB color, these secondary colors are in direct opposition, so that, for example, lowering blue gamma effectively raises the yellow gamma, and vice versa.

The HSB model includes all six individual channels, which means that if a given channel is too bright or over-saturated, you can dial back its Brightness & Saturation levels, or you can shift Hue toward a different part of the spectrum without unduly affecting the other primary and secondary colors. This can even be an effective way to reduce blue or green spill (Chapter 6).

More Color Tools and Techniques

This section has laid the foundation for color correction in After Effects using its most fundamental tools. The truth, of course, is that there are lots of ways to adjust the color levels of an image, with new ones emerging all the time. Alternatives used to create a specific look—layering in a color solid, creating selections from an image using the image itself along with blending modes, and more—are explored in Section III of this book.

Color Finesse and Magic Bullet Looks

Color Finesse is a sophisticated color correction system included with After Effects Professional; because it runs as a separate application and does not allow you to adjust corrections in the context of a composite, it is more suitable for overall color look adjustments. It is interesting to notice that it is in many ways a collection of the tools in this section, assembled into one toolset.

An alternative approach can be found in Magic Bullet Looks from Red Giant Software. This package also operates via a separate application and is thus more suited to overall color looks than compositing and matching. It uses a novel metaphor—that of the actual production pipeline—and

TIP

When in doubt about the amount of color in a given channel, try boosting its Saturation to 100%, blowing it out—this makes the presence of that tone in pixels very easy to spot.

TIP

One alternative usage of these basic color correction tools is to apply them via an adjustment layer, because you can then dial them back simply by adjusting the layer's opacity or hold them out from specific areas of the image using masks or track matte selections.

includes filters designed to emulate lighting effects, matte box filters, lens effects, and film stocks.

Much of what these tools do can be recreated with the simpler tools previously described, plus a few extras. However, most artists, particularly those just learning, find that they prefer the more intuitive approach of these higher-level tools for complex color corrections.

Three-Way Color

One thing sorely missing from After Effects is a three-way color corrector, typically featuring color wheels to adjust three distinct color ranges: shadows, midtones, and highlights. Look at any contemporary feature film or major television show and you're likely to find strong color choices that strongly deviate from how the original scene must have looked: In an ordinary day-lit scene the shadows might be bluish, the midtones green, and the highlights orange.

Chapter 12 includes a "roll your own" recipe and Animation Preset for cheap and cheerful three-way color correction.

A third-party tool, Magic Bullet Colorista from Red Giant Software makes this type of correction quick and intuitive in After Effects (**Figure 5.23**); a demo version is included on the book's disc.

Figure 5.23 Red Giant Software's Colorista adds color wheels to control shadows, midtones, and highlights (or lift, gamma, gain); this makes it possible to radically transform the color look of an image and achieve the kind of look a colorist might aim for.

Color Matching

Having examined the color correction tools in depth, it's now time for the bread and butter work of compositing: to match separate foreground and background elements such that the scene appears to have been shot at once.

Although it certainly requires artistry to do well, this is a learnable skill with measurable objective results. The process obeys such strict rules that you can do it without an experienced eye for color. Assuming the background (or whatever source element you're matching) has already been color-graded, you even can satisfactorily complete a shot on a monitor that is nowhere near correctly calibrated, and the result will not even suffer from your own color blindness, if that's an issue.

How is that possible?

As with so much visual effects work, the answer is derived by correctly breaking down the problem. In this case, the job of matching one image to another obeys rules that can be observed channel-by-channel, independent of the final, full-color result.

Of course, effective compositing is not simply a question of making colors match; in many cases that is only the first step. You must also obey rules you will understand from the careful observation of nature described in the previous chapter. And even if your colors are correctly matched, if you haven't interpreted your edges properly (Chapter 3) or pulled a good matte (Chapter 6), or if such essential elements as lighting (Chapter 12), the camera view (Chapter 9), or motion (Chapter 8) are mismatched, the composite will not succeed.

These same basic techniques will work for other situations in which your job is to match footage precisely—for example, color correcting a sequence to match a *hero* shot (the one determined to have the right color juju), a process also sometimes known as *color timing*.

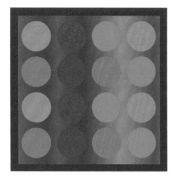

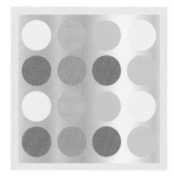

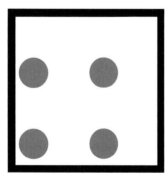

Figure 5.24 There are no yellow dots in the top image, and no blue dots in the middle image; the four dots shown in the bottom image are identical to their counterparts in the other two images.

The Fundamental Technique

Integration of a foreground element into a background scene often follows the same basic steps:

1. First match overall contrast without regard to color, using Levels (and in most cases, working only on the Green channel). When matching the black and white points, pay attention to atmospheric conditions.

2. Next, study individual color channels and use Levels to match the contrast of each channel (as needed—not all images contain so fundamental a color imbalance).

3. Match the color of the midtones (gamma), channel by channel, using Levels or Curves. This is sometimes known as *gray matching* and is easiest when an object in the background scene is known to be colorless gray (or something close).

4. Evaluate the overall result for other factors influencing the integration of image elements—lighting direction, atmospheric conditions, perspective, grain or other ambient movement, and so on (all of which and more are covered in this book).

The overall approach, although not complicated or even particularly sexy, can take you to places your naked eye doesn't readily understand when it is looking at color. Yet, when you see the results, you realize that nature beats logic every time.

The sad truth is that even an experienced artist can be completely fooled by the apparent subjectivity of color. **Figure 5.24** shows an example in which seeing is most definitely *not* believing. Far from some sort of crutch or nerdy detail, channel-by-channel analysis of an image provides fundamental information as to whether a color match is within objective range of what the eye can accept.

Ordinary Lighting

We begin with a simple example: inserting a 3D element lit with ordinary white lights into a daylight scene. As you can see in **Figure 5.25**, the two elements are close enough in color range that a lazy or hurried compositor might be tempted to leave it as is.

Figure 5.25 An unadjusted foreground layer (the plane) over a day-lit background.

With only a few minutes of effort, you can make the plane look as though it truly belongs there. Make sure the Info palette is somewhere that you can see it, and for now, choose Percent (0–100) in that palette's wing menu to have your values line up with the ones discussed here (you can, of course, use whatever you want, but this is what I'll use for discussion in this section).

This particular scene is a good beginner-level example of the technique because it is full of elements that would appear monochromatic under white light; next we'll move on to scenes that aren't so straightforward. The background is dominated by colorless gray concrete, and the foreground element is a silver aircraft.

Begin by looking for suitable black and white points to use as references in the background and foreground. In this case, the shadow areas under the archways in the background and underneath the wing of the foreground plane are just what's needed for black points—they are not the very darkest elements in the scene, but they contain a similar mixture of reflected light and shadow cast onto similar surfaces, and you can expect them to fairly nearly match. For highlights, you happily have the top of the bus shelter to use for a background white point, and the top silver areas of the plane's tail in the foreground are lit brightly enough to contain pure white pixels at this point.

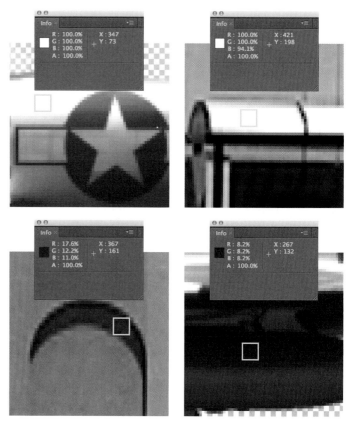

Figure 5.26 The target highlight and shadow areas for the foreground and background are outlined in yellow; levels corresponding to each highlight (in Percent values, as set in the panel menu) are displayed in the adjacent Info palette.

Figure 5.26 shows the targeted shadow and highlight regions and their corresponding readings in the Info palette. The shadow levels in the foreground are lower (darker) than those in the background, while the background shadows have slightly more red in them, giving the background warmth absent from the unadjusted foreground. The top of the plane and bus shelter each contain levels at 100%, or pure white, but the bus shelter has lower blue highlights, giving it a more yellow appearance.

To correct for these mismatches, apply Levels to the foreground and move the Output Black slider up to about 7.5%. This raises the level of the blackest black in the image, lowering the contrast.

Having aligned contrast, it's time to balance color. Because the red levels in the background shadows are higher than blue or green, switch the Composition panel to the red channel (click on the red marker at the bottom of the panel or use the **Alt+1/Option+1** shortcut), causing a thin red line to appear around the viewer. You can now zoom in on an area that shows foreground and background shadows (**Figure 5.27**).

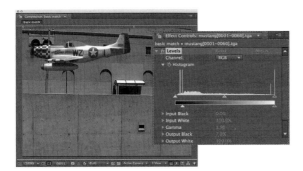
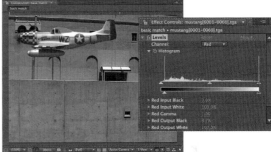

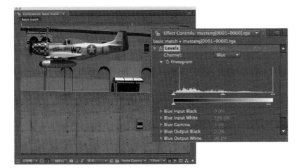

Figure 5.27 Evaluate and match black and white levels on individual channels. In this case the image is "green matched," with the RGB adjustment first made for the green channel, then the red and blue channels are adjusted individually. These subtle adjustments are all that's needed in this case to match the element.

Black levels in the red channel are clearly still too low in the foreground, so raise them to match. Switch the Channel pop-up in Levels to Red, and raise Red Output Black slightly to about 3.5%. You can move your cursor from foreground to background and look at the Info palette to check whether you have it right, but the great thing about this method is that your naked eye usually evaluates variations in luminance correctly without the numerical reference.

Now for the whites. Because the background highlights have slightly less blue in them, switch to the blue channel (clicking the blue marker at the bottom of the Composition panel or using **Alt+3/Option+3**). Pull back slightly to where you can see the top of the bus shelter and the back of the plane. Switching Levels to the blue channel, lower the Blue Output White setting a few percentage points to match the lower blue reading in the background. Back in RGB mode (**Alt+3/Option+3** toggles back from blue to RGB), the highlights on the plane take on a more sunlit, yellow quality. It's subtle, but it seems right.

What about the midtones? In this case, they're taking care of themselves because both the foreground and background are reasonably well balanced and these corrections are mild.

Figure 5.28 displays the result, with the same regions targeted previously, but with the levels corrected. To add an extra bit of realism, I also turned on motion blur, without yet bothering to precisely match it (something you will learn more about in Chapter 8). You see that the plane is now more acceptably integrated into the scene.

Work on this composite isn't done either; besides matching the blur, you can add some sun glints on the plane as it passes, similar to those on the taxi. On the other hand, you can tell that the blur on the plane is too heavy for the pilot's absence from the cockpit to be noticeable, a good example of how an initial pass at a composite can save a lot of extra work.

TIP

The human eye is more sensitive to green than red and blue. Often, when you look at a shot channel by channel, you will see the strongest brightness and contrast in the green channel. For that reason, a sensible approach to matching color may be to get the overall match in the ballpark so that the green channels match perfectly, and then adjust the other two channels to make green work. That way, you run less risk of misadjusting the overall brightness and contrast of your footage.

Figure 5.28 This is a better match, particularly in the shadow areas; motion blur helps sell the color adjustment as well.

Dramatic Lighting

Watch a contemporary feature film objectively for color and you may be shocked at how rare ordinary day-lit scenes such as the plane example are. Dramatic media—not just films but television and theater—use color and light to create mood, to signify key characters and plot points, and more. If you're working with a daring cinematographer, or even heed the advice in the Foreword, you'll be happy to know that this matching technique is even more impressive with strong lighting.

The composite in **Figure 5.29** clearly does not work; the foreground element does not even contain the scene's dominant color, and is white-lit. That's fine; it will better demonstrate the effectiveness of this technique.

It helps that both the foreground and the background elements have some areas that you can logically assume to be flat gray. The bridge has concrete footings for the steel girders along the edges of the road, while the can has areas of bare exposed aluminum.

NOTES

This section discusses colors expressed as percentages; to see the same values in your Levels effect, use the wing menu of the Info palette to choose Percent for the Color Display.

Figure 5.29 Not only is it clear that the can does not belong in the color environment of the background, the mismatch is equally apparent on each color channel. (Image courtesy of Shuets Udono via Creative Commons license.)

The steps to color match a scene like this are as follows:

1. Apply Levels to the foreground layer.

2. Switch the Comp view to Green (**Alt+2**/**Option+2**). Not only is this the dominant color in this particular scene, but it is dominant in human vision, so green-matching is the first step in most scenes, not just this one.

3. Begin as if you are looking at a black-and-white photo-graph, and match the element to this dark contrasty scene using Levels in the RGB channel. If the element needs more contrast in the shadows and highlights, as this one does, raise Input Black and lower Input White; if it needs less, adjust the Output controls instead. Finally, adjust the gamma; in this scene, should it come down to match the darkness of the scene or up so the element stands out more? The end result should look like a monochrome photo whose elements match believably (**Figure 5.30a**).

4. Switch the view (**Alt+1**/**Option+1**) and the Levels control to the Red channel and repeat the grayscale match-ing process. Clearly, the foreground element is far too bright for the scene. Specifically, the darkest silver areas of the can are much brighter than the brightest areas of the concrete in the background. Therefore, adjust the gamma down (to the right) until it feels more like they inhabit the same world. Now have a look at the high-lights and shadows; the highlights look a little hot, so lower Red Output White (**Figure 5.30b**).

5. Now move over to Blue in the view (**Alt+3**/**Option+3**) and in Levels. In this case, there is almost no match whatsoever. The can is much brighter and more washed out than the background. Raise Input Blue and bring gamma way down. Now the can looks believably like it belongs there (**Figure 5.30c**).

It's strange to make all of these changes without ever look-ing at the result in full color. So now, go ahead and do that. Astoundingly, that can is now within range of looking like it belongs in that scene; the remaining adjustments are subjective. If you want the can to pick up a little less green from the surroundings as I did, lower Green Input White. Back in the RGB channel, adjust Gamma according to how

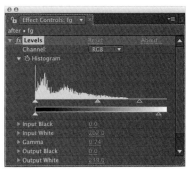

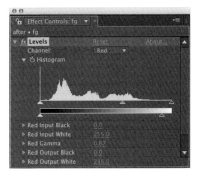

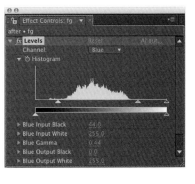

Figures 5.30a, b, and c (top to bottom) It's fun and satisfying to pull off an extreme match like this channel by channel. The Levels settings come from looking for equivalent black/white/midpoints in the image and just analyzing whether the result looks like a convincing black-and-white image on each channel.

much you want this element to pop. And of course finish compositing it: Defocus slightly with a little fast blur, add a shadow, and you start to believe it (**Figure 5.31**).

Figure 5.31 The result includes a subtle shadow that has been color matched as well as a final adjustment to the white contrast.

When There's No Clear Reference

The previous examples have contained fairly clear black, white, and gray values in the foreground and background elements. Life, of course, is not always so simple.

Figure 5.32 is a scene that lacks any obvious gray values to match; the lighting is so strong, it's hard to tell what color anything in the scene was originally, or whether there were any neutral black, white, or gray items.

Figure 5.32 Sometimes a source scene will have completely crazy lighting. Once you are confident about how to match it, you may say to an image that is blown out and overbalanced in one direction, "bring it on." (Image courtesy of Jorge L. Peschiera via Creative Commons license.)

Figure 5.33 This one requires as much intuition as logic, but the channel-by-channel approach completely works.

The technique still works in this case, but it may require more in the way of trial and error, or artist's intuition. Looking at each individual color channel, only green is even close to a plausible match right off the bat; the red channel contains blown-out whites, and the blue channel is so dark (and grainy) it hardly exists.

Once again, just try to get the brightness and contrast adjusted, working channel by channel, and you get an initial result something like **Figure 5.33**. Considering how subjective the adjustments are by necessity in this case, this isn't half bad; and fine adjustments to the RGB channel can bring it where it needs to go.

The ability to match color without seeing an image in full color is so powerful that it can seem almost magical the first few times you try it. Why, then, do so few artists work this way? I would have to say that laziness and ignorance are the main culprits here. Switching channels seems like a pain, and few untrained artists clearly realize that color works like this.

NOTES

It's often a good idea to take a break when trying to finalize fine color adjustment. When you come back, even to a labored shot, you regain an immediate impression that can save you a lot of noodling.

Direction and Position

These examples use simple 8-bit 3D elements rendered on a single pass. The skill of dealing with these is a basic skill of compositing—color matching—but it's not as if, having mastered this skill, you are prepared to match anything anywhere. An ideal element generated in 3D software would of course have multiple passes, giving you more control (Chapter 12); even short of that, if the lighting and perspective of an element are wrong, there's no practical way to make it match (**Figure 5.34**).

Figure 5.34 All of the 2D compositing trickery in the world can't change the fact that this element is angled wrong. It is also lit from the wrong side. (Source clip from "Jake Forgotten," courtesy of John Flowers.)

On the other hand, compositing has consistently freed artists from spending too long hanging around in 3D software trying to solve everything. **Figure 5.35** shows the simplest solution to the previous problem: match the camera angle and basic lighting by observing what's in the scene. From looking at the pool balls and shadows, it seems apparent that there are a couple of overhead lights nearby and that the one off camera right is particularly strong.

Figure 5.35 The angle and lighting have been roughly matched in 3D; rather than tweaking it further there, work on getting a quicker and more accurate result in 2D.

I match the angle by placing the background shot into the background of the 3D software's camera view, and I make sure that there are a couple of lights roughly matched to that of the scene so that they produce the correct shading and specular highlights. From there, I have an element that does not match perfectly, but I'm done with what I need to do in 3D if I want to be done.

More complex and dynamic perspective, interactive lighting, animation, global illumination, and so on certainly make more things that can be done in 3D, yet at the end of the day, the smart computer graphics artist kicks a scene over to 2D as soon as the elements are within range (**Figure 5.36**).

Figure 5.36 The color-matched final includes a shadow.

Gamma Slamming

Maybe you've seen an old movie on television—the example I think of first is *Return of the Jedi* (before the digital re-release)—in which you see black rectangular garbage mattes dancing around the Emperor's head, inside the cloak, that you obviously shouldn't be seeing. *Jedi* was made prior to the digital age, and some of the optical composites worked fine on film, but when they went to video, subtleties in the black levels that weren't previously evident suddenly became glaringly obvious.

Don't let this happen to you! Now that you know how to match levels, put them to the test by *slamming the gamma* of the image. The simplest way to do this is just to adjust the Exposure control at the lower right of the Viewer up or down. You can also make an adjustment layer, set it as a guide layer so that it cannot render, and add a Curves or Levels effect to push gamma up or down (different than exposure—you may prefer it).

Slamming (**Figure 5.37**) exposes areas of the image that might have been too dark to distinguish on your monitor; if the blacks still match with the gamma slammed up, you're in good shape. Similarly, slamming up will give you a clear glimpse of grain matching (and slamming the alpha, even more so). Slamming down can reveal whether highlight levels match; it's particularly useful if you're working in linear HDR with over-range values (Chapter 11).

Figure 5.37 Slamming gamma is like shining a bright light on your scene. In this case it reveals the need for grain and a mismatch in the shadow color.

This is a useful habit anywhere that there is a danger of subtle discrepancies of contrast; you can use it to examine a color key, as you'll learn in the next chapter, or a more extreme change of scene lighting. Every big effects studio I've worked at examines footage this way before it's sent for final.

Conclusion

This chapter has covered some of the basics for adjusting and matching footage. Obviously there are exceptional situations, some of which occur all of the time: depth cueing, changes in lighting during the shot, backlighting, interactive light, and shadow. There are even cases in which you can, to some degree, relight a shot in After Effects, introducing light direction, exchanging day for night, and so on. You'll discover more in Chapter 12.

6

Color Keying

Slow down, I'm in a hurry.

— Franz Mairinger (Austrian Equestrian)

Color Keying

Color keying was devised in the 1950s as a clever means to combine live-action foreground footage and backgrounds that could come from virtually anywhere. What was once a fragile and expensive proposition is now fully mainstream; whole films such as *300*, now rely on this technique, while the Colbert Report invites anyone with a computer to try the "Green Screen Challenge" (and runs entries from none less than John Knoll).

The process goes by many names: color keying, blue screening, green screening, pulling a matte, color differencing, and even chroma keying—a term from analog color television, the medium defined by chroma and heavily populated with weather forecasters.

The purpose of this chapter is to help you not only with color keying of blue- and green-screen footage but with all cases in which pixel values (hue, saturation, and/or brightness) stand in for transparency, allowing compositors to effectively separate the foreground from the background based on color data.

NOTES

For those reading nonlinearly, this chapter extends logically from fundamental concepts about mattes and selections in Chapter 3.

All of these methods extract luminance information that is then applied to the alpha channel of a layer (or layers). The black areas become transparent, the white areas opaque, and the gray areas gradations of semi-opacity; it's the gray areas that matter.

Good Habits and Best Practices

Before we get into detail about specific keying methods and when to use them, I'll share some top-level advice to remember when creating any kind of matte.

Figure 6.1 The background influences what you see. Against black, almost no detail is visible (left). Checkerboard reveals shadows (middle), but flaws in the matte are clearest with a bright, solid, contrasting background (right). (Source footage courtesy of Pixel Corps.)

▶ **Introduce contrast.** Use a bright, saturated, contrasting background (**Ctrl+Shift+B**/**Cmd+Shift+B**) such as yellow, red, orange, or purple (**Figure 6.1**). If the foreground is to be added to a dark scene, a dark shade is okay, but in most cases bright colors better reveal matte problems. Solo the foreground over the background you choose.

▶ **Protect edge detail.** This is the name of the game (and the focus of much of this chapter); the key to winning is to isolate edges as much as possible and focus just on them so as to avoid crunchy, chewy mattes (**Figure 6.2**).

Figure 6.2 A matte like this could be called "chewy," and is typically the result of clamping the foreground or background (or both) too far.

▶ **Keep adjustments simple, and be willing to start over.** Artists spend hours on keys that could be done more effectively in minutes, simply by beginning in the right place. There are many complex and interdependent steps involved with creating a key; if you're hung up on one, it's time to try a different approach.

▶ **Constantly scan frames and zoom into detail.** When possible, start with a tricky area of a difficult frame; look for motion blur, fine detail, excessive color spill, and so on, and keep checking various areas in various modes (**Figure 6.3**).

Figure 6.3 A glimpse of the alpha channel can reveal even more problems, such as faint holes in the foreground, which should be solid white.

▶ **Break it down into multiple passes.** This is the single most important concept novices miss. Most mattes will benefit from separate garbage, core, and edge passes—a process detailed later in this chapter—and in many cases it helps to create a separate pass just for delicate edges: hair, a translucent costume, motion blur, and so on.

I encourage you to review this list again once you've explored the rest of this chapter.

Linear Keyers and Hi-Con Mattes

There are cases in which edge detail is less of a factor because the matte is used to adjust, not layer, an element; for example, you could hold out the highlight areas of an image for adjustment using a *high-contrast* (*hi-con*) matte. You might create this matte with a *linear keyer*.

Linear keyers are relatively simple and define a selection range based on a single channel only. This could be it red, green, or blue, or just overall luminance. They're useful in a wide variety of cases outside the scope of blue- and green-screen shots, although similar principles apply with Keylight. (Keylight is covered later in this chapter.)

The most useful linear keyers are

▶ Extract

▶ Linear Color Key

The keyers to avoid are

▶ Luma Key

▶ Color Key

because each is limited to a bitmap (black and white) selection. Only by choking and blurring the result with Edge Thin and Edge Feather controls can you add threshold adjustment.

The Extract and Linear Color Key

Extract is useful for *luminance (luma) keying*, because it uses the black and white points of an image or any of its individual channels. Linear Color Key is a more appropriate tool to use to isolate a particular color (or color range).

Extract

The Extract key includes a histogram to help you isolate thresholds of black and white; these are then graded with black and white softness settings. You can work with averaged RGB luminance, or you can access histogram controls for each of the color channels.

CLOSE-UP

When, Exactly, Is Linear Keying Useful?

Keying using a single channel (or the average of multiple channels) is useful to matte an element using its own luminance data, in order to hold out specific portions of the element for enhancement. For example, you duplicate a layer and matte its highlights to bloom them (see Chapter 12).

Figure 6.4 When extracting an image using luminance, it's better to examine all three channels and choose the one that is closest to the matte you want than to simply rely on averaged luminance.

All Channels Are Not Created Equal

If you set an RGB image as a luma matte, the red, green, and blue channels are averaged together to determine the luminance of the overall image. However, they are not weighted evenly, because that's not how the eye sees them. Details about how to work with this fact can be found in Chapter 12.

If you find yourself wanting to use a particular channel as a luma matte, use Effect > Channel > Shift Channels; set Take Alpha From as Full On and the other three channels to whichever channel—red, green, or blue—is most effective.

One of the three color channels nearly always has better defined contrast than overall luminance, which is merely an average of the three. Either green or red is typically the brightest and most contrasty channel, while blue generally has higher noise (**Figure 6.4**).

Extract is interactive and easy to use and is a cousin to Levels. Its histogram shows the likely white or black thresholds on each channel. You bring in the White Point or Black Point (the upper of the two small square controls below the histogram) and then threshold (soften) that adjustment with the White Softness or Black Softness controls (the lower of the two small squares).

Linear Color Key

The Linear Color Key offers direct selection of a key color using an eyedropper tool. The default 10% Matching

Softness setting is arbitrary and defines a rather loose range. I often end up with settings closer to 1%.

Note that there are, in fact, three eyedropper tools in the Linear Color Key effect. The top one defines Key Color, and the other two add and subtract Matching Tolerance. I tend not to use these because they don't work in the Comp viewer; the main Key Color eyedropper and the Matching sliders work for me (**Figure 6.5**).

Figure 6.5 Suppose you wish to make a change to the distant, out-of-focus area of this shot. By selecting a prominent object in the foreground, the sweater, and adjusting the selection, you can create a matte that separates the foreground and background. (Image courtesy of Eric Escobar.)

There's a hidden trick to getting better results with Linear Color Key. Because it is linear, it will pick up hues that seem unrelated. To reduce the effect of these, you can add a second instance of Linear Color Key. Under Key

Operation, changing the default Key Colors setting to Keep Colors does nothing if it's the first instance except annul the effect. On the second instance, Keep Colors is unaffected by the first instance and can bring back hues that were already keyed. The one-two punch will often deliver the best result (**Figure 6.6**).

Figure 6.6 By adding a second instance of Linear Color Key set to Keep Colors, I'm able to get rid of the extra selection areas in the background, apply the matte, and add a glow effect that influences only the background.

Difference Mattes

A *difference matte* is simple in principle: Frame two shots identically, the first containing the foreground subject, the other without it (commonly called a *clean plate*). Compare the two images and remove everything that matches identically, leaving only the foreground subject. It sounds like the type of thing a computer was built to do.

In practice, of course, there are all sorts of criteria that preclude this from actually working very well, specifically

▶ Both shots must be locked off or motion stabilized to match, and even then, any offset—even by a fraction of a pixel—can kill a clean key.

▶ The foreground element may be rarely entirely unique from the background; low luminance areas, in particular, tend to be hard for the Difference Matte effect to discern.

▶ Grain, slight changes of lighting, and other real-world variables can cause a mismatch between two otherwise identical shots. Raising the Blur Before Difference setting helps correct for this, but only by introducing inaccuracy.

To try this for yourself, begin with a locked-off shot containing foreground action, ideally one in which a character enters the frame. Duplicate the layer, and lock off an empty frame of the background using Layer > Time > Freeze Frame. Apply Difference Matte to the top layer. Adjust Tolerance and Softness; if the result is noisy, try raising the Blur Before Difference value.

Figure 6.7 shows the likely result of attempting to key this footage using only Difference Matte. It's not a terrible way to isolate something when clean edges are not critical, but it cannot compare with more sophisticated methods for removing a solid color background.

Figure 6.7 I was hoping to grab just the shadows on the floor with a difference matte applied to the image on the left using the middle image as a Difference Layer; unfortunately, subtle stuff like that tends to be indistinguishable from noise, even with clean, low-grain source.

Luma Mattes

The honest truth is that I don't use the above effects very often; there are less immediately obvious but more powerful ways to generate transparency from color data:

▶ Blending modes

▶ Blending modes with color adjustments

▶ Shift channels and levels

In the interest of full disclosure, I often use track mattes (as detailed in Chapter 3) with a duplicate of the layer, instead of luminance keys applied directly to the layer. With a track matte, I can use Levels to work with color ranges on all channels in order to refine transparency. Other artists may consider this approach more cumbersome, preferring to work with a single layer and an effect, so the choice as always is yours.

Blue and Green Screen Keys

Keylight is useful in many keying situations, not just studio-created blue- or green-screen shots. For example, you can use Keylight for removal of a murky blue sky (**Figure 6.8**). You wouldn't use Keylight to pull a luminance key, however, or when you're simply trying to isolate a certain color range within the shot; its effectiveness decreases the further you get from the three primary colors.

Keylight is most typically used on footage shot against a uniform, saturated, primary color background, where preservation of edge detail is of utmost importance.

Figure 6.8 Keylight knocks out the background in one pass, with no adjustments, despite low saturation in the sky.

Figure 6.9 outlines the basic keying process detailed in the following pages. No two complex shots are the same, but something like this approach should help you pull a good matte, regardless of the tools used. The next section reviews these steps, specifically using Keylight.

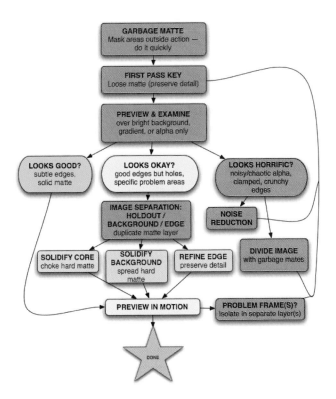

Figure 6.9 This chart summarizes steps that can yield a successful color key.

The basic steps are

1. **Garbage matte** any areas of the background that can easily be masked out. "Easily" means you do not have an articulated matte (you don't animate individual mask points). As a rule of thumb, limit this to what you can accomplish in about 20 minutes or less (**Figure 6.10**).

Figure 6.10 The quick-and-dirty garbage matte isolates the action; you don't waste time on areas of the frame that aren't overlapped by action.

2. Attempt a **first pass** quickly, keeping this matte on the loose side (preserving as much edge detail as possible) to be refined later.

3. **Preview** this at full resolution, in full motion, against a bright primary color. In rare cases, you're done, but before you throw up your arms in victory, carefully examine the alpha channel of the toughest frames (usually the ones with the most motion, reflection, or semi-opaque detail). Note any obvious holes in the foreground or areas of the background that have failed to disappear, as well as any noise in the solid areas of the matte (**Figure 6.11**).

Figure 6.11 The shadows need to be eliminated with a hard matte; they go up the wall and off set. A hard matte negatively influences fine detail such as motion blur and hair, any of which may require its own holdout matte.

If things look noisy and chaotic in the alpha channel or the edges are clamped and chewy, you can

▶ Start over and try a new pass

▶ Apply noise reduction to the plate, then start over (see "Noise Suppression" later in this chapter)

▶ Articulate or track garbage/holdout mattes to isolate problem portions of the footage (see "Beyond Keylights: Better Mattes," later in this chapter)

4. If necessary, **separate the plate for multiple passes**. At the very least, it's often useful to create a solid core and a completely transparent background so that you can focus only on the edge (detailed in the next section). You may also need to separate individual parts of a layer for a separate keying pass, such as hair or a fast-moving, motion blurred limb.

5. **Refine the edge.** Zoom in on a challenging area of the foreground edge (200% to 400%), and refine the key to try to accommodate it, using strategies outlined in the steps that follow. Challenging areas may include

  ▶ Fine detail such as hair

  ▶ Motion blurred foreground elements

  ▶ Cast shadows

You must also watch out for, and consider rotoscoping, foreground features that can threaten an effective key, such as

  ▶ Areas of the foreground that reflect the background color

  ▶ Edge areas whose color nearly matches the background

  ▶ Areas of poor contrast (typically underlit regions of the shot)

6. **Preview the shot in full motion.** Again, note holes and noise that crop up on individual frames, and use the strategies outlined in the section "Beyond Keylights: Better Mattes" to overcome these problems. Approaches you may add at this stage are

  ▶ More holdout mattes (typically masks), either for the purpose of keying elements individually or rotoscoping them out of the shot (**Figure 6.12**)

  ▶ Isolation of the matte edge, for the purpose of refining or blurring it (see "Matte Problems" later in this chapter)

Holdout Mattes

A *holdout matte* isolates an area of an image for separate treatment. I recommend that you think of a color key as an edge matte surrounded by two holdout mattes: one for the core, one for the background.

You can follow along with the steps using the blueScrn_mcu_HD.mov footage included in this chapter's Pixel Corps folder on the book's disc. Completed versions of several of the examples from this chapter are contained in the 06_colorKey.aep project.

Figure 6.12 Holdout mattes seem tedious to create and animate, but for true tedium try spending hours keying a shot in one pass that could have been broken down into a series of 10 minute roto masks.

Figure 6.13 Even with a well-shot, high-definition source (left), it is imperative that you get the Screen Colour setting right to preserve all of the transparent detail in this shot. Choosing a darker background color (center) creates a more solid initial background, but a lighter color selection (right) preserves far more detail. (Source footage courtesy of Pixel Corps.)

Keylight

The first decision in Keylight is most important: sampling a color for the Screen Colour setting (Keylight reveals its UK origins at Framestore CFC with that u). Specific tips to do so are up ahead in the section, "Generate the Screen Matte."

In the best-case scenario, you create any necessary garbage mattes and then follow these steps:

1. Use the Screen Colour eyedropper to sample a typical background pixel. View defaults to Final Result so you get a matte instantly; set the background to a bright color and solo the plate layer, or examine the alpha channel (**Alt+4/Option+4**).

2. If in doubt about the Screen Colour setting, turn the effect off and set another instance, repeating as necessary until you have one that eliminates the maximum unwanted background (**Figure 6.13**); you can then delete the rest.

Now, as needed, look for areas to refine.

3. Switch View to Status. Opaque pixels are displayed as white, transparent pixels are black, and those containing any amount of transparency are gray (**Figure 6.14**). It's an exaggerated view of the alpha channel matte.

CLOSE-UP

The Eyedropper and the Info Panel

With the Info panel active, sample a pixel in After Effects, either using an eyedropper tool or simply by moving your cursor around a viewer. The Info panel then displays the value that belongs to the exact pixel underneath the selection point of the cursor (the lower-left corner of the eyedropper, the upper-left corner of the pointer).

As in Photoshop, the After Effects eyedropper samples only the color state of a pixel; transparency of any given pixel is always evaluated as if 100%.

Figure 6.14 What looks like a good initial Combined Matte (left) turns out to have a lot of semi-transparent pixels where you ideally want full opacity or full transparency in Status view (right).

4. Still in Status view, you have the option to try Screen Balance at settings of 5.0, the default 50.0, and 95.0, although Keylight will preselect it based on your background color selection. This setting controls the weighting between the primary matte color (blue, green, or red) and each of the secondaries.

5. If the background is not solid black, you can boost Screen Gain until the gray mostly disappears in Status view, although the ideal is not to raise this value at all (the next section explains how). Use this setting as sparingly as possible.

6. Optionally, set the Despill Bias using the eyedropper. Sample an area of the foreground that has no spill and should remain looking as is (typically a bright and saturated skin tone area). I very rarely do this (see Notes).

NOTES

Keylight's built-in spill suppression can and will enhance the appearance of graininess, particularly with 4:2:2 or another compressed source. The workaround (detailed ahead) is to apply the keyed layer as a track matte instead.

The rare perfect footage is now completely keyed. If it isn't perfect (**Figure 6.15**), this is a decision point; how can you best divide this matte into multiple passes?

Figure 6.15 Not bad for a single pass, although just between you and me, this matte has some light foreground holes that need closing. A multi-pass approach will improve even a simple matte like this.

The Apple Shake-based implementation of Keylight adds inputs for a garbage matte and a holdout matte. This method of isolating and focusing on the edge inspired me to devise the following workflow to achieve the same result in an After Effects precomp, with as few extra steps as possible.

The Three-Pass Method

This breakdown will work with any software keyer, but it's especially helpful if you're trying to get the most out of Keylight.

1. Rename the Keylight effect by selecting it and pressing the Return key. Rename it Keylight gMatte.

   The first goal is to create a background matte that is 100% transparent and outside of all edge detail by several pixels. To do so, follow these steps:

   a. In Keylight Status or Combined Matte view (depending on your preference), raise Clip Black just enough to remove gray pixels from the background in Status view, then lower the Clip White setting just above the same number (**Figure 6.16**).

Figure 6.16 The garbage matte, or gMatte, has been crushed; Clip Black has been raised just enough to eliminate the noise in the lower-left corner (from 6.14, right), Clip White has been lowered near the same number for a hard matte. This is then spread with a negative Simple Choker setting and the layer blending mode has been set to Stencil Alpha to isolate the exterior of the edge.

   b. Important step: set View to Intermediate Result.

   c. If necessary, choke this matte further to eliminate tracking markers and other small bits of noise. You can lower the Screen Shrink/Grow setting (under Screen Matte in Keylight) or apply a Simple Choker effect and raise the Choke Matte number. Quick and dirty is fine here.

d. Whether or not you've choked the matte, the most essential step is to spread it until it's well outside the foreground edge. You can apply Simple Choker and lower the Choke Matte setting to a negative value, quite possibly in the double digits, even using a second instance if the maximum setting of −100 is reached without completely exceeding the foreground boundary.

e. Garbage matte any items in the background that have not disappeared and hand-animate the matte as needed (refer back to Figure 6.12).

You should see a generous blue (or green) buffer around the foreground edge (**Figure 6.17**).

Figure 6.17 Eliminating non-overlapping areas of the background with a garbage matte is step one.

2. Duplicate the layer and rename it Core. Reset the Simple Choker effects and solo the layer.

This matte fills in all holes inside the matte edge without coming close to overlapping that edge. To create this layer

a. In Keylight Status or Combined Matte view (your preference), lower Clip White until the foreground is completely opaque. Raise Clip Black to a value just below the same number.

b. If necessary, spread this matte to eliminate foreground holes by raising the Screen Shrink/Grow setting (under Screen Matte in Keylight). You can also lower the Choke Matte setting in Simple Choker to a negative value.

c. Whether or not you've spread the matte, choke it until it's well inside the foreground edge. If there was no spread operation, use Screen Shrink/Grow in Keylight; otherwise, use Simple Choker.

d. Add a layer and garbage matte; any remaining holes resulting from extra-stubborn shiny, reflective costumes or props.

e. Soften this layer as needed with a Fast Blur; with all three layers on, toggle the cMatte on and off to make sure it has little or no effect on the edge (**Figure 6.18**).

Figure 6.18 The core matte isn't pretty; it's job is to sit within the edge and fill holes. Here it is blurred to assure that any threshold with the actual edge is not noticeable.

3. Apply a second instance of Keylight on the layer containing the gmatte. If you like, rename this effect Keylight Edge. You have isolated the edge to the maximum extent possible (**Figure 6.19**).

Figure 6.19 The final result allows an Edge matte that has no adjustments to Keylight whatsoever: a maximally subtle edge.

Now just work on that edge layer—starting over with its key, if you want, because it's now a much simpler problem that demands the lightest possible touch. Your goal should be to use three controls only to refine it: Screen Colour,

Clip Black, and Clip White. If possible, do not adjust Screen Gain.

This is not the furthest you can go to break down a color keyed matte; problematic footage will require further steps, described in the following section.

Get the Best Out of Keylight

You're no doubt familiar with the areas where you want to take a good look when you're evaluating the quality of a matte:

▶ Hair detail: Are all of the "wispies" coming through? (**Figure 6.20a**)

▶ Motion blur or, in unusual cases with a defocus, lens blur: Do blurred objects appear chunky or noisy, or do they thin out and partially disappear? (**Figure 6.20b**)

▶ Screen contamination areas: Do holes remain in the foreground? (**Figure 6.20c**)

▶ Shadows: Are they keying as desired (usually all or nothing)? (**Figure 6.20d**)

A

B

C

D

Figures 6.20a through d Fun challenges you may encounter when pulling a color key include wispy hair (a), motion blur (b), contamination of foreground elements by the background color (c), and shadows (d).

TIP

Switch a RAM Preview to Alpha Channel view (**Alt+4/Option+4**); the cache is preserved (a note for those who remember when this was not the case).

There may also be fundamental problems, including

▶ Ill-defined foreground/background separation or semitransparency throughout the foreground or background

▶ *Crunchy*, *chewy*, or *sizzling* edges (other terms include *boiling*, which is more often applied to roto, and *chunky* or *clumpy* fine detail)

▶ Noise

▶ Excessive fringing or choking

▶ Errors in the spill suppression

There are specific tools to deal with these; before getting to those, it's a good idea to make sure you're not fighting the fundamentals.

Generate the Screen Matte

A few decisions are absolutely essential in Keylight and the rest are essentially compensatory. I have seen artists spend literally days on keys that sadly could be improved in under an hour with a different approach.

The core of Keylight is *screen matte* generation, and the most essential step is choosing the exact color to key. From that, Keylight makes weighted comparisons between its saturation and hue and that of each pixel, as detailed in **Table 6.1**. From this, you see that the ideal background is distinct and saturated.

TABLE 6.1 How Keylight Makes Its Key Decisions

Compared to Screen Color, Pixel Is	Keylight Will
Of a different hue	Consider it foreground, making it opaque
Of a similar hue and more saturated	Key it out completely, making it transparent
Of a similar hue, but less saturated	Subtract a mathematically weighted amount of the screen color and make it semitransparent

This section details the other tools that contribute to the screen matte:

► **Screen Gain** emphasizes the saturation of the background pixels

► **Screen Balance** delineates the background hue from the other primary colors.

► **Bias** is for color-correction.

Screen Gain

Before I describe Screen Gain, a disclaimer: The ideal Screen Gain setting is 100, no change to the default. This adjustment is compensation for a poorly lit matte, and while raising it may make the matte channel look better, you are also likely to see increased color grain and lost edge detail with values above the default.

A clear symptom that the background lacks sufficient intensity is that areas of the background are of a consistent hue yet fail to key easily. Similarly, a clear symptom that your foreground is contaminated with reflected color from the background is that it appears semi-opaque. Screen Gain is designed to help in these cases.

Screen Gain boosts (or reduces, although I've never used a setting lower than the default) the saturation of each pixel before comparing it to the screen color. This effectively brings more desaturated background pixels into the keying range.

A major point of holding out the edge using the three-pass method described above is to avoid having to use Screen Gain whatsoever; it can be useful to quickly refine a crude one-pass key.

The controls atop Keylight (from Screen Colour down to Alpha Bias) differ fundamentally from the rest; they work together to generate the actual matte, while the rest adjust the result of that operation.

A Rosco Ultimatte Blue screen contains quite a bit of green—much more than red, unless improperly lit. Ultimatte Green screens, meanwhile, are nearly pure green (**Figure 6.21**).

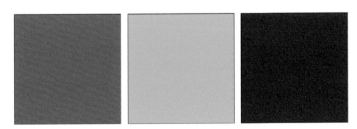

Figure 6.21 The Rosco colors: Ultimatte Blue, Ultimatte Green, and Ultimatte Super Blue. Blue is not pure blue, but double the amount of green, which in turn is double the amount of red. Ultimatte Green is more pure, with only a quarter the amount of red and no blue whatsoever. Lighting can change their hue (as does converting them for print in this book).

Screen Balance

Keylight is designed to expect one of the three RGB color values to be the dominant background color. It is even more effective, however, if it knows whether one of the two remaining colors is more prevalent, and if so, which. Screen Balance compensates for a dominant secondary background color.

On this theory, you would employ a balance of 95% with blue screens and leave it at 50% for green screens, and in version 1.2 of Keylight, that is exactly how the plug-in sets Screen Balance depending on whether you choose a blue or green Screen Colour setting. I hardly touch this control because Keylight added this automatic adjustment in version 1.1.

The generalized recommendation from The Foundry is to set it "near 0, near 100, and compare" these to the default setting of 50 to evaluate which one works best. In other words, imagine there are three settings (instead of 100) and try 5%, 50%, and 95%.

Bias

The Bias settings are Despill Bias and Alpha Bias. These color correct the image in the process of keying by scaling the primary color component up or down (enhancing or reducing its difference from the other two components).

The Foundry recommends that in most cases you leave Alpha Bias at the default and that you click the Despill Bias eyedropper on a well-lit skin tone that you wish to preserve; despill pivots around this value.

Like Screen Gain, Bias has an unpleasant side effect: it can significantly increase the graininess of keyed footage. There are other despill methods available (later in this chapter) that don't add this complication.

Refinement

When you spot an area that looks like a candidate for refinement, save (to hold an undo point should you need to use File > Revert), zoom in, and create a region of interest around the area in question.

Now take a look at the tools provided by Keylight to address some common problems.

Holes and Edges

The double-matte method (core and edge) shortcuts a lot of the tug of war that otherwise exists between a solid foreground and subtle edges. Even with this advantage, both mattes may require adjustments to the **Clip White** or **Clip Black** controls.

Keep the largest possible difference (or *delta*, if you prefer) between these two settings, as this is where all of your gray, semitransparent alpha pixels live. The closer the two numbers get, the closer you are to a bitmap alpha channel, in which each pixel is pure black or white—a very bad thing indeed (**Figure 6.22**).

Figure 6.22 Here's how the hair looks without a separated edge matte. Not nice.

If you push too far, you can try restoring back toward the initial matte with **Clip Rollback**. Its value is the number of pixels from the edge that are rolled back relative to the original, unclipped screen matte. So if your edges were subtle but sizzling on the first pass, but removing noise from the matte hardened them, then this tool may restore subtlety.

**Chroma Subsampling: The 411 on
4:1:1, 4:2:2, and 4:2:0**

Video images are RGB on your computer, but video devices themselves use Y'CrCb, the digital equivalent of YUV. Y' is the luminance or brightness signal (or "luma"); Cr and Cb are color-difference signals (roughly corresponding to red-cyan and blue-yellow)—you could call them chrominance or "chroma."

It turns out that the human eye is much more particular about gradations in luma than chroma, as is amply demonstrated in **Figure 6.23**.

The standard types of digital video compression take advantage of this fact. **Figure 6.24** shows the difference between straight RGB and 4:2:2 compression, which is common to popular formats including DVCPRO HD and DVCPRO50, ProRes 422 and cameras such as the Sony F900, as well as 4:1:1, which is used by DVCPRO and NTSC DV. Almost as bad for keying purposes is 4:2:0, the MPEG-2 (DVD), HDV, and PAL DV format.

As you might imagine, chromatic compression is far less than ideal for color keying (**Figure 6.25**), hence the workarounds in this section.

Noise Suppression

For seriously sizzling mattes, Keylight includes a **Screen Pre-blur** option that I would reserve for footage with a clearly evident noise problem, such as heavy compression. Blurring source footage before keying adds inaccuracy and is something of a desperation move. The footage itself does not appear blurred, but the matte does.

A better alternative for a fundamentally sound matte is **Screen Softness**, under the Screen Matte controls. This control blurs the screen matte itself, so it has a much better chance of retaining detail than a pre-blur approach. As was shown in Chapter 3, edges in nature are slightly soft, and a modest amount of softness is appropriate even with a perfectly healthy matte.

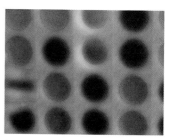

Figure 6.23 The source (top-left image) is then converted to YUV and blurred 100 pixels, first just the UV or chroma (lower-left image) and then just the Y or luma (right). Even very heavy Chroma Blur can be accepted by the eye—it even adds a softness to the highlights—whereas heavy luma blur is completely unacceptable.

Figure 6.24 4:4:4 is just pixels, no chroma subsampling, where 4:2:2 and 4:1:1 groups the nearest neighboring pixels, giving them identical luminance according to the patterns shown here.

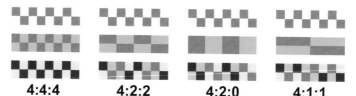

4:4:4   4:2:2   4:2:0   4:1:1

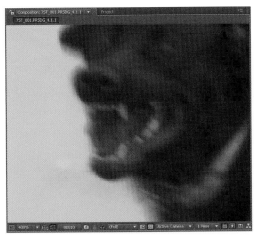 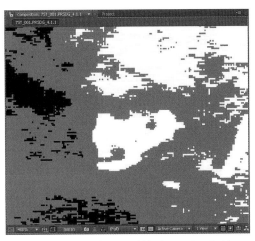

Figure 6.25 Key a 4:1:1 image (left) and Keylight's Status view (right) clearly shows the horizontal blocks associated with that type of chroma subsampling (images are zoomed 4x).

The Despot cleanup tools are meant to fill matte holes, but at sufficiently high levels they add blobbiness, so they are rarely useful. An alternative approach, particularly with DV formats (which, by the way, are guaranteed to add compression noise and are not recommended for blue-screen and green-screen work), is to

1. Convert the footage to YUV using Channel Combiner (the From pop-up menu). This will make the clip look very strange, because your monitor displays images as RGB. Do not be alarmed (**Figure 6.26**).

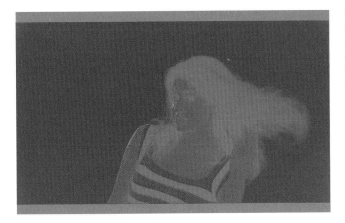

Figure 6.26 This is how an image converted to YUV should look on an RGB monitor—weird. The point is not how YUV looks, but what you can do to adjust it before using Channel Combiner to round-trip it back to RGB.

2. Apply Channel Blur to the green and blue channels only, at modest amounts (to gauge this, examine each channel as you work—press **Alt+2/Option+2** or **Alt+3/Option+3** while zoomed in on a noisy area). Make sure Repeat Edge Pixels is checked.

3. Round-trip back from YUV to RGB, using a second instance of Channel Combiner.

4. Apply Keylight.

Fringing and Choking

Fringing (excess edge opacity) and choking (lost edge detail) are the ultimate tests of an otherwise problem-free matte.

Screen Grow/**Shrink** deals with this issue directly; ideally this control would be used for Garbage and Core passes (described earlier) but not the Edge itself; otherwise it may be a symptom of a more fundamental problem, an indication that it's time to start over.

It's also not the last resort for choking and spreading a matte; alternatives follow in "Beyond Keylights: Better Mattes."

Spill Suppression

Keylight suppresses *color spill* (foreground pixels contaminated by reflected color from the background) as part of the keying operation. Thus spill-kill can be practically automatic if you pull a good initial key.

There are a surprising number of cases in which Keylight's spill suppression is not what you want, for the following reasons:

▶ Dramatic hue shifts occur to items whose colors are anywhere near green (for example, cyan) or opposite green (for example, magenta). It's challenging enough to keep green off of a green set, let alone its neighboring and opposite hues.

▶ These hue shifts can also add graininess, even to footage that was shot uncompressed and has little or no source grain.

Figure 6.27 Her face doesn't even look the same without the highlights reflected with the green. Even worse, at this magnification, it's easy to see that the amount of grain noise has increased significantly. It's a definite case for pulling the matte on one pass and applying spill suppression separately.

In **Figure 6.27**, notice how the whole shape of the girl's face seems to change due to the removal of highlights via spill suppression.

Should Keylight's spill suppression become unwieldy or otherwise useless for the preceding reasons, there is an easy out: ordinarily View is set to Final Result, but set it to Intermediate Result for the matte applied to the Alpha without any change to RGB. The CC Composite effect does the same thing, eliminating all RGB changes from preceding effects but keeping the alpha.

Keylight itself also includes spill suppression tools, under Edge Colour Correction, that influence only the edge pixels. Enable its checkbox and adjust the controls below, softening or growing the edge as needed to increase the area of influence. Sometimes adjusting Luminance or Saturation of edges is a quick fix.

There are better ways than Keylight to kill spill, detailed in the next section, which moves beyond this tool.

Beyond Keylight: Better Mattes

So, to recap, the number one thing you can do to improve a matte is to break it down into component parts:

▶ Garbage, Core, and Edge mattes (isolate the threshold areas)

▶ Holdout masks for problematic areas of the frame (big hair, fast motion, varied lighting, and shadow)

▶ Temporal split (if light conditions change as the shot progresses)

All other tricks fall short if you're not willing to take the trouble to do this. Here are other steps to take to ensure a good matte.

On Set

Your time is often considered cheaper than that of a full crew on set—in many cases, justifiably so. That means—shocking, I know—you'll be fixing things in post that shoulda coulda woulda been handled differently on set. If, on the other hand, you have the opportunity to supervise on set, knowledge is power.

A hard *cyclorama*, or *cyc* (pronounced like "psych") is far preferable to soft materials, especially if the floor is in shot. If you can't rent a stage that has one, the next best thing might be to invest in a roll of floor covering and paint it, to get the smooth transition from floor to wall, as in **Figure 6.28** (assuming the floor is in shot).

Regarding the floor, don't let anyone walk across it in street shoes, which will quickly contaminate it with very visible dust. There are white shoe-cover booties often used specifically to avoid this, and you can also lay down big pieces of cardboard for the crew to use setting up. Be pedantic about this if you're planning to key shadows.

Figure 6.28 On a set with no hard cyclorama, you can create the effect of one—the curve where the wall meets the floor—using a soft blue-screen instead. It doesn't behave as well (note the hotspot on the curve), but it will certainly do in a pinch and is much preferable to removing the seam caused by the corner between the wall and floor.

Lighting is, of course, best left to an experienced Director of Photography (D.P.) or gaffer (one who has shot effects before is hugely helpful), and any kind of recommendations for a physical lighting setup are beyond the scope of this book. Because you'll spend more time examining this footage than anyone else, here are a few things to watch for on set:

▸ Light levels on the foreground and background should have matching intensity. A spot light meter tells you if they do.

▸ Diffuse lights are great for the background (often a set of large 1 K, 2 K, or 5 K lights with a silk sock covering them, **Figure 6.29**), but fluorescent lights will do in a pinch, on a smaller set. With fluorescents you just need more instruments to light the same space. Kino Flo lights are a popular option for smaller sets as well.

Figure 6.29 The larger the set, the more diffuse white lights you'll see in the grid, to eliminate hotspots in the background.

▸ Maintain space between the foreground and background. Ten feet is ideal.

▸ Avoid unintentional shadows, but by all means light for shadows if you can get them and the floor is clean. Note that this works only when the final shot also has a flat floor.

▸ Where possible, avoid having talent sit, kneel, or lie down directly on the floor or any other keyable surface;

CLOSE-UP

The Right Color

The digital age lets shooters play fast and loose with what they consider a keyable background. You will likely be asked (or attempt) to pull mattes from a blue sky, from a blue swimming pool (like I did for *Pirates of the Caribbean*), or from other monochrome backgrounds.

How different must the background color be from the foreground? The answer is "not as much as you probably think." I have had little trouble keying a girl in a light blue dress or a soldier in a dress blue uniform. This is where it can be hugely helpful to have any type of capture device on set—even a point and shoot camera—and pull a test matte.

not only does an astonishing wash of shadow and reflection result, but there is no realistic interaction with the surface, which is especially noticeable if they are to end up on carpet, or grass, or the beach. If possible, use real surfaces and furniture in these cases.

▶ Here's a novel idea: Shoot exteriors outside where possible, forgoing the cyc and controlled lighting environment for chromatic tarps and the sun, which is a hard lighting source to fake.

▶ Record as close to uncompressed as possible. Even prosumer HD cameras these days almost always have an HDMI port that outputs live, uncompressed signal; pair this with a workstation or laptop containing a video capture card and high-speed storage and you can get 4:2:2 or better practically for free.

▶ Shoot clean plate: a few frames of the set only, particularly on a locked-off shot and each time a new set-up occurs.

In this day and age of quick camera to laptop transfer, it's great to have the means on-set to pull test comps; they not only help ensure that the result will key properly, they give the D.P. and talent a better idea of where they are, and where they can lead to more motivated light from the D.P. and more motivated action from the talent, who otherwise must work in a void.

Matte Problems

There are specific tools to help you manipulate transparency once a matte exists.

Minimax is powerful but imprecise, operating as it does in whole pixel increments. It provides a quick way to spread or choke pixel data, even without alpha channel information (it can also operate on individual channels of luminance).

Simple Choker allows you to choke or spread alpha channel data (via a positive or negative number, respectively) at the sub-pixel level (in other words, use decimal values). That's all it does. You can push it hard and even use more than one instance if the 100 pixel limit gets in your way, as it can with garbage mattes.

Shoot a lot of reference of the set, anything and everything you can think of. If you plan to recreate the lighting, it's also a great idea to take HDR images using bracketed exposures—the same image shot at various f-stops. Photoshop includes the File > Automate > Merge to HDR function to combine these into a 32 bpc linear light image.

Matte Choker looks and even sounds more deluxe than Simple Choker (something about that that "Simple" label) but it merely adds softness controls that can just complicate a bad key. I use Simple Choker most of the time, and I don't feel like a simpleton for doing so.

Edge Selection

Earlier in this chapter the three-pass method for deriving a matte was introduced; using this method is one way to derive an edge matte. However, the simplest means to this end is probably as follows:

1. **Apply Shift Channels**. Set Take Alpha From to Full On and all three color channels to Alpha.

2. **Apply Find Edges** (often mistaken for a useless psychedelic effect because, as with Photoshop, it appears in the Stylize menu). Check the Invert box for an edge highlighted in white.

   Minimax is useful to help choke or spread this edge matte. The default setting under Operation in this effect is Maximum, which spreads the white edge pixels by the amount specified in the Radius setting. Minimum chokes the edge in the same manner. If the result appears a little crude, an additional Fast Blur will soften it (**Figure 6.30**).

TIP

A useful third-party alternative to Minimax is Erodilation from ObviousFX (www.obviousfx.com). It can help do heavier choking (eroding) and hole-filling (dilating), and its controls are simple and intuitive (choose Erode or Dilate from the Operation menu and the channel—typically Alpha).

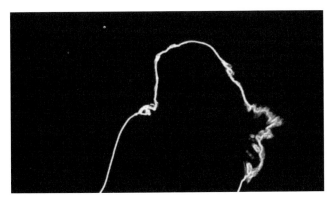

Figure 6.30 An edge matte can be used to blur background and foreground together, or to match the intensity and saturation to the background. The matte can itself be softened with a blur, and Minimax, set to Maximum and Color, can be used to grow the matte by increasing the Radius setting.

3. **Apply the result via a luma matte to an adjustment layer.** You should not need to precomp before doing so.

You can then use Fast Blur to soften the blend area between the foreground and background, which often works better than simply softening a chewy matte. A Levels adjustment will darken or brighten the composited edge to better blend it. Hue/Saturation can be used to desaturate the edge, similar to using a gray edge replacement color in Keylight.

Close Holes

When holes open up in your foreground or background, the best fix is usually to take care of these in the individual Garbage and Core passes; in fact, hole-closing is the main point of the three-pass method described earlier. The basic method is as follows:

1. Choke (Garbage matte) or Spread (Core matte) the holes until they disappear.

2. Spread or Choke (the opposite of the previous step) an equivalent or greater amount.

This will of course destroy all edge subtlety, which is why it only works well on a matte intended to be crude and inside or outside the delicate foreground edges.

Alpha Cleaner, part of the Key Correct set from Red Giant Software, has an automated tool to do this without destroying edges, but it can have unintended consequences, filling small gaps that should remain transparent (**Figure 6.31**).

Figure 6.31 Mind the gaps; choking and spreading a matte, or using tools to do so automatically, such as the third-party Key Correct tools, is liable to close small holes like this; they may require their own special hold-out mattes.

Therefore, there are occasions where you have to roto-scope, usually because the holes are too close to the edge. It can help to create an animated mask (Chapter 7) or track in a paint stroke (Chapter 8).

Color Spill

If Keylight (or another tool) is not doing spill suppression as you would like, the following alternatives are available:

Effect > Keying > Spill Suppressor uses a simple channel multiplication formula to pull the background color out of the foreground pixels. All you need to do is select a sample from the background color (you can sample the Keylight Screen Colour selection) and leave the setting at 100%.

Effect > Color Correction > Hue/Saturation is the option I use most nowadays. It takes practice, which can easily be done; try the following on a source blue or green screen image (no key—just so you can see everything):

1. Apply Effect > Color > Hue/Saturation.

2. Under Channel Control, choose your primary (Greens or Blues—plural for some reason).

3. Lower the Saturation value for that channel to zero.

4. Use the Channel Range sliders to eliminate the key color.

5. Boost Saturation to 100% to see if other colors are being desaturated that should be kept; adjust accordingly.

6. Now with the key applied, try some mixture of the following to eliminate spill:

   ▶ Lower Saturation (still on the individual color channel).

   ▶ Shift Hue between about 30 and 90 degrees to either direction (depending on your target background).

Some combination of desaturation and hue shift with a carefully targeted range usually does the trick; the worst that will happen is that other color artifacts will appear, in which case the trick is usually to go back and adjust the range again.

The Channel Range is the most important part of this, which is why I suggest cranking Saturation all the way down and all the way up to see it clearly. The inside rectangular sliders are the range, the outside, triangular sliders are the threshold area; I tend to be generous with the latter (**Figure 6.32**).

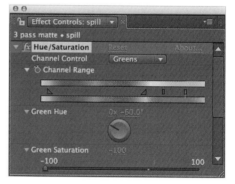

Figure 6.32 Isolate the Greens channel in Hue/Saturation to avoid killing neighboring colors along with green spill suppression. Expand the core and threshold hash marks to a wider range, and then both hue-shift and desaturate the result. Desaturation affects the core colors, and the hue shifts those in the threshold, which are thrown more to the range that would otherwise be missing.

There may be cases where it is difficult or impossible to avoid affecting some part of a costume or set with spill suppression; for example, a cyan colored shirt will change color when the actor is corrected for green. The above method should let you work around this better than most of the automated tools, especially Keylight itself, but there are cases where you might have to use loose roto to isolate the costume and bring its color back.

To correct only the edges, see the section above about how to isolate the edge and use it as a track matte.

Conclusion

Primatte Keyer (included as a demo in the book's disc) is a viable alternative to Keylight, especially because it uses an entirely different internal model to create a key. Whereas Keylight must, by design, be used only for blue, green or red, Primatte is a geometric keyer that treats R, G and B (or H, S and B) internally as a three-dimensional array of color—a box of hues. As you add and subtract from the key selection, a geometric blob grows and shrinks inside that box. You can't see this "blob" but the colors fully within it are keyed, and it has an outer threshold region as well. It takes some practice to master, but once you do, you should find more success getting a good key on one pass (forgoing the three-pass method discussed earlier) with Primatte than with Keylight.

The next chapter offers hands-on advice for situations where procedural matte generation must be abandoned in favor of hand matte generation, also known as rotoscoping.

7

Rotoscoping and Paint

It's a small world, but I wouldn't want to paint it.

—Steven Wright

Rotoscoping and Paint

Rotoscoping is something many artists strive to avoid, yet denial can be costly; although usually quicker and easier, procedural solutions can bog down. Adding roto into the mix solves the problem straightforwardly. *Rotoscoping* (or roto) is simply the process of adjusting a shot frame by frame, generally using masks. Cloning and filling using paint tools are variations on this task.

After Effects is not famed as a rotoscoping tool, but the truth is that there is a lot of ignorance as to how to use it most effectively for this purpose. Not only can the masking and previewing tools be made less cumbersome if applied correctly, but you can often combine paint and roto with tracking and keying.

Here are some overall guidelines for roto and paint:

▶ Keep it simple. In particular, pay attention to strategies using the fewest possible number of keyframes.

▶ Consider your options in the following order of difficulty and automation: keying, tracking, animated masks, paint. Paint is almost always slower and more painstaking than animating masks and should be reserved for times when it's truly the most expedient method.

▶ Review constantly at full speed (taking care to use the setup described next).

▶ Combine strategies. A color key or hi-con matte may take your matte 80 to 90% of the way there, so that roto merely completes the job. Stabilizing an element prior to rotoscoping it can save a lot of extra work. The tracker can be combined with individual adjustments rather than relying only on one or the other.

It can be satisfying to knock out a seamless rotoscope, especially when you avoid fighting the tools.

NOTES

"Rotoscoping" was invented by Max Fleischer, the animator responsible for bringing Betty Boop and Popeye to life, and patented in 1917. It involved tracing over live-action movement, a painstaking form of motion capture. The term has come to stand for any frame-by-frame manipulation of a moving image.

Articulated Mattes

An "articulated" matte is one in which individual mask points are adjusted to detail a shape in motion.

Each adjustment that you make to an animated mask requires the entire frame to redraw, whether in the Comp or Layer viewer. Good rotoscoping requires eliminating this delay, as details are clear only when seen in motion. Doing so is simple:

NOTES

"Keyframing" began at Disney, in the 1930s, where top animators would create the key frames—the top of the heap, the moment of impact—and lower-level artists would add the in-between frames thereafter.

1. Create a comp containing only the source plate.

2. Add a solid layer above the plate.

3. Turn off the solid layer's visibility.

4. Lock the plate layer.

5. Select the solid layer and draw the first mask shape, then press **Option+Shift+M/Alt+Shift+M** to keyframe it.

Now any changes you make to the masked solid have no effect on the plate layer or the cache; you can RAM Preview the entire section and it is preserved, as is each frame as you navigate to it and keyframe it. When it comes time to apply the masks, you can either apply the solid as a track matte or copy the masks and keyframes to the plate layer itself. Genius!

NOTES

There's one major downside to masking on a layer with its visibility off: You cannot drag-select a set of points (although you can Shift-select each of them).

Specific strategies make effective rotoscoping of complex organic shapes possible, regardless of tools:

▶ Use multiple overlapping masks instead of a single mask on a complex, moving shape (**Figure 7.1**).

Figure 7.1 It is crazy to mask a complex articulate figure with a single mask shape; the sheer number of points will have you playing whack-a-mole. Separated segments let you focus on one area of high motion while leaving another area that moves more steadily more or less alone.

One key to working quickly is to intentionally create overlapping, separate mask shapes for different parts of your masked area that you know will move independently, or be revealed and concealed (in this case, because of a simple perspective shift). A shape with 20 or more points will be difficult to manage over time.

► When working with multiple masks, you can lock, hide, or show unselected masks to get them out of the way (and bring them back): context-click > Mask > Lock Other Masks/Hide Locked Masks/Show All Masks.

► Define a shape beginning on a frame where it can be drawn with the fewest possible points, adding more points as needed as you go. As a rule of thumb, no articulated mask should contain more than a dozen or so points.

► Go through the clip and look for the natural keyframe points, where a change of direction, speed, or shape begins or ends, and block in keyframes before you animate them.

► To replace a Mask shape, in Layer view, select the shape from the Target menu and start drawing a new one; whatever you draw replaces the previous shape. Beware: The first vertex point of the two shapes may not match, creating strange in-between frames. To set the first vertex point, context-click on any mask vertex.

► Use a mouse—a pen and tablet system makes exact placement of points difficult.

► Use the arrow keys to move points. The increments change according to the zoom level of the current view.

► Select a set of points and use the Tranform Box to offset, scale, or rotate them together instead of moving them individually (**Figure 7.2**). Most objects shift perspective more than they fundamentally change shape, and this method uses that fact to your advantage.

Block in and refine the first shape, then refine as necessary. Check the result at full speed against a contrasting background, just as you do with color keys. Then move on to the next shape.

NOTES

Always make certain that Preferences > General > Preserve Constant Vertex Count when Editing Masks is toggled on, as it is by default.

TIP

Enable Cycle Mask Colors in Preferences > User Interface Colors to generate a unique mask color with each new mask. You can customize the color if necessary to make it visible by clicking its swatch in the Timeline.

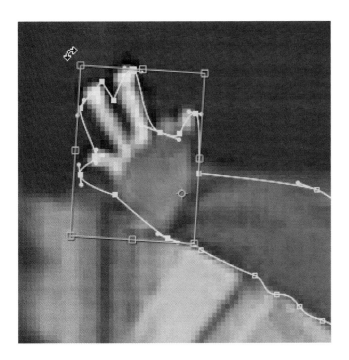

Figure 7.2 Select and double-click a set of mask vertices and manipulate them together using a transform box, offsetting its center point as needed.

Rotobeziers

Rotobezier shapes are designed to animate a mask over time; they're like Bézier shapes (discussed in Chapter 3) without the handles, which means less adjustment and less chance of pinching or loopholes when points get close together (**Figure 7.3**). Rotobeziers aren't universally beloved, partly because it's difficult to get them right in one pass; adjoining vertices change shape as you add points.

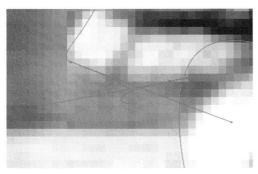 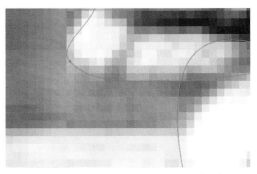

Figure 7.3 Overlapping Bézier handles result in kinks and loopholes (left); switching the mask to Rotobezier (right) eliminates the problem.

TIP

You can freely toggle a shape from Bézier to Rotobezier mode and back, should you prefer to draw with one and animate with the other.

Activate the Pen tool (**G** key) and check the Rotobezier box in the Tools menu, then click the layer to start drawing points; beginning with the third point, the segments are, by default, curved at each vertex.

The literal "key" to success with Rotobeziers is the **Alt/Option** key. At any point as you draw the mask, or once you've completed and closed it by clicking on the first point, hold **Alt/Option** to toggle the Convert Vertex tool ⌐. Dragging it to the left increases tension, and makes the vertex a sharp corner, like collapsed Bézier handles. Drag in the opposite direction, and the curve rounds out. You can freely add ⌖₊ or subtract ⌖₋ points as needed by toggling the Pen tool (**G** key).

TIP

If the Selection tool (V) is active, **Ctrl+Alt/Cmd+Option** activates the Adjust Tension pointer.

The real advantage of the Rotobezier is that it's impossible to kink up a mask as with long overlapping Bézier handles; other than that, Rotobeziers are essentially what could be called "automatic" Béziers (**Figure 7.4**). By drawing enough Bézier points to keep the handles short, however, you may find that you don't need them.

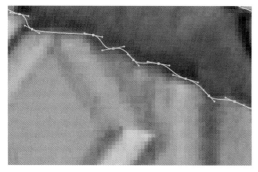 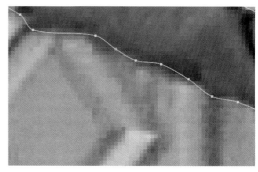

Figure 7.4 You can carefully avoid crossing handles with Béziers (left); convert this same shape to Rotobeziers (right) and you lose any angles, direction, or length set with Bézier handles.

Beyond Built-in Limitations

As mentioned earlier, masks in After Effects haven't evolved as a feature in quite some time. Here are some common limitations, followed by tips to work around them.

▸ After Effects has no built-in method for applying a tracker to a mask. There is, however, a way to do this thanks to at least one third-party script (credited in the front of the book): TrackerViz, detailed in the following chapter, lets you convert trackers to mask vertices.

▸ You can't translate multiple mask keyframes at once; even if you select multiple keyframes, the move is applied only at the current frame.

▸ After Effects lacks the ability to specify whether a feather is applied to the inside or outside of a mask, nor can you vary feather settings on a per-vertex basis (**Figure 7.5**). If you really need this ability, check out PV Feather from RE:Vision Effects.

TIP

Preferences > General includes a preference, on by default, to preserve a constant vertex count when editing masks. Practically the only reason to disable this is if you're creating keyframes on every frame, with no in-betweens.

Figure 7.5 After Effects mask feather controls the entire mask; the PV Feather plug-in allows you to use two masks to control the inside and outside feather.

▸ Adding points to an animated mask has no adverse effect on adjacent mask keyframes. Delete a point, however, and it is removed from all keyframes, usually deforming them.

▸ There is no dedicated morphing tool in After Effects. The tools to do a morph, however, do exist, along with solid deformation tools generally.

The following sections elaborate upon the above points in depth.

Tracking and Translating

There seems to be no way to motion track a mask (other than the aforementioned TrackerViz) nor to move a set of Mask Path keyframes together. Here are some workarounds that help when a mask needs to move:

▶ If movement of a masked object is from camera motion and occurs in the entire scene, you can essentially stabilize the layer, animate the mask in place, and then reapply motion to both. Chapter 8 goes into more detail about this.

▶ To translate an entire animated mask, you can make the masked layer a track matte applied to the same layer (without masks); you can then track or translate the entire track matte.

Mask shapes can be linked together directly with expressions. **Alt/Option**-click the Mask Path stopwatch, then use the pickwhip to drag to the target Mask Path. Only a direct link is possible, no mathematical or logical operations, so all linked masks behave like instances of the first.

Mask Motion Blur

To mask motion blur would seem to be something of a nightmare, as its edges defy careful observation. It's not easy by any means, but masks respect the motion blur settings of the composition; a masked element in motion can be set with motion blurred edges that obey the same composition settings as any other animated element.

That means you have a chance of matching the motion blur using a mask whose contours would fit the shape of the object in its stationary state (**Figure 7.6**). To make the mask work with the moving element is a matter of getting the composition's Shutter Angle and Shutter Phase settings to match. (For details, see Chapter 2.)

Morph

Let's talk about morphing—that's right, that craze of the early '90s, the breakout success on Michael Jackson's *Black or White* video by PDI.

Thing is, morphing can come in handy, without being so blatant and obvious, if you consider it a concealing tool. It's useful when you don't want anyone to notice a transition between two objects or even a transition between one object and itself at a different point in time. Or heck, go crazy morphing together members of your extended family to see if you look anything like the result.

What exactly is a morph? It is, quite simply, a combination of two warps and a dissolve. Given two images, each with a corresponding shape (say, the features of the face), you warp the source image's face shape to the face shape of the target, warp the target from something that matches the source to its face shape, fading the target in over the source.

After Effects has no tool called "Morph," and for a long time, the program offered no good way to pull off this effect. However Reshape is a warping tool that lays the groundwork for simple morphs. You can build these up into more complex morphs, with separate individual transitions occurring to create an overall transition.

Figure 7.7 Me and my evil twin, and that awkward adolescent phase in between.

Reshape

Unfortunately, creating a morph with Reshape is nowhere near a one-button process. This book generally steers away from step-by-step recipes in favor of helping you solve larger problems creatively, but in this case, it's easy to get confused. So here is a step-by-step, using a demonstration of my own resemblance transitioning to that of my evil twin (**Figure 7.7**):

1. Start with two elements that have some basic similarities in their relative position of features. The subtler the distortion required, the more you can get away with.

2. Isolate the two elements you will be morphing from their backgrounds to prevent contamination. If you're working with elements shot against a blue screen, key them out first. Otherwise, mask them. In my example, I created masks for each layer.

3. Ascertain that the two layers are the same size in the X and Y dimensions and as closely aligned as possible. If they are not, precompose one layer to match the other. *This step is important because it will make matching the source and target masks much, much simpler.* Name the two layers **Source** and **Target** (as they are in the example) if it helps you follow along.

4. Choose matching sections from your two clips for the duration of your transition (say, 24 frames). If you have still elements, no worries. The closer your moving elements are to still, the more likely you'll get a clean result.

5. Draw a mask around the boundary that is going to morph in both layers. Be as precise as possible, erring to the inside if at all (**Figure 7.8**). This could be the masks created in step 2, if you created masks there. It need not be active; if you don't need it to mask out the background, set it to None. Rename each mask something descriptive like **outer** (the name used in my example).

Figure 7.8 The outline of each head is carefully masked. These two masks need not correspond to one another; they are defining the boundary for the Reshape effect and can have differing numbers and orders of points. This mask prevents Reshape from pulling bits of background into the morph region.

6. Create a mask around the area of the Source layer that is the focus of the morph. In my example, the focus is facial features: the eyes, nose, and mouth (**Figure 7.9**). Make this mask as simple as you can; use Rotobeziers and as few points as will work to outline the features in question.

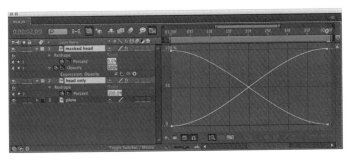

Figure 7.9 Here's the full setup along with the top layer enabled at 100% and color corrected. It begins the final animation at 0% Opacity, reaching 100% at the end of the transition.

7. Set the mask mode to None; this mask is your first shape, you don't need it to influence the layer at all; you will use it for the Reshape effect only. Give it a name (mine is called **me**).

8. Copy this mask shape and paste it in the Target layer. If the two layers are the same dimensions, it should be an identical size and position as it was in the Source layer.

9. Duplicate the mask. Give it a different color and re-name it. In my case, I called the mask **it**.

10. First scale and rotate, then if necessary move individual points (as little as possible!) so that the it mask surrounds the equivalent area of the Target layer that

NOTES

As of version 7.0, mask names are copied along with masks; the copied mask in step 8 remains named me in the new layer.

me does of the source: in my example, the eyes, nose, and mouth.

11. Copy the resulting it mask shape, and paste it to the Source layer to create a new, third mask.

12. You now have three masks for each of the Source and Target layers. Now apply the Reshape effect to each layer.

13. Starting with the Source layer, set the Source Mask (me), the Destination Mask (it), and the Boundary Mask (outer). Set Elasticity to Liquid (you can experiment with other settings later if need be). Set Interpolation to Smooth.

14. At the first frame of the morph transition, still in Source, set a keyframe for Percent (at the default, 0.0%, meaning no reshaping is occurring). At the last frame, set Percent to, you guessed it, 100.0%. Now sit back and wait for the gruesome transformation. Don't worry about how it looks yet.

15. Repeat steps 12 and 13 for the Target layer, with the following changes: Set Source Mask to it and Destination Mask to me. The Percent keyframes should be set to 0.0 at the *last* frame of the transition (where it is keyframed to 100.0 on the Source layer) and, you guessed it, 100.0 at the first frame.

16. You've created the warps, now you just need the cross dissolve. Set an Opacity keyframe for Target at the last frame of the transition (leaving it at the default 100.0%), and then add a 0.0% Opacity keyframe at the first frame.

You should now be ready to preview. The preview may take a long time to build the first frame; subsequent frames render much more quickly, so be patient. The main question to resolve is whether the features line up properly; if not, you must adjust the source and destination mask shapes accordingly, watching the median frame to see whether the changes are improving matters.

TIP

The Correspondence Points in Reshape can be raised from the default of 1 to make the distortion more precise (and in some cases, less twisted). The downside is that this slow effect thus becomes even slower. Better to simplify what you're attempting to do with your masks and fix things there; raise this value only as a last resort.

TIP

If at any point during setup it becomes difficult to interact with the UI because After Effects is taking so long updating a frame, enable **Caps Lock** on your keyboard to prevent any further frame rendering until you're done.

At this point my example may be looking good in terms of the face transition, but, of course, I've made life hard on myself by transitioning from a head of one size to a larger one, and the edges just kind of fade in. Therefore—and this is where it can get really complicated—I add a second morph, using the same steps as before, but with all new masks.

Why complicated? Why new masks? These two questions are interrelated. If you set a second Reshape effect, the key is to avoid influencing the result of the first Reshape effect at all. Therefore, on the second instance the Boundary mask should be the boundary of the object *minus the area occupied by the original source and destination masks.* My second set of shapes covers the ears and top of the head but avoids the area of the previous masks completely (**Figure 7.10**).

Because I know this is complicated, I've included the source and the final result as projects on the book's DVD-ROM. Please do not use the result as the centerpiece of your horror feature.

Figure 7.10 The full setup to do more than one morph on a single image quickly becomes pretty gnarly. Here are two non-overlapping holdout areas containing two sets of transition curves. This setup also takes exponentially longer to render.

223

Now, a quick look at a detail I left out (by having you duplicate the Source and Destination masks in step 9, for example, rather than draw them from scratch).

First Vertex and Target Mask

The Reshape tool heavily relies on the First Vertex to determine which point on the source mask corresponds to which on the destination mask. In this morph example, it is easiest to duplicate the source mask to create the destination mask to automatically satisfy the two criteria most essential for a smooth Reshape effect:

▶ Placement of the First Vertex corresponds on both masks

▶ Each mask has the same number of points

If either is not fulfilled, Reshape will execute some not-so-nice compensatory measures, probably deforming the in-between frames in undesirable ways. The easiest solution is usually to duplicate the source mask and edit it, keeping the same number of points. The next easiest method would be to draw a new mask with the same number of points, in the same direction (clockwise or counterclockwise), and to set the First Vertex where you need it (by context-clicking on the mask and choosing Select First Vertex from the menu).

To draw a new mask, go to the Layer viewer and choose Masks from the View menu. If the layer has a mask, a Target menu appears along the bottom of the viewer (**Figure 7.11**). Choose the mask you want to replace from this menu and draw or paste a new one. If the Mask Path has keyframes, it will deform from the previous mask shape to the new one, and if the First Vertex and vertex direction match, the transition will be clean.

Figure 7.11 In the Layer panel, the View menu (highlighted in yellow) lets you choose any applied masks, effects or paint strokes; if you want to disable the effect of the selected item, uncheck Render (in green). If you select a Target mask (in orange) you can then simply start drawing or paste, and the existing mask is replaced at that frame.

Puppet

Reshape is old-school compared with the Puppet tools. To get started with Puppet, select a layer (preferably a foreground element with a shape defined by transparency, such as an alpha channel or mask), and add the Puppet Pin tool ✖ (**Ctrl+P**/**Cmd+P**) by clicking points on areas you want to animate. Click two points, drag the third, and behold: The layer is now pliable in a very organic, intuitive way.

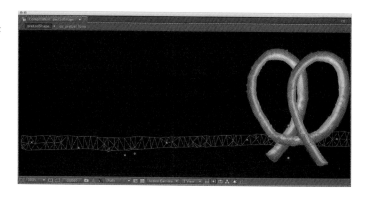

Figure 7.12 The outline of the pretzel source can be seen in wireframe view; this is the Puppet mesh. The pins, in yellow, are effectively the joints.

Perhaps just because I could, I created a pretzel (**Figure 7.12**). Puppet can be used for much subtler stuff, but this example clearly demonstrates something previously impossible in After Effects.

Here are the basic steps to create a deformation animation:

1. Use the Puppet Pin tool to add three pins to a foreground layer. Experimentation will tell you a lot about where to place these, but they're very similar to the places on a marionette where the wires connect: the center, joints, and ends.

2. Move one of them, and observe what happens to the overall image.

3. Add points as needed to further articulate the deformation.

4. To animate by positioning and timing keyframes: Expose the numbered Puppet Pin properties in the Timeline (**UU**); these have X and Y Position values matching many other properties in After Effects.

5. To animate in real time: Hold **Ctrl/Cmd** as you move your cursor over a pin, and a stopwatch icon appears; click and drag that pin, and a real-time animation of your cursor movement records from the current time until you release the mouse. You can specify an alternate speed for playback by clicking Record Options in the toolbar.

TIP

To animate an image from its initial position once you've already deformed it, create keyframes for the pins that have moved, go to the frame that should have the initial position, and click Reset for those pin properties. Only keyframes at the current time are reset.

Try these steps with virtually any matted image and see what happens; you'll quickly get the feel for how Puppet is used. To refine the result, you have some options.

In the toolbar is a toggle to show the mesh. The mesh not only gives you an idea how Puppet actually works, it can be essential to allow you to properly adjust the result. I like to leave it on.

The Expansion and Triangles properties use defaults that are often just fine for a given shape. Raising Expansion can help clean up edge pixels left behind in the source. Raising Triangles makes the deformation more accurate, albeit slower. The default number of triangles varies according to the size and complexity of the source.

More Tools

The Puppet Pin tool does the heavy lifting, but **Ctrl/ Cmd+P** cycles through two other Puppet tools that help in special cases.

The pretzel example requires specific control over which parts of the deformation overlap as two regions cross; this is handled by the Puppet Overlap tool. The mesh must be displayed to use Puppet Overlap, and you apply the Overlap point on the original, undeformed mesh shape, not the deformation (**Figure 7.13**).

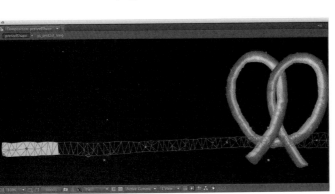

Figure 7.13 The blue starch pin is placed where the tail of the pretzel had mistakenly been below all over-lapping segments, and then its Extent is raised near 500 (to highlight and bring forward more polygons) and its In Front setting raised to 100%.

> **TIP**
>
> Pins disappeared? To display them, three conditions must be satisfied: the layer is selected, the Puppet effect is active, and the Puppet Pin tool is currently selected.

Overlap is not a tool you animate (except perhaps its numerical settings, which are found in the Timeline). Instead, you place it at the center of the area that should overlap others and then adjust the settings as to how much "In Front" it's meant to be and its Extent (how far from the pin this overlap area reaches). You can leave the In Front setting at the default until you start mixing more than one overlap; the higher the value, the closer to the viewer (and negative values will be further away than those with no setting, which default to 0).

The Starch 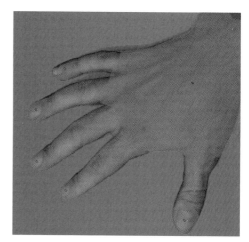 tool prevents an area from deforming. It's not meant to anchor a region of the image but instead to sit between animated pins, preventing the highlighted area (expanded or contracted with the tool's Extent setting) from being squished or stretched (**Figure 7.14**).

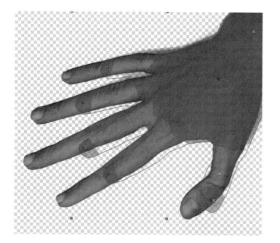

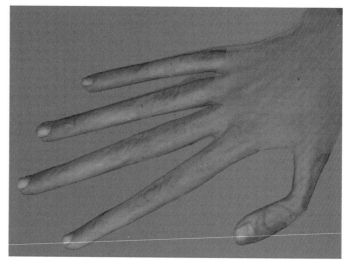

Figure 7.14 Without starch pins applied to the hand and fingertips, such a grotesque extension of the fingers would distort the fingernails and back of the hand along with the fingers. Starch gives you control over what should not be stretched or distorted.

Paint and Cloning

Paint is generally a last resort when roto is impractical, and for a simple reason: Paint work is typically painstaking and more likely to show flaws than approaches involving masks. Of course, there are exceptions. The ability to track clone brushes offers a huge advantage over masks, which are not so easy to track, and painting in the alpha channel is akin to masking with paint.

For effects work, paint controls in After Effects have at least a couple of predominant uses:

▶ Clean up an alpha channel mask by painting directly to it in black and white

▶ Clone Stamp to overwrite part of the frame with alternate source

Once you fully understand the strengths and limitations of paint, you can come up with your own uses.

Paint Fundamentals

Two panels, Paint and Brush Tips, are essential to the three brush-based tools in the Tools palette: Brush ✐, Clone Stamp ♨, or Eraser ◢. These can be revealed by choosing the Paint Workspace.

The After Effects paint functionality is patterned after Photoshop, but with a couple of fundamental differences. After Effects offers fewer customizable options for its brushes (you can't, for example, design your own brush tips). More significantly, Photoshop's brushes are raster based, while After Effects brushes are vector based, allowing them to be edited and animated at any stage.

Suppose that you have an alpha channel in need of a touch-up; for example, the matte shown in **Figure 7.15** is a difficult key without matte cleanup due to tracking markers and shadows. With the Brush tool active, go to the Paint palette and set Channels to Alpha (this palette remembers the last mode you used); the foreground and background color swatches in the palette become grayscale, and you can make them black and white by clicking the tiny black-over-white squares just below the swatches.

Figure 7.15 Touch up an alpha channel matte (for example, remove a tracking marker): In the Paint palette, select Alpha in the Channels menu, then display the alpha channel (**Alt/ Option+4**).

To see what you are painting, switch the view to the Alpha Channel (**Alt+4/Option+4**); switch back to RGB to check the final result.

When using the paint tools

▶ Brush-based tools operate only in the Layer panel.

▶ Brushes include a Mode setting (analogous to Transfer Modes).

▶ With a tablet, you can use the Brush Dynamics settings at the bottom of the Brush Tips palette to set how the pressure, angle, and stylus wheel of your pen affect strokes.

▶ The Duration setting and the frame where you begin painting are crucial.

▶ Preset brushes and numerical settings for properties such as diameter and hardness (aka feather) live in the Brush Tips panel.

Much more fun and interactive than the Brush Tips panel are the following shortcuts. With the Brush tool active in the Layer viewer

TIP

The older Vector Paint effect (Pro only) remains useful for painting in the context of a comp viewer, but it won't clone and it's not intuitive; I prefer to open two viewers (Comp and Layer).

- ▶ Hold **Ctrl/Cmd** and drag to scale the brush.

- ▶ Add the **Shift** key to adjust in larger increments, and **Alt/Option** for fine adjustments.

- ▶ With the mouse button still held, release **Ctrl/Cmd** to scale hardness (an inner circle appears representing the inside of the threshold, **Figure 7.16**).

- ▶ **Alt/Option**-click to use the eyedropper (with brushes) or clone source (with the clone brush).

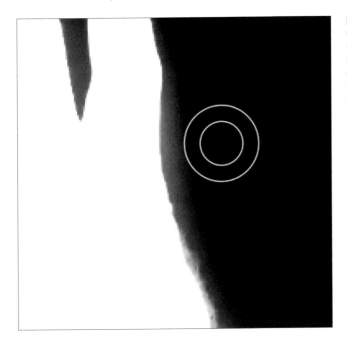

Figure 7.16 Modifier keys (**Ctrl/Cmd** to scale, **Alt/Opt** to feather, all with mouse button held) let you define a brush on the fly. The inner circle shows the solid core; the area between it and the outer circle is the threshold (for feathering).

By default, the Duration setting in the Paint menu is set to Constant, which means that any paint stroke you create on this frame continues to the end of the layer. For cleaning up an alpha channel, this is typically not a desirable setting because you're presumably painting stray holes in your matte here and there, on single (or just a few) frames. The Single Frame setting confines your stroke to just the current frame on which you're painting, and the Custom setting allows you to enter the number of frames that the stroke will persist.

The other option, Write On, records your stroke in real time, re-creating the motion (including timing) when you

TIP

There is a major gotcha with Constant (the default mode): Paint a stroke at any frame other than the first frame of the layer, and it does not appear until that frame during playback. It's apparently not a bug, but it is certainly an annoyance.

replay the layer; this stylized option can be useful for such motion graphics tricks as handwritten script.

The Brush Tips panel menu includes various display options and customizable features: You can add, rename, or delete brushes, as well. You can also name a brush by double-clicking it. Brush names do not appear in the default thumbnail view except via tooltips when you move your cursor above each brush.

For an alpha channel, you will typically work in Single Frame mode (under Duration in the Paint panel), looking only at the alpha channel (**Alt+4/Option+4**) and progressing frame by frame through the shot (pressing **Page Down**).

After working for a little while, your Timeline may contain dozens of strokes, each with numerous properties of its own. New strokes are added to the top of the stack and are given numerically ordered names; to select one to edit or delete, you may more easily find it using the Selection tool (**V**) to directly select it in a viewer panel.

Cloning Fundamentals

When you clone moving footage, the result retains grain and other natural features that still images lack. Not only can you clone pixels from a different region of the same frame, you can clone from a different frame of a different clip at a different point in time (**Figure 7.17**), as follows:

▶ **Clone from the same frame:** This works just as in Photoshop. Choose a brush, **Alt/Option**-click on the area of the frame to sample, and begin painting. Remember that by default, Duration is set to Constant, so any stroke created begins at the current frame and extends through the rest of the composition.

▶ **Clone from the same clip, at a different time:** Look at Clone Options for the offset value in frames. Note that there is also an option to set spatial offset. To clone from the exact same position at a different point in time, set the Offset to 0, 0 and change the Source Time.

TIP

As in Photoshop, the **X** key swaps the foreground and background swatches with the Brush tool active.

NOTES

The Aligned toggle in the Paint panel (on by default) preserves 1:1 pixel positions even though paint tools are vector-based. Nonaligned clone operations tend to appear blurry.

Figure 7.17 Clone source overlay is checked (left) with Difference mode active, an "onion skin" that makes it possible to line up precisely two matching shots (middle and right images). Difference mode is on, causing all identical areas of the frame to turn black when the two layers are perfectly aligned.

▶ **Clone from a separate clip:** The source from which you're cloning must be present in the current composition (although it need not be visible and can even be a guide layer). Simply open the layer to be used as source, and go to the current time where you want to begin; Source and Source Time Shift are listed in the Paint panel and can also be edited there.

▶ **Mix multiple clone sources without having to reselect each one:** There are five Preset icons in the Paint panel; these allow you to switch sources on the fly and then switch back to a previous source. Just click on a Preset icon before selecting your clone source and that source remains associated with that preset (including Aligned and Lock Source Time settings).

That all seems straightforward enough; there are just a few things to watch out for, as follows.

Tricks and Gotchas

Suppose the clone source time is offset, or comes from a different layer, and the last frame of the layer has been reached—what happens? After Effects helpfully loops back to the first frame of the clip and keeps going. This is dangerous only if you're not aware of it.

Edit the source to take control of this process. Time remapping is one potential way to solve these problems; you can time stretch a source clip or loop it intentionally.

You may need to scale the source to match the target. Although temporal edits, including time remapping, render before they are passed through, other types of

TIP

To clone from a single frame only to multiple frames, toggle on Lock Source Time in the Paint panel.

NOTES

Clone is different from many other tools in After Effects in that Source Time Shift uses frames, not seconds, to evaluate the temporal shift. Beware if you mix clips with different frame rates, although on the whole this is a beneficial feature.

edits—even simple translations or effects—do not. As always, the solution is to precompose; any scaling, rotation, motion tracking, or effects to be cloned belong in the subcomposition.

Finally, Paint is an effect. Apply your first stroke and you'll see an effect called Paint with a single checkbox, Paint on Transparent, which effectively solos the paint strokes. You can change the render order of paint strokes relative to other effects. For example, you can touch up a green-screen plate, apply a keyer, and then touch up the resulting alpha channel, all on one layer.

The View menu in the Layer panel (**Figure 7.18**) lists, in order, the paint and effects edits you've added to the layer. To see only the layer with no edits applied, toggle Render off; to see a particular stage of the edit—after the first paint strokes, but before the effects, say—select it in the View menu, effectively disabling the steps below it. These settings are for previewing only; they will not enable or disable the rendering of these items.

Figure 7.18 Isolate and solo paint strokes in the View menu of the Layer panel.

You can motion track a paint stroke. To do so requires the tracker, covered in the next chapter, and a basic expression.

Wire Removal

Wire removal and rig removal are two common visual effects needs. Generally speaking, *wire removal* is cloning over a wire (typically used to suspend an actor or prop in mid-air). *Rig removal*, meanwhile, is typically just an animated garbage mask over any equipment that appeared in shot.

After Effects has nothing to compete with the state-of-the-art wire removal tool found in The Foundry's Furnace plug-ins (which sadly are available for just about every compositing package besides After Effects, although Adobe did license the Kronos toolset from Furnace to become Timewarp).

The CC Simple Wire Removal tool is indeed simple: It replaces the vector between two points by either displacing pixels or using the same pixels from a neighboring frame. There are Slope and Mirror Blend controls allowing you a little control over the threshold and cloning pattern, and you can apply a tracker to each point via expressions and the pickwhip (usage described in Chapter 10).

The net effect may not be so different from drawing a two-point clone stroke (sample the background by **Alt/Option**-clicking, then click one end of the wire, and **Shift**-click the other end). That stroke could then be tracked via expressions.

Rig removal can very often be aided by tracking motion, because rigs themselves don't move, the camera does. The key is to make a shape that mattes out the rig, then apply that as a track matte to the foreground footage and track the whole matte.

Dust Bust

This is in many ways as nitty-gritty and low-level as rotoscoping gets, although the likelihood of small particles appearing on source footage has decreased with the advent of digital shooting and the decline of film. Most of these flaws can be corrected only via frame-by-frame cloning, sometimes known as *dust busting*. If you've carefully read this section, you already know what you need to know to do this work successfully, so get to it.

Conclusion

And so, like rain, into every effects artist's life a little rotoscoping must fall. The tools outlined here are mostly sufficient for the type of rotoscoping work that compositors will have to do. Dedicated rotoscope artists would likely choose software other than After Effects or perhaps employ Silhouette as an After Effects plug-in. As long as

CLOSE-UP

Photoshop Video

Photoshop offers an intriguing alternative to the After Effects vector paint tools; you can work with moving footage in Photoshop. The After Effects paint tools are heavily based on those in Photoshop, but with one key difference: Photoshop strokes are bitmaps (actual pixels) and those from After Effects are vectors. This makes it possible to use custom brushes, as are common in Photoshop (and which are themselves bitmaps). There's not as much you can do overall with the stroke once you've painted it as in After Effects, but if you like working in Photoshop, it's certainly an option. After Effects can open Photoshop files containing video.

rotoscoping isn't your stock in trade, however, the After Effects tools will usually allow you to finish the shot without having to look for other software.

The next chapter completes the picture by adding motion tracking to your areas of expertise. As mentioned, motion tracking plus rotoscoping can equal a shortcut around tedious tasks.

8

Effective Motion Tracking

Never mistake motion for action.

—Ernest Hemingway

Effective Motion Tracking

There is more that can be done with tracking than simply sampling the motion of one layer and applying it to another, even though that's fundamentally what it does; because you can track in several different ways using a variety of points, the methods and applications go far beyond the obvious.

Native tracking possibilities have been further expanded in After Effects CS4 thanks to the licensing and inclusion of MochaAE from Imagineer Systems. Previously available as a third-party application, Mocha uses a fundamentally different approach (planar tracking) than that of the built-in After Effects point tracker and it solves a problem (corner pinning) that had exposed weaknesses in that tracker.

It is also possible to use third-party 3D tracking software to import 3D camera data matched to real-world motion into After Effects, via a methodology that is described at the end of this chapter.

All of these automated trackers are astoundingly accurate, often sampling motion at a detail level that would be impossible for you to pick up by eye. It's not a fully automated process, however, and so you must understand how to

▶ Choose effective track regions

▶ Customize settings based on the particular scene

▶ Rescue tracks that seem to have gone astray (or abandon and restart, provided you understand what to try instead)

▶ Handle motion blur

This chapter addresses these techniques and more. Once you grasp these, you can use tracking to go beyond the ordinary:

▶ Match multiple elements to a single track using the 3D camera

▶ Stabilize a handheld or other moving camera shot

▶ Continue tracks when the object being tracked leaves the visible frame

▶ Import and use 3D tracking data

There are so many cases where effective tracking can help accomplish the seemingly impossible; it's worth knowing this stuff inside out.

Point Tracking Essentials

Step one is to be able to get a good basic track right in After Effects. You may find your tracks going astray after reviewing the clear After Effects documentation on how to use the tracker. Here are some background fundamentals.

Tracking is a two-step process: The tracker analyzes the clip and stores its analysis as a set of layer properties that don't actually do anything. The properties must be applied to take effect. Both steps, setting the tracking target and applying the track, occur in the Tracker Controls panel when matching or stabilizing motion in After Effects.

Choose a Feature

Success with the After Effects tracker relies on your ability to choose a feature that will track effectively (**Figure 8.1**).

Figure 8.1 Objects with clear contours, definition, and contrast make the best track targets.

Search and feature regions don't have to be square! Widen the feature region to match a wide, short target feature. With unidirectional motion—say, a right-to-left pan—widen and offset the search region in the direction of the pan (**Figure 8.2**).

Figure 8.2 Offset the track region in the direction of uniform motion, if any exists.

Ideally, the feature you plan to track

▶ Is unique from its surroundings

▶ Has high-contrast edges—typically a corner or point—entirely within the feature region

▶ Is identifiable throughout the shot

▶ Does not have to compete with similar distinct features within the search region at any point during the track

▶ Is close to the area where the tracked object or objects will be added

Figure 8.3 shows the many draggable features of the tracker control. It's very easy to grab the wrong thing, so pay close attention to the icon under your cursor as you set up the track.

Figure 8.3 Many interactive controls are clustered close together in the tracker. Identified here are: A. Search region, B. Feature region, C. Keyframe marker, D. Attach point, E. Move search region, F. Move both regions, G. Move entire track point, H. Move attach point, I. Move entire track point, J. Resize region. Zoom in to ensure you're clicking the right one.

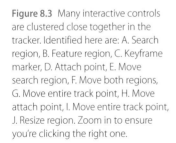
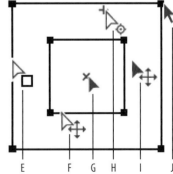

The main decisions when setting up a track regard the size and shape of the Search and Feature regions. Keep the following in mind:

▶ A large Feature region averages pixel data, producing a smoother but possibly less accurate track.

▶ A small Feature region may pick up noise and grain as much as trackable detail, creating an accurate but jittery track.

▶ The bigger the Search region, the slower the track.

▶ The Feature region doesn't have to contain the area of frame you want to match. One way to offset a track is to move the attach point—that little x at the center of the tracker. A better solution is to apply the track to a null, as is discussed later.

Most features that you'll track are unreliable—they change perspective, lighting or color throughout the course of the shot. The following sections explain what to do when you don't have a constant, trackable feature exactly where you want your target to go.

Tweak the Tracker

There are five types of track listed under the Track Type menu in the Tracker panel (**Figure 8.4**).

Figure 8.4 The various available track types are set in the Tracker Controls panel.

Stabilize and *Transform* tracks are virtually identical until applied. Edit Target shows the singular difference between them: Stabilize tracks are always applied to the *anchor point of the tracked layer*. Transform tracks are applied to the *position of a layer other than the tracked layer*.

Using Stabilize, the animated anchor point (located at the center of the image by default) moves the layer in opposition to Position. Increasing the anchor point's X value (assuming Position remains the same, which it does when you adjust the Anchor Point value directly in the Timeline) moves the layer to the left, just as decreasing the Position value does.

Corner Pin tracks are very different; in After Effects these require three or four points to be tracked, and the data is applied to a Corner Pin plug-in to essentially distort the perspective of the target layer. Because these tracks are notoriously difficult and unreliable, the happy truth is that MochaAE, which also generates data that can be applied to a corner pin, more or less supersedes Corner Pin tracking.

Raw tracks generate track data only, graying out the Edit Target button. What good is track data that isn't applied anywhere? It can be used to drive expressions or saved to be applied later. It's no different than simply never clicking Edit Target; the raw track data is stored within the source layer (**Figure 8.5**).

Figure 8.5 Tracker data is stored under the tracked layer and can be accessed at any time.

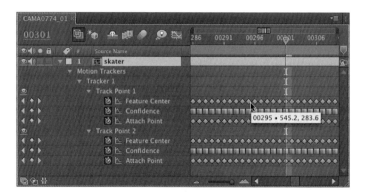

Position, Rotation, and/or Scale

You can't uncheck the Position toggle in the Tracker panel (thus avoiding the unsolvable riddle, what is a motion track without Position data?), but you can add Rotation and Scale. Enable either toggle, and a second track point is automatically added.

Figure 8.6 These two points are not suitable for a two-point track because they exist on different planes of depth relative to the camera; the rear one covers more distance in this pan shot.

Additionally tracking rotation and scale data is straightforward enough, employing two track points instead of one. Typically, the two points should be roughly equidistant from the camera due to the phenomenon of parallax (**Figure 8.6**).

Tracks that add rotation and scale usually have features that change appearance through the course of the shot (because they themselves may rotate and scale). Tracker > Options contains the Adapt Feature on Every Frame toggle.

By default, the tracker is set to adapt the track feature if confidence slips below 80%. Adapt Feature on Every Frame is like restarting the track on each and every frame, comparing each frame to the previous one instead of the one you originally chose. For ordinary tracks this adds an unwanted margin of error, but in a case where a feature is changing each frame anyhow, because the scale, orientation or blurriness is in constant flux, this can help.

Subpixel Motion

The key feature of the After Effects tracker is subpixel positioning, on by default in Motion Tracker Options. You could never achieve this degree of accuracy manually; most supposedly "locked off" scenes require stabilization despite that the range of motion is less than a full pixel; your vision is actually far more acute than that.

As you watch a track in progress, the trackers move in whole pixel values, bouncing around crudely, but unless you disable subpixel positioning, this does not reflect the final track, which is accurate to ¹⁄₁₀,₀₀₀ of a pixel (four places below the decimal point).

If a track keeps slipping going forward, try starting at the end of the clip and tracking in reverse (note that the "play" icons in Tracker Controls go both directions). It's best to start where your feature is largest and most prominent so that it doesn't outgrow the boundaries of the Feature region.

Confidence

At the bottom of Motion Tracker Options is a submenu of options related to After Effects' mysterious Confidence settings. Every tracked frame gets a Confidence setting, an evaluation of how accurate the track was at that frame. This may or may not be indicative of the actual accuracy, but my experience is that you're almost guaranteed to be fine with values above 90%, and real problems will cause this value to drop way down, even to 30% or less (**Figure 8.7**).

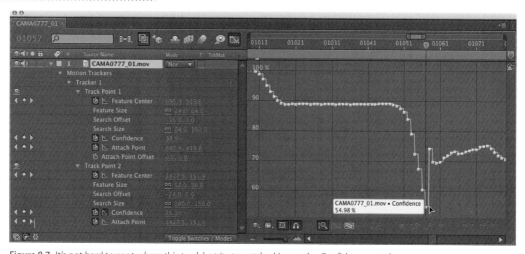

Figure 8.7 It's not hard to spot where this track lost its target, looking at the Confidence graph.

To reveal the current track in the Timeline with the Track Controls active, use the **SS** (show selected) shortcut.

Depending on this setting, you can (**Figure 8.8**)

▶ Continue Tracking. Just power ahead no matter what.

▶ Stop Tracking. So you can reset the tracker manually right at the problem frame.

▶ Extrapolate Motion. Let After Effects guess based on how it was moving on the previously tracked frames.

This is for cases where the tracked item disappears for one or a few frames.

▶ Adapt Feature. The default behavior is to go ahead and change the reference Feature region to the previous frame if there is low Confidence, indicating the feature has suddenly changed appearance.

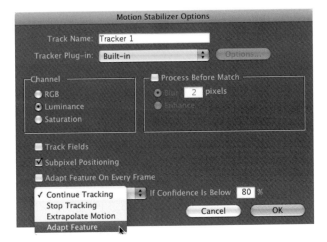

Figure 8.8 This menu specifies what to do when the Confidence rating drops below a certain threshold during the track.

Whichever you choose, you also have the option to go back to the frame where a track went wrong, reset the feature region by hand, and restart the track.

Solve Problems with Nulls

I almost always apply track data to a null object layer and then use parenting to apply the motion to other layers. This offers a bunch of advantages:

▶ Offset and relocate tracks: It doesn't matter whether the track attach point is in the right location; the null picks up the relative motion, and any layer parented to it can be repositioned or animated on its own (**Figure 8.9**).

▶ Optionally lock the tracked layer once you're happy with it, so you don't inadvertently move it.

▶ Use a Stabilization track to peg multiple object to a scene (next section).

▶ Parent one motion track to another if you need to switch to a different track target mid-shot.

NOTES

Most of the other Motion Tracker Options are rarely adjusted. If your footage has contrast only on one color channel, you can try RGB instead of Luminance; I've never seen footage that has trackable contrast in Saturation, although it must exist. You don't need to Track Fields if you removed them on import. You can blur a jittery track before match, or enhance low-contrast footage, but adjusting the size of the Feature region or choosing a different feature, can do a better job making your track more or less precise.

One common problem is that a track is good only until a given point in the scene, and if you then move the tracker to search a different location, the whole track jumps. By adding a new track and another null, you can create and apply as many individual tracks as you like, parenting one to the next.

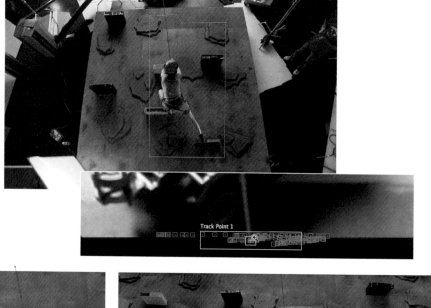

Figure 8.9 The rope must be painted and tracked to reach the edge of the frame (top). The point where the rope meets the edge of the set can be tracked (middle), and a two-point mask with a Stroke effect can be added to replace it (bottom left). The final animation offsets the track to match the rope angle (bottom right).

Track Averaging and Mask Tracking

A couple of techniques have long been popular but
reserved to the select few willing to set them up; with the
addition of a script called TrackerViz (credited at the front
of the book), there's no need to undergo the pain in order
to get the benefit.

If you are having a difficult time getting an After Effects
track to stick, there's an alternative to continually rework-
ing a single track; several not-so-accurate tracks, averaged
together, will often be more accurate than any alternative
approach. The setup involved is a slight pain, however,
which is where the script comes in (**Figure 8.10**).

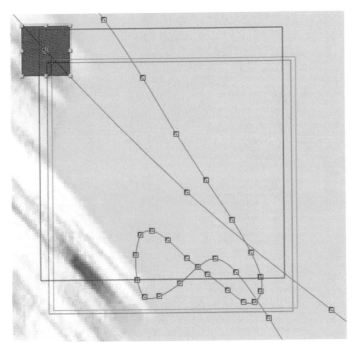

Figure 8.10 The TrackerViz script takes a set of passes tracking the same object
and averages them; the small red solid is a layer created as the average of the
three tracked nulls.

TrackerViz also lets you interchange tracked nulls and mask
points, making it possible to effectively track in a mask. You
first track a set of nulls, each with a unique name, corresponding to vertices on the shape. Select them in the order

that you would draw them, and in TrackerViz choose and apply Layers to Shape in the Function menu. The result is not a shape layer but much more usefully, a solid with a key-framed mask applied to it. The mask can be used to replace any equivalent hand-drawn masks applied to layers.

Match Motion Blur

Don't neglect the possibility of motion blur! It can be your friend until it appears unwanted, like a malingering house-guest, impossible to ignore.

A good track won't look right until its motion blur also matches that of the background plate. Matching motion blur is similar to color or grain matching; you do it by eye, most often zooming in to an area of the frame where it is apparent in both the foreground and background.

Motion blur settings are not interactive; they reside in Composition Settings (**Ctrl+K/Cmd+K**) > Advanced, where you don't see the effect of your changes until you clear the dialog by clicking OK. As described back in Chapter 2, adjust Shutter Angle and Shutter Phase until you see a good match, raising (or in the odd case, lowering) Samples per Frame and Adaptive Sample Limit to match (**Figure 8.11**).

Figure 8.11 Motion tracking can't work without matching motion blur. This shot uses the standard film camera blur: a 180 degree shutter angle, with a phase of –90.

If you're trying to stabilize a scene that contains motion blur, you have a bigger problem, one that needs to be avoided when shooting (by boosting the shutter speed of the camera, where possible, **Figure 8.12**). In such cases it's no doubt preferable to smooth camera motion rather than lock the stabilization (see "Smooth a Camera Move" later in this chapter).

Figure 8.12 If shooting with the intention of stabilizing later, raise the film shutter speed and reduce camera motion to minimize motion blur and a huge image gutter, which both soften the image beyond the point of being useful.

Match Multiple Objects

In the real world, objects sit in an environment, and if that environment or the point of view changes, they remain in place. You knew this. You may not know how to make a 2D After Effects track re-create it.

The key is to stabilize the background layer and then parent a camera to that stabilization, restoring the motion. The motion of the source camera is captured and applied to a virtual camera so that any elements you add to the scene pick up on that motion. It's quite cool.

The AE Camera as a Tracking Tool

Suppose you have an arbitrary number of foreground layers to match to a background plate: not just objects, but color corrections, effects with hold-out masks, you name it. Applying track data to each of those layers individually is a time-consuming headache, and even parenting them all to a tracked null may not work properly if there is rotation or scale data, as that null then becomes the center of those translations.

Instead, the following method allows you to stabilize the background scene, add static foreground elements, and then reapply the scene motion.

1. With the background layer selected, choose Stabilize Motion (either by context-clicking the layer or by choosing it from the Animation menu).

2. Stabilize the layer for Position, Rotation, and Scale, using two points equidistant from the camera.

3. The stabilized layer offsets and rotates in the frame (**Figure 8.13**). Return to the first frame of the track (quite possibly frame 0 of the comp). Turn on the stabilized layer's 3D switch.

Figure 8.13 Gaps open up around the edges of the image as the track points are held in place.

NOTES

A 50 mm camera lens in After Effects offers a neutral perspective; toggle any layer to 3D and it should appear the same as in 2D.

4. Add a 3D camera (context-click in an empty area of the Timeline); in the Camera Settings, give it a name like trackerCam, use the 50mm preset, and click OK.

5. Parent the camera layer to the stabilized layer (**Figure 8.14**).

Figure 8.14 The relevant Transform properties are copied and pasted to a null, to which the camera is then parented.

Everything now appears back to normal, with one intriguing twist: Any new item added to the scene picks up the scene motion as soon as you toggle its 3D switch. All you have to do is drop it in and enable 3D. Any layer that shouldn't follow the track, such as an adjustment layer, can remain 2D (**Figure 8.15**).

Figure 8.15 Extra layers for a new clock face and child's artwork along with a shadow are added as 3D layers, so they pick up the motion of the scene as captured by the tracked camera.

2.5D Tracking

You can even fake 3D parallax by offsetting layers in Z space. Any layer that is equidistant from the camera with the motion track points has a Z-depth value of 0. Offsetting layers is tricky as there is no frame of reference for where they should be placed in Z space—not even a grid (**Figure 8.16**).

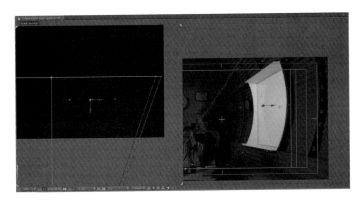

Figure 8.16 Rotoscoped shapes can be tracked so that they "stick" in a scene; you don't have to animate the shape itself unless it is also a matte that needs to be articulated around a moving figure. Here it is even offset in 3D to match the parallax of the wall nearer camera.

NOTES

2.5D tracking will even stick foreground layers to a zoomed shot; the Scale stabilization scales the parented camera, making it appear to zoom.

This is what I call "2.5D tracking": a 3D camera paired with two-dimensional tracking points and layers. Any 3D offset derived from a 2D track is only approximately accurate, so this is a big cheat; if your scene has areas of frame closer or further than the track points that you wish to match, you can try to guess where in 3D space to place a layer and you may just get lucky.

If your shot tracks (the camera moves), it probably requires a real 3D camera track (see "Try It Out for Yourself" at the end of this chapter).

Stabilize a Moving Shot

After Effects doesn't provide you with a workflow to take a shot with a moving camera—handheld, aerial, crane, or dolly—and smooth bumps in the motion while retaining the move. But you can do it.

Figure 8.17 features an aerial shot of Silicon Valley (look closely and you'll see Adobe headquarters). It wasn't taken in a helicopter with a gyro, but rather from a camera attached to a 2 × 4 wooden plank, C-clamped to the open door of a Cessna aircraft. The pilot did his best to keep the plane steady, but even on a calm day that type of aircraft bobs and weaves, which is why you might pay ten times more money to get the helicopter with the gyro.

Figure 8.17 Track two co-planar points at whatever distance the eye is focused—here the near-horizon—and stabilize for position, rotation and scale.

Ah, but it's so much fun to fix it in post. To stabilize a shot like this, first decide where the viewer's attention will be, because that's the area that you want to stabilize. Objects in the near foreground move more than those in the distance; stabilizing them adds motion on the horizon. In this case, the viewer's attention is likely on the near-horizon, below the foothills. Begin by creating a Position/Rotation/Scale stabilization based on two points at that depth.

The basic setup replicates the first four steps from the last section, but instead of parenting the camera to the stabilized source layer, follow these steps:

1. Create a null named Stabilizer (or your choice), and enable 3D.

2. Select all of the Anchor Point keyframes from the stabilized background plate.

3. Copy and paste the Anchor Point keyframe data to Stabilizer.

4. Apply smoothing to this duplicated smoothing data.

5. Parent the camera to the Stabilizer layer (**Figure 8.18**).

Figure 8.18 The camera is parented to a null whose transform data matches that of the stabilized plate.

You have a couple of options to "apply smoothing": Window > Smoother is an automatic but destructive solution; the smooth() expression is a vastly superior technique, because you can view the smoothed motion in the Graph Editor without affecting the source keyframes. If, later on, it turns out you need to adjust it again, you can (**Figure 8.19**).

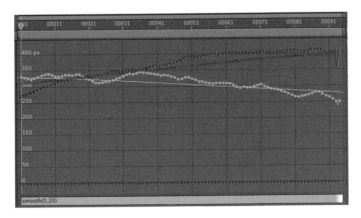

Figure 8.19 The smooth() expression is displayed as a reference graph adjacent to the actual tracked keyframes and does not rewrite them. The control to enable the expressions graph is grouped with the other expression controls under the property.

To apply a smooth() expression

1. **Alt/Option**-click on the Anchor Point stopwatch of the layer to which the camera is parented.

2. With the default expression (anchorPoint) still highlighted, go to the Expressions menu icon 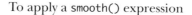 and under Property choose the smooth default: smooth(width = .2, samples = 5, t = time).

   This works, but as a starting setting, I recommend discarding the third argument ("t = time") and the other hints ("width =" and "samples =") to get the leaner, meaner and more powerful setting like smooth(2, 48).

The expression works as follows: It gives a command (smooth()) followed by three settings known as *arguments*. The third one, time, is used only to offset the result, and it's optional, so I have a habit of deleting it. The hints for the other two (width = and samples =) are also not needed to make the expression work—they are there just to remind you what they do.

Width determines how much time (before and after the current time) is averaged to create the result. A setting of 2 samples 2 seconds means 1 second before and 1 second after the current time. The samples argument determines how many individual points within that range are actually sampled for the result; generally, the more samples, the smoother the curve. A setting of 48 means that over that 2 seconds, 48 individual frame values will be averaged (the maximum for 24 fps footage).

It's also possible to smooth rotation in this manner, although I find a lighter touch (fewer samples) works best with rotation. However, the best way to find out for your individual shot is by trying different settings, looking at how smooth the resulting curve (not to mention the actual motion) appears.

It's a little hard to imagine that you can smooth the motion data for the camera, causing it to go out of sync with the background, and not have a mismatch. What is actually happening, though, is that the scene motion is removed completely and then restored in a smoother state.

Incorporate MochaAE

After Effects CS4 has added a whole separate tracking application: MochaAE, licensed from Imagineer Systems. MochaAE is not in any way integrated directly into After Effects; it was originally sold as stand-alone software and remains a separate application (now found in the same folder as After Effects itself), which you can fire up as needed.

When is it needed? Mocha is a planar tracker, which means that it does not analyze individual points or feature regions like the After Effects tracker (and most other trackers) but instead looks at entire plane of motion.

Look around the environment where you are right now and you will see numerous two dimensional planes: walls, table tops, the backs of chairs, or maybe the trunk of a tree, or the side, front, top, wheel, hood, window (and on and on) of a passing truck (**Figure 8.20**). If you were sitting on the moon reading this book, the surface of earth, though curved, would track as a plane; you wouldn't track the tip of Florida or New Zealand, but the whole planet.

Figure 8.20 A plane does not have to be flat and rectilinear in order for Mocha to track it; look around and you will see many coplanar objects.

Thus Mocha is most plainly useful for Corner Pin tracking: replacing a surface with four discernable corners with another such surface. This type of track has long been the Achilles heel of the After Effects tracker, and Mocha provides such welcome relief that I've omitted coverage of corner pinning with the After Effects tracker from this book.

Mocha can, in fact, be used for just about any type of 2D tracking. It's less convenient to use outside software than to track directly in After Effects, but once you become comfortable with Mocha, you may find that the extra precision is worth the trouble of doing so.

The Basics

Mocha is an application all unto itself with its own manual, longer than this chapter (just click Guide on the Mocha Welcome dialog). It's not a bad read. Because it's a new feature, here's a look at how best to get up and running.

First of all, Mocha is limited to a subset of footage formats that you might use in an After Effects project. Cineon log files are okay, but several other higher-than-8-bpc formats seem to be off-limits, so you may need to render a special version of your source clip to be compatible. (I suggest Animation compressed QuickTime; it's imperative to get the frame rate correct and having it embedded in the source file helps you avoid careless errors with image sequences.)

The wizard to set up a project results in the creation of the Mocha project file before you get started—either in a location you specify or adjacent to the shot. The most crucial thing to get right in this three-page process is frame rate (which is only an issue with an image sequence); the difference between, for example, 23.976 and 24 frames per second is crucial; a mismatch will result in a track that slips.

Once your shot appears in Mocha, the next step is to scrub to a frame that clearly shows the planar area you wish to track. The rules are entirely different than with a point tracker: You don't need to see the entire plane or any of its boundaries; you're just looking for coplanar details that are most consistent through the shot. "Consistent" means not obscured by foreground motion or light flares and reflections, although there are workarounds for both.

On that starting frame, you use one of two tools to draw out a mask shape: Bézier splines 🔲 or the less familiar but preferable Mocha X-splines 🔲. Select either and tap a few points—it doesn't matter how many—around the target details (**Figure 8.21**). It's helpful if these points correspond to some recognizable detail for fine-tuning later, but they don't have to. Close the shape by clicking back on the first point.

Figure 8.21 Mocha shows a close-up of the selected point of the X-spline shape around the target. Mocha is a planar tracker and doesn't track this individual point like After Effects would, but these points help you gauge whether the shape continues to line up, so it's helpful to align them with a feature you can easily identify.

At this point, with an easy track, you can use the forward and backward controls and watch Mocha work its magic.

If the track sticks to its target, the next step is to fine-tune it. Assuming you're exporting corner pin data, you must at minimum enable Surface under the View Controls and place the corners where you want them in the result.

If all is still well, you can now click Export Tracking Data on the Track panel and copy or save After Effects CS4 Corner Pin Data. If you copy, you can then paste directly into the target layer in After Effects at the first frame of the source; Mocha creates a keyframe on every frame (**Figure 8.22**). If you instead choose to save a text file, you can then copy and paste its data from an ordinary text editor.

NOTES

Mocha is typically used for corner pinning, but you can instead choose to export After Effects Transform Data and use it like regular tracker data.

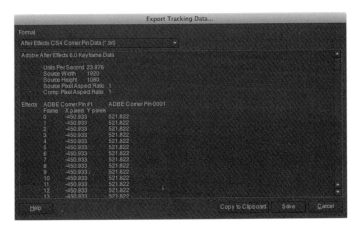

Figure 8.22 The bridge from Mocha back to After Effects is this export dialog. If you've never seen it, this is the format that After Effects keyframe data takes when it's pasted into a text file, which is how Mocha exports it; you then open the text file, select all, copy, and paste it into the target layer to be corner-pinned.

The Nitty Gritty

It's normal for a track to be slightly more complicated than this, usually due to motion or perspective shifts within the track area. This can be the result of foreground objects passing across the track region or the appearance of the region itself changing over time.

Figure 8.23 shows an otherwise straightforward track of a handheld game unit with the following challenges: flares and reflections play across the screen, the hands move back and forth across the unit, and the perspective of the screen changes from flat to face-on.

Figure 8.23 The tracking markers on the screen are not necessary for Mocha to track this handheld unit for screen replacement, it's the reflective screen itself and the movement of the thumbs across it that present Mocha with a challenge.

There are two standard solutions to any track that slips:

▶ Sudden slippage is often the result of foreground motion or light changing the appearance of the tracked area; the solution is to mask out the area containing the disturbance.

▶ Small, gradual slippage is often the result of shifts in perspective and can be keyframed.

The clip shown in Figure 8.23 requires both techniques. A track of the entire face of the unit shifts slightly as it is tilted and a lot as the thumbs move across the track area and reflections play across the screen.

Big shifts in the track region are caused by changes in the track area, so I fix those first, adding an additional spline (or splines) containing the interruptive motion. The Add X-spline 🖾 and Add Bézier Spline 🖾 create a subtractive shape (or shapes) around the areas of the first region that contain any kind of motion. **Figure 8.24** shows that these can be oddly defined; they track right along with the main planar track.

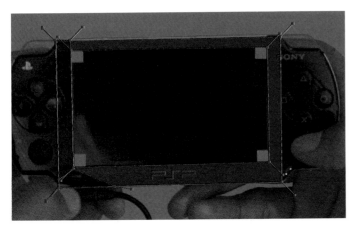

Figure 8.24 Holdout masks are added to eliminate areas where the screen picks up reflections and the left thumb moves around. Notice that the tracking markers aren't even used; there is plenty of other detail for Mocha to track without them.

Retracking with these additional hold-out masks improves the track a good amount; all that is required to perfect this track is a keyframe at one point where the unit is tilted about 15 degrees toward camera. I look for the frame where the plane settles into its new, offset position and highlight one corner of the main track mask (not the hold-outs).

When I highlight the point, zoomed views with crosshairs appear at the upper-left or right corner (**Figure 8.25**). At the right under Keyframe Controls, Autokey is on by default. This is where it becomes helpful to have aligned mask points with recognizable features, as the idea is to move the points to match the adjacent position. This creates a green keyframe along the main Timeline. Mocha uses these keyframes as extra points of comparison, rather than simply averaging their positions.

You need not rely on luck and manual labor to get points to match over time. Open the AdjustTrack panel. Under Nudge are controls allowing Mocha to automatically guess where the point should move to match the Master, along with controls to move it in fine increments. If Mocha isn't finding your point automatically, you can try adjusting the neighboring AutoNudge controls. If it seems as though you've started with a reference point that isn't representative, you can reset the Master under Reference Point.

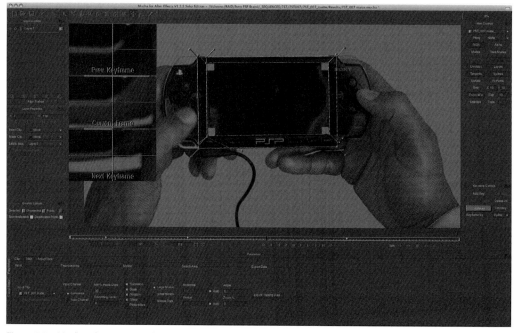

Figure 8.25 Mocha relies on you to fix the position of the mask vertex by hand if it slips, helpfully offering close-up views to allow you to match the cross-hairs to the same feature, automatically creating a new keyframe when the Autokey button is on (in red, at the right).

In this example it's also helpful to check Perspective under Motion in the Track tab; this allows the change in proportions from the tilting of the screen to be included in the Corner Pin export.

Still in beta at this writing, the Red Giant Corner Pin effect included in its Warp collection is ready-made for usage with Mocha (**Figure 8.26**).

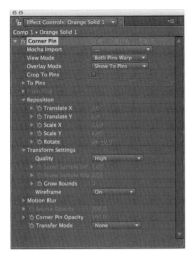

Figure 8.26 The Red Giant Corner Pin effect not only includes a Mocha Import function, up top, it allows "from" as well as "to" pins— so your corner pin content can be tracked from a moving source as well—and even adds motion blur capabilities. It puts After Effects' built-in Corner Pin tool to shame.

If you get into trouble, you'll want to know how to delete keys (under Keyframe Controls) or reference points (in the AdjustTrack tab). You also need to know a few new keyboard shortcuts, such as **X** for the hand tool and arrow keys to navigate one frame. This discussion omits the many actual compositing features included with Mocha (the Layer Controls), which you assumedly don't need, because you have After Effects.

Use Tracking with Expressions

Expressions and tracking data go together like peanut butter and chocolate. You don't even have to apply raw tracking data in order to put it to use; you can pickwhip any property containing X and Y position data directly to other properties.

For example, to track in a paint clone operation in a single layer

1. Set up a track with the paint target as the feature center (the center of the Feature Region).

2. Move the attach point to the area from which you wish to clone.

3. Track motion; you can set Track Type to Raw or simply don't apply it.

4. Add a clone stroke with appropriate settings.

5. Pickwhip Stroke Options > Clone Position to the Attach Point and Transform: Clone 1 > Position to the Feature Center.

This works equally well applied to another layer.

Continue Loop

Sometimes a track point will disappear before the track is completed, either because it is obscured by a foreground object or because it has moved offscreen. Mocha can generally deal with this—if any part of the tracked plane remains in frame, it is tracked.

Nonetheless it's useful to do this right in After Effects. First make certain there are no unwanted extra tracking keyframes beyond where the point was still correctly tracked; this expression uses the difference between the final two keyframes to estimate what will happen next.

Reveal the property that needs extending (Position in this case), and **Alt/Option**-click on its stopwatch. In the text field that is revealed, replace the text (position) by typing loopOut("continue"). Yes, that's right, typing; don't worry, you're not less of an artist for doing it (**Figure 8.27**).

This expression uses the delta (velocity and direction) of the last two frames. It creates matching linear motion (not a curve) moving at a steady rate, so it works well if those last two frames are representative of the overall rate and direction of motion.

Chapter 10 offers many more ideas about how to go beyond these simple expressions and to customize them according to specific needs.

Figure 8.27 A continue loop is handy anywhere you have motion that should continue at the pace and in the direction at the first or last keyframe. Notice in this example that although it could help as the skater disappears behind the post, it doesn't do curves; motion continues along a linear vector.

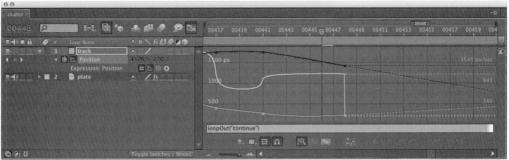

Import 3D Tracking Data

After Effects does not include a dedicated 3D tracker, but it can import 3D tracking data created in a separate application, such as 2D3's Boujou, Pixel Farm's PF Track, or SynthEyes, from Andersson Technologies. Nor does it work with 3D mesh objects (it's the "postcards in space" model of 2D in a 3D environment), so the 3D tracking workflow operates as follows:

1. Track the scene with a 3D tracking application. This generates 3D camera data, typically exportable in various 3D formats; included with these is usually an option to export a .ma file for After Effects.

   The track will ideally also generate nulls corresponding to the track points and an axis centered on the "floor," the ground plane of the shot, although you may have to specify these.

2. (Optional) Import the camera data into a 3D animation program and render 3D elements. You can also massage the 3D data for After Effects here, leaving, for example, only helpful nulls.

3. Import the camera data into After Effects; it imports in the form of a composition with an animated 3D camera and nulls (potentially many layers of them). Add your background plate and foreground elements; those that are 2D can be freely matched with 3D elements, which will pick up the camera movement.

Figure 8.28 shows the final result from the baseball plate; the camera follows the pitch all the way to the plate, where the batter hits it out of the park (of course). This shot is a complete mishmash of 2D and 3D elements. The ball, field, and front of the stands are computer generated, but the crowd was lifted from footage of an actual game.

Figure 8.28 True 3D tracking (done in 2D3's Boujou for this shot) is essential to this composite because the feet of the characters must be locked to the computer-generated ground, and a camera on dolly tracks wobbles and bounces. The full shot follows the ball to the plate.

Figure 8.29 shows a completely different type of shot that also began with a 3D track in Boujou. The fires that you see in the after shot are actually dozens of individual 2D fire and smoke layers, staggered and angled in 3D space as the camera flies over to give the sense of perspective. You'll find more on this shot and how it was set up in Chapter 14.

Figure 8.29 Just because you're stuck with 2D layers in After Effects doesn't mean you can't stagger them all over 3D space to give the illusion of depth, as with this fly-by shot. Tracking nulls from Boujou helped get the relative scale of the scene, this was important because the depth of the elements had to be to exact scale for the parallax illusion to work. (Final fire image courtesy of ABC-TV.)

3D Tracking Data

Many people don't realize that After Effects can import Maya scenes (.ma files); but they have to be properly prepped and include only rendering cameras (with translation and lens data) and nulls. The camera data should be "baked," which is Maya parlance meaning that it should have a keyframe at every frame (search on "baking Maya camera data" in the online help for specifics on this).

3D trackers operate a bit differently than the After Effects tracker. Generally you do not begin by setting tracking points with these; instead, the software creates a swarm of hundreds of points that come and go throughout the shot, and it "solves" the camera using a subset of them.

Besides Position and Rotation, the Camera may also contain Zoom keyframes. Unless Sergio Leone has started making spaghetti westerns again, zoom shots are not the norm and any zoom animation should be checked against a camera report (or any available anecdotal data) and eliminated if bogus (it might be a push or even an unstable camera). Most 3D trackers allow you to specify that a shot was taken with a prime lens (no zoom).

TIP

Because After Effects offers no proportional 3D grids in the viewers, nulls imported with a 3D scene can be essential to scale and position elements in 3D. The scale of the scene is otherwise arbitrary.

Import a Maya Scene

You import a .ma scene the same way you would any element; make sure it has the .ma extension to be recognized properly. After Effects will import either one or two compositions: one for a Maya project with a square pixel aspect ratio, and two for nonsquare (a square pixel version is nested in the nonsquare one).

Your camera may be *single-node* (in which case the camera holds all of the animation data) or *targeted*, in which case the transformation data resides in a parent node to which the camera is attached.

Instead of exporting a .ma scene, Maxon's Cinema 4D software offers its own support for After Effects integration via a plug-in available from Maxon (www.maxon.net).

Any null object with the word "null" in its name is also imported. Depending on your tracker and your scene, you may import so many nulls with the scene that it becomes cumbersome. A composition with 500 layers, even nulls, quickly becomes unwieldy, so if possible, weed out the useless nulls, paring it down to a couple dozen of them (adding descriptive names) in the tracking software or 3D program. It's usually easy to make out what the nulls correspond to in the scene if you watch them over the background plate; they tend to cluster around certain objects.

If all of those nulls make their way into After Effects, find the dozen or two that are useful to you in the scene, and select those in the Timeline along with the camera and its parent null (if any). Context-click on the selected layers and choose Invert Selection to select the potentially hundreds of other unused nulls. Delete them.

3D tracking data uses 0,0,0 as a center point; as you create new 3D layers in After Effects, zero out their position values to match. It's much simpler to work this way than to translate the tracked scene to the comp center.

If the nulls come in with tiny values—say, all in the single digits—you can add a null, make it 3D and set its Position to 0,0,0, parent all layers of the imported Maya comp to it, and scale up the null. Now hold down the **Option/Alt** key and un-parent all of those layers; the scaled values stick. You can also use this method to invert a scene that comes in upside-down.

Try It Out for Yourself

If you'd like to try out a 3D tracker, look no further than the book's DVD-ROM. It includes a demo of SynthEyes, a reasonably priced 3D tracker from Andersson Technologies that has been used on feature films (**Figure 8.30**). For about the cost of a typical After Effects plug-in set, you can own your own 3D tracking software (Mac or Windows). The demo is the full version but with a time limit, and projects cannot be saved, so you must execute and export your track start to finish before quitting. The output data, however, is fully usable.

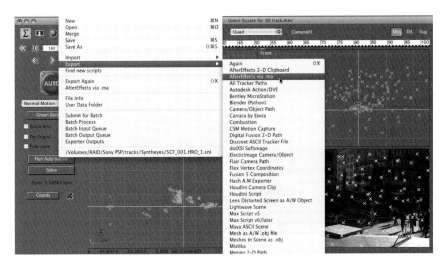

Figure 8.30 SynthEyes is one of several third-party software options that will output a Maya .ma file suitable for import as an After Effects composition. The tracking markers are included as null objects that can help orient you when you place objects into the resulting 3D space.

TIP

To learn more about the complex art of match moving, check out *Matchmoving: The Invisible Art of Camera Tracking* (Sybex Inc.) by Tim Dobbert, a colleague from The Orphanage.

There are also sample files to try out before you create a scene of your own. You may have luck simply importing your shot into SynthEyes, clicking Full Automatic, and exporting the result as AfterEffects via .ma. If there's more involved in getting a good track, however, you will need to learn a bit more about how the software works, and it's beyond the scope of this chapter to document it. SynthEyes is the type of application that yields much better results if you carefully read the online documentation, which is available from the Help menu.

Conclusion

Despite all attempts to make it standardized and automatic, tracking remains as much art as it is science, which is probably why most large effects facilities retain a staff of match movers. Even if you've understood everything in this chapter and followed along closely, working on your own shots will open a process of trial and error.

The next chapter will delve further into the ways in which After Effects can replicate what a physical camera can do, expanding on some of the concepts touched on earlier in the "2.5D Tracking" section.

9

The Camera and Optics

A film is never really good unless the camera is an eye in the head of a poet.

— Orson Welles

The Camera and Optics

It seems as if visual effects is all about simulating the look of the real world, but that's not quite the goal; as a visual effects compositor, your actual job is to simulate the real world *as it appears through the lens of a camera.* The distinction is critical, because when photographed the world looks different—more or less real, and possibly both.

It's not too grandiose to say that cinematography is essential to compositing, because After Effects offers the opportunity to re-create and even change essential shooting decisions long after the crew has struck the set and called it a wrap. Your shot may be perfectly realistic on its own merits, but it will only belong in the story if it works cinematically. Factors in After Effects that contribute to good cinematography include

- Field of view
- Depth of focus
- The shooting medium and what it tells about the storyteller
- Planar perspective and dimensionality
- Camera motion (handheld, stabilized, or locked) and what it implies about point of view

These seemingly disparate points all involve understanding how the camera sees the world and how film and video record what the camera sees. All of them transcend mere aesthetics, influencing how the viewer perceives the story itself.

Cameras: Virtual and Real

We begin our exploration of virtual cinematography with the After Effects camera, which relates closely to an actual motion picture camera without actually being anything like one. Following is an examination of how 3D operates in After Effects and how the application's features—not only the camera, but also lights and shading options—correspond to real world counterparts.

See with the Camera

Toggle a layer to 3D and voila, its properties contain three axes instead of two—but enabling 3D without a camera is a little bit like racing a car with automatic transmission: You can't really maneuver, and before long you're bound to slam into something.

The Camera Settings dialog (**Figure 9.1**) uniquely includes a physical diagram that helps tell you what you need to know about how settings in the 3D camera affect your scene.

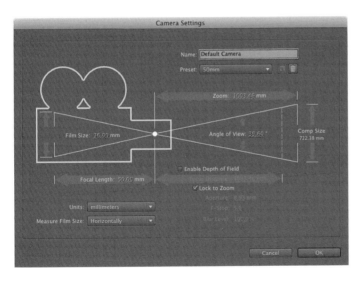

Figure 9.1 Artists love a visual UI, and the Camera Settings dialog provides one to help elucidate settings that might otherwise seem a bit abstract. The 50 mm preset selected in the Preset menu is the neutral (default) setting; use it when you want no change in perspective by the simple act of adding a camera.

Lens Settings

Although it is not labeled as such, and although After Effects displays previous camera settings by default, the true default lens preset in Camera Settings is 50 mm. This setting (**Figure 9.2**) is neither wide (as with lower values, **Figure 9.3**) nor long (as with higher values, **Figure 9.4**); and it introduces no shift in perspective.

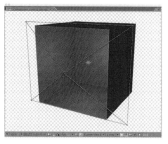  

Figure 9.2 The default lens (50 mm setting). If the Z Position value is the exact inverse of the Zoom value, and all other settings are at the default, this is the view you get, and it matches the appearance of setting no After Effects camera whatsoever.

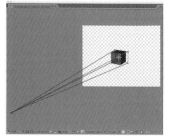 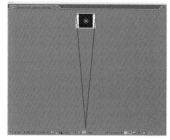 

Figure 9.3 The extreme wide or *fisheye* lens pointed inside an evenly proportioned 3D box. Note that the "long" look of the box is created by this "wide" lens, which tends to create very strange proportions at this extreme. A physical lens with anything like this angle would include extremely distorted lens curvature.

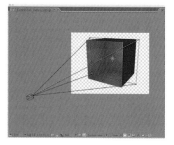 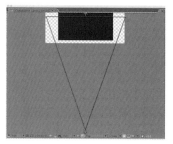 

Figure 9.4 A telephoto lens (using the 200 mm setting) pushes items together in depth space, shortening the distance between the front and back of the box dramatically.

"50 mm" is a virtually meaningless term because virtual space doesn't contain millimeters any more than it contains kilograms, parsecs, or bunny rabbits. This is the median lens length of a 35 mm SLR camera, the standard professional still image camera.

Motion picture cameras are not so standardized. The equivalent lens on a 35 mm film camera shooting Academy ratio itself has a 35 mm length. A miniDV camera, on the other hand, has a tiny neutral lens length of around 4 mm. The length corresponds directly to the size of the backplate or video pickup, the area where the image is projected inside the camera.

Lens length, then, is a somewhat arbitrary and made-up value in the virtual world of After Effects. The corresponding setting that applies universally is Angle of View, which can be calculated whether images were shot in IMAX or HDV or created in a 3D animation package.

Real Camera Settings

To understand the relationship of the After Effects camera to those of a real-world camera, look again at the Camera Settings diagram introduced in Figure 9.1. Four numerical fields—Film Size, Focal Length, Zoom, and Angle of View—surround a common hypotenuse.

A prime (or fixed) lens would have static values for all four. A zoom lens would of course work with a fixed Film Size, but would allow Zoom and Focal Length to be adjusted, changing the Angle of View. These four settings, then, are interrelated and interdependent, as the diagram implies, and the relationship is just the same as with a real camera, which the Film Size can even help emulate. Lengthen the lens by increasing Focal Length and you decrease Angle of View.

The settings you actually use are Zoom (to animate) and Angle of View (to match the real-world source).

Angle of View is the radius, in degrees, that fits in the view. If you're matching it, note that Camera Settings lets you specify a horizontal, vertical, or diagonal measurement in the Measure Film Size menu.

NOTES

A fifth numerical field in Camera Settings, Focus Distance, is enabled by checking Enable Depth of Field; it corresponds to a camera's aperture setting.

273

In After Effects, the Zoom value is the distance of the camera, in pixels, from the plane of focus. Create a camera and its default Z Position is the inverse of the Zoom value, perfectly framing the contents of the comp at their default Z Position, 0.0 (**Figure 9.5**). This makes for easy reference when you're measuring depth of field effects, and it lets you link camera position and zoom together via expressions (for depth of field and multiplane effects, discussed later).

Figure 9.5 Comp Size (at the right) is the frame size, in pixels. The diagram shows it as vertical (right), but here it is measured horizontally according to Measure Film Size (left). Units can be inches or millimeters, helpful when matching a physical camera (described later in this chapter).

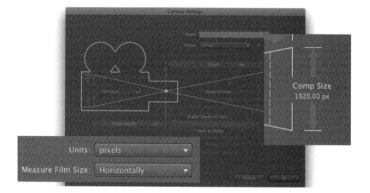

Emulate a Real Camera

Other considerations when matching a real-world camera include

▶ **Depth of field:** This is among the most filmic and evocative additions you can make to a scene. Like any computer graphics program, After Effects naturally has limitless depth of field, so you have to re-create the shallow depth of real-world optics to bring a filmic look to a comp.

▶ **Zoom or push:** A move in or out is used for dramatic effect, but a zoom and a push communicate very different things about point of view.

▶ **Motion blur and shutter angle:** These are composition (not camera) settings; introduced in Chapter 2 and further explored here.

▶ **Lens angle:** The perspective and parallax of layers in 3D space change according to the angle of the lens used to view them.

- ▶ **Lens distortion:** Real lenses introduce curvature to straight lines, which is most apparent with wide-angle or "fisheye" lenses. An After Effects camera has no lens, hence, no distortion, but it can be created or removed (see the section "Lens Distortion").

- ▶ **Exposure:** Every viewer in After Effects includes an Exposure control (Aperture icon, lower right); this (along with the effect with the same name) is mathematically similar but different in practice from the aperture of a physical camera. Exposure and color range is detailed in Chapter 11.

- ▶ **Boke, halation, flares:** All sorts of interesting phenomena are generated by light when it interacts with the lens itself. The appeal of this purely optical phenomenon in a shot is subjective, yet they can offer a unique and beautiful aesthetic and lend realism to a scene shot under conditions where we would expect to see them (whether we know it or not).

A *camera report* is a record of the settings used when the footage was taken, usually logged by the camera assistant (or equivalent).

The Camera Report

With accurate information on the type of camera and the focal length of a shot, you know enough to match the lens of that camera with your After Effects camera.

Table 9.1 on the next page details the sizes of some typical film formats. If your particular brand and make of camera is on the list, and you know the focal length, use these to match the camera via Camera Settings. The steps are

1. Set Measure Film Size to Horizontally. (Note that hFilmPlane stands for "Horizontal Film Plane.")

2. Set Units to Inches.

3. Enter the number from the Horizontal column of the chart that corresponds to the source film format.

4. Set Units to Millimeters.

5. Enter the desired Focal Length.

TIP

A potentially easier alternative to the listed steps, for those who like using expressions, is to use the following expression on the camera's Zoom property:

```
FocalLength = 35 //
➥change to your value,
➥in mm
hFilmPlane = 24.892
➥//change to film size,
➥in mm (horizontal);
➥multiply values in
➥inches by 25.4
this_comp.width*(Focal
➥Length/hFilmPlane)
```

TABLE 9.1 Typical Film Format Sizes

FORMAT	HORIZONTAL	VERTICAL
Full Aperture Camera Aperture	0.980	0.735
Scope Camera Aperture	0.864	0.732
Scope Scan	0.825	0.735
2:1 Scope Projector Aperture	0.838	0.700
Academy Camera Aperture	0.864	0.630
Academy Projector Aperture	0.825	0.602
1.66 Projector Aperture	0.825	0.497
1.85 Projector Aperture	0.825	0.446
VistaVision Aperture	0.991	1.485
VistaVision Scan	0.980	1.470
16 mm Camera Aperture	0.404	0.295
Super-16 Camera Aperture	0.493	0.292
HD Full 1.78	0.378	0.212 (Full Aperture in HD 1.78)
HD 90% 1.78	0.340	0.191 (90% Safe Area used in HD 1.78)
HD Full 1.85	0.378	0.204 (Full Aperture in HD 1.85)
HD 90% 1.85	0.340	0.184 (90% Safe Area used in HD 1.85)
HD Full 2.39	0.3775	0.158 (Full Aperture in HD 2.39)
HD 90% 2.39	0.340	0.142 (90% Safe Area used in HD 2.39)
RED One Mysterium	0.960	0.539

Courtesy of Stu Maschwitz The Orphanage

Once the Angle of View matches the footage, any objects that you track in (perhaps using techniques described in Chapter 8) maintain position in the scene as the shot progresses. It's vital to get this right when the camera moves during the shot, especially if a particularly wide or long lens was used.

Lens Distortion

A virtual camera with a wide-angle view (like the one back in Figure 9.2) has a dramatically altered 3D perspective, but it has no lens to distort objects the way a real camera lens does. A virtual camera can widen the view area in a completely linear fashion.

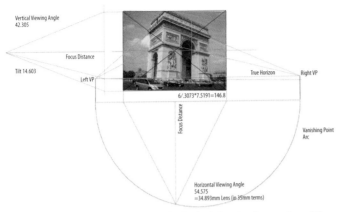

NOTES

If you're lacking Angle of View data from a shoot, it can be cleverly derived (**Figure 9.6**).

Figure 9.6 This diagram shows the result of calculating the view angle and thus the lens length used to take this shot. Check out the 12-minute video description by Mike Seymour of how this was done (on the book's disc). Image and video excerpted from the Background Fundamentals course at fxphd.com.

A physical lens curves light to project it properly across the camera backplate with physical width and height, no matter how small. To show up properly the reflected imagery must be perpendicular to the surface of the lens glass, so a wide-angle view requires not only a short lens length but also a convex lens in order to gather the full range of view.

At the extremes, this causes easily visible lens distortion; items in the scene known to contain straight lines don't appear straight at all, but bent in a curve (**Figure 9.7**). In a fisheye lens shot, it's as if the screen has been inflated like a balloon.

Figure 9.7 The nearly psychedelic look of extreme lens distortion; the lens flare itself is extremely aberrated. You can create just as wide a lens with the 3D camera, but there would be no lens distortion because there is no lens.

Figure 9.8 It is simply not possible to make all four corners and edges of a yellow solid line up properly with the side of a distorted building.

Figure 9.9 Optics compensation takes place in a composition larger than the source; the padding gives the corners of the image space. The Beam effect can serve as a virtual plumb line, or you can use **Ctrl/Command+"** to superimpose a grid.

As you refine your eye, you may notice that many shots that aren't as extreme as a fisheye perspective contain a degree of lens distortion. Or you might find that motion tracks match on one side of the frame but slip on the opposite side, or proportions go out of whack, or things just don't quite line up as they should (**Figure 9.8**).

There's no way to introduce lens distortion directly to a 3D camera, but the Optics Compensation effect is designed to add or remove it directly on the 2D layer or stack. **Figure 9.9** shows this effect in action. Increasing the Field of View makes the affected layer more fish-eyed in appearance; to correct a shot coming in with lens distortion, check Reverse Lens Distortion and raise the Field of View (FOV) value.

This process is not exactly scientific. You typically eye-match the setting, because Field of View doesn't correspond to measurable data in the camera report, such as the Lens Angle.

1. Having identified lens distortion (Figure 9.8), precomp the background into a new composition that is at least 20% larger than the plate (to allow room at the borders to distort).

2. Add an adjustment layer above the plate layer, and apply Optics Compensation to that layer. With a wide angle lens, check Reverse Lens Distortion and raise the Field of View (FOV) setting until all straight lines appear straight.

3. Add a Beam effect to the adjustment layer (below the Optics Compensation effect, unaffected by it). To get away from the distracting light saber look, match Inside Color and Outside Color to some easily visible hue, then align the Starting Point and Ending Point along an apparently straight line near the edge of the frame. Fine-tune the Field of View setting a little more until the line is plumb (Figure 9.9).

4. Precompose all of these layers and set this new composition as a guide layer. In **Figure 9.10**, you can see that the corner pin is now successful.

Figure 9.10 Over the undistorted background plate, you can freely position, animate, and composite elements as if everything were normal. Note that the perspective is still that of a very wide-angle lens, but without the curvature.

5. To complete the shot, restore the original field of view, including distortion. First create a new comp with the original background plate (no Optics Compensation) and the precomp with the assembled foreground elements.

6. Copy Optics Compensation with the settings added in step 2 and paste it to the foreground element. Toggle Reverse Lens Distortion off. The Field of View of the background is restored, but the foreground elements match (**Figure 9.11**).

Here is an original Stu Maschwitz haiku summing it up:

undistort, derive
reunite distorted things
with an untouched plate

Figure 9.11 The composited layer is distorted to match the curvature of the original background.

2D and 3D

The point of matching a 3D lens angle is typically to composite in 3D over a 2D plate background. After Effects helps this process in the following ways:

▶ A 2D background layer remains in place no matter what happens with the camera and 3D layers.

▶ 2D adjustment layers set to comp size and default position affect all layers below them, including 3D layers.

▶ 3D layers can use 2D Blending Modes (over 2D elements, they obey layer order, and with other 3D elements, z-space depth).

You just need to be careful:

▶ Joining a 3D track matte to a 3D layer is almost never the right idea, particularly with an animated camera. A 3D layer can use a 2D layer as a track matte; it is applied just as it would be to a 2D layer. A 2D layer can use a 3D layer as a track matte; the 3D perspective of the track matte renders first and is then applied. But combine two 3D layers in this manner and the matte is first translated by the camera perspective once, then applied, and then effectively translated again as the affected layer also obeys camera perspective.

▶ Paradoxically, the only layers in After Effects that themselves can contain true 3D effects are 2D layers (which may nonetheless make use of the 3D camera perspective, **Figure 9.12**).

Figure 9.12 Particles generated by Trapcode Particular fill the volume of 3D space, as is evident in a perspective view, although the effect is applied to a 2D layer.

▶ A precomped set of 3D layers behaves like a single 2D layer unless Collapse Transformations is enabled on that layer. As described back in Chapter 4, this toggle passes through all 3D data from the precomp as if those layers lived right in the master composition.

Each point provides advantages provided you understand how the image pipeline works.

Photoshop CS4 3D

One of the most intriguing new features of the CS4 version of Adobe software is the ability to bring 3D models into After Effects as Photoshop 3D layers. You might expect this feature to radically change what can be done with an After Effects 3D scene; however, there are many limitations to its use—enough, in fact that it may rarely be worth the trouble.

To really take advantage of using 3D models directly in After Effects, you would want them to preview quickly (perhaps using OpenGL), to allow fine tuning of lighting, texturing, anti-aliasing, and motion blur, not to mention animating or deforming the mesh itself. Instead

▸ You can control texture, lighting, and anti-aliasing only in Photoshop CS4.

▸ To adjust Photoshop-only features (even changing anti-aliasing from Draft quality so you can work quickly to Best quality for rendering) you must choose the image layer and use Edit Original (**Ctrl/Command+E**).

▸ After Effects lighting, material options, and motion blur have no effect.

Figure 9.13 shows a 3D model imported into After Effects; although the source Photoshop file has a single layer, the After Effects Comp contains three: a camera, a Controller layer, and the 3D image itself. You can replace or even eliminate the camera layer, but the other two must remain together or the layer becomes ordinary again, like Cinderella after midnight.

To transform the 3D object, you work with the controller layer, a null. You can apply any standard image effects to the layer that contains the image itself. More fundamental changes to the appearance of the model are hardly more convenient than if it were rendered in third-party software such as Maya; lighting and surface changes can only happen in Photoshop.

Figure 9.13 The Photoshop Import dialog has changed to accommodate Live Photoshop 3D layers; to get this option, import the PSD as a composition. The resulting comp contains a camera, the image and a controller layer; the image has a Live Photoshop 3D effect applied to it, which links it to the Controller via a set of expressions (in red).

The lack of motion blur seems like the main deal-killer; there are workarounds if you're willing to take the render hit. You can try adding an adjustment layer at the top of the comp containing your 3D animation and then

▶ Apply the Timewarp effect to that layer. Change speed to 100 and toggle Enable Motion Blur, then set the other Motion Blur settings to get the motion blur look you want.

▶ For a less render-intensive approach, you can try applying CC TimeBlend; it won't work with heavy motion and is a bit eccentric to preview (if it looks strange, try hitting the Clear button at the top of the effect and re-previewing).

These are the same workarounds you would use if for some reason your 3D render had no motion blur; it's a less accurate and, especially in the case of Timewarp, more render-intensive approach. More about using Timewarp to generate motion blur can be found in Chapter 2.

Storytelling and the Camera

Locked-off shots are essential to signature shots by Welles, Hitchcock, Kubrick, and Lucas, among others, but they're the exception, not the norm. In contemporary films in particular, the camera point of view often implies a human point of view, hence the popularity of the hand-held shot since the 1970s.

In the bad old days of optical compositing, it was scarcely possible to composite anything but a static camera point of view. Nowadays, most directors aren't satisfied being limited to locked-off shots, yet the decision to move the camera might not happen on set, or it might have to be altered in post-production.

It's helpful to create a rough assemble with camera animation as early in the process of creating your shot as possible, because it will tell you a lot about what you can get away with and what needs dedicated attention. The "Sky Replacement" section in Chapter 13 contains an example in which a flat card stands in for a fully dimensional skyline

TIP

Always keep in mind where the audience's attention is focused—a successful visual effects artist employs the magician's technique, misdirection, all the time.

(**Figure 9.14**). The audience should instead be focused on watching the lead character walk through the lobby, wondering what he has in his briefcase; if not, the film has more problems than can be fixed with more elaborate visual effects elements.

Figure 9.14 Prominent though it may appear in this still image, the audience isn't focused on that San Francisco skyline outside the window. There's no multiplaning as the camera moves because the background skyline is a still image; no one notices because viewer attention is on the foreground character. (Image courtesy of The Orphanage.)

Camera Animation

The most common confusion about the After Effects camera stems from the fact that by default, it includes a *point of interest*, a point in 3D space at which the camera always points, for auto-orientation. The point of interest is *fully optional*, yet the setting is among the least discoverable in After Effects. To clarify

Figure 9.15 So many After Effects 3D camera tragedies could have been avoided had only more users known about this dialog box (**Ctrl+Alt+O/ Cmd+Option+O**). By disabling auto-orientation, you are free to move the camera anywhere without changing its direction.

▶ Layer > Transform > Auto-Orient (**Ctrl+Alt+O/ Cmd+Option+O**) contains the toggles to disable auto-orientation and the point of interest (making the camera a *free* camera, **Figure 9.15**).

▶ In that same dialog, you can instead orient the camera along its path of camera motion so that its rotation maintains tangency; in other words, it follows the path.

▶ You might want to use the point of interest but transform it and the camera together. To do this, don't attempt to match keyframes for the two properties— this is sheer madness! Parent the camera to a null and translate that instead.

TIP

The new Unified Camera Tool (**C**) lets you use a three-button mouse to orbit, track, and zoom the camera without having to cycle through the tools.

▶ Orientation works differently depending on whether auto-orientation is on (causing it to revolve around the point of interest) or not (in which case it rotates around its own center).

▶ The auto-oriented camera always maintains an upright position; cross over the X/Y plane above the center and the camera flips. To avoid this behavior, use a free camera.

The Y axis is upside down in After Effects 3D, just as in 2D; an increased Y value moves a layer downward.

The preceding points come into play only with more elaborate camera animations; more modest use of the 3D camera, such as a simple camera push, raises other questions.

Push and Zoom

A camera *push* moves the camera closer to the subject; a *zoom* lengthens the lens while the camera remains stationary. **Figure 9.16** demonstrates the difference in perspective, which is just as noticeable with multiple 3D elements in After Effects as with objects in the real world. The zoom has a more extreme effect on the foreground/background composition of the shot and calls more attention to the camera itself.

Figure 9.16 Frame a similar shot with a long (left) and wide (right) lens and you see the difference between a zoom and a push. A zoomed image has a flattened perspective.

Dramatic zooms for the most part had their heyday in 1960's-era Sergio Leone movies, although they have recurred any time a filmmaker wants the live feel of a camera operator reaching quickly for a shot. And that's really the point; because your eye does not zoom, this move calls attention to the camera apparatus itself, and to the camera operator. Its use is therefore limited.

The push, on the other hand, is a dramatic staple. The question when creating one in After Effects is, does it require a 3D camera when you can simply scale 2D layers?

Scaling a 2D layer (or several, parented to a null) works for a small move; however, to re-create progression through Z space, the rate of scaling must increase logarithmically, which complicates things. Not only does a 3D camera move create this effect naturally, it makes it simple to add eases, stops, and starts, a little bit of destabilization—whatever works.

Natural camera motion will contain keyframe eases (Chapter 2), for the human aspect. A little bit of irregularity lends the feeling of a camera operator's individual personality (**Figure 9.17**), or even dramatic interest (hesitation, caution, intrigue, a leap forward—the possibilities are many).

NOTES

Animation > Keyframe Assistant > Exponential Scale is the old-school, pre-3D way to fake the illusion of a camera move on a 2D layer. There is no good reason to employ this feature when you can instead animate a 3D camera.

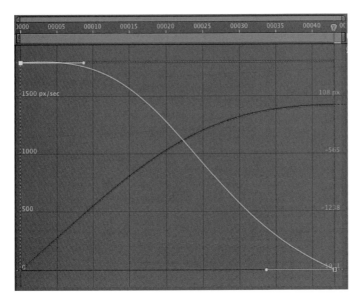

Figure 9.17 The Graph Editor shows where you've created organic motion in ease curves, although the smoothness of this camera push as it eases to a stop may itself lack that extra human imperfection, which would also show up in the curves.

A move in or out of a completely 2D shot can easily look wrong due to the lack of parallax. Likewise, all but the subtlest tracking and panning shots, crane-ups, and other more elaborate camera moves will blow the 2.5D gag, so if you do them, that had better be your intention.

TIP

Do you have a bunch of coplanar layers you're making 3D just so you can push in on them? Precomp them together first to avoid little rounding errors that can easily occur where they overlap in 3D.

Certain types of elements—soft, translucent organic shapes, such as clouds, fog, smoke, and the like—can be layered together and staggered in 3D space, fooling the eye into seeing 3D volume. Chapter 13 shows how to do this.

Camera Projection

Camera projection (or *camera mapping*) typically begins with a still photo, which is then projected onto 3D objects that match the dimensions and placement of objects in the photo. You can then move the 3D camera—typically only along the Z axis—providing the illusion that the photo is fully dimensional (right up until things start to tear and break as areas and perspectives that aren't there are revealed).

Figure 9.18 shows a camera projection that ambitiously features two military vehicles parked in the foreground. A dozen separate white solids with masks were created to form a crude 3D model, ready to receive a projected image (**Figure 9.19**). This example shows both the magic of this technique—deriving perspective shifts from a flat, still image—and the associated problems of image tearing when an area of the frame is revealed that had previously been obscured in the source photo.

The setup is key: How is it that the one "texture" (the photo) sticks to the 3D objects? The fundamental concept is actually relatively simple; it's a virtual version of a slide projector and a bunch of angled screens. Getting the setup right is a question of managing details, and that part is fairly advanced and not for the faint of heart (which is why mention of a third-party option follows this description). The steps to projecting any still image into 3D space (an example of which, 09_cameraProjection.aep, can be found on this book's disc) are as follows:

1. Begin with an image that can be modeled as a series of planes.

2. Create a white solid for each dimensional plane in the image. Enable 3D for each, and under Material Options, change the Accepts Lights option to Off.

Figure 9.18 The progression from the source image (left) through the camera move. By the final frame (right), image warping and tearing are evident, but the perspective of the image is essentially correct for the new camera position. The tearing occurs simply because as the camera moves it reveals areas of the image that don't exist in the source.

3. Add a camera named Projection Cam; if you know the Angle of View of your source image, add that value.

4. Add a Point light called Projector Light. Set its position to that of Projection Cam, then parent it to Projection Cam. Set Casts Shadows to On.

5. Duplicate the source image, naming this layer Slide. Enable 3D, and in Material Options, change Casts Shadows to Only and Light Transmission to 100%.

6. Slide not located properly? Add a null object called Slide Repo; set its position to that of Projection Cam, and parent it to Projection Cam. Now parent Slide to it, and adjust its scale downward until the image is cast onto the white planes, as if projected.

7. Now comes the challenge: masking, scaling, and repositioning those white solids to build the model, ground plane, and horizon onto which the slide is projected. Toggle on the reference layer and build your model to match that, checking it with the slide every so often.

8. If planes that you know to be at perpendicular 90 degree angles don't line up, you need to adjust the Zoom value of the Projection Cam, scaling the model and slide as needed to match the new Zoom value. The example file includes an expression applied to the Scale value of the Slide layer so that the slide scales up or down to match however you adjust the Zoom of the camera, which is not necessary but is helpful.

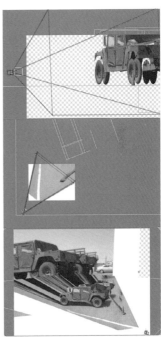

Figure 9.19 This shows the rather complicated setup for this effect, now aided by a script on this book's disc. From the top and side views you can see the planes that stand in for the vehicles and the orange cone, which appears stretched along the ground plane.

This edition of the book newly includes a script that Jeff Almasol and I designed to accomplish the basic camera projection setup automatically. You can find it on the disc.

9. Once everything is lined up, duplicate Projection Cam, and rename the duplicate (the one on the higher layer) Anim Cam. Freely move this camera to take advantage of the new dimensional reality of the scene.

10. To get everything looking sharp, go to Composition Settings > Advanced > and click Options; boost the Shadow Map Resolution from its default Comp Size to a higher number as needed (check the image at Full resolution to see if it becomes sharper). I tend to max out this setting and take the render hit.

The best way to learn about this is probably to study the example file included on this book's disc.

Camera Blur

Camera blur, also known as lens blur, results from objects in a scene falling outside focal range. It has unique characteristics when compared with an ordinary image blur operation.

Ironically, although the standard consumer video camera has a very wide depth of field and rarely produces lens blur, this is considered a major disadvantage of video to most filmmakers. Narrow focal depth not only produces a beautiful image one would almost automatically call "cinematic," it focuses the viewer's attention and thus provides the director with a powerful storytelling tool.

It can be a lot of work to re-create depth of field effects in After Effects; it's better to get them in camera if possible. Nonetheless you can create specific cinematic blur effects such as a *rack focus* shot, in which the plane of focus shifts from a subject at one distance to another. This is a device to create anticipation and change the object of attention while creating a beautiful aesthetic.

Limited focal range is a natural part of human vision, but camera lenses contribute their own unique blur characteristics that in the contemporary era are often considered aesthetically pleasing the world over. There is even a Japanese term (literally meaning "fuzzy") to describe the quality of out-of-focus light as viewed through a lens, *boke* (also *bokeh*, more phonetic but clunkier).

You can create these effects and more in After Effects, using a combination of tools built in to the software, third-party tools to support the process, and a careful observation of optics and nature.

Image Planes and Rack Focus

Any time you can divide a shot into distinct planes of depth with each plane as its own layer, you can rack focus. All you need is a focal point to animate and a depth of field narrow enough to create blur everywhere but the immediate plane of focus.

Narrow depth of field is created on a real camera by lowering the f-stop value, which lowers exposure as well. Not so with the After Effects 3D camera. Its Aperture and F-Stop settings (**Figure 9.20**) affect only focal depth, not exposure or motion blur. The two settings have an inverse relationship. F-Stop is the setting more commonly referenced by camera operators, and yet only Aperture appears as a property in the Timeline.

A solid description of boke with links lives on the Web at http://en.wikipedia.org/wiki/Bokeh.

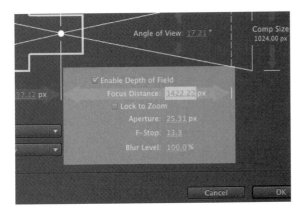

Figure 9.20 Check Enable Depth of Field in Camera Settings to activate Focus Distance (the distance in pixels of the focal point, which can be toggled to Lock to the Zoom). A low F-Stop (or high Aperture) with a Blur Level of 100% creates a shallow focal effect.

After Effects depth of field settings can be matched to a camera report, provided that it includes the f-stop setting used when the footage was shot. If so, open up the Camera Settings dialog (**Ctrl+Shift+Y/Cmd+Shift+Y**, or double-click on the Camera in the Timeline panel), check the box labeled Enable Depth of Field, and enter the value.

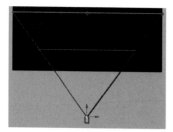

Figure 9.21 With Enable Depth of Field on, the Focus Distance is denoted by a red boundary line, easily viewed and animated in isometric views.

The key here is to offset at least one layer in Z space so that it falls out of focal range. Now, in the Top view, set the Focus Distance (under Options) to match the layer that will be in focus at the beginning of the shot, add a keyframe, then change the Focus Distance at another frame to match a second layer later in the shot (**Figure 9.21**).

A static focus pull doesn't look quite right; changing focus on a real camera will change the framing of the shot slightly. To sell the example shot, which starts on a view of the city and racks focus to reveal a sign in the foreground, I animate the camera pulling back slightly, augmented by a nice shift that then occurs in the offset planes of focus (**Figure 9.22**).

Figure 9.22 The final shot combines a rack focus with a gentle pull-back, using ease keyframes to animate Position and Focus Distance.

Boke Blur

Racking focus in this manner generates camera blur that is accurate relative to the plane of focus, but it does not truly create the look of a defocused lens, because the lens itself is a major participant in that look.

Boke connotes the phenomenon whereby points of light become discs of light (also called *circles of confusion*) that take on the character of the lens itself as they pass through the camera lens and aperture. Like lens flares (covered in Chapter 12) these are purely a phenomenon of the camera lens, not human vision; they can add beauty and suspense to a shot.

Illuminated out of focus elements in a shot are, after all, mysterious. Visual intrigue is created as the shot resolves in or out of a wash of color and light (**Figure 9.23**).

Figure 9.23 With shallow depth of field, highlights in the foreground retain blur even in a focused shot.

A perfect lens passes a defocused point of light to the back of the camera as a soft, spherical blur. A bright point remains bright, but is larger and softer. Ordinary blur of a low-dynamic-range image in 8 or 16 bit per channel color mode instead merely dims the highlights (**Figure 9.24**).

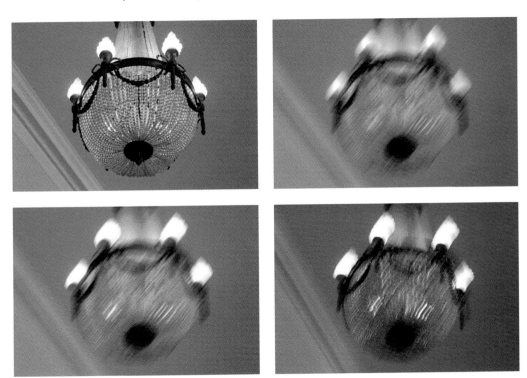

Figure 9.24 Begin with a source image that includes bright highlights (top left); blur it via conventional means and the result is gray and desaturated (top right), unless the source image is HDR and the comp is 32 bpc (bottom left), which approaches the look of real camera motion blur (bottom right).

Most camera lenses are not perfect, so instead of perfect blurred spheres, boke spheres may be brighter toward the edges than in the middle. An anamorphic lens will show squashed spheres, and as with lens flares, the shape of the aperture itself may be visible in the circles, making them hexagonal (or pentagonal, and so on, depending on the number of blades in the opening).

Go for Boke

To accurately create the bloom of highlights as they are blurred requires 32 bit per channel color and source highlights that are brighter than what would be called full white in 8 or 16 bpc. The process of creating such an image is explored and explained in Chapter 11.

The Lens Blur effect does not operate in 32 bpc—it instead mimics the behavior of bright highlights through a lens. It's more or less a direct port from Photoshop; as such, it can be slow and cumbersome in After Effects. It won't blur beyond 100 pixels, and the effect does not understand non-square pixels (it creates a perfect circle every time).

Instead of 3D camera or layer data, Lens Blur can use a Depth Map Layer, using pixel values (brightness) from a specified Depth Map Channel. You can rack focus by adjusting Blur Focal Distance. Iris Shape defines polygons around the highlights, corresponding to the number of blades in the iris; these can also have a specified Iris Blade Curvature and Iris Rotation (this rotates the polygon).

The actual amount of blur is determined by Iris Radius, the bloom by Specular Threshold (all pixels above this value are highlights) and Specular Brightness, which creates the simulation of highlight bloom. These are the controls you'll tweak most (**Figure 9.25**).

The Noise controls are designed to restore noise that would be removed by the blur operation; they don't relate to the blur itself and can be ignored in favor of grain techniques described in the following section.

NOTES

The most respected third-party tool for lens blurs is Frischluft's Lenscare. The default settings are not reliable, but with adjustments and depth maps (for 3D footage), you can derive some lovely results (you'll find Lenscare at www.frischluft.com and on the book's DVD).

Figure 9.25 The result of a Lens Blur effect (left) doesn't look so hot compared it to the real thing (center), while the Lens-care plug-in from Frischluft (right) is remarkably close. Sometimes the tools matter.

By no means do the settings in Lens Blur (or for that matter, third-party alternatives such as Lenscare from Frischluft) exhaust the possibilities for how defocused areas of an image might appear, especially when illuminated. Keep looking at the reference and thinking of ways to re-create what you see in it (**Figure 9.26**).

Figure 9.26 Does an image with shallow depth of field look more cinematic? What do you see happening in the defocused background?

The Role of Grain

Once the image passes through the lens and is recorded, it takes on another characteristic: grain. Grain is essentially high-frequency noise readily apparent in each channel of most recorded footage, although progress in image gathering technology has led to a gradual reduction of grain. Grain can, however, be your friend, adding life to static imagery and camouflaging edge detail.

Grain management is an essential part of creating high-quality moving images; properly done, it is not simply switched on or off, but requires careful per-channel adjustment. There are two basic factors to consider:

▶ Size of the grain, per channel

▶ Amount of grain, or amount of contrast in the grain, per channel

The emphasis here is that these factors typically vary from channel to channel. Blue is almost universally the channel likeliest to have the most noise; happily, the human eye is less sensitive to blue than red or green.

How much grain is enough? As with color in Chapter 5, the goal is typically to match what's there already. If your shot has a background plate with the proper amount of grain in it, match foreground elements to that. A computer-generated still or scene might have to be grain-matched to surrounding shots.

Grain Management Strategies

After Effects Professional includes a suite of three tools for automated grain sampling, grain reduction, and grain generation: Add Grain, Match Grain, and Remove Grain. Add Grain relies on your settings only, but Match Grain and Remove Grain can generate initial settings by sampling a source layer for grain patterns.

I often caution against the automated solution, but not in this case. Match Grain is not even appreciably slower with grain sampling than Add Grain, which does not sample but includes all of the same controls. Match Grain usually comes up with a good first pass at settings; it gets you 70–80% there and is just as adjustable thereafter. In either case

1. Look for a section of your source footage with a solid color area that stays in place for 10 to 20 frames. Most clips satisfy these criteria (and those that don't tend to allow less precision).

2. Zoom to 200% to 400% on the solid color area, and create a Region of Interest around it. Set the Work Area to the 10 or 20 frames with little or no motion.

NOTES

Excessive grain is often triggered by a low amount of scene light combined with a low-quality image-gathering medium, such as miniDV, whose CCD has poor light-gathering abilities.

Figure 9.27 Even without slamming the image it's clear that the added window looks too flat in this grainy scene, but doing so with the addition of a gradient gives you a clear target.

3. Add a solid small enough to occupy part of the Region of Interest. Apply a Ramp effect to the solid, and use the eyedropper tools to select the darkest and lightest pixels in the solid color area of the clip. The lack of grain detail in the foreground gradient should be clearly apparent (**Figure 9.27**).

4. Apply the Match Grain effect to the foreground solid. Choose the source footage layer in the Noise Source Layer menu. As soon as the effect finishes rendering a sample frame, you have a basis from which to begin fine-tuning. You can RAM Preview at this point to see how close a match you have. In most cases, you're not done yet.

5. Twirl down the Tweaking controls for Match Grain, and then twirl down Channel Intensities and Channel Size. You can save yourself a lot of time by doing most of your work here, channel by channel.

6. Activate the green channel only in the Composition panel (**Alt+1/Option+1**) and adjust the Green Intensity and Green Size values to match the foreground and background. Repeat this process for the green and blue channels (**Alt+2/Option+2** and **Alt+3/Option+3**). If you don't see much variation channel-to-channel, you can instead adjust overall Intensity and Size (**Figure 9.28**). RAM Preview the result.

7. Adjust Intensity, Size, or Softness controls under Tweaking according to what you see in the RAM Preview. You may also find it necessary to reduce Saturation under Color, particularly if your source is film rather than video.

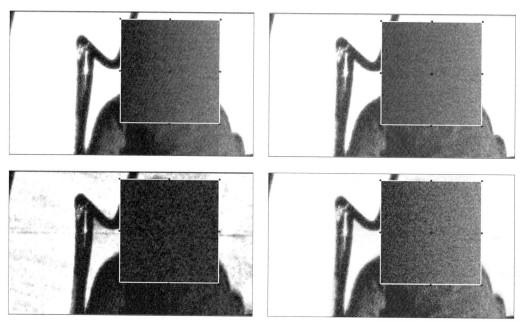

Figure 9.28 In this unusual case there is little variation of grain channel to channel, and the automatic match is pretty good; a slight boost to the overall Intensity setting under the "Tweaking" controls does the trick.

In most cases, these steps yield a workable result (**Figure 9.29**). The effect can then be copied and pasted to any foreground layers that need grain. If the foreground layer already contains noise or grain, you may need to adjust the Compensate for Existing Noise percentage for that layer.

Figure 9.29 Even in this printed figure the matching grain is somewhat evident. Grain matching is often best reviewed in motion with a boosted exposure.

Obviously, whole categories of controls within Match Grain remain untouched with this approach; the Application category, for example, contains controls for how the grain is blended and how it affects shadows, midtones, and highlights individually. These are typically overkill, as are the Sampling and Animation controls, but how far you go in matching grain before your eye is satisfied is, of course, up to you.

Grain Removal

Removing grain, or sharpening an image in general, is an entirely different process from adding grain. On a well-shot production, you'll rarely have a reason to reach for the Remove Grain tool.

If you do, the reason for doing so may be unique to your particular footage. In such cases, you may very well find that leaving Remove Grain at the default settings gives you a satisfactory result. If not, check into the Fine Tuning and Unsharp Mask settings to adjust it.

Use Noise as Grain

Prior to the addition of Add Grain and Match Grain to version 6.5 Professional, the typical way to generate grain was to use the Noise effect. The main advantage of the Noise effect over Match Grain is that it renders about 20 times faster. However, After Effects doesn't make it easy for you to separate the effect channel by channel, and scaling requires a separate effect (or precomping).

You can employ three solid layers, with three effects applied to each layer: Shift Channels, Noise, and Transform. You use Shift Channels to set each solid to red, green, or blue, respectively, set Blending Modes to Add, and set their Opacity very low (well below 10%, adjusting as needed). Next, set the amount of noise and scale it via the Transform effect.

If the grain is meant to affect a set of foreground layers only, hold them out from the background plate either via precomping or track mattes. If this sounds complicated, it is, which is why Match Grain is preferable unless the rendering time is really killer.

Remove Grain is often best employed stealthily—not necessarily across the entire frame (**Figure 9.30**), or as part of a series of effects. It is a reasonably sophisticated solution (compared with the current alternatives) that can really help in seemingly hopeless situations; this book's technical editor reports having used it extensively on a feature film in which the aging lead actor needed a lot of "aesthetic" facial work done (removing wrinkles and so on).

Figure 9.30 The left side of frame is clearly less grainy than the right as a result of applying Remove Grain and letting it automatically sample the footage.

TIP

If you're using Remove Grain to improve a blue-screen or green-screen key, consider applying the result as an alpha track matte. This offers the best of both worlds: a clean matte channel and preservation of realistic grain on the source color layer.

When to Manage Grain

The most obvious candidates for grain addition are computer-generated or still image layers that lack the moving grain found in film or video footage. As soon as your shot has to match anything that came from a camera, and particularly in a large format such as HD or film, you must manage grain.

Blurred elements may also need grain addition, even if they originate as source footage. Blurry source shots contain as much grain as focused ones because the grain is an artifact of the medium recording the image, not the subject itself. Elements that have been scaled down in After Effects contain scaled-down grain, which may require restoration. Color keying can also suppress grain in the channel that has been keyed out.

Other compositing operations will instead enhance grain. Sharpening, unless performed via Remove Grain, can strongly emphasize grain contrast in an element, typically in a not-so-desirable manner. Sharpening also brings out any nasty compression artifacts that come with footage that uses JPEG-type compression, such as miniDV video.

Lack of grain, however, is one of the big dead giveaways of a poorly composited shot. It is worth the effort to match the correct amount of grain into your shot even if the result isn't apparent as you preview it on your monitor.

Film and Video Looks

If you flipped to this section intentionally, you may be trying to do one of two things with a given shot or project:

▶ Achieve the look of a different camera

▶ Maximize the production value of your video to make it "filmic"

There are so many issues connected to the second one above and beyond what you can achieve in an After Effects comp that Stu Maschwitz went and wrote a whole book about it. *The DV Rebel's Guide: An All-Digital Approach to Making Killer Action Movies on the Cheap* (Peachpit Press, 2006) is an excellent resource, not only for After Effects knowledge, but for the whole process of low-budget digital filmmaking. The first chapter lists the major factors that influence production value. Many of these, including image and sound quality, location and lighting, cannot entirely be created in After Effects, which must be why Stu's book includes a bunch of information on how to actually shoot. Stu is also a big proponent of shallow depth of field as a necessary component of visual storytelling.

Achieving the look of a different camera is well within the realm of tricks you can pull off consistently in After Effects, and some of the following play into both developing a look and maximizing production value:

▶ **Lens artifacts:** In addition to those already discussed in this chapter, such as boke and chromatic aberration, are such filmic visual staples as the vignette and the lens flare.

Garbage In, Garbage Out

You don't need me to tell you how difficult it is to bring a poorly shot image back from the dead, but check *The DV Rebel's Guide* for a thorough rundown of factors that go into a well-shot image, and if possible go on set to offer supervision and help eliminate flaws that will be difficult to fix in post. Among the less obvious points from the book

▸ When shooting digitally, keep the contrast low and overall light levels well below maximum; you are shooting the negative, not the final (**Figure 9.31**).

▸ If using a small, light camera, mount it to something heavy to move it; that weight reads to the viewer as more expensive and more natural motion.

Figure 9.31 Shooting low-contrast (top) with a camera that has a healthy contrast range allows you to bring out hidden detail and color, even tone-mapping to do so only in specific areas of frame (bottom).

▸ **Frame rate:** Change this and you can profoundly alter the viewer's perception of footage.

▸ **Aspect ratio:** The format of the composition makes a huge perceptual difference as well, although it's not so simple as "wider = better."

▸ **Color palette:** Nothing affects the mood of a given shot like color and contrast. It's a complex subject further explored in Chapter 12.

Lens Artifacts Aren't Just Accidents

Because this chapter is all about reality as glimpsed by the camera lens, several types of lens artifacts, visual phenomena that occur only through a lens, have already appeared in this chapter, including lens distortion and lens blur (or boke).

You won't be surprised to hear that this isn't all: potentially in your palette are more phenomena of the type that professional cinematographers tended to avoid until the 1970s (when they started to be considered cool). These include lens flares, vignettes, and chromatic aberration. None of these occur with the naked eye, but remember, your target is the look of the real world as seen through the camera.

Lens Flares

Optical flares are caused by secondary reflections bouncing around between the camera elements. Because they occur within the lens, they appear superimposed over the image, even when partially occluded by objects in the foreground.

Unlike your eye, which has only one very flexible lens, camera lenses are made up of a series of inflexible lens elements; the longer the lens, the more elements within it. Each element is coated to prevent reflection under normal circumstances, but with enough light flooding directly in, reflection occurs.

Artists sometimes like to get goofy and creative with lens flares; how many of us, after all, are experts in how they should look? And yet this is one more area where seemingly unsophisticated viewers can smell something fake under their noses, so certain rules apply.

Zoom lenses contain many focusing elements and tend to generate a complex-looking flare with lots of individual reflections. Prime lenses generate fewer reflections and a simpler flare.

Just as with boke, aperture blades within the lens can contribute to the appearance of flares. Their highly reflective corners often result in streaks, the number corresponding to the number of blades. The shape of the flares sometimes corresponds to the shape of the aperture (a pentagon for a five-sided aperture, a hexagon for six). Dust and scratches on the lens also reflect light.

You can create a lens flare look by hand using solids and blending modes, but most people don't have the time for this. The Lens Flare effect that ships with After Effects is a rather paltry offering and includes little in the way of customization; you're best off with Knoll Light Factory, which is highly customizable and is derived from careful study of lens behaviors, although if you already own Tinderbox 2 from The Foundry, the T_LensFlare is still a vast improvement over the After Effects default.

More about the behavior and application of lens flares appears in Chapter 12.

Vignettes

Vignetting is a reduction in image brightness around the edges of an image. It's generally an undesired by-product of certain lenses (particularly wide-angle fisheyes), but it is sometimes deliberately chosen because of how it helps focus attention on the center of frame. I can say with authority that several underwater shots from *Pirates of the Caribbean: At World's End* contain vignettes, because I added them myself.

It's an easy effect to create:

1. Create a black solid the size of your frame as the top layer and name it Vignette.

2. Double-click the Ellipse tool in the toolbar; an elliptical mask fills the frame.

Figure 9.32 A vignette is created with a feathered mask applied to a solid (top). If the image is reframed for display in another format, such as anamorphic, you may have to use that framing instead of the source (bottom).

3. Highlight the layer in the Timeline and press **F** to reveal Mask Feather.

4. Increase the Mask Feather value a lot—somewhere in the triple digits is probably about right.

5. Lower the Opacity value (**T**) until the effect looks right; you might prefer a light vignette (10 to 15%) or something heavier (40 to 50%).

Note that the vignette is elliptical, not perfectly round, and if your project is to be seen in more than one format (see later in the chapter) you'll have to decide which is the target (**Figure 9.32**). There would be no reason for a realistic vignette to appear offset.

Chromatic Aberration

Even further down the road of questionably aesthetic visual phenomena is chromatic aberration, a fringing or smearing of light that occurs when a lens cannot focus various colors on the spectrum to a single point, because of the differing wavelengths. The effect is similar to that of light passing through a prism and dispersing into a rainbow of colors.

Like vignettes, and optically related to lens flares and boke, chromatic aberration is something higher-end lenses are designed to avoid, yet it can occur even under relatively expensive and high-end shooting circumstances, particularly if there is any type of lens conversion happening.

Unlike the others, it can really look like a mistake, so it's not the kind of thing you would probably add to a clip in order to make it look cool; instead you might add it to a shot or element to match another shot or background plate in which it appears. My recommendation in such a case?

1. Duplicate the layer twice and precompose all three.

2. Use the Shift Channels effect to leave only red, green or blue on for each layer (so you end up with one of each).

3. Set the top two layers to Add mode.

Figure 9.33 A simulation of chromatic aberration (right), the color ringing which is caused when different wavelengths of light have different focal lengths; most lenses correct for it with an added diffractive element.

4. Scale the green channel to roughly 101% and the blue channel to roughly 102%.

5. Add a small amount of Radial Blur (set to Zoom, not the default Spin).

A before and after comparison appears in **Figure 9.33**.

Frame Rate Isn't Just Speed

One could probably write a whole book or thesis on this one topic alone, but it's no accident that film images are displayed at 24 frames per second and that newer digital formats, which could theoretically be optimized for just about any frame rate, also aim for this rate (despite how difficult it is to find a low-end camera that shoots 24p natively, with no interlacing).

The question that would generate all of the chatter is "why?" There is no logical answer, and many attempts have been made to explore alternatives. The simple truth seems to be that frame rates of 30 fps and higher feel more like direct reality, but 24 fps is just above the threshold where persistence of vision breaks down, giving it a more ephemeral and dream-like quality, just as do other cinematic conventions such as light bloom and shallow depth of field.

If you have a choice on a given project and you want it to have a cinematic look, try creating it at 24 fps and judge for yourself. After Effects is quite forgiving about letting you change frame rates mid-stream compared with most video applications; details on how the conversion actually works appeared back in Chapter 2.

29.97 fps Videotape Never Took Over

The debate between using 24 fps film and 29.97 fps videotape in the U.S. and other countries with NTSC has been raging since long before the digital era. It began with the advent of videotape in the 1950s, when tape was cheap and fast, if cumbersome by today's standards.

One particular experiment from this era stands out. For six episodes, the producers of *The Twilight Zone* tried tape before they evidently realized it was ruining the show's mystique.

Video's higher frame rate and harder look instantly turned one of the most intriguing and ironic series of all time into something that looked more like a soap opera. To judge for yourself, rent DVDs from Season 2 that include the following videotaped episodes: "Static," "Night of the Meek," "The Lateness of the Hour," "The Whole Truth," "Twenty-Two," or "Long Distance Call."

Even though videotape was always much cheaper and more convenient than film, there seem to be dramatic reasons for why it never took over.

The numbers "1.85" and "2.35" give the width, relative to a height of 1, so it's like saying 1.85:1 or 2.35:1. The 16:9 format, which has become popular with digital video and HD, is equivalent to a 1.77:1 ratio, slightly narrower than Academy, but wide compared to the standard television format of 4:3 (1.33: 1).

If you have no choice but to work at 29.97 fps, you still have a choice: progressive versus interlaced. It's not necessarily an error to render animation without adding interlacing; in fact, step through your favorite animated series on television and you may find that it's animated at 15 fps or less (and basically never at 59.94 fps, which is effectively what 29.97 fps interlaced means in animation terms). *South Park* doesn't count.

Format Isn't Just Display Size

As the world transitions from standard-definition to high-definition broadcast television, formats are undergoing the same transition that they made in film half a century ago. The nearly square 4:3 aspect is being replaced as standard by the wider 16:9 format, but 1.85 Academy aperture and 2.35 Cinemascope also appear as common "widescreen" formats.

A lot of artists (students, particularly) fall in love with the widescreen look for how it conjures *Star Wars* and *Lawrence of Arabia*, but if these formats aren't shown at 24 fps and don't obey other cinematic conventions outlined here, the result tends to appear a bit cheesy. So remember, it's a convention we associate with film, whether or not we know the following history.

In response to the growing popularity of television in the 1950s, Hollywood conjured up a number of different widescreen formats through experiments with anamorphic lenses and film stocks as wide as 70 mm. These systems—CinemaScope, VistaVision, Panavision, and so on—haven't completely faded away, but their presence in the modern era is mostly felt in the way that films are displayed, not how they are shot. 35 mm is once again the most popular shooting format, specifically the full-aperture version known as Super 35 mm.

Standard 35 mm film has an aspect ratio of 4:3, which is not coincidentally the same as a television. Almost all current movies are filmed in this format as if originally intended for the small screen. When shown in a theater using a widescreen aspect of 1.85:1 (also known as 16:9, the HDTV standard) or 2.35:1 (CinemaScope/Panavision), the full 4:3 negative is cropped (**Figure 9.34**). Theater patrons actually pay $10 to see less than if they waited for the movie to get broadcast full screen on cable!

Less Color Can Be More

The influence of color decisions on the final shot, and by extension on the story being told in the shot, is an immense topic, hashed over by cinematographers and colorists the world over. Any attempt to distill this into a few pithy paragraphs would be a disservice.

One thing you may notice as you study your favorite films and videos is that they are limited to a distinct palette, and scenes that you would think of as "full color" may in fact be dominated by one, two or at most three basic hues.

Thus, if you're new to the idea of developing a color look for a film or sequence, look at references. Study other people's work for the effect of color on the mood and story in a shot, sequence, or entire film. There are also great color brainstorming tools such as the one shown in **Figure 9.35**, designed specifically to give a particular look or mood to your shot.

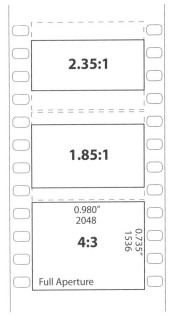

Figure 9.34 The "wider" film formats might more accurately be called "shorter" because they typically involve cropping the original 4:3 image.

Figure 9.35 Looks 3, from Red Giant Software, is both an After Effects plug-in and a stand-alone tool called Looks Builder. Not only does it have an innovative color pipeline based on real-world optics, it lets you window-shop through dozens of strong, preset looks (and create more of your own) so it's great for brainstorming.

Conclusion

And really, you've just scratched the surface of what's possible. The inventive compositor can and should always look for new methods to replicate the way that the camera sees the world, going beyond realism to present what we really want to see—realism as it looks through the lens.

10

Expressions

Dan Ebberts

Music is math.

—Michael Sandison and Marcus Eoin
(Boards of Canada)

Expressions

Expressions are very cool. You can use them to create amazing procedural effects that would otherwise be impossible (or at least impractical). You can also use them to create complex relationships between various parameters. Unfortunately, many After Effects users are afraid of expressions. Don't be.

The fact that you're reading this chapter indicates that you are at least curious about expressions. That's a good start. By the end of the chapter, you'll see how expressions can open new doors for you, and, hopefully, you'll have the confidence to give them a try.

The best way to learn about expressions is to examine working examples to figure out what makes them tick. The examples in this chapter focus on how you can use expressions to create or control effects.

As you work through the examples (don't be discouraged if you need a couple passes to understand it all), please keep in mind that I'm mainly a code guy—not a special effects or motion graphics artist. My examples may not be very visually impressive, but using these same techniques, I'm convinced that you'll be able to create your own dazzling effects.

What Expressions Are

The After Effects expression language is a powerful set of tools with which you can control the behavior of a layer's properties. Expressions can range in complexity from ridiculously simple to mind-numbingly complicated. At the simple end of the spectrum, you can use expressions to link one property to another or to set a property to a static value. At the other extreme, you can create complex linkages, manipulate time, perform calculations in 3D space, set up tricky procedural animations, and more.

Sometimes you'll use expressions instead of keyframes (most properties that can be keyframed can be controlled by expressions). In other cases you'll use expressions to augment the keyframed behavior. For example, you could use keyframes to move a layer along a specific path and then add an expression to add some randomness to the motion.

CLOSE-UP

Expressions Have Limitations

Although the After Effects expression language presents you with an impressive arsenal of powerful tools, it's important to understand the limitations of expressions so that you can avoid making assumptions that lead you astray.

▶ An expression may generally be applied only to a property that can be keyframed, and it can affect only the value of that property. That is, a expression can affect one, and only one thing: the value of the property to which it is applied. This means there are no global variables. This also means that although an expression has access to many composition and layer attributes (layer width and height, for example) as well as the values of other properties, it can only read, not change, them.

▶ Expressions can't create objects. For example, an expression cannot spawn a new layer, add an effect, create a paint stroke, change a blend mode—the list goes on and on. Remember, if you can't keyframe it, you can't create an expression for it.

▶ Expressions can't access information about individual mask vertexes.

▶ Expressions can't access text layer formatting attributes, such as font face, font size, leading, or even the height and width of the text itself.

▶ Expressions cannot access values they created on previous frames, which means expressions have no memory. If you've had a little Flash programming experience, you might expect to be able to increment a value at each frame. Nope. Even though you can access previous values of the property using valueAtTime(), what you get is the pre-expression value (the static value of the property plus the effect of any keyframes). It's as if the expression didn't exist. There is no way for an expression to communicate with itself from one frame to the next. Note, however, just to make things more confusing, the post-expression value of a property *is* available to any other expression, just not the one applied to that property. In fact, the post expression value is the *only* value available to expressions applied to other properties. To summarize: an expression has access only to the pre-expression value of the property to which it is applied, and it only has access to the post-expression values for other properties with expressions. It's confusing at first, but it sinks in eventually.

Creating Expressions

The easiest way to create an expression is to simply **Alt/Option**-click the stopwatch of the property where you want the expression to go. After Effects then creates a default expression, adds four new tool icons, changes the color of the property value to red (indicating that the value is determined by an expression), and leaves the expression text highlighted for editing (**Figure 10.1**).

Figure 10.1 When you create an expression, After Effects creates a default expression with the text highlighted for editing, changes the color of the property value to red, and adds four new tool icons: an enable/disable toggle, a Graph Editor toggle, a pickwhip, and an Expression Language menu fly-out.

At this point you have a number of options. You can simply start typing, and your text will replace the default expression. Note that while you're in edit mode, the **Enter/Return** key moves you to a new line in the expression (this is how you can create multiline expressions) and leaves you in edit mode.

Another option while the text is highlighted is to paste in the text of an expression that you have copied from a text editor. This is the method I generally use if I'm working on a multiline expression.

Instead of replacing all the default text by typing or pasting, you can click somewhere in the highlighted text to create an edit point for inserting additional text.

Alternatively, you can drag the expression's pickwhip to another property or object (the target can even be in another composition), and After Effects will insert the appropriate text when you let go. Note that if an object or property can be referenced using the pickwhip, a rounded rectangle appears around the name as you drag the pickwhip over it. If this doesn't happen, you won't be able to pickwhip it.

Finally, you can also use the Expression Language menu to insert various language elements.

After creating your expression, exit edit mode by clicking somewhere else in the Timeline or pressing **Enter** on the numeric keypad. If your expression text contains an error, After Effects displays an error message, disables the expression, and displays a little yellow warning icon (**Figure 10.2**). You can temporarily disable an expression by clicking on the enable/disable toggle.

Figure 10.2 If your expression contains an error, After Effects disables the expression, changes the enable/disable toggle to the disabled state, returns the Property value to its normal color, displays an error icon, and displays an error message dialog box.

Working with existing expressions is as easy as creating them. Some common operations are

▶ **Editing.** Click in the expression text area to select the entire expression; you now have the same options as when creating a new expression. If your expression consists of multiple lines, you may need to expand the expression editing area to be able to see all (or at least more) of it by positioning the cursor over the line below the expression text until you see a double-ended arrow and then clicking and dragging.

▶ **Deleting.** Simply **Alt/Option**-click the property's stopwatch, or you can delete all the text for the expression and press **Enter** on the numeric keypad.

▶ **Exposing.** Select a layer in the Timeline and press **EE** to expose any expressions applied to that layer.

▶ **Copying.** In the Timeline, select a layer property containing an expression and choose Edit > Copy Expression Only to copy just the property's expression. You now can select as many other layers as you'd like and Edit > Paste to paste the expression into the appropriate property of the other layers.

The Language of Expressions

The After Effects expression language is based on a subset of JavaScript. JavaScript is a scripting language used largely for web page design and includes many features specifically aimed at that task. The JavaScript implementation for expressions includes the core features only. That means there's a lot about JavaScript that you won't need to know, but it also means that any JavaScript reference you pick up (and you're going to need one if you really want to master expressions) is going to have a lot of content that will be of little or no use to you.

The rest of the expression language consists of extensions that Adobe has added specifically for After Effects. This means that in addition to a good JavaScript reference, you'll also be frequenting Adobe's *After Effects Expression Element Reference*. The most up-to-date version of this reference can be found at Adobe's Help on the Web. For machines with an Internet connection, the After Effects Help menu will take you there: Help > After Effects Help. Alternatively, you can go to www.adobe.com/go/learn_ae_cs4helphome.

This chapter focuses on working examples rather than the details of JavaScript. The book's disc, however, contains an abbreviated JavaScript guide, and I recommend that you glance through it before you really dive into the sample expressions discussed here. In addition, I'll point you to the appropriate sections of that guide as you encounter new JavaScript elements for the first time.

Linking an Effect Parameter to a Property

Here's the scenario: You want to link an effect to an audio track. Specifically, you want to link the Field Of View (FOV) parameter of the Optics Compensation effect to the amplitude of an audio layer. Expressions can't access audio levels directly, so first you have to use a keyframe assistant (Animation > Keyframe Assistant > Convert Audio to Keyframes) to create a null layer named Audio Amplitude with Slider Controls keyframed for the audio levels of the Left, Right, and Both channels (for a stereo source).

Next, you just **Alt/Option**-click the stopwatch for the FOV parameter of the Optics Compensation effect and drag the pickwhip to the Both Channels Slider property of the Audio Amplitude layer (**Figure 10.3**). Doing so generates this expression

```
thisComp.layer("Audio Amplitude").effect("Both
➥Channels")("Slider")
```

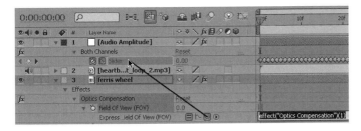

Figure 10.3 Select the Both Channels slider with the pickwhip to replace the highlighted default expression text.

Take a closer look at its syntax: From JavaScript, the After Effects expression language inherits a left-to-right "dot" notation used to separate objects and attributes in a hierarchy. If your expression references a property in a different layer, you first have to identify the composition. You can use `thisComp` if the other layer happens to be in the same composition (as in this example). Otherwise, you would use `comp("other comp name")`, with the other composition name in quotes. Next you identify the layer using `layer("layer name")` and finally, the property, such as `effect("effect name")("property name")` or possibly `transform.rotation`.

In addition to objects and properties, the dot notation hierarchy can include references to an object's attributes and methods. An attribute is just what you would guess: a property of an object, such as a layer's height or a composition's duration. In fact, in JavaScript documentation, attributes are actually referred to as properties, but in order to avoid confusion with the layer properties such as Position and Rotation (which existed long before expressions came along), in After Effects documentation (and here) they're referred to as attributes. For example, each layer has a height attribute that can be referenced this way:

```
comp("Comp 1").layer("Layer 1").height
```

Methods are a little harder to grasp. Just think of them as actions or functions associated with an object. You can tell the difference between attributes and methods by the parentheses that follow a method. The parentheses may enclose some comma-separated parameters.

It's important to note that you don't have to specify the full path in the dot notation hierarchy if you're referencing attributes or properties of the layer where the expression resides. If you leave out the comp and layer references, After Effects assumes you mean the layer with the expression. So, for example, if you specify only width, After Effects assumes you mean the width of the layer, not the width of the composition.

Let's forge ahead. You linked the amplitude of your audio layer to your effect parameter, but suppose you want to increase the effect that the audio level has on the parameter. You can use a little JavaScript math to multiply the value by some amount, like this

```
thisComp.layer("Audio Amplitude").effect("Both
↪Channels")("Slider") * 3
```

Towards the end of the chapter you'll see a much more complicated and powerful way of linking an effect to audio.

Using a Layer's Index

A layer's index attribute can be used as a simple, but powerful tool that allows you to create expressions that behave differently depending on where the layer is situated in the layer stack. The index attribute corresponds exactly to the number assigned to the layer in the Timeline window. So, the index for the layer at the top of the stack is 1, and so on.

Time Delay Based on Layer Index

Suppose you keyframed an animation for one layer. Now you want to create a bunch of identical layers, but you want their animations to be delayed by an amount that increases as you move down the layer stack. You also want to rotate each copy by an amount proportional to its position in the

NOTES

If you're not familiar with JavaScript arithmetic operators (such as the * for multiplication used in this example), you might want to take a look at the "Operators" section of the JavaScript guide.

layer stack. To do so, you first apply an expression like this to the top layer's animated properties

```
delay = 0.15;
valueAtTime(time - (index-1)*delay)
```

Then you apply an expression like this to the Rotation property:

```
offsetAngle = 3;
value +(index-1)*offsetAngle
```

Finally, duplicate the layer a bunch of times. The animation of each layer will lag behind the layer above it by 0.15 seconds and the rotation of each layer will be 3 degrees more than the layer above (**Figure 10.4**).

Figure 10.4 Notice how the blaster shot created by each layer lags that of the previous layer and is at a slightly different angle.

What's going on here? In the first expression, the first line defines a JavaScript variable named delay and sets its value to 0.15 seconds. The second line is where all the action is and it's packed with new things. For example, notice the use of time. It represents the current composition time, in seconds. In other words, time represents the time at which the expression is currently being evaluated.

NOTES

If you're not familiar with JavaScript variables, see the "Variables" section of the JavaScript guide on the accompanying disc.

You use `valueAtTime()` to access a property's pre-expression value at some time other than the current comp time (to access the pre-expression value at the current comp time, use `value()` instead, as in the Rotation expression). The parameter passed to `valueAtTime()` determines that time:

```
time - (index-1)*delay
```

Subtracting 1 from the layer's `index` and multiplying that result by the value of the `delay` variable (0.15) gives the total delay (in seconds) for this layer. Subtracting 1 from `index` means that the delay will be zero for the first layer. So, for Layer 1, the total delay is zero, for Layer 2 it is 0.15, for Layer 3 it is 0.30, and so on. You then subtract the total delay from the current comp `time`. The result of this is that Layer 1's animation runs as normal (not delayed). Layer 2's animation lags behind Layer 1 by 0.15 seconds, and so on.

The Rotation expression is very similar except that it doesn't reference `time`. The reason for this is that the first expression is used to offset a keyframed animation in time, while the second expression simply creates a static (not animated) offset for the Rotation property. The first line of the expression defines a variable named `offsetAngle`. This variable defines the rotation amount (in degrees) by which each layer will be offset from the layer above it. The second line tells After Effects to calculate the layer's offset and add it to the pre-expression `value` of the property.

You'll see other ways to use `index` in later examples.

Looping Keyframes

The expression language provides two convenient ways to loop a sequence of keyframes: `loopOut()` and `loopIn()`.

Suppose you keyframed a short animation and you want that sequence to repeat continuously. Simply add this expression to the keyframed property

```
loopOut("cycle")
```

and your animation will loop for the duration of the comp (**Figure 10.5**).

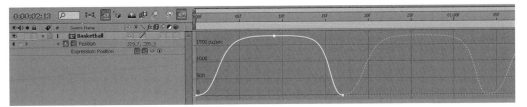

Figure 10.5 The solid line in the graph represents the keyframed bounce action. The dotted line represents the subsequent bounces created by `loopOut("cycle")`.

There are three other variations of `loopOut()`, as well:

▶ `loopOut("pingpong")` Runs your animation alternately forward then backward.

▶ `loopOut("continue")` Extrapolates the animation beyond the last keyframe, so the value of the property keeps moving at the same rate (and in the same direction, if you're animating a spatial property such as Position) as the last keyframe. This can be useful, for example, if you're tracking an object that has moved off screen and you want After Effects to extrapolate where it would be if it kept moving at the same speed and in the same direction.

▶ `loopOut("offset")` Works similarly to "cycle", except that instead of returning to the value of the first keyframe, each loop of the animation is offset by an amount equal to the value at the end of the previous loop. This produces a cumulative or stair-step effect.

`loopIn()` operates the same way as `loopOut()`, except that the looping occurs before the first keyframe instead of after the last keyframe. Both `loopIn()` and `loopOut()` will accept a second, optional parameter that specifies how many keyframes to loop. Actually, it's easier to think of it as how many keyframed segments to loop. For `loopOut()` the segments are counted from the last keyframe toward the layer's In point. For `loopIn()` the segments are counted from the first keyframe toward the layer's Out point. If you leave this parameter out (or specify it as 0), all keyframes are looped. For example, this variation loops the segment bounded by the last and next-to-last keyframes:

```
loopOut("cycle",1)
```

TIP

A small glitch in the `cycle` version of `loopOut()` drops the first keyframe from each of the loops. If you want the frame with the first keyframe to be included, add a duplicate of the first keyframe one frame beyond the last keyframe.

Two variations on the expressions—loopOutDuration() and loopInDuration()—enable you to specify the time (in seconds) as the second parameter instead of number of keyframed segments to be looped. For loopOutDuration(), the time is measured from the last keyframe toward the layer's In point. For loopInDuration(), the time is measured from the first keyframe toward the layer's Out point. For example, this expression loops the two-second interval prior to the last keyframe:

```
loopOutDuration("cycle",2)
```

If you leave out the second parameter (or specify it as 0), the entire interval between the layer's In point and the last keyframe will be looped for loopOutDuration(). For loopInDuration(), the interval from the first keyframe to the Out point will be looped.

Using Markers

The expression language gives you access to the attributes of layer (and composition) markers. This can be extremely useful for synchronizing or easily establishing timing relationships between animated events.

The marker attributes that appear most frequently in expressions are time and index. As you might guess, the time attribute represents the time (in seconds) where the marker is located on the Timeline. The index attribute represents the marker's order on the Timeline, where 1 represents the left-most marker. You can also retrieve the marker nearest to a time that you specify by using nearestKey(). For example, to access the layer marker nearest to the current comp time use

```
marker.nearestKey(time)
```

This can be handy, but more often you'll want to know the most recent previous marker. The code necessary to retrieve it looks like this

```
n = 0;
if (marker.numKeys > 0){
  n = marker.nearestKey(time).index;
  if (marker.key(n).time > time){
    n--;
  }
}
```

Note that this piece of code by itself is not very useful. When you do use it, you'll always combine it with additional code that makes it suitable for the particular property to which the expression will be applied. Because it's so versatile, and can show up in expressions for virtually any property, it's worth looking at in detail.

The first line creates a variable, n, and sets its value to 0. If the value is still 0 when the routine finishes, it means that at the current time no marker was reached or that there are no markers on this layer.

The next line, a JavaScript if statement, checks if the layer has at least one marker. If there are no layer markers, After Effects skips to the end of the routine with the variable n still set to 0. You need to make this test because the next line attempts to access the nearest marker with the statement

```
n = marker.nearestKey(time).index;
```

If After Effects attempted to execute this statement and there were no layer markers, it would generate an error and the expression would be disabled. It's best to defend against these kinds of errors so that you can apply the expression first and add the markers later if you want to.

If there is at least one layer marker, the third line of the expression sets n to the index of the nearest marker. Now all you have to do is determine if the nearest marker occurs before or after the current comp time with the statement

```
if (marker.key(n).time > time){
    n--;
}
```

NOTES

For more explanation of if statements, check out the "Conditionals" and "Comparison Operators" sections of the JavaScript guide.

NOTES

If you're wondering about the JavaScript decrement operator (--), it's described in the "Operators" section of the JavaScript guide.

This tells After Effects to decrement n by 1 if the nearest marker occurs later than the current time.

The result of all this is that the variable n contains the index of the most recent previous marker or 0 if no maker has yet been reached.

So how can you use this little routine? Consider a simple example.

Trigger Animation at Markers

Say you have a keyframed animation that you want to trigger at various times. All you need to do is drop a layer marker (just press * on the numeric keypad) wherever you want the action to be triggered. Then, apply this expression to the animated property:

```
n = 0;
if (marker.numKeys > 0){
  n = marker.nearestKey(time).index;
  if (marker.key(n).time > time){
    n--;
  }
}if (n == 0){
  valueAtTime(0);
}else{
  t = time - marker.key(n).time;
  valueAtTime(t)
}
```

As you can see, it's the previous marker routine with six new lines at the end. These lines tell After Effects to use the property's value from time 0 if there are no previous markers. Otherwise, variable t is defined to be the time since the most recent previous marker, and the value for that time is used.

The result of this is that the animation will run, beginning at frame zero, wherever there is a layer marker.

Play Only Frames with Markers

Suppose you want to achieve a stop motion animation effect by displaying only specific frames of your footage, say playing only the frames when your actor reaches the apex of a jump so he appears to fly or hover.

First enable time remapping for the layer, then scrub through the Timeline and drop a layer marker at each frame that you want to include. Finally, apply this expression to the Time Remap property:

```
n = marker.numKeys;
if (n > 0){
   f = timeToFrames(time);
   idx = Math.min(f + 1, n);
   marker.key(idx).time
}else{
   value
}
```

In this expression, the variable n stores the total number of markers for the layer. The if statement next checks whether there is at least one marker. If not, the else clause executes, instructing After Effects to run the clip at normal speed. If there are markers, the expression first calculates the current frame using timeToFrames(), which converts whatever time you pass to it into the appropriate frame number. Here, it receives the current comp time and returns the current frame number, which is stored in variable f.

Next you need to convert the current frame number to a corresponding marker index for the frame you actually want to display. It turns out that all you need to do is add 1. That means when the current frame is 0, you actually want to show the frame that is at marker 1. When frame is 1, you want to show the frame at marker 2, and so on. The line

```
idx = Math.min(f + 1, n);
```

calculates the marker index and stores it in the variable idx. Using Math.min() ensures the expression never tries to access more markers than there are (which would generate an error and disable the expression). Instead, playback freezes on the last frame that has a marker.

Finally, you use the idx variable to retrieve the time of the corresponding marker. This value becomes the result of

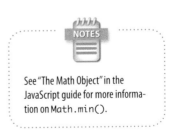

NOTES

See "The Math Object" in the JavaScript guide for more information on Math.min().

the expression, which causes After Effects to display the frame corresponding to the marker (**Figure 10.6**).

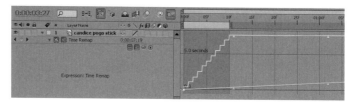

Figure 10.6 The bottom line in the graph represents how the Time Remap property would behave without the expression. As you would expect, it is a linear, gradual increase. The upper, stair-stepped line is the result of the expression. Because the expression only plays frames with markers (represented in the graph by small triangles) time advances much more quickly.

Time Remapping Expressions

There are many ways to create interesting effects with time remapping expressions. You've already seen one (the last expression in the previous section). Here are a few more illustrative examples.

Jittery Slow Motion

Here's an interesting slow motion effect where frames 0, 1, 2, and 3 play, followed by frames 1, 2, 3, and 4, then 2, 3, 4, and 5, and so on. First, enable time remapping for the layer and then apply this expression to the Time Remap property:

```
cycle = 4;
f = timeToFrames();
framesToTime(Math.floor(f/cycle) + f%cycle);
```

NOTES

For more detail on Math.floor() and the % modulo operator, see "The Math Object" and "Operators" sections of the JavaScript guide.

The first line sets the value of the variable cycle to the number of frames After Effects will display in succession (4 in this case). The second line sets variable f to the frame number corresponding to the current comp time. Next comes a tricky bit of math using JavaScript's Math.floor() method and its % modulo operator. The result is a repeating sequence (whose length is determined by the variable cycle) where the starting frame number increases by 1 for each cycle.

Wiggle Time

This effect uses multiple copies of the same footage to achieve a somewhat creepy echo effect. This effect actually involves three short expressions: one for Time Remap, one for Opacity, and one for Audio Levels. First, you enable time remapping for the layer. Then apply the three expressions and duplicate the layer as many times as necessary to create the look you want (**Figure 10.7**).

Figure 10.7 The time-wiggling effect with multiple layers.

Note that this time-wiggling effect is interesting, even with a single layer. The Opacity and Audio Levels expressions are necessary only if you want to duplicate the layer.

The expression for the Time Remap property is

```
Math.abs(wiggle(1,1))
```

`wiggle()` is an extremely useful tool that can introduce a smooth or fairly frenetic randomness into any animation, depending on your preference. `wiggle()` accepts five parameters, but only `frequency` and `amplitude` are required. Check the After Effects documentation for an explanation of what the remaining three optional parameters do.

The first parameter, `frequency`, represents the frequency of the wiggle in seconds; `wiggle(1,1)` varies the playback speed at the rate of once per second. The second parameter is the amplitude of the wiggle, given in the units of the parameter to which `wiggle()` is applied, which in this case is also seconds. So, `wiggle(1,1)` lets the playback time deviate from the actual comp time by as much as one second in either direction.

You use `Math.abs()` to make sure that the wiggled time value never becomes less than zero, which would cause the layer to sit at frame zero.

The Opacity expression gives equal visibility to each layer. Here's what it looks like:

```
(index/thisComp.numLayers)*100
```

This is simply the ratio of the layer's index divided by the total number of layers in the comp, times 100%. That means if you duplicate the layer four times (for a total of five layers), the top layer will have an Opacity of 20%, the second layer will have an Opacity of 40%, and so on, until the bottom (fifth) layer, which will have an Opacity of 100%. This allows each layer to contribute equally to the final result.

If the footage has audio, you have a couple of choices. You can turn the audio off for all but one of the layers, or you can use an expression for Audio Levels that normalizes them so that the combined total audio level is roughly the same as it would be for a single layer. I think the second option enhances the creepiness of the effect; here's the Audio Levels expression for a stereo audio source (for a mono source you could just leave out the second line of the expression):

```
db = -10*Math.log(thisComp.numLayers)/Math.log(10);
[db,db]
```

This is just a little decibel math that reduces the level of each layer based on how many total layers there are (using the comp attribute `numLayers`). You'll also notice a couple of JavaScript elements you haven't encountered before: `Math.Log()` and an array (the second line of the

NOTES

For more detail on `Math.abs()`, see "The Math Object" section of the online JavaScript guide.

expression). In expressions, you specify and reference the value of a multidimensional property, such as both channels of the stereo audio level, using array square bracket syntax.

Random Time

In this example, instead of having the time of each layer wander around, the expression offsets each layer's playback time by a random amount. The expression you need for the Time Remap property is

```
maxOffset = 0.7;
seedRandom(index, true);
time + random(maxOffset);
```

The first thing to notice about this expression is the use of `seedRandom()` and `random()` and the relationship between these functions. If you use `random()` by itself, you get a different random number at each frame, which is usually not what you want. The solution is `seedRandom()`, which takes two parameters. The first is the seed. It controls which random numbers get generated by `random()`. If you specify only this parameter, you will have different random numbers on each frame, but they are an entirely new sequence of numbers. It's the second parameter of `seedRandom()` that enables you to slow things down. Specifying this parameter as `true` tells After Effects to generate the same random numbers on each frame. The default value is `false`, so if you don't specify this parameter at all, you get different numbers on each frame. It's important to note that `seedRandom()` doesn't generate anything by itself. It just defines the subsequent behavior of `random()`.

Here's an example. This Position expression randomly moves a layer to a new location in the comp on each frame:

```
random([thisComp.width,thisComp.height])
```

This variation causes the layer to stay in one random location:

```
seedRandom(1,true);
random([thisComp.width,thisComp.height])
```

NOTES

For more information on `Math.log()` see the "Math Object" section of the JavaScript guide on the accompanying disc; for more on arrays see the "Arrays" section.

This version is the same as the previous one, except that it generates a different, single random location because the value of the seed is different:

```
seedRandom(2,true);
random([thisComp.width,thisComp.height])
```

Let's get back to the Time Remap expression. The first line creates the variable maxOffset and sets it to the maximum value, in seconds, that each layer's playback time can deviate from the actual comp time. The maximum for the example is 0.7 seconds.

The next line tells After Effects that you want the random number generator (random()) to generate the same random number on each frame.

The last line of the expression calculates the final Time Remap value, which is just the sum of the current comp time plus a random offset between 0 and 0.7 seconds.

Next, you would apply the Opacity and Audio Levels expressions from the wiggle() example so that each layer's video and audio will be weighted equally. Duplicate the layer as many times as necessary to get the effect you like.

Layer Space Transforms

In the world of expressions, layer space transforms are indispensible, but they present some of the most difficult concepts to grasp. There are three coordinate systems in After Effects, and layer space transforms provide you with the tools you need to translate locations from one coordinate system to another.

One coordinate system represents a *layer's own space*. This is the coordinate system relative (usually) to the layer's upper-left corner. In this coordinate system [0, 0] represents a layer's upper-left corner, [width, height] represents the lower-right corner, and [width, height]/2 represents the center of the layer. Note that unless you move a layer's anchor point, it too will usually represent the center of the layer in the layer's coordinate system.

More About random()

There are several ways to use random(). If you call it with no parameters, it will generate a random number between 0 and 1. If you provide a single parameter (as in the Random Time example), it will generate a random number between 0 and the value of the parameter. If you provide two parameters, separated by a comma, it will generate a random number between those two parameters. It's important to note that the parameters can be arrays instead of numbers. For example, this expression will give you a random 2D position somewhere within the comp:

```
random ([thisComp.width,
➥thisComp.height])
```

In addition to random(), After Effects provides gaussRandom(), which operates in much the same way as random() except that the results have more of a Gaussian distribution to them. That is, more values are clustered toward the center of the range, with fewer at the extremities. Another difference is that with gaussRandom(), sometimes the values may actually be slightly outside the specified range, which never happens with random().

The second coordinate system represents *world space*. World coordinates are relative to [0, 0, 0] of the composition. This starts out at the upper-left corner of a newly created composition, but it can end up anywhere relative to the comp view if the comp has a camera and the camera has been moved, rotated, or zoomed.

The last coordinate system represents *comp space*. In this coordinate system, [0, 0] represents the upper-left corner of the camera view (or the default comp view if there is no camera), no matter where the camera is located or how it is oriented. In this coordinate system, the lower-right corner of the camera view is given by [thisComp.width, thisComp.height]. In comp space, the Z coordinate really doesn't have much meaning because you're only concerned with the flat representation of the camera view (**Figure 10.8**).

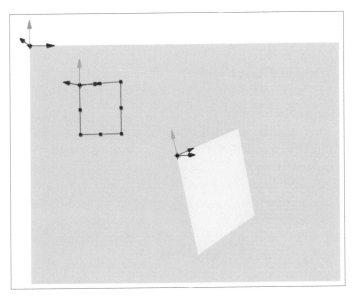

Figure 10.8 This illustration shows the three coordinate systems of After Effects. Positions in the yellow layer's coordinate system are measured relative to its upper-left corner. The 3D null is positioned at [0,0,0] in the comp so that it shows the reference point of the world coordinate system (which, in this case is exactly the same as the null's layer coordinate system). The comp's coordinate system is always referenced to the upper-left corner of the Comp view, which in this case no longer matches the world coordinate system because the camera has been moved and rotated.

So when would you use layer space transforms? One of the most common uses is probably to provide the world coordinates of a layer that is the child of another layer. When you make a layer the child of another layer, the child layer's Position value changes from the world space coordinate system to layer space of the parent layer. That is, the child layer's Position becomes the distance of its anchor point from the parent layer's upper-left corner. So a child layer's Position is no longer a reliable indicator of where the layer is in world space. For example, if you want another layer to track a layer that happens to be a child, you need to translate the child layer's position to world coordinates. Another common application of layer space transforms allows you to apply an effect to a 2D layer at a point that corresponds to where a 3D layer appears in the comp view. Both of these applications will be demonstrated in the following examples.

Effect Tracks Parented Layer

To start, consider a relatively simple example: You have a layer named star that's the child of another layer, and you want to rotate the parent, causing the child to orbit the parent. You have applied CC Particle Systems II to a comp-sized layer and you want the Producer Position of the particle system to track the comp position of the child layer. The expression you need to do all this is

```
L = thisComp.layer("star");
L.toComp(L.transform.anchorPoint)
```

The first line is a little trick I like to use to make the following lines shorter and easier to manage. It creates a variable L and sets it equal to the layer whose position needs to be translated. It's important to note that you can use variables to represent more than just numbers. In this case the variable is representing a layer object. So now, when you want to reference a property or attribute of the target layer, instead of having to prefix it with thisComp.layer("star"), you can just use L.

In the second line the toComp() layer space transform translates the target layer's anchor point from the layer's own space to comp space. The transform uses the anchor point because it represents the layer's position in its own layer space. Another way to think of this second line is "From the target layer's own layer space, convert the target layer's anchor point into comp space coordinates."

This simple expression can be used in many ways. For example, if you want to simulate the look of 3D rays emanating from a 3D shape layer you can create a 3D null and make it the child of the shape layer. You then position the null some distance behind the shape layer. Then apply the CC Light Burst 2.5 effect to a comp-sized 2D layer and apply this expression to effect's Center parameter (**Figure 10.9**):

```
L = thisComp.layer("source point");
L.toComp(L.anchorPoint)
```

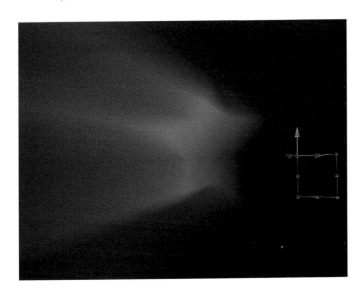

Figure 10.9 The Center parameter for the CC Light Burst Effect is obtained by converting the null's position in 3D world space to its corresponding position in comp space.

(Notice that this is the same expression as in the previous example, except for the name of the target layer: source point, in this case). If you rotate the shape layer, or move a camera around, the rays seem to be coming from the position of the null.

Apply 2D Layer as Decal onto 3D Layer

Sometimes you may need to use more than one layer space transform in a single expression. For example, you might want to apply a 2D layer like a decal to a 3D layer using the Corner Pin effect. To pull this off you need a way to mark on the 3D layer where you want the corners of the 2D layer to be pinned. Apply four Point Controls to the 3D layer, and you can then position each of the 2D layer's corners individually on the surface of the 3D layer. To keep things simple, rename each of the Point Controls to indicate the corner it represents, making the upper-left one UL, the upper-right UR, and so on. Once the Point Controls are in place, you can apply an expression like this one for the upper-left parameter to each parameter of the 2D layer's Corner Pin effect:

```
L = thisComp.layer("target");
fromComp(L.toComp(L.effect("UL")("Point")))
```

Expression Controls

Expression Controls are actually layer effects whose main purpose is to allow you to attach user interface controls to an expression. These controls come in six versions:

- ▶ Slider Control
- ▶ Point Control
- ▶ Angle Control
- ▶ Checkbox Control
- ▶ Color Control
- ▶ Layer Control

All types of controls (except the Layer Control) can be keyframed and can themselves accept expressions. The most common use, however, is to enable you to set or change a value used in an expression calculation without having to edit the code. For example, you might want to be able to easily adjust the `frequency` and `amplitude` parameters of a `wiggle()` expression. You could accomplish this by applying two Slider Controls to the layer with the expression (Effects > Expression Controls). It's usually a good idea to give your controls descriptive names; say you change the name of the first slider to frequency and the second one to amplitude. You would then set up your expression like this (using the pickwhip to create the references to the sliders would be smart):

```
freq = effect("frequency")("Slider");
amp = effect("amplitude")("Slider");
wiggle(freq, amp)
```

Now, you can control the frequency and amplitude of the wiggle via the sliders. With each of the control types (again, with the exception of the Layer Control) you can edit the numeric value directly, or you set the value using the control's gadget.

One unfortunate side note about expression controls is that because you can't apply effects to cameras or lights, neither can you apply expression controls to them.

The first line is just the little shorthand trick so that you can reference the target layer (the 3D layer in this case) more succinctly. The second line translates the position of Point Controls from the 3D layer's space to the layer space of the 2D layer with the Corner Pin effect. There are no layer-to-layer space transforms, however, so the best you can do is transform twice: first from the 3D layer to comp space and then from comp space to the 2D layer. (Remember to edit the expression slightly for each of the other corner parameters so that it references the corresponding Point Control on the 3D layer.)

So, inside the parentheses you convert the Point Control from the 3D layer's space into comp space. Then you convert that result to the 2D layer's space. Nothing to it, right?

Reduce Saturation Away From Camera

Let's change gears a little. You want to create an expression that reduces a layer's saturation as it moves away from the camera in a 3D scene. In addition, you want this expression to work even if the target layer and the camera happen to be children of other layers. You can accomplish this by applying the Color Balance (HLS) effect to the target layer and applying this expression to the Saturation parameter:

```
minDist = 900;
maxDist = 2000;

C = thisComp.activeCamera.toWorld([0,0,0]);
dist = length(toWorld(transform.anchorPoint), C);
ease(dist, minDist, maxDist, 0, -100)
```

The first two lines define variables that will be used to set the boundaries of this effect. If the target layer's distance from the camera is less than `minDist`, you'll leave the Saturation setting unchanged at 0. If the distance is greater than `maxDist` you want to completely desaturate the layer with a setting of -100.

The third line of the expression creates variable C, which represents the position of the comp's currently active camera in world space. It's important to note that cameras and lights don't have anchor points, so you have to convert a specific location in the camera's layer space. It turns out that, in its own layer space, a camera's location is represented by the array [0,0,0] (that is, the X, Y, and Z coordinates are all 0).

The next line creates another variable, `dist`, which represents the distance between the camera and the anchor point of the target layer. You do this with the help of `length()`, which takes two parameters and calculates the distance between them. The first parameter is the world location of the target layer and the second parameter is the world location of the camera, calculated previously.

All that's left to do is calculate the actual Saturation value based on the layer's current distance from the camera. You do this with the help of `ease()`, one of the expression language's amazingly useful interpolation methods. What this line basically says is "as the value of `dist` varies from `minDist` to `maxDist`, vary the output of `ease()` from 0 to –100."

Interpolation Methods

After Effects provides some very handy global interpolation methods for converting one set of values to another. Say you wanted an Opacity expression that would fade in over half a second, starting at the layer's In point. This is very easily accomplished using the `linear()` interpolation method:

```
linear(time, inPoint, inPoint + 0.5, 0, 100)
```

As you can see, `linear()` accepts five parameters (there is also a seldom-used version that accepts only three parameters), which are in order

▶ Input value that is driving the change

▶ Minimum input value

▶ Maximum input value

▶ Output value corresponding to the minimum input value

▶ Output value corresponding to the maximum input value

In the example, time is the input value (first parameter), and as it varies from the layer's In point (second parameter) to 0.5 seconds beyond the In point (third parameter), the output of linear() varies from 0 (fourth parameter) to 100 (fifth parameter). For values of the input parameter that are less than the minimum input value, the output of linear() will be clamped at the value of the fourth parameter. Similarly, if the value of the input parameter is greater than the maximum input value, the output of linear() will be clamped to the value of the fifth parameter. Back to the example, at times before the layer's In point the Opacity value will be held at 0. From the layer's In point until 0.5 seconds beyond the In point, the Opacity value ramps smoothly from 0 to 100. For times beyond the In point + 0.5 seconds, the Opacity value will be held at 100. Sometimes it helps to read it from left to right like this: "As the value of time varies from the In point to 0.5 seconds past the In point, vary the output from 0 to 100."

The second parameter should always be less than the third parameter. Failure to set it up this way can result in some bizarre behavior.

Note that the output values need not be numbers. Arrays work as well. If you want to slowly move a layer from the composition's upper-left corner to the lower-right corner over the time between the layer's In point and Out point, you could set it up like this:

```
linear(time, inPoint, outPoint, [0,0],
➥[thisComp.width, thisComp.height])
```

There are other equally useful interpolation methods in addition to linear(), each taking exactly the same set of parameters. easeIn() provides ease at the minimum value side of the interpolation, easeOut() provides it at the maximum value side, and ease() provides it at both. So if you wanted the previous example to ease in and out of the motion, you could do it like this:

```
ease(time, inPoint, outPoint, [0,0], [thisComp.width,
➥thisComp.height])
```

Fade as Move Away From Camera

Just as you can reduce a layer's saturation as it moves away from the camera, you can reduce its Opacity. The expression is, in fact, quite similar:

```
minDist = 900;
maxDist = 2000;


C = thisComp.activeCamera.toWorld([0,0,0]);
dist = length(toWorld(transform.anchorPoint), C);
ease(dist, minDist, maxDist, 100, 0)
```

The only differences between this expression and the previous one are the fourth and fifth parameters of the ease() statement. In this case, as the distance increases from 900 to 2000 the opacity fades from 100% to 0%.

From Comp Space to Layer Surface

There's a somewhat obscure layer space transform that you haven't looked at yet, namely fromCompToSurface(). This translates a location from the current comp view to the location on a 3D layer's surface that lines up with that point (from the camera's perspective). When would that be useful?

Imagine you have a 2D comp-sized layer named Beam, to which you have applied the Beam Effect. You want a Lens Flare effect on a 3D layer to line up with the ending point of the Beam effect on the 2D layer. You can do it by applying this expression to the Flare Center parameter of the Lens Flare effect on the 3D layer:

```
beamPos = thisComp.layer("beam").effect("Beam")
➡("Ending Point");
fromCompToSurface(beamPos)
```

First, store the location of the ending point of the Beam effect into the variable beamPos. Now you can take a couple of short cuts because of the way things are set up. First, the Ending Point parameter is already represented as a location in the Beam layer's space. Second, because the Beam layer is a comp-sized layer that hasn't been moved or scaled, its layer space will correspond exactly to the Camera view (which is the same as comp space). Therefore, you can assume that the Ending Point is already represented in comp space. If the Beam layer were a different size than the comp, located somewhere other than the comp's center, or scaled, you couldn't get away with this. You would have to convert the Ending Point from Beam's layer space to comp space.

Now all you have to do is translate the `beamPos` variable from comp space to the corresponding point of the surface of the layer with the Lens Flare, which is accomplished easily with `fromCompToSurface()`.

You'll look at one more example of layer space transforms in the big finale "Extra Credit" section at the end of the chapter.

Color Sampling and Conversion

Here's an example that demonstrates how you work with colors in a expression. The idea here is that you want to vary the opacity of an animated small layer based on the lightness (or luminosity) of the pixels of a background layer that currently happen to be under the moving layer. The smaller layer will become more transparent as it passes over dark areas of the background and more opaque as it passes over lighter areas. Fortunately, the expression language supplies a couple of useful tools to help out.

Before examining the expression, we need to talk about the way color data is represented in expressions. An individual color channel (red, blue, green, hue, saturation, lightness, or alpha) is represented as a number between 0.0 (fully off) and 1.0 (fully on). A complete color space representation consists of an array of four such channels. Most of the time you'll be working in red, blue, green, and alpha (RGBA) color space, but you can convert to and from hue, saturation, lightness, and alpha (HSLA) color space. This example uses `sampleImage()` to extract RGBA data from a target layer called background. Then `rgbToHsl()` converts the RGBA data to HSLA color space so that you can extract the lightness channel, which will then be used to drive the Opacity parameter of the small animated layer. Here's the expression:

More About sampleImage()

You can sample the color and alpha data of a rectangular area of a layer using the layer method `sampleImage()`. You supply up to four parameters to `sampleImage()` and it returns color and alpha data as a four-element array ([red, green, blue, alpha]), where the values have been normalized so that they fall between 0.0 and 1.0. The four parameters are

▶ Sample point
▶ Sample radius
▶ Post-effect flag
▶ Sample time

The sample point is given in layer space coordinates, where [0, 0] represents the center of the layer's top left pixel. The sample radius is a two-element array ([x radius, y radius]) that specifies the horizontal and vertical distance from the sample point to the edges of the rectangular area being sampled. To sample a single pixel, you would set this value to [0.5, 0.5] (half a pixel in each direction from the center of the pixel at the sample point). The post-effect flag is optional (its default value is true if you omit it) and specifies whether you want the sample to be taken after masks and effects are applied to the layer (true) or before (false). The sample time parameter specifies the time at which the sample is to be taken. This parameter is also optional (the default value is the current composition time), but if you include it, you must also include the post-effect flag parameter. As an example, here's how you could sample the red value of the pixel at a layer's center, after any effects and masks have been applied, at a time one second prior to the current composition time:

```
mySample = sampleImage([width/
  height]/2, [0.5,0.5], true,
  time - 1);
myRedSample = mySample[0];
```

```
sampleSize = [width, height]/2;
target = thisComp.layer("background");
rgba = target.sampleImage(transform.position,
sampleSize, true, time);
hsla = rgbToHsl(rgba);
hsla[2]*100
```

First you create the variable sampleSize and set its value as an array consisting of half the width and height of the layer whose opacity will be controlled with the expression. Essentially this means that you'll be sampling all of the pixels of the background layer that are under smaller layers at any given time.

The second line just creates the variable target, which will be a shorthand way to refer to the background layer. Then sampleImage() retrieves the RGBA data for the area of the background under the smaller layer and stores the resulting array in the variable rgba. See the sidebar "More About sampleImage()" earlier in the chapter for details on all the parameters of sampleImage().

Next rgbToHsl() converts the RGBA data to HSLA color space and stores the result in variable hsla. Finally, because the lightness channel is the third value in the HSLA array you use the array index of [2] to extract it (see the "Arrays" section of the JavaScript guide if this doesn't make sense to you). Because it will be a value between 0.0 and 1.0, you just need to multiply it by 100 to get it into a range suitable to control the Opacity parameter (**Figure 10.10**).

Figure 10.10 The small blue layer becomes more transparent as it passes over darker areas of the background image.

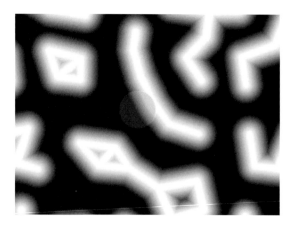

Extra Credit

Congratulations on making it this far. The remaining examples build on concepts covered earlier, but I have saved them for this section because they are particularly tricky or involve some complex math. I'm presenting them mainly to entice you to take some time and figure out how they work.

Fade as Turn Away From Camera

Let's briefly return to the world of layer space transforms and examine a simple idea that requires only a short expression, but one with a lot of complicated vector math going on under the hood. The idea is that you want a 3D layer to fade out as it turns away from the camera. This needs to work not only when the layer rotates away from the camera, but also if the camera orbits the layer. And of course, it should still work if either the layer or the camera happens to be the child of another layer. Take a look at an expression for Opacity that will accomplish this:

```
minAngle = 20;
maxAngle = 70;

C = thisComp.activeCamera.toWorld([0,0,0]);
v1 = normalize(toWorld(transform.anchorPoint) - C);
v2 = toWorldVec([0,0,1]);
angle = radiansToDegrees(Math.acos(dot(v1, v2)));
ease(angle, minAngle, maxAngle, 100, 0)
```

The first two lines just create two variables (minAngle and maxAngle) that establish the range of the effect. Here you set their values so that when the layer is within 20 degrees of facing the camera, it will be at 100% Opacity and its Opacity will fade from 100% to 0% as the angle increase to 70 degrees. Beyond 70 degrees, Opacity will be 0%.

Next you create a variable C that represents the position of the comp's active camera in world space. You've seen this before, in the expression where the layer fades as it moves away from the camera.

Now starts the vector math. Things get a little bumpy from here. Briefly, a *vector* is an entity that has a length and a direction, but has no definite position in space. I like to think of vectors as arrows that you can move around, but they always keep the same heading. Fortunately the expression language provides a pretty good arsenal of tools to deal with vectors.

To figure out the angle between the camera and the layer with the expression, you're going to need two vectors. One will be the vector that points from the center of the layer towards the camera. The other will be a vector that points outward from the center of the layer along the Z axis.

To calculate the first vector (variable v1), convert the layer's anchor point to world space coordinates and subtract from that value the location of the camera in world space. What you're doing is subtracting two points in space. Remember, in After Effects, each 3D position in space is represented by an array: [x,y,z]. The result of subtracting two points like this gives you a vector. This vector has a magnitude representing the distance between the two points and a direction (in this case, the direction from the layer to the camera). You can use `normalize()` to convert the vector to what is known as a unit vector, which maintains the direction of the original vector, but sets its length to 1. This simplifies the upcoming determination of the angle between two vectors.

Next you create the second vector (variable v2). You can create the necessary unit vector in one step this time by using `toWorldVec([0,0,1])` to create a vector of length 1 pointed along the layer's Z axis.

Now you have your two vectors. To calculate the angle between two vectors, you use what is known as the vector dot product. I won't go into great detail about how it works (there's a lot of information on the Internet if you're curious), but it turns out that if you use unit vectors, the vector dot product will directly give you the arc cosine of the angle between the two vectors. Luckily, the expression language gives us a built-in function, `dot()`, to calculate the dot product.

So now you can calculate the angle you need (and store it in variable `angle`) in three steps. First you take the dot product of the two vectors, producing the arc cosine of the angle. Then you use `Math.acos()` to convert that to an angle (see the "Math Object" section of the JavaScript guide for more information). Because the result of `Math.acos()` will be in radians, you need to convert it to degrees so that it will be in the same units as the limits `minAngle` and `maxAngle`. Fortunately, the expression language provides `radiansToDegrees()` to make the conversion.

The final step is to use the interpolation method `ease()` to smoothly execute the fade as the angle increases.

Audio Triggers Effect

Earlier, you learned about linking an effect to an audio level. You can take that idea one step further and use audio to trigger an animated effect. The difference is subtle, but significant. In the earlier examples, the effect tracked the audio level precisely, leaving the result at the mercy of the shape of the audio level's envelope. Here, you're going to use the transitioning of the audio level above some threshold to trigger an animation. The animation will run until there is another trigger event, which will cause the animation to start again from the beginning.

This is a powerful concept and there are many ways to use it. This example triggers a decaying oscillation that is actually contained within the expression, but you could easily adapt this to run a keyframed animation using `valueAtTime()` or to run a time remapped sequence.

The heart of this expression is what I would call a "beat detector." The expression basically walks backward in time, frame-by-frame, looking for the most recent event where the audio level transitioned from below the threshold to above the threshold. It then uses the difference in time between the triggering event and the current comp time to determine how far along it should be in the animation. At each new beat, this time resets to zero and runs until the next beat. Take a look at this monster:

```
threshold = 20.0;

A = thisComp.layer("Audio Amplitude").effect("Both
➥Channels")("Slider");

// beat detector starts here

above = false;
frame = timeToFrames();
while (true){
  t = framesToTime(frame);
  if (above){
    if (A.valueAtTime(t) < threshold){
      frame++;
      break;
    }
  }else if (A.valueAtTime(t) >= threshold){
    above = true;
  }
  if (frame == 0){
    break;
  }
  frame--
}
if (! above){
  t = 0;
}else{
  t = time - framesToTime(frame);
}

// animation starts here

amp = 75;
freq = 5;
decay = 2.0;

angle = freq * 2 * Math.PI * t;
amp * (-Math.cos(angle)+1)/ Math.exp(decay * t);
```

This expression has three sections. The first section defines
the audio level that you want to trigger the animation
and stores it into the variable threshold. It then defines

variable A to use as shorthand notation for the Slider Control containing the keyframed data for the audio level.

The next section is the actual beat detector. In general, the expression starts at the current comp time and determines if the level is currently above the threshold. If it is, the expression moves backward in time, frame-by-frame until it finds the most recent frame where the audio level was below the threshold. It then determines that the triggering event occurred on frame after that (the most recent frame where the level transitioned from below the threshold to above it). That transition frame is converted to time using framesToTime(), that value is subtracted from the current comp time, and the result (the time, in seconds, since the triggering event) is stored into variable t.

However, if instead, the audio level at the current comp time is *below* the threshold, the expression has more work to do. It first moves backward from the current comp time, frame-by-frame until it finds a frame where the audio level is above the threshold. Then it continues on, looking for the transition from below the threshold to above it. The elapsed time since the triggering event is then calculated and stored in variable t.

There are some other things going on in this routine, but they mostly have to do with special cases, such as the case where there hasn't yet been a triggering event (in which case the animation is held at the first frame), or where the level is above the threshold but it has been there since the first frame.

There are some JavaScript elements in this section that you haven't seen before. // denotes the start of a comment. The routine consists mainly of a giant while() loop. This loop is unusual in that its terminating condition is set to true, so it will never end on its own. It will continue to loop until one of the break statements is executed.

When After Effects arrives at the last section of the expression, variable t contains the necessary information: how long it has been since the last triggering event. The final section uses it to drive a decaying oscillation routine with Math.cos() and Math.exp(). First you define the amplitude

NOTES

See the "Comments" section of the JavaScript guide for more details on comments and the "Loops" section for more information about while(), break, and loops in general.

You might want to visit "The Math Object" section of the JavaScript guide for more information on Math.cos() and Math.exp().

of the oscillation with the variable amp. Then you define the frequency of the oscillation (oscillations per second) with the variable freq. Variable decay determines how fast the oscillation decays (a higher number means a faster decay).

Math.cos() creates an oscillating sine wave with amplitude amp and frequency freq, then Math.exp() reduces the amplitude of the oscillating wave at a rate determined by variable decay (**Figure 10.11**).

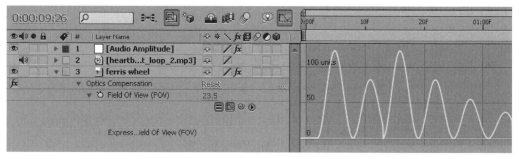

Figure 10.11 The graph shows the decaying oscillation triggered whenever the audio threshold level is crossed.

Conclusion

This chapter covered a lot of ground, but still it really only provided a hint of what's possible with expressions. Here are a few resources where you can find a lot of additional information:

▶ **www.aenhancers.com:** A forum-based site where you can get your questions answered and take a look at expressions contributed by others

▶ **http://forums.creativecow.net/forum/adobe_after_effects_expressions:** A forum dedicated to expressions

▶ **www.adobeforums.com:** Adobe's own After Effects forum, which has a sub-forum on expressions

▶ **www.adobe.com/go/learn_ae_cs4helphome:** The online version of After Effects Help

▶ **www.motionscript.com:** My own Web site, which has a lot of examples and analysis

11

32-Bit HDR Compositing and Color Management

True realism consists in revealing the surprising things which habit keeps covered and prevents us from seeing.

—Jean Cocteau (French director, painter, playwright, and poet)

32-Bit HDR Compositing and Color Management

Whether you are directly aware of limitations or not, you no doubt realize that there are limits to the ways images are processed and displayed on a computer. Your monitor likely only displays 8 bits of color per channel, and while its size (in pixel dimensions) has steadily increased over the last few years, this color depth limitation has hardly budged.

You may also be aware that although an After Effects project, by default, operates in the same limited 8-bit-per-channel mode as your monitor, this is hardly the optimal way to create an image. Other modes, models, and methods for color are available, including high-bit depths, alternate color spaces, and color management, and few topics in After Effects generate as much curiosity or confusion as these. Each of the features detailed here improves upon the standard digital color model you know best, but at the cost of requiring better understanding on your part.

In After Effects CS4 the process centers around Color Management, whose name would seem to imply that it is an automated process to manage colors for you, when in fact it is a complex set of tools allowing (even requiring) you to effectively manage color.

On the other hand, 32-bit High Dynamic Range (HDR) compositing is routinely ignored by artists who could benefit from it, despite that it remains uncommon for source files to contain over-range color data, which are pixel values too bright for your monitor to display.

Film can and typically does contain these over-range color values. These are most often brought into After Effects as 10-bit log Cineon or DPX files, and importing, converting, and writing this format requires a bit of special knowledge. It's an elegant and highly standardized system that has relevance even when you're working with the most up-to-date, high-end digital cameras.

Color Management: Why Bother?

It's normal to wish Color Management would simply go away. So many of us have produced footage with After Effects for years and devised our own systems to manage color through each stage of production. We've assumed, naively perhaps, that a pixel is a pixel and as long as we control the RGB value of that pixel, we maintain control over the appearance of the image.

The problem with this way of thinking is that it's tied to the monitor. The way a given RGB pixel looks on your monitor is somewhat arbitrary—I'm typing this on a laptop, and I know that its monitor has higher contrast than my desktop monitors, one of which has a bluer cast than the other if I don't adjust them to match. Not only that, the way that color operates on your monitor is nothing like the way it works in the real world, or even in a camera. Not only is the dynamic range far more limited, but also an arbitrary gamma adjustment is required to make images look right.

Color itself is not arbitrary. Although color is a completely human phenomenon—"color" as such does not exist except in our vision system and that of other higher primates—it is the result of measurable natural phenomena. Because the qualities of a given color are measurable to a large degree, a system is evolving to measure them, and Adobe is attempting to spearhead the progress of that system with its Color Management features.

Completely Optional

The Color Management feature set in After Effects is completely optional and disabled by default. Its features become necessary in cases including, but not necessarily limited to, the following:

▶ A project relies on a color managed file (with an embedded ICC Profile). For example, a client provides an image or clip with specific managed color settings and requires that the output match.

▶ A project will benefit from a linearized 1.0 gamma working space. If that means nothing to you, read on; this is the chapter that explains it.

▶ Output will be displayed in some manner that's not directly available on your system.

▶ A project is shared and the color is adjusted on a variety of workstations, each with a calibrated monitor. The goal is for color corrections made on a given workstation to match once the shot moves on from that workstation.

To achieve these goals requires that some old rules be broken and new ones established.

Related and Mandatory

Other changes introduced in After Effects CS4 seem tied to Color Management but come into play even if you never enable it:

▶ A video file in a DV or other Y'CrCb (YUV) format requires (and receives) automatic color interpretation upon import into After Effects, applying settings that would previously have been up to you to add. This is done by MediaCore, a little known Adobe application that runs invisibly behind the scenes of Adobe video applications (see "Input Profile and MediaCore," later in this chapter).

▶ QuickTime gamma settings in general have become something of a moving target as Apple adds its own form of color management, whose effects vary from codec to codec. As a result, there are situations in which imported and rendered QuickTimes won't look right. This is not the fault of Color Management, although you can use the feature set to correct the problems that come up (see "QuickTime," below).

▶ Linear blending (using a 1.0 gamma only for pixel-blending operations without converting all images to linear gamma) is possible without setting a linearized Project Working Space or enabling Color Management (see the section "Blend Colors Using 1.0 Gamma").

Because these issues also affect how color is managed, they tend to get lumped in with the Color Management system when in fact they can be unique from it.

A Pixel's Journey Through After Effects

Join me now as we follow color through After Effects, noting the various features that can affect its appearance or even its very identity—its RGB value. Although it's not mandatory, it's best to increase that pixel's color flexibility and accuracy, warming it up to get it ready for the trip, by raising project bit depth above 8 bpc. Here's why.

16-Bit-Per-Channel Composites

A 16-bit-per-channel color was added to After Effects 5.0 for one basic reason: to eliminate color *quantization*, most commonly seen in the form of banding where subtle gradients and other threshold regions appear in an image. In 16 bpc mode there are 128 extra gradations between each R, G, B, and A value contained in the familiar 8 bpc mode.

Those increments are typically too fine for your eye to distinguish (or your monitor to display), but your eye easily notices banding, and when you start to make multiple adjustments to 8 bpc images, as may be required by Color Management features, banding is bound to appear in edge thresholds and shadows, making the image look bad.

You can raise color depth in your project by either **Alt/Option**-clicking on the color depth setting at the bottom of the Project panel or via the Depth menu in File > Project Settings. The resulting performance hit typically isn't as bad as you might think.

NOTES

Many but not all effects and plug-ins support 16 bpc color. To discern which ones do, with your project set to the target bit depth (16 bpc in this case), choose Show 16 bpc-Capable Effects Only from the Effects & Presets panel menu. Effects that are only 8 bpc aren't off-limits; you should just be careful to place them where they are least likely to cause banding—typically either at the beginning or the end of the image pipeline.

Most digital artists prefer 8 bpc colors because we're so used to them, but switching to 16 bpc mode doesn't mean you're stuck with incomprehensible pixel values of 32768, 0, 0 for pure red or 16384, 16384, 16384 for middle gray. In the panel menu of the Info panel, choose whichever numerical color representation works for you; this setting is used everywhere in the application, including the Adobe color picker (**Figure 11.1**). The following sections use 8 bpc values despite referring to 16 bpc projects.

Figure 11.1 Love working 16 bpc but hate analyzing 16-bit values that go up to 32768? Choose 8 bpc in the Info Panel Menu to display familiar 0 to 255 values. Or better yet, use Decimal values in all bit depths.

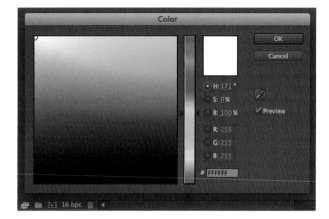

Monitor Calibration

Sometimes it becomes obvious that RGB values alone cannot describe pure colors; if you don't know what I'm talking about, connect a still-working decade-old CRT monitor to your system and see how it looks. You can imagine that a 255,255,255 white would be likely to look blue or yellow.

Assuming your monitor isn't that far out of whack, third-party color calibration hardware and software can be used to generate a profile that is then stored and set as a system preference. This monitor profile accomplishes two things:

▶ Defines a color space for compositing unique from what is properly called *monitor color space.*

▶ Offers control over the color appearance of the composition. Each pixel has not only an RGB value but also an actual precise and absolute color.

In other words, the color values and how they interrelate change, as does the method used to display them.

Color Management: Disabled by Default

Import a file edited in another Adobe application such as Photoshop or Lightroom and it likely contains an embedded ICC color profile. This profile can tell After Effects how the colors should be interpreted and appear, instead of remaining as raw electrical signals.

A file called sanityCheck.tif can be found on the book's disc; it contains data and color gradients that will help you understand linear color later in the chapter. Import this file into After Effects and choose File > Interpret Footage > Main (**Ctrl+F/Cmd+F**, or context-click instead). The Interpret Footage includes a Color Management tab.

Figure 11.2 shows how this tab appears with the default settings. Assign Profile is grayed out because, as the Description text explains, Color Management is off and color values are not converted. Color Management is enabled as soon as you assign a *working space*.

NOTES

Is there an external broadcast monitor attached to your system (set as an Output Device in Preferences > Video Preview)? Color Management settings do not apply to that device.

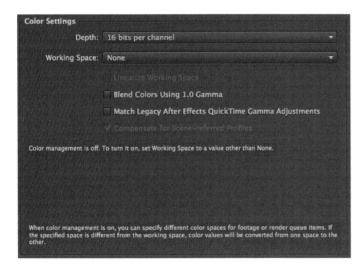

Figure 11.2 Until Color Management is enabled for the entire project, the embedded profile of a source image is not displayed in the Project panel, nor is it used.

Project Working Space

The proper choice of a working space is the one that typically matches the "output intent," the color space corresponding to the target device. The Working Space menu containing all possible choices is located in File > Project Settings (**Ctrl+Alt+K/Cmd+Opt+K,** or just click where you see the "bpc" setting along the bottom of the Project panel).

Profiles above the line are considered by Adobe to be the most likely candidates. Those below might include profiles used by such unlikely output devices as a color printer (**Figure 11.3**).

Figure 11.3 For better or worse, all of the color profiles active on the local system are listed as Working Space candidates, even such unlikely targets as the office color printer.

By default, Working Space is set to None (and thus Color Management is off). Choose a Working Space from the menu and Color Management is enabled, triggering the following:

▶ Assigned profiles in imported files are activated and displayed atop the Project panel when it's selected.

▶ Imported files with no assigned profile are assumed to have a profile of sRGB IEC61966-2.1, hereafter referred to as simply *sRGB*.

▶ Actual RGB values *can and will change* to maintain consistent color values.

Choose wisely; it's a bad idea to change working space mid-project once you've begun adjusting color, because it will change the fundamental look of source footage and comps.

Okay, so it's a cop-out to say "choose wisely" and not give actual advice. There's a rather large document, included on the disc and also available at www.adobe.com/devnet/ aftereffects/articles/color_management_workflow.html, that includes a table itemizing each and every profile included in After Effects.

We can just forego that for the moment in favor of a concise summary:

▶ For HD display, HDTV (Rec. 709) is Adobe-sanctioned, but sRGB is similar and more of a reliable standard.

▶ For monitor playback, sRGB is generally most suitable.

▶ SDTV NTSC or SDTV PAL theoretically let you forego a preview broadcast monitor, although it's also possible to simulate these formats without working in them ("Display Management and Output Simulation," below).

▶ Film output is an exception and is discussed later in this chapter.

To say that a profile is "reliable" is like saying that a particular brand of car is reliable: It has been taken through a series of situations and has caused the least problems under various types of duress. I realize that with color management allegedly being so scientific and all, this sounds squirrelly, but it's just the reality of an infinite variety of images heading for an infinite variety of viewing environments. There's the scientifically tested reliability of the car and then there are real-world driving conditions.

Gamut describes the range of possible saturation, keeping in mind that any pixel can be described by its hue, saturation, and brightness as accurately as its red, green, and blue. The range of hues accessible to human vision is rather fixed, but the amount of brightness and saturation possible is not—32 bpc HDR addresses both. The idea is to match, not outdo (and definitely not to undershoot) the gamut of the target.

Working spaces change RGB values. Open sanityCheck.tif in a viewer and move your cursor over the little bright red square; its values are 255, 0, 0. Now change the working space to ProPhoto RGB. Nothing looks different, but the values are now 179, 20, 26, meaning that with this wider gamut, color values do not need to be nearly as large in order to appear just as saturated, and there is headroom for far more saturation. You just need a medium capable of displaying the more saturated red in order to see it properly with this gamut. Many film stocks can do it, and your monitor cannot.

NOTES

A small yellow + sign appears in the middle of the Show Channel icon to indicate that Display Color Management is active (**Figure 11.4**).

Figure 11.4 When Use Display Color Management is active in the View menu (the default after you set a working space) this icon adds a yellow plus symbol at its center.

Figure 11.5 Any imported image with no color profile gets sRGB by default to bring it into the color management pipeline. You can override this setting in Interpret Footage > Color Management.

In many ways, MediaCore's automation is a good thing. After Effects 7.0 had a little checkbox at the bottom of Interpret Footage labeled "Expand ITU-R 601 Luma Levels" that obligated you to manage incoming luminance range. With MediaCore, however, you lose the ability to override the setting. Expanded values above 235 and below 16 are pushed out of range, recoverable only in 32 bpc mode.

Input Profile and MediaCore

If an 8 bpc image file has no embedded profile, sRGB is assigned (**Figure 11.5**), which is close to monitor color space. This allows the file to be color managed, to preserve its appearance even in a different color space. Toggle Preserve RGB in the Color Management tab and the appearance of that image can change with the working space—not, generally, what you want, which is why After Effects goes ahead and assigns its best guess.

Video formats (QuickTime being by far the most common) don't accept color profiles, but they do require color interpretation based on embedded data. After Effects uses an Adobe application called MediaCore to interpret these files automatically; it operates completely behind the scenes, invisible to you.

You know that MediaCore is handling a file when that file has Y'CbCr in the Embedded Profile info, including DV and YUV format files. In such a case the Color Management tab is completely grayed out, so there is no option to override the embedded settings.

Display Management and Output Simulation

And in the middle of all of this great responsibility comes a genuinely fun feature, Output Simulation, which simulates how your comp will look on a particular device. The "device" in question can include film projection, and the process of representing that environment on your monitor works better than you might expect.

Suppose you need to know how an image (**Figure 11.6**) would appear on NTSC and PAL standard definition television, and you don't have a standard def broadcast monitor to preview either of those formats.

No problem. With the viewer selected choose View > Simulate Output > SDTV NTSC. Here's what happens:

▶ The appearance of the footage changes to match the output simulation. The viewer displays After Effects' simulation of an NTSC monitor.

Figure 11.6 The source image (courtesy of Michael Scott) is adjusted precisely in a color managed project.

▶ Unlike when you change the working space, color values do not change due to output simulation.

▶ The image is actually assigned two separate color profiles in sequence: a scene-referred profile to simulate the output profile you would use for NTSC (SDTV NTSC) and a second profile that actually simulates the television monitor that would then display that rendered output (SMPTE-C). To see what these settings are, and to customize them, choose View > Simulate Output > Custom to open the Custom Output Simulation dialog (**Figure 11.7**).

Figures 11.7 This Custom Output Simulation dialog now nicely shows the four stages from source RGB image to the monitor. The middle two stages are those set by Output Simulation; the first occurs on import, the final when the image is displayed.

Interpretation Rules

A file on your system named interpretation rules. txt defines how files are automatically interpreted as they are imported into After Effects. To change anything in this file, you should be something of a hacker, able to look at a line like

```
# *, *, *, "sDPX", * ~ *, *, *,
➥*, "ginp", *
```

and, by examining surrounding lines and comments, figure out that this line is commented out (with the # sign at the beginning), and that the next to last argument, `"ginp"` in quotes, assigns the Kodak 5218 film profile if the file type corresponds with the fourth argument, `"sDPX"`. If this makes you squirm, don't touch it, call a nerd. In this case, removing the # sign at the beginning would enable this rule so that DPX files would be assigned a Kodak 5218 profile (without it, they are assigned to the working space).

If this isn't your cup of tea, as it won't be for most artists, leave it to someone willing to muck around with this stuff.

Figure 11.8 The result of Output Simulation shows bluer highlights, deeper blacks (which may not read on the printed page) and a less saturated red dress. If you wanted the image to appear different when projected, you would now further adjust it with this view active. It might then look "wrong" with Output Simulation off, but "right" when finally filmed out and projected.

This gets really fun with simulations of projected film (**Figure 11.8**)—not only the print stock but the appearance of projection is simulated, allowing an artist to work directly on the projected look of a shot instead of waiting until it is filmed out and projected.

Here's a summary of what is happening to the source image in the example project:

1. The source image is interpreted on import (on the Footage Settings > Color Management tab) according to its Working Space setting.

2. The image is transformed to the Project Working Space; its color values will change to preserve its appearance.

3. With View > Simulate Output and any profile selected

   a. Color values are transformed to the specified Output Profile.

   b. Color appearance (but not actual values) is transformed to a specified Simulation Profile.

4. With View > Display Color Management enabled (required for step 3) color appearance (but not actual values) is transformed to the Monitor Profile (the one that lives in system settings, that you created when you calibrated your monitor, remember?)

That leaves output, which relies only on steps 1 and 2. The others are only for previewing, although you may wish to render an output simulation (to show the filmed-out look

TIP

Having trouble with View > Simulate Output appearing grayed-out? Make sure a viewer window is active when you set it; it operates on a per-viewer basis.

NOTES

In Photoshop, there is no Project Working Space, only the document Working Space, because there are no projects (no need to accommodate multiple sources together in a single nondestructive project).

on a video display in dailies, for example). To replicate the two-stage color conversion of output simulation:

1. Apply the Color Profile Converter effect, and match the Output Profile setting to the one listed under View > Simulate Output > Custom. Change the Intent setting to Absolute Colorimetric.

2. Set a second Color Profile Converter effect, and match the Input Profile setting to the Simulation Profile under View > Simulate Output > Custom (leaving Intent as the default Relative Colorimetric).

The Output Profile in the Render Queue then should match the intended display device.

Now let's leave simulation behind and look at what happens when you try to preserve actual colors in rendered output. (Which is, after all, the whole point, right?)

Output Profile

By default, After Effects uses Working Space as the Output Profile, usually the right choice. Place the comp in the Render Queue and open the Output Module; on the Color Management tab you can select a different profile to apply on output. The pipeline from the last section now adds a third step to the first two:

1. The source image is interpreted on import (on the Footage Settings > Color Management tab).

2. The image is transformed to the working space; its color values will change to preserve its appearance.

3. The image is transformed to the output profile specified in Output Module Settings > Color Management.

If the profile in step 3 is different from that of step 2, color values will change to preserve color appearance. If the output format supports embedded ICC profiles (presumably a still image format such as TIFF or PSD), then a profile will be embedded so that any other application with color management (presumably an Adobe application such as Photoshop or Illustrator) will continue to preserve those colors.

In the real world, of course, rendered output is probably destined to a device or format that doesn't support color management and embedded profiles. That's okay, except in the case of QuickTime, which may further change the appearance of the file, almost guaranteeing that the output won't match your composition without special handling.

QuickTime

QuickTime continues to have special issues of its own separate from, but related to Adobe's color management. Because Apple constantly revises QuickTime and the spec has been in some flux, the issues particular to the version of QuickTime at this writing (7.5.5) and how After Effects handles it may continue to evolve.

The current challenge is that Apple has begun implementing its own form of color management without sharing the specification publicly or letting anyone know when it changes. The gamma of QuickTime files can be specifically tagged, and the tag is then interpreted uniquely by each codec, so files with Photo-JPEG compression have a different gamma than files with H.264 compression. Even files with the default Animation setting, which are effectively uncompressed and assumedly neutral, display an altered gamma, and at this writing, that gamma will display differently depending on which application is displaying it. Gamma handling is not even consistent among Apple video applications.

The Match Legacy After Effects QuickTime Gamma Adjustments toggle in Project Settings is not only the longest-titled checkbox in the entire application, it is an option you should not need, in theory at least, unless you've opened up an old 7.0 (or earlier) project, or you need a Composition to match what you see in QuickTime Player.

However, many of us deliver client review files as QuickTime movies, so your best bet is to enable Color Management for any project intended to output QuickTime video. The option to disable the Match Legacy toggle is reserved for cases in which that approach doesn't work; these do unfortunately crop up and remain a moving target as new versions of QuickTime are released, further revising the standard.

To Bypass Color Management

Headaches like that make many artists long for the simpler days of After Effects 7.0 and opt to avoid Color Management altogether, or to use it only selectively. To completely disable the feature and return to 7.0 behavior:

1. In Project Settings, set Working Space to None (as it is by default).

2. Enable Match Legacy After Effects QuickTime Gamma Adjustments.

Being more selective about how color management is applied—to take advantage of some features while leaving others disabled for clarity—is really tricky and tends to stump some pretty smart users. Here are a couple of final tips that may nonetheless help:

▶ To disable a profile for incoming footage, check Preserve RGB in Interpret Footage (Color Management tab). No attempt will be made to preserve the appearance of that clip.

▶ To change the behavior causing untagged footage to be tagged with an sRGB profile, in interpretation rules.txt find this line

```
# soft rule: tag all untagged footage with an sRGB
➥profile
*, *, *, *, * ~ *, *, *, *, "sRGB", *
```

and add a # at the beginning of the second line to assign no profile, or change "sRGB" to a different format (options listed in the comments at the top of the file).

▶ To prevent your display profile from being factored in, disable View > Use Display Color Management and the pixels are sent straight to the display.

▶ To prevent any file from being color managed, check Preserve RGB in Output Module Settings (Color Management tab).

Note that any of the preceding tips may lead to unintended consequences. Leaving a working space enabled and disabling specific features is tricky and potentially dangerous to your health and sanity. Add your own further disclaimers here.

Film and Dynamic Range

The previous section showed how color benefits from precision and flexibility. The precision is derived with the steps just discussed; flexibility is the result of having a wide dynamic range, because there is a far wider range of color and light levels in the physical world than can be represented on your 8-bit-per-channel display.

However, there is more to color flexibility than toggling 16 bpc in order to avoid banding, or even color management, and there is an analog image medium that is capable of going far beyond 16 bpc color, and even a file format capable of representing it.

Film and Cineon

To paraphrase Mark Twain, reports of film's demise have been exaggerated; not only that, but new formats make use of tried and true filmic standards. Here's a look at the film process and the digital files on which it relies.

After film has been shot, the negative is developed, and shots destined for digital effects work are scanned frame by frame. During this, the Telecine process, some initial color decisions are made before the frames are output as a numbered sequence of Cineon files, named after Kodak's now-defunct film compositing system. Both Cineon files and the related format, DPX, store pixels uncompressed at 10 bits per channel. Scanners are usually capable of scanning 4 K plates, and these have become more popular for visual effects usage, although many still elect to scan at half resolution, creating 2 K frames around 2048 by 1536 pixels and weighing in at almost 13 MB.

Working with Cineon Files

Because the process of shooting and scanning film is pretty expensive, almost all Cineon files ever created are the property of some Hollywood studio and unavailable to the general public. The best known free Cineon file is Kodak's original test image, affectionately referred to as Marcie (**Figure 11.9**) and available from Kodak's Web site (www.kodak.com/US/en/motion/-support/dlad/) or the

book's disc. To get a feel for working with film, drop the
file called dlad_2048X1556.cin into After Effects, which
imports Cineon files just fine.

Figure 11.9 This universal sample
image has been converted from film
of a bygone era to Cineon format
found on the book's disc.

The first thing you'll notice about Marcie is that she looks
funny, and not just because this photo dates back to the
'80s. Cineon files are encoded in something called log
color space. To make Marcie look more natural, open the
Interpret Footage dialog, select the Color Management
tab, click Cineon Settings and choose the Over Range
preset (instead of the default Full Range). Ah, that looks
better; the log image is now converted to the monitor's
color space.

It would seem natural to convert Cineon files to the monitor's color space, work normally, and then convert the end
result back to log, but to do so would be to throw away
valuable data. Try this: Apply the Cineon Converter effect
and switch the Conversion Type from Linear to Log. This
is a preview of how the file would be written on output
back to a Cineon log file. Upon further examination of
this conversion, you see a problem: in an 8 bpc (or even
16 bpc) project, the bright details in Marcie's hair don't
survive the trip (**Figure 11.10**).

NOTES

Also included on the book's disc
is a Cineon sequence from the
RED Camera (and courtesy of
fxphd.com), showing off that digital
camera's dynamic range and overall
image quality. This is one example
of Cineon format that is remaining
viable with digital source.

Figure 11.10 When you convert an image from log space (left) to linear (center) and then back to log (right), the brightest details are lost.

As becomes evident later in the chapter, the choice of the term "linear" as an alternative to "log" space for Cineon Converter is unfortunate, because "linear" specifically means neutral 1.0 gamma; what Cineon Converter calls "linear" is in fact gamma encoded.

What's going on with this mystical Cineon file and its log color space that makes it so hard to deal with? And more importantly, why? Well, it turns out that the engineers at Kodak know a thing or two about film and have made no decisions lightly. But to properly answer the question, it's necessary to discuss some basic principles of photography and light.

Dynamic Range

The pictures shown in **Figure 11.11** were taken in sequence from a roof on a winter morning. Anyone who has ever tried to photograph a sunrise or sunset with a digital camera should immediately recognize the problem at hand. With a standard exposure, the sky comes in beautifully, but foreground houses are nearly black. Using longer exposures you can bring the houses up, but by the time they are looking good the sky is completely blown out.

Figure 11.11 Different exposures when recording the same scene clearly produce widely varying results.

The limiting factor here is the digital camera's small dynamic range, which is the difference between the brightest and darkest things that can be captured in the same image. An outdoor scene has a wide array of brightnesses, but any digital device can read only a slice of them. You can change exposure to capture different ranges, but the size of the slice is fixed.

Our eyes have a much larger dynamic range and our brains have a wide array of perceptual tricks, so in real life the houses and sky are both seen easily. But even eyes have limits, such as when you try to see someone behind a bright spotlight or use a laptop computer in the sun. The spotlight has not made the person behind any darker, but when eyes adjust to bright lights (as they must to avoid injury), dark things fall out of range and simply appear black.

White on a monitor just isn't very bright, which is one reason we work in dim rooms with the blinds pulled down. When you try to represent the bright sky on a dim monitor, everything else in the image has to scale down in proportion. Even when a digital camera can capture extra dynamic range, your monitor must compress it in order to display it.

A standard 8-bit computer image uses values 0 to 255 to represent RGB pixels. If you record a value above 255—say 285 or 310—that represents a pixel beyond the monitor's dynamic range, brighter than white or overbright. Because 8-bit pixels can't actually go above 255, overbright information is stored as floating point decimals where 0.0 is black and 1.0 is white. Because floating point numbers are virtually unbounded, 0.75, 7.5, or 750.0 are all acceptable values, even though everything above 1.0 will clip to white on the monitor (**Figure 11.12**).

In recent years, techniques have emerged to create HDR images from a series of exposures—floating point files that contain all light information from a scene (**Figure 11.13**). The best-known paper on the subject was published by Malik and Debevec at SIGGRAPH '97 (www.debevec.org has details). In successive exposures, values that remain within range can be compared to describe how the camera

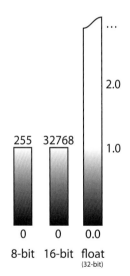

Figure 11.12 Monitor white represents the upper limit for 8-bit and 16-bit pixels, while floating point can go arbitrarily higher (depending on format) or lower; the range also extends below absolute black, 0.0—values that are theoretical and not part of the world you see (unless you're in outer space, staring into a black hole).

is responding to different levels of light. That information allows a computer to connect bright areas in the scene to the darker ones and calculate accurate floating point pixel values that combine detail from each exposure.

— Darker Sky: 1.9

— Bright Sky: 7.5

— Dark Tree: 0.03

— Houses: 0.8

Figure 11.13 Consider the floating point pixel values for this HDR image; they relate to one another proportionally, and continue to do so whether the image is brightened or darkened, because the values do not need to clip at 1.0.

Photoshop's Merge to HDR feature allows you to create your own HDR images from a series of locked-off photos at varied exposures.

But with all the excitement surrounding HDR imaging and improvements in the dynamic range of video cameras, many forget that for decades there has been another medium available for capturing dynamic range far beyond what a computer monitor can display or a digital camera can capture.

That medium is film.

Cineon Log Space

A film negative gets its name because areas exposed to light ultimately become dark and opaque, and areas unexposed are made transparent during developing. Light makes dark. Hence, negative.

Dark is a relative term here. A white piece of paper makes a nice dark splotch on the negative, but a lightbulb darkens the film even more, and a photograph of the sun causes the negative to turn out darker still. By not completely exposing to even bright lights, the negative is able to capture the differences between bright highlights and really bright highlights. Film, the original image capture medium, has always been high dynamic range.

If you were to graph the increase in film "density" as increasing amounts of light expose it, you'd get something like **Figure 11.14**. In math, this is referred to as a logarithmic curve. I'll get back to this in a moment.

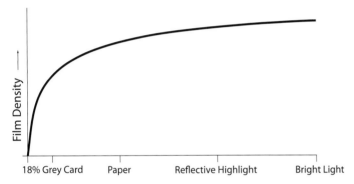

Figure 11.14 Graph the darkening (density) of film as increasing amounts of light expose it and you get a logarithmic curve.

Digital Film

If a monitor's maximum brightness is considered to be 1.0, the brightest value film can represent is officially considered by Kodak to be 13.53 (although using the more efficient ICC color conversion, outlined later in the chapter, reveals brightness values above 70). Note this only applies to a film negative that is exposed by light in the world as opposed to a film positive, which is limited by the brightness of a projector bulb, and is therefore not really considered high dynamic range. A Telecine captures the entire range of each frame and stores the frames as a sequence of 10-bit Cineon files. Those extra two bits mean that Cineon pixel values can range from 0 to 1023 instead of the 0 to 255 in 8-bit files.

Having four times as many values to work with in a Cineon file helps, but considering you have 13.53 times the range to record, care must be taken in encoding those values. The most obvious way to store all that light would simply be to evenly squeeze 0.0 to 13.53 into the 0 to 1023 range. The problem with this solution is that it would only leave 75 code values for the all-important 0.0 to 1.0 range, the same as allocated to the range 10.0 to 11.0, which you are far less interested in representing with much accuracy. Your eye can barely tell the difference between two highlights that bright—it certainly doesn't need 75 brightness variations between them.

A proper way to encode light on film would quickly fill up the usable values with the most important 0.0 to 1.0 light and then leave space left over for the rest of the negative's range. Fortunately, the film negative itself with its logarithmic response behaves just this way.

Cineon files are often said to be stored in log color space. Actually it is the negative that uses a log response curve and the file is simply storing the negative's density at each pixel. In any case, the graph in **Figure 11.15** describes how light exposes a negative and is encoded into Cineon color values according to Kodak, creators of the format.

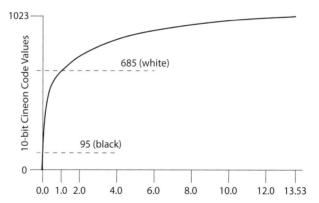

Figure 11.15 Kodak's Cineon log encoding is also expressed as a logarithmic curve, with labels for the visible black and white points that correspond to 0 and 255 in normal 8-bit pixel values.

One strange feature in this graph is that black is mapped to code value 95 instead of 0. Not only does the Cineon file store whiter-than-white (overbright) values, it also has some blacker-than-black information. This is mirrored in the film lab when a negative is printed brighter than usual and the blacker-than-black information can reveal itself. Likewise, negatives can be printed darker and take advantage of overbright detail. The standard value mapped to monitor white is 685, and everything above is considered overbright.

Although the Kodak formulas are commonly used to transform log images for compositing, other methods have emerged. The idea of having light values below 0.0 is dubious at best, and many take issue with the idea that a single curve can describe all film stocks, cameras, and shooting environments. As a different approach, some visual effects facilities take care to photograph well-defined photographic charts and use the resultant film to build custom curves that differ subtly from the standard Kodak one.

As much as Cineon log is a great way to encode light captured by film, it should not be used for compositing or other image transformations. This point is so important that it just has to be emphasized again:

Encoding color spaces are not compositing color spaces.

To illustrate this point, imagine you had a black pixel with Cineon value 95 next to an extremely bright pixel with Cineon's highest code value, 1023. If these two pixels were blended together (say, if the image was being blurred), the result would be 559, which is somewhere around middle gray (0.37 to be precise). But when you consider that the extremely bright pixel has a relative brightness of 13.5, that black pixel should only have been able to bring it down to 6.75, which is still overbright white! Log space's extra emphasis on darker values causes standard image processing operations to give them extra weight, leading to an overall unpleasant and inaccurate darkening of the image. So, final warning: If you're working with a log source, don't do image processing in log space!

All About Log

You may first have heard of logarithmic curves in high school physics class, if you ever learned about the decay of radioactive isotopes.

If a radioactive material has a half-life of one year, half of it will have decayed after that time. The next year, half of what remains will decay, leaving a quarter, and so on. To calculate how much time has elapsed based on how much material remains, a logarithmic function is used.

Light, another type of radiation, has a similar effect on film. At the molecular level, light causes silver halide crystals to react. If film exposed for some short period of time causes half the crystals to react, repeating the exposure will cause half of the remaining to react, and so on. This is how film gets its response curve and the ability to capture even very bright light sources. No amount of exposure can be expected to affect every single crystal.

The description of gamma in video is oversimplified here somewhat because the subject is complex enough for a book of its own. An excellent one is Charles Poynton's *Digital Video and HDTV Algorithms and Interfaces* (Morgan Kaufmann).

Video Gamma Space

Because log space certainly doesn't look natural, it probably comes as no surprise that it is a bad color space to work in. But there is another encoding color space that you have been intimately familiar with for your entire computer-using life and no doubt have worked in directly: the video space of your monitor.

You may have always assumed that 8-bit monitor code value 128, halfway between black and white, makes a gray that is half as bright as white. If so, you may be shocked to hear that this is not the case. In fact, 128 is much darker—not even a quarter of white's brightness on most monitors.

A system where half the input gives you half the output is described as linear, but monitors (like many things in the real world) are nonlinear. When a system is nonlinear, you can usually describe its behavior using the gamma function, shown in **Figure 11.16** and the equation

```
Output = inputgamma 0 <= input <= 1
```

In this function, the darkest and brightest values (0.0 and 1.0) are always fixed, and the gamma value determines how the transition between them behaves. Successive applications of gamma can be concatenated by multiplying them together. Applying gamma and then 1/gamma has the net result of doing nothing. Gamma 1.0 is linear.

Figure 11.16 Graph of monitor gamma (2.2) with file gamma (0.4545) and linear (1.0). These are the color curves in question, with 0.4545 and 2.2 each acting as the direct inverse of the other.

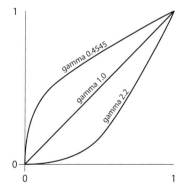

Mac monitors have traditionally had a gamma of 1.8, while the gamma value for PCs is 2.2. Because the electronics in your screen are slow to react from lower levels of input

voltage, a 1.0 gamma is simply too dark in either case; boosting this value compensates correctly.

The reason digital images do not appear dark, however, is that they have all been created with the inverse gamma function baked in to prebrighten pixels before they are displayed (**Figure 11.17**). Yes, all of them.

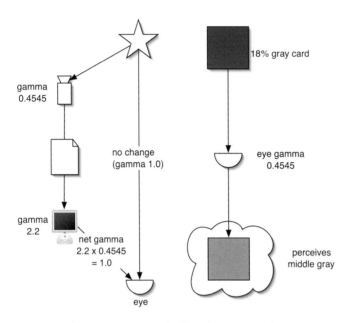

Figure 11.17 The gamma settings in the file and monitor complement one another to result in faithful image reproduction.

Because encoding spaces are not compositing spaces, working directly with images that appear on your monitor can pose problems. Similar to log encoding, video gamma encoding allocates more values to dark pixels, so they weigh more than they should. Video color space is not much more valid than Cineon color space for recreating the way light behaves in the world at large.

Linear Floating Point HDR

In the real world, light behaves linearly. Turn on two lightbulbs of equivalent wattage where you previously had one and the entire scene becomes exactly twice as bright.

Gamma-rama

In case all this gamma talk hasn't already blown your mind, allow me to clarify how monitor gamma and human vision work together. The question often comes up—why is middle gray 18% and not 50%? And why does 50% gray look like middle gray on my monitor, but not on a linear color chart?

. . . .

It turns out that your eyes also have a nonlinear response to color—your vision brightens low light, which helps you to see where it's dim, a survival advantage. The human eye is very sensitive to small amounts of light, and it gets less sensitive as brightness increases. Your eye effectively brightens the levels, and objects in the world are, in fact, darker than they appear—or, they become darker when we represent their true linear nature.

. . . .

The fact that 18% gray (or somewhere around that level; there is some disagreement about the exact number) looks like middle gray to your eye tells us that the eye does its own gamma correction of roughly 0.36: $50\% \times 0.36 = 18\%$.

A linear color space lets you simulate this effect simply by doubling pixel values. Because this re-creates the color space of the original scene, linear pixels are often referred to as scene-referred values, and doubling them in this manner can easily send values beyond monitor range.

The Exposure effect in After Effects converts the image to which it is applied to linear color before doing its work unless you specifically tell it not to do so by checking Bypass Linear Light Conversion. It internally applies a .4545 gamma correction to the image (1 divided by 2.2, inverting standard monitor gamma) before adjusting.

NOTES

To follow this discussion, choose Decimal in the Info panel menu (this is the default for 32 bpc). 0.0 to 1.0 values are those falling in Low Dynamic Range, or LDR—those values typically described in 8 bit as 0 to 255. Any values outside this range are HDR, 32 bpc only.

A common misconception is that if you work solely in the domain of video you have no need for floating point. But just because your input and output are restricted to the 0.0 to 1.0 range doesn't mean that overbright values above 1.0 won't figure into the images you create. The 11_sunrise.aep project included on your disc shows how they can add to your scene even when created on the fly.

The examples in **Table 11.1** show the difference between making adjustments to digital camera photos in their native video space and performing those same operations in linear space. In all cases, an unaltered photograph featuring the equivalent in-camera effect is shown for comparison.

The table's first column contains the images brightened by one stop, an increment on a camera's aperture, which controls how much light is allowed through the lens. Widening the aperture by one stop allows twice as much light to enter. An increase of three stops brightens the image by a factor of eight ($2 \times 2 \times 2$, or 2^3).

To double pixel values in video space is to quickly blow out bright areas in the image. Video pixels are already encoded with extra brightness and can't take much more.

The curtain and computer screen lose detail in video space that is retained in linear space. The linear image is nearly indistinguishable from the actual photo for which camera exposure time was doubled (another practical way to brighten by one stop).

TABLE 11.1 Comparison of Adjustments in Native Video Space and in Linear Space

	BRIGHTEN ONE STOP	LENS DEFOCUS	MOTION BLUR
Original Image			
Filtered in Video Space			
Filtered in Linear Space			
Real-World Photo			

The second column simulates an out-of-focus scene using Fast Blur. You may be surprised to see an overall darkening with bright highlights fading into the background—at least in video space. In linear, the highlights pop much better. See how the little man in the Walk sign stays bright in linear but almost fades away in video because of the extra emphasis given to dark pixels in video space. Squint your eyes and you notice that only the video image darkens overall. Because a defocused lens doesn't cause any less light to enter it, regular 8 bpc blur does not behave like a true defocus.

The table's third column uses After Effects' built-in motion blur to simulate the streaking caused by quick panning as the photo was taken. Pay particular attention to the highlight on the lamp; notice how it leaves a long, bright streak in the linear and in-camera examples. Artificial dulling of highlights is the most obvious giveaway of nonlinear image processing.

Artists have dealt with the problems of working directly in video space for years without even knowing we're compensating all the time. A perfect example is the Screen transfer mode, which is additive in nature but whose calculations are clearly convoluted when compared with the pure Add transfer mode. Screen uses a multiply-toward-white function with the advantage of avoiding the clipping associated with Add. But Add's reputation comes from its application in bright video-space images. Screen was invented only to help people be productive when working in video space, without overbrights; Screen darkens overbrights (**Figure 11.18**). Real light doesn't Screen, it Adds. Add is the new Screen, Multiply is the new Hard Light, and many other blending modes fall away completely in linear floating point.

Figure 11.18 Watch those highlights. Adding in video space blows out (left), but Screen in video looks better (center). Adding in linear is best (right).

HDR Source and Linearized Working Space

Should you in fact be fortunate enough to have high-bit-depth source images with over-range values, there are indisputable benefits to working in 32-bit linear, even if your final output uses a plain old video format that cannot accommodate these values.

In **Figure 11.19**, the lights are severely clipped by video space, which is not a problem so long as the image is only displayed; all of the images look fine printed on this page or displayed on your monitor. Add motion blur, however, and you see the problem at its most exaggerated; the points of light should not lose their intensity simply by being put into motion.

TIP

Linear blending is available without 32 bpc HDR; in Project Settings, choose Blend Colors using 1.0 Gamma. This feature is described in detail near the end of the chapter.

Figure 11.19 An HDR image is blurred without floating point (left) and with floating point (center), before being shown as low dynamic range (right).

The benefits of floating point aren't restricted to blurs, however; they just happen to be an easy place to see the difference. Every operation in a compositing pipeline gains extra realism from the presence of floating point pixels and linear blending.

Figure 11.20 features an HDR image on which a simple composite is performed, once in video space and once using linear floating point. In the floating point version, the dark translucent layer acts like sunglasses on the bright window, revealing extra detail exactly as a filter on a camera lens would. The soft edges of a motion-blurred object also behave realistically as bright highlights push through. Without floating point there is no extra information to reveal, so

CLOSE-UP

Terminology

Linear floating point HDR compositing uses *radiometrically linear*, or *scene-referred*, color data. For the purposes of this discussion, this is perhaps best called "linear light compositing," or "linear floating point," or just simply, "linear." The alternative mode to which you are accustomed is "gamma-encoded," or "monitor color space," or simply, "video."

Figure 11.20 A source image with over-range values in the highlights (top) is composited without floating point (bottom left) and with floating point (bottom right).

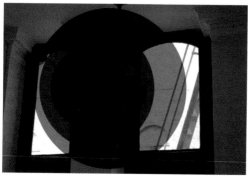

the window looks clipped and dull and motion blur doesn't interact with the scene properly.

32 Bits per Channel

Although it is not necessary to use HDR source to take advantage of an HDR pipeline, it offers a clear glimpse of this brave new world. Open 11_treeHDR_lin.aep; it contains a comp made up of a single image in 32 bit EXR format (used to create Figure 11.19). With the Info panel clearly visible, move your cursor around the frame.

As your cursor crosses highlights—the lights on the tree, specular highlights on the wall and chair, and most especially, in the window—the values are seen to be well above 1.0, the maximum value you will ever see doing the same in 8 bpc or 16 bpc mode. Remember that you can quickly toggle between color spaces by **Alt/Option**-clicking the project color depth identifier at the bottom of the Project panel.

NOTES

Included on the disc are two similar images, sanityCheck.exr and sanityCheck.tif. The 32 bpc EXR file is linearized, but the 8 bpc TIFF file is not. Two corresponding projects are also included, one using no color profile, the other employing a linear profile. These should help illustrate the different appearances of a linear and a gamma-encoded image.

Any experienced digital artist would assume that there is no detail in that window—it is blown out to solid white forevermore in LDR. However, you may have noticed an extra icon and accompanying numerical value that appears at the bottom of the composition panel in a 32 bpc project (**Figure 11.21**). This is the Exposure control; its icon looks like a camera aperture and it performs an analogous function—controlling the exposure (total amount of light) of a scene the way you would stop a camera up or down (by adjusting its aperture).

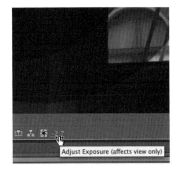

Figure 11.21 Exposure is an HDR preview control that appears in the Composition panel in 32 bpc mode.

Drag to the left on the numerical text and something amazing happens. Not only does the lighting in the scene decrease naturally, as if the light itself were being brought down, but at somewhere around -10.0, a gentle blue gradient appears in the window (**Figure 11.22**, left).

Figure 11.22 At −10 Exposure, the room is dark other than the tree lights and detail becomes visible out the window. At +3, the effect is exactly that of a camera that was open 3 stops brighter than the unadjusted image.

Drag the other direction, into positive Exposure range, and the scene begins to look like an overexposed photo; the light proportions remain and the highlights bloom outward (**Figure 11.22**, right).

The Exposure control in the Composition panel is a preview-only control (there is an effect by the same name that renders); scan with your cursor, and Info panel values do not vary according to its setting. This control offers a quick way to check what is happening in the out-of-range areas of a composition. With a linear light image,

NOTES

Keep in mind that for each 1.0 adjustment upward or downward of Exposure, you double (or halve) the light levels in the scene. Echoing the earlier discussion, a +3.0 Exposure setting sets the light levels 8× (or 2^3) brighter.

each integer increment represents the equivalent of one photographic stop, or a doubling (or halving) of linear light value.

Mixed Bit Depths and Compander

Most effects don't, alas, support 32 bpc, although there are dozens that do. Apply a 16 bpc or (shudder) 8 bpc effect, however, and the overbrights in your 32 bpc project disappear—all clipped to 1.0. Any effect will reduce the image being piped through it to its own color space limitations. A small warning sign appears next to the effect to remind you that it does not support the current bit depth. You may even see a warning explaining the dangers of applying this effect.

Of course, this doesn't mean you need to avoid these effects to work in 32 bpc. It may mean you have to cheat, and After Effects includes a preset allowing you to do just that: Compress-Expand Dynamic Range (contained in Effects & Presets > Animation Presets > Image – Utilities. Make certain Show Animation Presets is checked in the panel menu).

This preset actually consists of two instances of the HDR Compander effect, which was specifically designed to bring floating point values back into LDR range. The first instance is automatically renamed Compress, and the second, Expand, which is how the corresponding modes are set. You set the Gain of Compress to whatever is the brightest overbright value you wish to preserve, up to 100. The values are then compressed into LDR range, allowing you to apply your LDR effect. The Gain (as well as Gamma) of Expand is linked via an expression to Compress so that the values round-trip back to HDR (**Figure 11.23**).

Additionally, there are smart ways to set up a project to ensure that Compander plays the minimal possible role. As much as possible, group all of your LDR effects together, and keep them away from the layers that use blending modes where float values are most essential. For example, apply an LDR effect via a separate adjustment layer instead of directly on a layer with a blending mode. Also, if possible, apply the LDR effects first, then boost the result

Floating Point Files

As you've already seen, there is one class of files that does not need to be converted to linear space: floating point files. These files are already storing scene-referred values, complete with overbright information. Common formats supported by After Effects are Radiance (.hdr) and floating point .tiff, not to mention .psd, but the most universal and versatile is Industrial Light + Magic's OpenEXR format. OpenEXR uses efficient 16-bit floating point pixels, can store any number of image channels, supports lossless compression, and is already supported by most 3D programs thanks to being an open source format.

After Effects CS4 offers expanded support of the OpenEXR format by bundling plug-ins from fnord software, which provide access to multiple layers and channels within these files. EXtractoR can open any floating point image channel in an EXR file, and Identifier can open the other, non-image channels such as Object and Material ID.

8 and 16 bpc effects clip only the image that they process. Apply one to a layer, you clip that layer *only*. Apply one to an Adjustment Layer and you clip everything below. Add an LDR comp or layer to an otherwise HDR comp in a 32 bpc project, it remains otherwise HDR.

into HDR range to apply any additional 32 bpc effects and blending modes.

Blend Colors Using 1.0 Gamma

After Effects CS4 contains a fantastic option to linearize image data only when performing blending operations: the Blend Colors Using 1.0 Gamma toggle in Project Settings. This allows you to take advantage of linear blending, which makes Add and Multiply blending modes actually work properly, even in 8 bpc or 16 bpc modes.

The difference is quite simple. A linearized working space does all image processing in gamma 1.0, as follows

```
footage --> to linear PWS ->
   Layer ->
      Mask -> Effects -> Transform ->
         Blend With Comp ->
   Comp -> from linear PWS to OM space ->
output
```

whereas linearized blending performs only the blending step, where the image is combined with the composition, in gamma 1.0

```
footage --> to PWS ->
   Layer ->
      Mask -> Effects -> Transform -> to linear PWS ->
         Blend With Comp -> to PWS ->
   Comp -> from PWS to OM space ->
output
```

(Special thanks to Dan Wilk at Adobe for detailing this out.)

Because effects aren't added in linear color, blurs no longer interact correctly with overbrights (although they do composite more nicely), and you don't get the subtle benefits to Transform operations; After Effects' much maligned scaling operations are much improved in linear floating point. Also, 3D lights behave more like actual lights in a fully linearized working space.

I prefer the linear blending option when in lower bit depths and there is no need to manage over-range values; it gives me the huge benefit of more elegant composites

Figure 11.23 Effects & Presets > Animation Presets > Presets > Image - Utilities includes the Compress-Expand Dynamic Range preset, also known as the Compander (Compressor/Expander). It consists of two instances of the HDR Compander effect, one named Compress and the other, Expand, wired with an expression to undo whatever Compress does. The idea is to place your 8 or 16 bpc effect (such as Match Grain, shown) between the two of them. This prevents clipping of over-range values. If banding appears as a result of Compress-Expand, Gamma can be adjusted to weight the compressed image more toward the region of the image (probably the shadows) where the banding occurs. You are sacrificing image fidelity in order to preserve a compressed version of the HDR pipeline.

and blending modes without forcing me to think about managing effects in linear color. Certain key effects, in particular Exposure, helpfully operate in linear gamma mode.

Output

Finally, what good is it working in linear floating point if the output bears no resemblance to what you see in the composition viewer? Just because you work in 32-bit floating point color does not mean you have to render your images that way.

Keeping in mind that each working space can be linear or not, if you work in a linearized color space and then render to a format that is typically gamma encoded (as most are), the gamma-encoded version of the working space will also be used. After Effects spells this out for you explicitly in the Description section of the Color Management tab.

To this day, the standard method to pass around footage with over-range values, particularly if it is being sent for film-out, is to use 10-bit log-encoded Cineon/DPX. This is also converted for you from 32 bpc linear, but be sure to choose the Working Space as the output profile and that in Cineon Settings, you use the Standard preset.

The great thing about Cineon/DPX with a standard 10-bit profile is that it is a universal standard. Facilities around the world know what to do with it even if they've never encountered a file with an embedded color profile. As was detailed earlier in the chapter, it is capable of taking full advantage of the dynamic range of film, which is to this day the most dynamic display medium widely available.

Conclusion

This chapter concludes Section II, which focused on the most fundamental techniques of effects compositing. In the next and final section, you'll apply those techniques. You'll also learn about the importance of observation, as well as some specialized tips and tricks for specific effects compositing situations that re-create particular environments, settings, conditions, and natural phenomena.

SECTION III

Creative Explorations

Chapter 12 Light   381

Chapter 13 Climate and the Environment   405

Chapter 14 Pyrotechnics: Heat, Fire, Explosions   429

12

Light

There are two kinds of light: the glow that illuminates and the glare that obscures.

—James Thurber

Light

There's more to understanding how light works in the world than knowing the science of it, although that is certainly essential. The work of a compositor is much like that of a painter or cinematographer, in that a combination of technical knowledge, interpretation, and even intuition are all part of getting a scene "right."

Other areas of digital production rely on elaborate models to simulate the way light works in the physical world. Like a painter, the compositor observes the play of light in the three-dimensional world to re-create it two-dimensionally. Like a cinematographer, you succeed with a feeling for how lighting and color decisions affect the beauty and drama of a scene and how the camera gathers them.

Several chapters in this book touch upon principles of the behavior of light. Chapter 5 was about the bread and butter work of the compositor—matching brightness and color of a foreground and background. Chapter 9 was all about how the world looks through a lens. Chapter 11 explored less straightforward ways in which After Effects can re-create the way color and light values behave.

This chapter is dedicated to practical situations involving light that you as a compositor must re-create. It's important to distinguish lighting conditions you can easily emulate and those that are essentially out of bounds—although, for a compositor with a good eye and patience, the seemingly "impossible" becomes a welcome challenge and the source of a favorite war story.

Source and Direction

In many scenes, there is clearly more involved with light than matching brightness and contrast channel by channel.

Light direction is fundamental, especially where the quality of the light is *hard* (direct) rather than *soft* (diffuse).

Such a huge variety of light situations are possible in a shot, and in an infinite array of combinations, that it becomes difficult to make any broad statements stand up about lighting. This section, however, tries to pin down some general guidelines and workflows for manipulating the light situation of your scene.

Location and Quality

You may have specific information about the lighting conditions that existed when source footage was shot. On a set, you can easily identify the placement and type of each light, and away from set, this information may be found in a camera report or on-set photos. For a naturally lit shot, it's mostly a question of the position of the sun relative to the camera and the reflectivity of the surrounding environment.

Sometimes the location and direction of light is readily apparent, but not as often as you might think. Hard, direct light casts clear shadows and raises contrast, and soft, diffuse light lowers contrast and casts soft shadows (if any). That much seems clear.

These, however, are broad stereotypes, which do not always behave as expected in the real world. Hard light aimed directly at a subject from the same direction as the camera actually flattens out detail, effectively decreasing contrast. And artificial lighting is usually multiple sources in a single scene, which work against one another to diffuse hard shadows (**Figure 12.1**).

Figure 12.1 Interior sets, like interior environments, are typically lit by more than one source, creating multiple soft highlights and shadows.

Neutralize Direction and Hotspots

When the direction or diffusion of light on a foreground element doesn't match the target background environment, that's potentially a big problem. The solution is generally to neutralize the mismatch by isolating and minimizing it, rather than actually trying to fix the discrepancy by attempting to simulate relighting the element in 2D.

Every shot in the world has unique light characteristics, but a couple of overall strategies apply. Once you've exhausted simple solutions such as flopping the shot (where lighting is on the wrong side), you can

▶ Isolate and remove directional clues around the element, such as cast shadows (typically by matting or rotoscoping them out).

▶ Isolate and reduce contrast of highlights and shadows in the element itself, typically with a Levels or Curves adjustment (potentially aided by a luma matte, described later in this chapter).

▶ Invert the highlights and shadows with a counter-gradient.

The simple way to undo evidence of too strong a key light in a scene is to create a counter-gradient as a track matte for an adjustment layer; a Levels or Curves effect on this layer affects the image proportionally to this gradient. The Ramp effect can be set and even animated to the position of a key light hotspot (**Figure 12.2**).

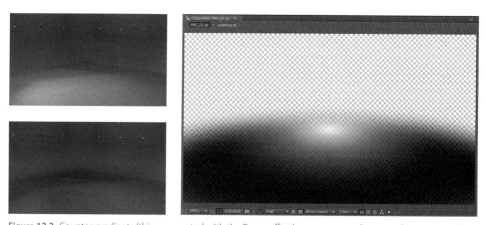

Figure 12.2 Counter-gradients (this one created with the Ramp effect) can serve an adjustment layer used to lower the brightness and contrast in the hotspot region.

A radial ramp is merely linear, which is not the correct model for light falloff. Light's intensity diminishes proportionally to its distance from the source squared, according to the *inverse square law*. An object positioned twice as far from a single light source is illuminated by one-quarter the amount of light. To mimic this with a gradient, precomp it, duplicate the radial gradient layer, and set the upper of the two layers to a Multiply blending mode (**Figure 12.3**).

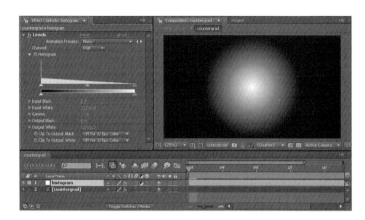

Figure 12.3 A standard Ramp gradient (top left) is linear, as can be seen in the Histogram, but light falls off in a logarithmic, inverse-square pattern, so the matte used in Figure 12.2 multiplies together two linear gradients (bottom left) with Linear blending enabled (bottom right) in Project Settings even though it's not a 32 bpc linear HDR project. Again, light works in linear.

Of course, you don't want to fight the fundamental source lighting in this way unless you absolutely have to do so; hopefully you will rarely have to "fix" lighting and will most often want to work with what you've got to make it even stronger and more dramatic.

Color Looks

Have you ever seen unadjusted source clips or behind-the-scenes footage from a favorite movie? It's a striking reminder about the bold and deliberate use of color in modern films. Look at the work prints or on-set making-of video—the magic more or less disappears.

In older films color looks had to be accomplished optically and photochemically. Strong color filters would be used in the camera's *matte box* to reduce or enhance the effect of the source lighting and color. The well-known *bleach-bypass method* would be used to strip certain colors out in the film lab. Nowadays, a digital production pipeline has made the photochemical approach rarer, although optical filters still play a large role in shooting. Meanwhile, it's becoming more and more common for an entire feature-length production to be graded through a *digital intermediate*, or *D.I.*

After Effects has an advantage over D.I. software such as a DaVinci system in that it is a true compositing system, with fine controls over image selection. After Effects was not created principally with the colorist in mind, so its primary color tools (as described in Chapter 5) are simpler and less interactive. Third-party solutions such as Colorista and Magic Bullet Looks, both from Red Giant, have appeared to help bridge this gap.

Keeping in mind that your job as a compositor is to emulate the world as it looks when viewed with a camera, it can be effective to begin by emulating physical lens elements.

The Virtual Lens Filter

Suppose a shot (or some portion of it) should simply be "warmer" or "cooler." With only a camera and some film, you might accomplish this transformation by adding a lens filter. It could be a solid color (blue for cooler, amber to warm things up) or a gradient (amber to white to change only the color of a sky above the horizon).

Add a colored solid and set its blending mode to Color. Choose a color that is pleasing to your eye, with brightness and saturation well above 50%. Use blue or green for a cooler look, red or yellow for a warmer one (**Figure 12.4**).

Figure 12.4 Here, the four color filters are applied as a test with a Color blending mode, and with the Linear mode, so that they behave a lot like lens filters of an equivalent color.

At 100%, this is the equivalent of a full-color tint of the image, which is too much. Dial Opacity down between 10% and 50%, seeking the threshold where the source colors remain discernable, filtered by the added color to set the look.

To re-create a graded filter, typically used to affect only the sky, apply the Ramp effect to the solid and change the Start Color to your tint color; an amber filter adds the look of an extremely smoggy urban day. This is best applied with an Add or Screen mode instead of Color because the default End Color, white, desaturates the lower part of the image.

Black and White

When removing color from an element entirely, there is a huge difference between using the Hue/Saturation effect and the likely alternatives. Counterintuitively, Hue/Saturation is typically not the best choice to create a black-and-white image because it maintains luminance proportions, and as was mentioned in a sidebar back in Chapter 6, that's not how the eye sees color. **Figure 12.5** illustrates the difference.

NOTES

The flag of Mars is a red, green, and blue tricolor selected by the Mars Society and flown into orbit by the Space Shuttle Discovery. It was not used by Marvin the Martian to claim Planet X.

Figures 12.5 This is the flag of Mars (left): it shows three fields of pure red, green, and blue (no earthly location was logical enough to choose this). Tint (center) compensates for the perceptual differences in human color vision when desaturating, Hue/Saturation (right) does not.

Even if converting an image to black and white is only an intermediate step, you're best off doing so either using the Tint effect at the default settings or a fully desaturated solid (black, white, or gray, it doesn't matter) with a Color blending mode. To really get the conversion right may involve adjusting or shifting color channels prior to the color-to-black-and-white conversion (**Figure 12.6**).

Figure 12.6 A real color to grayscale conversion may involve carefully rebalancing color, contrast, or saturation. Here, the face and lamp are important and get individual adjustments in color prior to conversion. (Images courtesy of 4charros.)

TIP

Many images benefit from a subtle reduction in overall Saturation using the Hue/Saturation tool. This moves red, green, and blue closer together and can reduce the "juicy" quality that makes bright colored images hard to look at.

Day for Night

Stronger optical effects are even possible, such as making a daytime scene appear as if it were shot on a moonlit night. Known in French as *la nuit américaine* (and immortalized in Francois Truffaut's ode to filmmaking of the same name), this involves a simple trick. Shoot an exterior scene under ordinary daylight with a dark blue lens filter to compensate for the difficulty of successful low light night shoots. If there is direct sunlight, it's meant to read as moonlight.

Lighting techniques and film itself have improved since this was a common convention of films, particularly westerns, but digital cameras tend to become noisy and muddy under low light.

Figure 12.7 An ordinary twilight shot of a house at dusk becomes a spooky Halloween mansion. Converting day for night avoids the problems associated with low-light shooting. (Images courtesy of Mars Productions.)

Figure 12.7 shows the difference between a source image that is blue and desaturated and an actual night look; if instead you're starting with a daylight image, look at the images on the book's disc, which take the image more in that direction. Overall, remember that the eye cannot see color without light, so only areas that are perceived to be well illuminated should have a hue outside the range between deep blue and black.

Color Timing Effects

Digital tools can of course go far beyond what is possible with lens filters. The industry standard tools rely on a *three-way color corrector*, which allows you to tint the image in three basic luminance ranges—highlights, midtones, and shadows—adjusting each separately via wheels which control hue and brightness.

Colorista from Red Giant is a three-way color corrector that opens the door to coloring footage the way it would be done with a feature film D.I. grade. Third-party plug-ins are generally considered beyond the scope of this book, and colorist work based on three-way color correction has merited whole books and courses of its own, but this plug-in opens the door to grading primary and secondary colors like a pro.

A primary grade might involve injecting unexpected hues into each range: blue shadows, pink highlights, green midtones. The secondary grade then isolates an area of the scene—often faces or other dramatically key elements—and determines how their color and contrast complements the scene as a whole.

The grade is then applied across several shots in what is traditionally called the *color timing* process—literally, making color consistent across time, which typically involves much more than simply applying the same adjustment to every shot. You can use the techniques described here and in Section II to first balance a shot, then add its color look, finally bringing out any key exceptional details; then voila, you are a colorist.

Source, Reflection, and Shadow

Sometimes you work with source footage that contains strong lighting and thus offers a clear target. Other times, it's up to you to add a strong look. Either way, reference is your friend. You will be surprised how much bolder and more fascinating nature's choices are than your own.

Unexpected surprises that simply "work" can be the *kiss of love* for a scene—that something extra that nobody requested but everyone who is paying attention appreciates. Details of light and shadow are one area where this extra effort can really pay off.

Big, bold, daring choices about light can and should become almost invisible if they are appropriate to a scene, adding to the dramatic quality of the shot instead of merely showing off what you as an artist can do.

Backlighting and Light Wrap

The conditions of a backlit scene are a classic example where the compositor often does not go far enough to match what actually happens in the real world.

This technique is designed for scenes that contain backlighting conditions and a foreground that, although it may be lit to match those conditions, lacks light wrapping around the edges (**Figure 12.8**).

TIP

If you don't like the idea of adding a third-party plug-in to your workflow, there is even a free alternative wired to a Color Balance (HLS) effect included in *The DV Rebel's Guide* by Stu Maschwitz (Peachpit Press) as RebelCC.

NOTES

New in this edition of the book, the light wrap formula outlined below has been converted to a script created by Jeff Almasol. You can find it on the book's disc as rd_Lightwrap. Select the matted source layer and let this script do the work.

Figure 12.8 The silhouetted figure is color corrected to match, but lacks any of the light wrap clearly visible around the figures seated on the beach.

Set up a light wrap effect as follows:

1. Create a new composition that contains the background and foreground layers, exactly as they are positioned and animated in the master composition. You can do this simply by duplicating the master comp and renaming it something intuitive, such as Light Wrap. If the foreground or background consists of several layers, it will probably be simpler to precompose them into two layers, one each for the foreground and background.

2. Set Silhouette Alpha blending mode for the foreground layer, punching a hole in the background.

3. Add an adjustment layer at the top, and apply Fast Blur.

4. In Fast Blur, check the Repeat Edge Pixels toggle on and crank up the blurriness.

5. Duplicate the foreground layer, move the copy to the top, and set its blending mode to Stencil Alpha, leaving a halo of background color that matches the shape of the foreground (**Figure 12.9**, top). If the light source is not directly behind the subject, you can offset this layer to match, producing more light on the matching side.

6. Place the resulting comp in the master comp and adjust opacity (and optionally switch the blending mode to Add, Screen, or Lighten) until you have what you're after. You may need to go back to the Light Wrap comp to further adjust the blur (**Figure 12.9**, bottom).

Figure 12.9 The background is blurred into the matte area (top) in a precomp and added back into the scene to better integrate the silhouette (bottom).

What Causes a Lens Flare?

Unlike your eye, which has only one very flexible lens, camera lenses are typically made up of a series of inflexible lens elements. These elements are coated to prevent light reflecting off of them under normal circumstances. Extreme amounts of light, however, are reflected somewhat by each element.

Zoom lenses contain many focusing elements and tend to generate a complex-looking flare with lots of individual reflections. Prime lenses generate fewer.

Many factors besides the lens elements contribute to the look of a flare. Aperture blades within the lens cause reflective corners that often result in streaks; the number of streaks corresponds to the number of blades. The shape of the flares sometimes corresponds to the shape of the aperture (a pentagon for a five-sided aperture, a hexagon for six). Dust and scratches on the lens also reflect light.

FInally, lens flares look very different depending on whether they were shot on film or video; excess light bleeds out in different directions and patterns.

When there is no fill light on the foreground subject whatsoever, most cameras are incapable of picking up as much detail in the foreground as your eye might see. In your reference photo, an unlit foreground subject might appear completely silhouetted. Because the foreground subjects are often the stars of the scene, you might have to compensate, allowing enough light and detail in the foreground that the viewer can see facial expressions and other important dramatic detail.

In other words, this might be a case where your reference conflicts with what is needed for the story. Try to strike a balance, but remember, when the story loses, nobody wins.

Flares

For our purposes a "flare" is any direct light source that appears in shot, not just a cheesy 17-element lens flare whenever the sun pokes around the moon in some science fiction television show from the early 1990s (or in several shots from the more recent movie *Hancock*). These don't come for free in After Effects; 3D lights don't even create a visible source if placed in shot until you add the Trapcode Lux effect (included on this book's disc).

Real lens flares are never cheesy: Our eyes accept them as natural, even beautiful artifacts without necessarily understanding anything about what actually causes them (**Figure 12.10**). *Transformers*, composited at ILM, is a recent example of a visual effects movie full of great looking light optics.

Figure 12.10 You might think of a lens flare as one of those element rings caused by a zoom lens pointing at the sun, but flares occur anytime a bright light source appears in or near frame. Here, the green traffic light causes a large flare without even appearing in frame, and numerous other lights bloom and flare. (Image from Quality of Life, courtesy of Benjamin Morgan.)

Therefore, to get lens flares or even simple glints right (not cheesy), good reference is often key. Only a tiny percentage of your viewers may know the difference between lens flares from a 50 mm prime and a 120 mm zoom lens, yet somehow, if you get it wrong, it reads as phony. Odd.

Here are some things you should know about lens flares:

Prior to the 1970s-era of *Easy Rider* and moon shots, flares were regarded as errors on the part of the cinematographer, and shots containing them were carefully noted on the camera report and retaken.

▶ They are consistent for a given lens. Their angles vary according to the position of the light, but not the shape or arrangement of the component flares.

▶ The big complex flares with lots of components are created by long zoom lenses with many internal lens elements. Wider prime lenses create simpler flares.

▶ Because they are caused within the lens, flares beyond the source appear superimposed over the image, even over objects in the foreground that partially block the source flare.

Moreover, not every bright light source that appears in frame will cause a lens flare—not even the sun.

The Lens Flare effect included with After Effects is rather useless as it contains only three basic presets. Knoll Light Factory, available from Red Giant Software, is much more helpful both because the presets correspond to real lenses and because the components can be fully customized in a modular fashion. The lens flare plug-in offered by The Foundry as part of Tinderbox also makes realistic-looking flares possible, although the included defaults are not so convincing.

Reflected Light

Reflected light is another "kiss of love" opportunity for a scene. You might not notice that it's missing, but a glimmer, glint, or full reflection can add not only realism but pizzazz to a shot.

Glints are specular flares that occur when light is reflected toward the camera from shiny parts of an element in scene, such as the chrome of the taxi in **Figure 12.11**, taken from the Chapter 5 color matching example.

Figure 12.11 This sequence shows the glint that plays off the chrome areas of the taxi as it passes a spot in the frame where the sun is reflected directly into the camera lens.

Figure 12.12 There's not a whole lot to a glint when you look at it closely, but it helps sell the plane.

The same plug-ins used for flares (Trapcode Lux, Knoll Light Factory, and Tinderbox) can be used to create glints, with more modest settings that don't create all the lens reflections. **Figure 12.12** shows that there's not necessarily a whole lot to a single glint. An Add mode makes these work even in 32 bpc HDR (in which case they create over-range values, just as they would on film).

Light Scattering and Volume

Light scatters as it encounters particles in the air, most dramatically causing the phenomena of volumetric light or God rays. Our atmosphere does not permit light to travel directly to the camera, uninterrupted, as it does in outer space. Instead, the light ricochets off tiny particles in the air, revealing its path.

The effect can be subtle. Lights that appear in the scene, casting their beams at the camera, tend to have a glowing halo around them. If the light traveled directly to the camera, the outline of the source light would be clear. Instead, light rays hit particles on their way to the camera and head off in slightly new directions, causing a halo (**Figure 12.13**).

Figure 12.13 You're so used to light halation that it looks wrong to lower the exposure so that it disappears.

Add more particles in the air (in the form of smoke, fog, or mist), and you get more of a halo, as well as the conditions under which volumetric light occurs. God rays are the result of the fact that light from an omnidirectional source, such as the sun, travels outward in a continuous arc (**Figure 12.14**).

Figure 12.14 The Devil Rays are a baseball team; these are God rays.

The CC Light Rays effect is probably most helpful among those included with After Effects to re-create volumetric light effects, and even God rays. It not only boosts and

Three-Way Blur

After Effects offers quite a few blur effects, but three are most common for general usage: Gaussian Blur, Fast Blur (which at best quality is no different), and Box Blur, which can match the other two but offers more flexibility.

At the default Iterations setting (1), a Box Blur can seem crude and, well, boxy, but it can approximate the look of a defocused lens without all the more complex polygons of Lens Blur; you can also hold it out to the horizontal or vertical axis to create a nice motion blur approximation (where Directional Blur is actually too smooth and Gaussian).

Raising the Box Blur Iterations setting above 3 not only amplifies the blur but refines the blur kernel beyond anything the other two effects are capable of producing. What actually occurs is that the blur goes from a square appearance (suiting the name box blur) to a softer, rounder look. You're more likely to notice the difference working with over-range bright values in 32 bit HDR.

Fast Blur and Box Blur also each include a Repeat Edge Pixels checkbox; enable this to avoid dark borders when blurring a full frame image. The same setting with these two effects will not, alas, produce the same amount of blur even if Box Blur is set to 3 iterations (to match Fast Blur).

causes halation around the source light, but it also adds rays coming straight at camera. These rays can be made more prominent by boosting radius and intensity, but in order to create a God rays effect and not overwhelm an entire image with rays, it's usually best to make a target source and apply the effect to that. For example, you can

1. Add a solid of your preferred color.

2. Apply Fractal Noise (default settings are acceptable to begin).

3. Mask the solid around the target God rays source area. Feather it heavily.

4. Apply CC Light Rays. Place the Center at the God rays target. Boost Intensity and Radius settings until the rays are prominent.

5. For rays only (no fractal noise) set Transfer Mode to None.

6. Set a Subtract mask or Alpha Inverted track matte to create occluded areas for the rays to wrap around, as in **Figure 12.15**.

Figure 12.15 The included CC Light Rays effect is essential to creating your own volumetric light effects in After Effects. Masks or mattes can be used to occlude rays.

NOTES

A more straightforward plug-in for volumetric light is Trapcode Lux, which can derive volume and a flare from any After Effects 3D light simply by applying it to an adjustment layer.

You can further hold out and mask out the rays as needed, even precomping and moving the source outside of frame if necessary. To make the rays animate, keyframe the Evolution property in Fractal Noise or add an expression such as `time*60` causing it to undulate over time. Different Fractal Type and Noise Type settings will also yield unique rays.

Shadows

As there is light, so must there be shadows. Unfortunately, they can be difficult to re-create in 2D because they interact with 3D space and volume, none of which 2D layers have. The behavior of shadows can be unpredictable, but luckily, your audience typically doesn't know how they should look in your scene either.

You can certainly cast a shadow from a matted layer onto a plane by positioning each of them in 3D space and properly positioning a light. Be sure that you first change Casts Shadows for the matted layer from its default Off setting to

On or Only (the latter option making it possible to create a precomp containing only the shadow).

You can instead corner pin the matte to the angle at which the shadow should fall and avoid the 3D setup altogether. In either case, the problem is that the illusion breaks if the light source is more than 10 degrees off-axis from the camera. The more you light a 2D element from the side, the more it just breaks (**Figure 12.16**).

Figure 12.16 Compare the fake 3D shadow with the real thing and you instantly grasp the problem with this approach. You can cast a good shadow head-on, but not at this steep an angle.

There's also the possibility of cheating: if it's easy to add ground surface that would obscure a shadow (for example, grass instead of dirt), do so, and no one will even expect to see a shadow because it no longer belongs there.

Contact Shadows and Indirect Light

For the most part, successful shading in a 2D scene relies on getting what you can practically, and getting creative when there are no practical shadows. There are plenty of cases where a full cast shadow would be correct and no shadow at all clearly looks wrong, but a simple contact shadow will at least remove glaring contrast.

A contact shadow is a lot like a drop shadow, basically just an offset, soft, dark copy directly behind the foreground. A drop shadow, however, is good only for casting a shadow onto an imaginary wall behind a logo, whereas a contact shadow is held out to only the areas of the foreground that have contact with the ground plane.

Figure 12.17 shows the foreground layer duplicated and placed behind the source. A mask is drawn around the base, and it is then offset downward. A blur is applied to soften the transparency channel. That gives you the matte.

Figure 12.17 A simple contact shadow can make the difference between an object that appears to sit on a surface and an object that appears to float in space.

A shadow is not just a black overlay; it's an area of reduced light and therefore, color. Instead of darkening down the matte itself to create the shadow, create an adjustment layer just below the contact shadow layer and set an Alpha track matte. Add a Levels (or if you prefer, Curves) effect and adjust brightness and gamma downward to create your shadow. Treat it like a color correction, working on separate channels if necessary; the result is more interesting and accurate than a pool of blackness (**Figure 12.18**).

Reflected light is another type of contact lighting that plays a role in how things look in the real world, and thus in your composited scenes. Most objects in the world have diffuse surfaces that reflect light; when the object is prominent or colorful enough, your eye expects it to affect other more neutral neighboring surfaces (**Figure 12.19**).

Figure 12.18 The obvious way to create a shadow is just to overlay a black layer and adjust opacity (top) but that approach looks bland, fails to match the shadows in the scene and flattens out detail. By applying the shadow layer as a track matte to an adjustment layer you can treat the shadow as a color correction and match the color and contrast of the scene's existing shadows (bottom).

Figure 12.19 The color influence of indirect light is not always so evident as with a bright saturated object, but it is always in play in a natural setting.

In 3D computer graphics this fact has been realized via global illumination, which considers light and surface interactions in a render. If you're working with a computer-generated scene, aim for a pass that includes these types of light interactions. If you have to create the effect from scratch, the method is similar to that of shadows or color matching: Create a selection of the area reflecting light, including any needed falloff (that may be the hard part), and use color correction tools to color match the adjacent object reflecting color.

Multipass 3D Compositing

Some artists, including a majority of those who work predominantly in 3D, labor under the delusion that you should finalize the look of a computer-generated element in one pass. Certainly, as it becomes more and more possible to adjust the look of a 3D model in real time (via the GPU, OpenGL) this becomes tempting.

However, it's possible to do better by dividing the render of a single element into multiple passes. This is different from rendering in layers, which while also useful for compositing is really only about separating foreground elements from the background. *Multipass rendering* is the technique of isolating individual surface qualities and creating a separate render for each. By surface qualities I mean things like specularity and wear and tear, also known as grunge. In his excellent book *Digital Lighting & Rendering, Second Edition* (Peachpit Press, 2006), Jeremy Birn calls out multiple benefits yielded by rendering a model on multiple passes:

▶ **Changes** can be made with little or no re-rendering. If a shadow is too dark or a glow is the wrong color, the adjustment can be made right in After Effects.

▶ **Integration** often requires multiple passes where the model interacts with the scene, casting a shadow on the ground or being reflected in water. If the cast shadow is simply part of a single render you lose all control over its appearance and cannot apply it as recommended in the previous section.

▶ **Reflections**, which often consume massive amounts of time to process, can be rendered at lower quality and blurred in After Effects.

▶ **Bump Maps** can be applied more selectively (held out by another pass such as a highlight or reflection pass).

▶ **Glows** can be created easily in 2D by simply blurring and boosting exposure of a specular pass.

▶ **Depth of Field** can be controlled entirely in 2D by using a Z pass as a matte for a blur adjustment layer.

▶ **Less render power and time** is required to render any one pass than the entire shaded model, so a lower powered computer can do more, and redoing any one element takes far less time than redoing the entire finished model.

Putting multiple passes to use is also surprisingly simple; the artistry is in all of the minute decisions about which combination of adjustments will bring the element to life. **Table 12.1** (on the next page) describes some common render passes and how they are typically used.

Other passes might include: a *Fresnel* (or *Incidence*) pass showing the sheen of indirect light and applied to an adjustment layer with a Luma Matte (raise Output Black in Levels to re-create sheen); a *Grunge* or *Dirt* map, applied as a Luma Inverted Matte, allowing you to dial in areas of wear and tear with Levels on an adjustment layer; a *Light* pass for any self-illuminated details; and a *Normal* pass showing the

NOTES

Got UV Maps? After Effects has the means to use them with the RE:Map plug-in from RE:Vision Effects. This allows you to map a texture to an object, using the UV map for coordinates, without returning to the 3D app that generated it or waiting for Live Photoshop 3D to support mapping in After Effects (which it doesn't in CS4).

TABLE 12.1 Ten Typical Multipass Render Layer Types

TYPE	COLOR/ GRAYSCALE	TYPICAL BLENDING MODE	DESCRIPTION	USE
Diffuse	Color	Normal	Full color render; includes diffuse illumination, color correction and texture, excludes reflections, highlights and shadows	Color basis for the element; main target for primary color
Specular	Color	Add or Screen	Isolated specular highlights	Control how highlights are rendered; can be reused to create a glow pass by simply blurring and raising exposure
Reflection	Color	Add or Screen	Self-reflections, other objects, environment	Control the prominence and color of reflections
Shadow	Grayscale	Luma Inverted Matte	Isolated translucent shadows in scene	Control appearance, color and softness of shadows; applied as a track matte to an adjustment layer with a Levels or Curves effect
Ambient	Color	Color	Color and texure maps without diffuse shading, specular highlights, shadows, or reflections	Color reference, can be used to make the color/texture of an object more pure and visible
Occlusion	Grayscale	Luma Inverted Matte	Shadows that result from soft illumination, simulating light from an overcast sky or well-lit room	Adds natural soft shadows to an object; these can be tinted to reflect the color of reflected light
Beauty	Color	Normal	A render of all passes	Reference: this is how the object or scene would appear if rendered in a single pass
Global Illumination	Color	Add or Screen	Indirect light added to the scene by global illumination, potentially including raytraced reflections and refractions	Control intensity of indirect lighting in scene
Matte/ Mask/ Alpha	Grayscale	Luma Matte	Can be used to contain multiple transparency masks for portions of the object or scene, one each on the red, green, blue, and alpha channels	
Depth/Z-depth/ Depth Map	Grayscale or non-image floating point	Luma Matte	Describes the distance of surface areas from the camera	Can be used to control depth effects such as fog and lens blur, as well as light fall-off

direction of surface normals for relighting purposes. Many, many more are possible—really anything that you can isolate in a 3D animation program. **Figure 12.20a** through **i** show a robot set up for multipass rendering and a few of its component render layers.

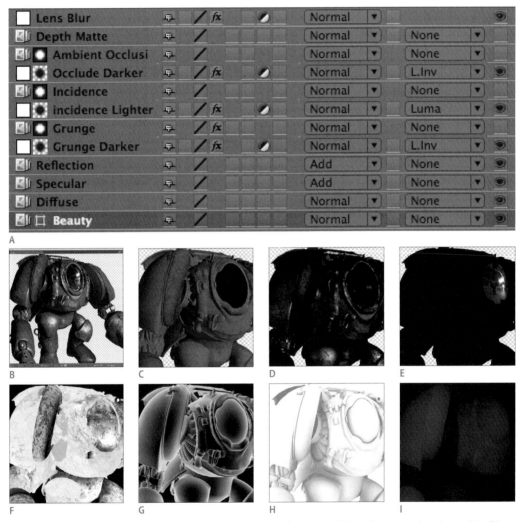

Figure 12.20a through i A basic multipass setup (a, above) with the beauty pass (b) as reference, and made up of the following color passes: diffuse (c), specular (d) and reflection (e) as well as grayscale passes applied as luma mattes to adjustment layers, each containing a Levels effect: grunge (f), incidence (g), and occlusion (h). A depth matte (i) can be applied in various ways; here it is used as reference for a lens blur on an adjustment layer (to give the appearance of shallow depth of field).

Note that none of these passes necessarily requires a transparency (alpha) channel, and at the biggest old-school effects houses it is customary not to render them, since multiple passes of edge transparency can lead to image multiplication headaches.

The general rules for multipass compositing are simple:

▶ Use the Diffuse layer as the base.

▶ Apply color layers meant to illuminate the base layer, such as specular and reflection, via Add or Screen blending modes.

▶ Apply color layers meant to darken the base layer, if any, via Multiply or Darken blending modes.

▶ Apply grayscale maps as luma mattes for adjustment layers. Apply Levels, Curves, and Hue/Saturation to allow these mattes to influence the shading of the object or scene.

▶ Control the strength of any layer using that layer's Opacity.

Note that multipass renders present an excellent case to enable Blend Colors Using 1.0 Gamma in Project Settings, whether or not you assign a Working Space (and whether or not that working space is linearized).

Multipass rendering is only partially scientific and accurate; successful use of multiple passes is a highly individualized and creative sport. With the correct basic lighting setup you can use multipass renders to place a given 3D element in a variety of environments without the need for a complete re-render.

Varied environments are themselves the subject of the following chapter.

CLOSE-UP

RPF and EXR

RPF files are an Autodesk update to RLA. After Effects offers limited native support for these files (via the effects in the 3D Channel menu) but more robust support for some of the finer features of RPF such as Normal maps is only available via third-party plug-ins. Commercially available plug-ins that can translate normal maps for use in After Effects include ZBornToy (which also does amazing things with depth maps; a demo is available on this book's disc) from Frischluft and WalkerFX Channel Lighting, part of the Walker Effects collection. There is a free option for Windows only called Normality (www.minning.de/software/normality).

As mentioned in Chapter 8, After Effects can also extract camera data from RPF files (typically generated in 3DS Max or Flame); place the sequence containing the 3D camera data in a comp and choose Animation > Keyframe Assistant > RPF Camera Import.

The most popular way to get a multipass render into After Effects these days is via the EXR format, which can store all of the various passes and related data in a single file. EXR is now supported directly in After Effects CS4 thanks to the inclusion of EXtractoR and IDentifier, two plug-ins from fnordware.

13

Climate and the Environment

Conversation about the weather is the last refuge of the unimaginative.

— Oscar Wilde

Yes, yes, let's talk about the weather.

— W. S. Gilbert, *The Pirates of Penzance, or the Slave of Duty*

Climate and the Environment

Even if you're not called upon to re-create extreme climate conditions (as someone once pointed out seems to be a theme in my work), even a casual glance out the window demonstrates that the meteorological phenomena are always in play: a breeze is blowing in the trees, or water and particulate in the air are changing the appearance of buildings and the land closest to the horizon.

This chapter offers methods to create natural elements such as particulate and wind effects, as well as to replace a sky, or add mist, fog, or smoke, or other various forms of precipitation. All of these are more easily captured with a camera than re-created in After Effects, but sometimes the required conditions aren't available on the day of a shoot. Mother nature is, after all, notoriously fickle, and shooting just to get a particular environment can be extraordinarily expensive.

It's rare indeed that weather conditions cooperate on location, and even rarer that a shoot can wait for perfect weather or can be set against the perfect backdrop. Transforming the appearance of a scene using natural elements is among the more satisfying things you can do as a compositor.

Particulate Matter

Particulate matter in the air influences how objects appear at different depths. What is this matter? Fundamentally, it is water and other gas, dust, or visible particulate usually known as pollution. Even in an ideal, pristine, pollution-free environment there is moisture in the air—even in the driest desert, where there also might be heavier forms of particulate like dust and sand. The amount of haze in the air offers clues as to

▶ The distance to the horizon and of objects in relation to it

▶ The basic type of climate; the aridness or heaviness of the weather

▶ The time of year and the day's conditions

▶ The air's stagnancy (think *Blade Runner*)

▶ The sun's location (when it's not visible in shot)

The color of the particulate matter offers clues to how much pollution is present and what it is, even how it feels: dust, smog, dark smoke from a fire, and so on (**Figure 13.1**).

NOTES

Particulate matter does not occur in outer space, save perhaps when the occasional cloud of interstellar dust drifts through the shot. Look at photos of the moon landscape, and you'll see that the blacks in the distance look just as dark as those in the foreground.

Figure 13.1 Same location, different conditions. Watch for subtleties: backlighting emphasizes even low levels of haze and reduces overall saturation; more diffuse conditions desaturate and obscure the horizon while emphasizing foreground color.

Essentially, particulate matter in the air lowers the apparent contrast of visible objects; secondarily, objects take on the color of the atmosphere around them and become slightly diffuse. This is a subtle yet omnipresent depth cue: With any particulate matter in the air, objects lose contrast further from camera; the apparent color can change quite a bit, and detail is softened. As a compositor, you use this to your advantage, not only to re-create reality, but to provide dramatic information.

Match an Environment

Figure 13.2 shows how the same object at the same size indicates its depth by its color. The background has great foreground and background reference for black and white levels; although the rear plane looks icy blue against gray, it matches the look of gray objects in the distance of the image.

Figure 13.2 One plane (white circle) is composited as if it is a toy model in the foreground, the other (black circle) as if it is crossing the sky further in the distance; a look at just the planes shows them to be identical but for their color (left). The difference between a toy model airplane flying close, a real airplane flying nearby, and the same plane in the distant sky is conveyed with the use of Scale, but just as importantly, with Levels that show the influence of atmospheric haze.

The technique used here is the same as the one outlined in Chapter 5 with the additional twist that now you understand how atmospheric haze influences the color of the scene. Knowing how this works from studying a scene like this one helps you create something similar from scratch even without such good reference.

The plane as a foreground element seems to make life easier by containing a full range of monochrome colors. When matching a more colorful or monochrome element, you can always create a small solid and add the default Ramp effect. With such a reference element, it is simple to add the proper depth cueing with Levels and then apply the setting to the final element (**Figure 13.3**).

Figures 13.3 If your foreground layer lacks the full range of values, match a grayscale gradient, then swap in the element. These gradient squares have the same settings as the planes in 13.2.

Create an Environment

To re-create depth cues in a shot from scratch, you must somehow separate the shot into planes of distance. If the source imagery is computer-generated, the 3D program that created it can also generate a depth map for you to use. If not, you can slice the image into planes of distance, or you can make your own depth map to weight the distance of the objects in frame (**Figure 13.4**).

Figure 13.4 This grayscale depth map is made up of individual roto shapes, each shaded for relative distance (further elucidated in *Advanced Rotoscoping Techniques for Adobe After Effects* by Pete O'Connell, Creative Cow).

There are several ways in which a depth map can be used, but the simplest approach is probably to apply it to an adjustment layer as a Luma (or Luma Inverted) Matte, and then add Levels or other color correction adjustment to the adjustment layer. Depth cueing would be applied to the furthest elements, so applying this matte as a Luma Inverted Matte and then *flashing* the blacks (raising the Output Black level in Levels) adds the effect of atmosphere on the scene.

TIP

Getting reference is easy for anyone with an Internet connection these days, thanks to sites and services like flickr.com and Google image search.

Figure 13.5 An RPF image close-up can be clearly seen to have jagged edge pixels, but a depth map does not have to be perfectly pristine. An EXR does not have this limitation. (Created by Fred Lewis; used with permission from Inhance Digital, Boeing, and the Navy UCAV program.)

One good reason to use a basic 3D render of a scene as the basis for a matte painting is that the perspective and lens angle can be used not only for reference, but to generate a depth map, even if the entire scene is painted over.

Depth data may also be rendered and stored in an RPF file, as in **Figure 13.5** (which is taken from an example included on the disc as part of 13_multipass.aep). RPF files are in some ways crude, lacking even thresholding in the edges (let alone higher bit depths), but they can contain several types of 3D data, as are listed in the 3D Channel menu. This data can be used directly by a few effects to simulate 3D, including Particle Playground, which accepts RPF data as an influence map.

More extreme conditions may demand actual 3D particles, which are saved for later in the chapter.

Sky Replacement

Sky replacement is among the most inexpensive and fundamental extensions that can be made to a shot. It opens up various possibilities to shoot faster and more cheaply. Not only do you not have to wait for ideal climate conditions, you can swap in a different sky or an extended physical skyline.

Skies are, after all, part of the story—often a subliminal one, but occasionally a starring element. An interior with a window could be anywhere, but show a recognizable skyline outside the window and locals will automatically gauge the exact neighborhood and city block of that location, along with the time of day, time of year, weather, outside temperature, and so on, possibly without ever really paying conscious attention to it.

You could spend tens (even hundreds) of thousands of dollars for that view apartment on Central Park East to film a scene at golden hour (the beautiful "hour" of sunset that typically lasts about 20 minutes and is missing on an overcast day). The guerilla method would be to use your friend's apartment, light it orange, shoot all day, and add the sunset view in post. In many cases, the real story is elsewhere, and the sky is a subliminal (even if beautiful) backdrop that must serve that story (**Figures 13.6**).

Figure 13.6 For an independent film with no budget set in San Francisco, the director had the clever idea of shooting it in a building lobby across the bay in lower-rent Oakland (top left), pulling a matte from the blue sky (top center), and match moving a still shot of the San Francisco skyline (from street level, top right) for a result that anyone familiar with that infamous pyramid-shaped building would assume was taken in downtown San Francisco (bottom). (Images courtesy of The Orphanage.)

The Sky Is Not (Quite) a Blue Screen

Study the actual sky (there may be one nearby as you read this) or even better, study reference images, and you may notice that the blue color desaturates near the horizon, cloudless skies are not always so easy to come by, and even clear blue skies are not as saturated as they might sometimes seem.

Some combination of a color keyer, such as Keylight, and a hi-con luminance matte pass or a garbage matte, as needed, can remove the existing sky in your shot, leaving nice edges around the foreground. Chapter 6 focuses on strategies for employing these, and Chapter 7 describes supporting strategies when keys and garbage mattes fail.

The first step of sky replacement is to remove the existing "sky" (which may include other items at infinite distance, such as buildings and clouds) by developing a matte for it. As you do this, place the replacement sky in the background; a sky matte typically does not have to be as exacting as a blue-screen key if the replacement sky is also fundamentally blue, or if the whole image is radically color corrected as in **Figure 13.7**.

Figure 13.7 A very challenging matte for several reasons, not the least of which is the uneven desaturated quality of the sky. Placing the pigeon in a radically different environment requires color and grain matching to compensate for a less than stellar source.

Infinite Depth

A locked-off shot can be completed with the creation of the matte and a color match to the new sky. If, however, there is camera movement in the shot, you might assume that a 3D track is needed to properly add a new sky element.

Typically, that's overkill. Instead, consider

▶ When matching motion from the original shot, if anything in the source sky can be tracked, by all means track the source.

▶ If only your foreground can be tracked, follow the suggestions in Chapter 8 for applying a track to a 3D camera: Move the replacement sky to the distant background (via a Z Position value well into four or five digits, depending on camera settings). Scale up to compensate for the distance; this is all done by eye.

▶ A push or zoom shot (Chapter 9 describes the difference), may be more easily re-created using a tracked 3D camera (but look at Chapter 8 for tips on getting away with a 2D track).

The basic phenomenon to re-create is the scenery at infinite distance that moves less than objects in the foreground. This is the parallax effect, which is less pronounced with a long, telephoto lens, and much more obvious with a wide angle. For the match in Figure 13.6, a still shot (no perspective) was skewed to match the correct angle and tracked in 2D; the lens angle was long enough and the shot brief enough that they got away with it. A simpler example is included on the disc.

Fog, Smoke, and Mist

An animated layer of translucent clouds is easy to re-create in After Effects. The basic element can be fabricated by applying the Turbulent Noise effect to a solid, then adding a blending mode such as Add or Screen with the appropriate Opacity setting. On the book's disc, 13_smokyFlyover. aep contains a simple example of layers of smoke laid out as if on a three-dimensional plane.

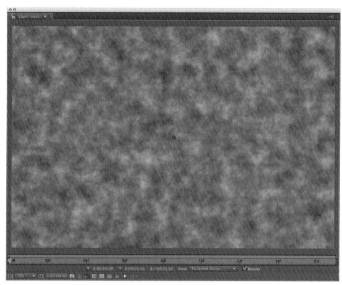

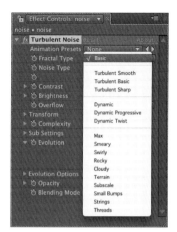

Figure 13.8 The new Turbulent Noise effect (shown at the default setting) is a decent stand-in for organic-looking ambient smoke and fog. Animate the Evolution if you want any billowing of the element. The same alternate Fractal Types as found in the older Fractal Noise effect are available, as seen in the pop-up menu.

Turbulent Noise at its default settings already looks smoky (**Figure 13.8**); switching the Noise Type setting from the default, Soft Linear, to Spline improves it. The main thing to add is motion, which I like to do with a simple expression applied to the Evolution property: `time*60` (I find 60 an appropriate rate in many situations, your taste may vary). The Transform properties within Fractal Noise can be animated, causing the overall layer to move as if being blown by wind.

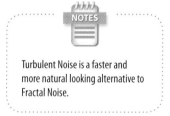

Turbulent Noise is a faster and more natural looking alternative to Fractal Noise.

Brightness, Contrast, and Scale settings influence the apparent scale and density of the noise layer. Complexity and Sub settings also affect apparent scale and density, but with all kinds of undesirable side effects that make the smoke look artificial. The look is greatly improved by layering at least two separate passes via a blending mode (as in the example project).

Masking and Adjusting

When covering the entire foreground evenly with smoke or mist, a more realistic look is achieved using two or three separate overlapping layers with offset positions (**Figure 13.9**). The unexpected byproduct of layering 2D particle layers in this manner is that they take on the illusion of depth and volume.

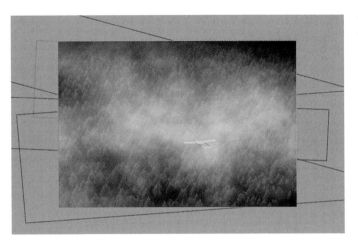

Figure 13.9 Overlay layers of fabricated smoke to add dimensionality and depth.

The eye perceives changes in parallax between the foreground and background and automatically assumes these to be a byproduct of full three-dimensionality, yet you save the time and trouble of a 3D volumetric particle render. Of course, you're limited to instances in which particles don't interact substantially with movement from objects in the scene; otherwise, you instantly graduate to some very tricky 3D effects (although I have seen it done in After Effects with warps).

Particle layers can be combined with the background via blending modes, or they can be applied as a Luma Matte to a colored solid (allowing you to specify the color of the particles without having a blending mode change it).

To add smoke to a generalized area of the frame, a big elliptical mask with a high feather setting (in the triple digits even for video resolution) will do the trick; if the borders of the smoke area are apparent, increase the mask feather even further (**Figure 13.10**).

NOTES

Fractal Noise texture maps maintain the advantage over Turbulent Noise in that they can loop seamlessly (allowing reuse on shots of varying length). In Evolution Options, enable Cycle Evolution, and animate Evolution in whole revolutions (say, from 0° 2 × 0.0°). Set the Cycle (in Revolutions) parameter to the number of total revolutions (2). The first and last keyframes now match, and a loopOut("cycle") expression continues this loop infinitely.

Figure 13.10 This mask of a single smoke element from the shot in Figure 13.8 has a feather value in the hundreds. The softness of the mask helps to sell the element as smoke and works well overlaid with other, similarly feathered masked elements.

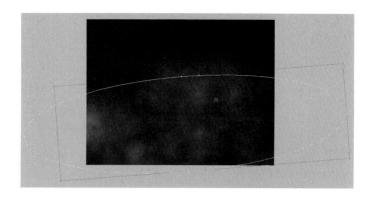

Moving Through the Mist

The same effect you get when you layer several instances of Turbulent or Fractal Noise can aid the illusion of moving forward through a misty cloud. That's done simply enough (for an example of flying through a synthetic cloud, see 13_smokyLayers.aep), but how often does your shot consist of just moving through a misty cloud? Most of the time, clouds of smoke or mist are added to an existing shot.

You can use the technique for emulating 3D tracking (see Chapter 8) to make the smoke hold its place in a particular area of the scene as the camera moves through (or above) it. To make this work, keep a few points in mind:

CLOSE-UP

Selling the Effect with Diffraction

There is more to adding a cloud to a realistic shot than a simple A over B comp; water elements in the air, whether in spray, mist, or clouds, not only occlude light but diffract it. This diffraction effect can be simulated by applying Compound Blur to an adjustment layer between the fog and the background and using a precomposed (or prerendered) version of the fog element as its Blur layer.

This usage of Compound Blur is is detailed further in the next chapter, where it is used to enhance the effect of smoky haze.

▶ Each instance of Fractal Noise should have a soft elliptical mask around it.

▶ The mask should be large enough to overlap with another masked instance, but small enough that it does not slide its position as the angle of the camera changes.

▶ A small amount of Evolution animation goes a long way, and too much will blow the gag. Let the movement of the camera create the interest of motion.

▶ Depending on the length and distance covered in the shot, be willing to create at least a half-dozen individual masked layers of Fractal Noise.

13_smokyFlyover.aep features just such an effect of moving forward through clouds. It combines the tracking of each shot carefully into place with the phenomenon of parallax, whereby overlapping layers swirl across one another in a believable manner. Mist and smoke seem to be a volume but they actually often behave more like overlapping, translucent planes—individual clouds of mist and smoke.

Billowing Smoke

Fractal Noise works fine to create and animate thin wispy smoke and mist. It will not, however, be much help if you need to fabricate thick, billowing clouds. Instead of a plug-in effect, all you need is a good still cloud element and you can animate it in After Effects. And all you need to create the element is a high-resolution reference photo—or even a bag of cotton puffs, as were used to create the images in **Figure 13.11**.

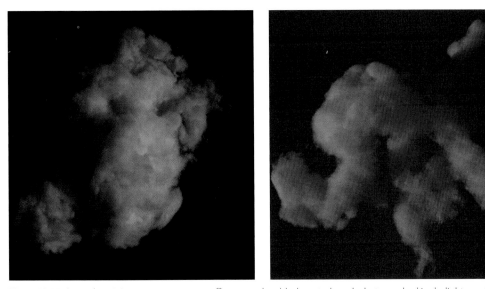

Figure 13.11 A good static image, even cotton puffs arranged on black posterboard, photographed in daylight, can be used as the foundation of billowing smoke.

To give clouds shape and contour, open the image in Photoshop, and use the Clone Stamp tool to create a cloud with the shape you want. You can do it directly in After Effects, but this is the kind of job for which Photoshop was designed. Clone in contour layers of highlights (using Linear Dodge, Screen, or Lighten blending modes) and shadows (with Blending set to Multiply or Darken) until the cloud has the look you're after (**Figure 13.12**).

Figure 13.12 The elements from Figure 13.11 are incorporated into this matte painting, and the final shot contains a mixture of real and composited smoke.

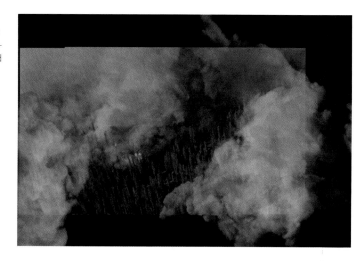

So now you have a good-looking cloud, but it's a still. How do you put it in motion? This is where After Effects' excellent distortion tools come into play, in particular Mesh Warp and Liquify. A project containing just such a cloud animation appears on the disc as 13_smokeCloud.aep.

Mesh Warp

Mesh Warp lays a grid of Bézier handles over the frame; to animate distortion, set a keyframe for the Distortion Mesh property at frame 0, then move the points of the grid and realign the Bézier handles associated with each point to bend to the vertices between points. The image to which this effect is applied follows the shape of the grid.

By default, Mesh Warp begins with a seven-by-seven grid. Before you do anything else, make sure that the size of the grid makes sense for your image; you might want to increase its size for a high-resolution project, and you can reduce the number of rows to fit the aspect ratio of your shot, for a grid of squares (**Figure 13.13**).

You can't typically get away with dragging a point more than about halfway toward any other point; watch carefully for artifacts of stretching and tearing as you work, and preview often. If you see stretching, realign adjacent points and handles to compensate. There is no better way to learn about this than to experiment.

TIP

Mesh Warp, like many distortion tools, renders rather slowly. As you rough in the motion, feel free to work at quarter-resolution. When you've finalized your animation, you can save a lot of time by pre-rendering it (see Chapter 4).

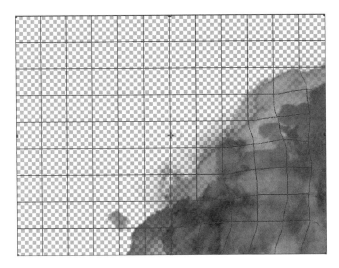

Figure 13.13 The Mesh Warp controls are simple, just a grid of points and vectors. You can preset the number and quality; more is not necessarily better (just more to control). Points can be multiselected and dragged, and each point contains Bézier handles for warping the adjacent vectors.

I have found that the best results with Mesh Warp use minimal animation of the mesh, animating instead the element that moves underneath it.

Liquify

Mesh Warp is appropriate for gross distortions of an entire element. The Liquify effect is a brush-based system for fine distortions. 13_smokeCloud.aep includes a composition that employs Liquify to swirl a cloud. Following is a brief orientation to this toolset, but as with most brush-based painterly tools, there is no substitute for trying it hands-on.

The principle behind Liquify is actually similar to that of Mesh Warp; enable View Mesh under View Options and you'll see that you're still just manipulating a grid, albeit a finer one that would be cumbersome to adjust point by point—hence the brush interface.

Of the brushes included with Liquify, the first two along the top row, Warp and Turbulence, are most often used (**Figure 13.14**). Warp has a similar effect to moving a point in Mesh Warp; it simply pushes pixels in the direction you drag the brush. Turbulence scrambles pixels in the path of the brush.

The Reconstruction brush (rightmost on the bottom row) is like a selective undo, reversing distortions at the default

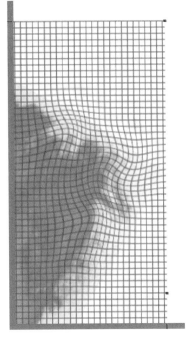

Figure 13.14 Liquify is also a mesh distortion tool, only the mesh is much finer than Mesh Warp's and it is controlled via brushes, allowing more specific distortions.

setting; other options for this brush are contained in the Reconstruction Mode menu (which appears only when the brush is selected).

Liquify has the advantage of allowing hold-out areas. Draw a mask around the area you want to leave untouched by Liquify brushes, but set the Mask mode to None, disabling it. Under Warp Tool Options, select the mask name in the Freeze Area Masked menu.

Liquify was a key addition to the "super cell" element (that huge swirling mass of weather) for the freezing of the New York City sequence in *The Day After Tomorrow*. Artists at The Orphanage were able to animate matte paintings of the cloud bank, broken down into over a dozen component parts to give the effect the appropriate organic complexity and dimension.

Smoke Trails and Plumes

Many effects, including smoke trails, don't require particle generation in order to be re-created faithfully. This section is included less because the need comes up often and more to show how, with a little creativity, you can combine techniques in After Effects to create effects that you might think require extra tools.

Initial setup of such an effect is simply a matter of starting with a clean plate, painting the smoke trails in a separate still layer, and revealing them over time (presumably behind the aircraft that is creating them). The quickest and easiest way to reveal such an element over time is often by animating a mask, as in **Figure 13.15**, or you could use techniques described in Chapter 8 to apply a motion tracker to a brush.

The second stage of this effect is dissipation of the trail; depending on how much wind is present, the trail might drift, spread, and thin out over time. That might mean that in a wide shot, the back of the trail would be more dissipated than the front, or it might mean the whole smoke trail was blown around.

Figure 13.15 No procedural effect is needed; animating out masks is quick, simple, and gives full control over the result.

One method is to displace with a black-to-white gradient (created with Ramp) and Compound Blur. The gradient is white at the dissipated end of the trail and black at the source (**Figure 13.16a**); each point can be animated or tracked in. Compound Blur uses this gradient as its Blur Layer, creating more blur as the ramp becomes more white. Another method, shown in **Figure 13.16b**, uses a different displacement effect, Turbulent displace, to create the same type of organic noise as in the preceding cloud layers.

Figures 13.16a and b To dissipate a smoke trail the way the wind would, you can do so using a gradient and Compound Blur, so that the smoke dissipates more over time, or using the Turbulent Displace effect that, like Turbulent Noise, adds fractal noise, using it to displace the straight trails from Figure 13.15.

Wind

What is wind doing in this chapter? You can't see it. Nevertheless, a static environment is rarely believable if it's not the surface of the moon, and because your job is to help the viewer suspend disbelief, you may have to consider adding the influence of wind to your scene.

The fact is that most still scenes in the real world contain ambient motion of some kind. Not only objects directly in the scene, but reflected light and shadow might be changing all the time in a scene we perceive to be motionless.

As a compositor, you always look for opportunities to add to them in ways that contribute to the realism of the scene without stealing focus. Obviously, the kinds of dynamics involved with making the leaves and branches of a tree sway are mostly beyond the realm of 2D compositing, but there are often other elements that are easily articulated and animated ever so slightly. Successful examples of ambient animation should not be noticeable, and they often will not have been explicitly requested, so it's an exercise in subtlety.

Adding and Articulating Elements

To make it easier on yourself, look for elements that can be readily isolated and articulated; you should be able to mask the element out with a simple roto or a hi-con matte if it's not separated to begin with. Look for the point where the object would bend or pivot, place your anchor point there, then animate a gentle rotation. 13_ambientAnim.aep (on the disc) offers a simple animation of the arm of a streetlight, held out from the background. A little warp on the clouds behind it, and this still image could convincingly be a brief moving shot (**Figure 13.17**).

You also have the option of acquiring and adding elements that indicate or add to the effect of wind motion. **Figure 13.18** is an element of blowing autumn leaves shot against a black background for easy removal and matting; granted, you could add an element this turbulent only to a scene that either already had signs of gusts in it or that contained only elements that would show no secondary motion from wind whatsoever.

Primary and Secondary

Primary animation is the gross movement of the object, the movement of the object as a whole. *Secondary animation* is the movement of individual parts of the object as a result of inertia. So, for example, a helicopter crashes to the ground: That's the primary animation. Its rotors and tail bend and shudder at impact: That's the secondary animation. For the most part, in 2D compositing, your work is isolated to primary animation.

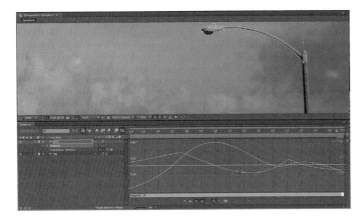

Figure 13.17 It's impossible to do a full wind dynamics simulation in After Effects, but if there should be a little ambient motion to go with some moving clouds, look for simple ways to add it, such as this `wiggle` expression tied to the top of the light pole.

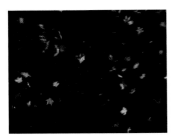 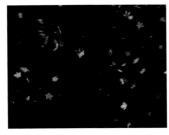 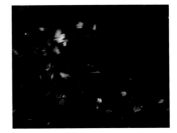

Figure 13.18 Sometimes you can find elements that will enliven your scene when comped in, such as this clip of blowing leaves shot over black. (Footage courtesy of Artbeats.)

Precipitation

You might want to create a "dry for wet" effect, taking footage that was shot under clear, dry conditions and adding the effects of inclement weather. Not only can you not time a shoot so that you're guaranteed shooting in a storm (not in most parts of the world, anyhow), but wet, stormy conditions limit shooting possibilities and cut down on available light. Re-creating a storm by having actual water fall in a scene is expensive, complicated, and not necessarily convincing.

I like to use the Trapcode Particular effect (demo on the book's disc) for the particles of accumulating rain or snow. This effect outdoes After Effects' own Particle Playground for features, flexibility, and fast renders. As the following example shows, Particular is good for more than just falling particles, as well.

The Wet Look

Study reference photographs of stormy conditions and you'll notice some things that they all have in common, as well as others that depend on variables. Here are the steps taken to make a sunny day gloomy (**Figure 13.19**):

Figure 13.19 An ordinary exterior where "it never rains" becomes a deluge.

1. Replace the sky: placid for stormy (**Figure 13.20a**).

2. Adjust Hue/Saturation—LA for Dublin—to bring out the green mossiness of those dry hills, I've knocked out the blues and pulled the reds down and around toward green (**Figure 13.20b**).

3. Exchange Tint—balmy for frigid—a bluish cast is common to rainy scenes (**Figure 13.20c**).

4. Fine-tune Curves—low light for daylight—aggressively dropping the gamma while holding the highlights makes things even moodier (**Figure 13.20d**).

That's dark, but it looks as dry as a lunar surface. How do you make the background look soaked? It seems like an impossible problem, again, until you study reference. Then it becomes apparent that all of that moisture in the air causes distant highlights to bloom. This is a win-win adjustment (did I really just type that?) because it also makes the scene lovelier to behold.

You can simply add a Glow effect, but it doesn't offer as much control as the approach I recommend.

Follow these steps:

1. Bring in the background layer again (you can duplicate it and delete the applied effects, **Ctrl+Shift+E/Command+Shift+E**).

2. Add an Adjustment Layer below it and set the duplicated background as a Luma Matte.

3. Use Levels to make the matte layer a hi-con matte that isolates the highlights to be bloomed.

4. Fast Blur the result to soften the bloom area.

5. On the Adjustment Layer, add Exposure and Fast Blur to bloom the background within the matte selection.

Figure 13.20e shows the result; it now looks like a wet, cold day, but where's the rain?

Create Precipitation

Particular contains all the controls needed to generate custom precipitation; it contains a lot of controls, period. A primer is helpful, to get past the default animation of little white squares emanating out in all directions (click under Preview in Effect Controls to see it). To get started making rain, create a comp-sized 2D solid layer, apply Particular, and

1. Twirl down Emitter and set an Emitter Type. For rain I like Box so that I can easily set its width and depth, but anything besides the default Point and Grid will work.

2. Set Emitter Size to at least the comp width in X, to fill the frame.

3. Set Direction to Directional.

4. Set X Rotation to –90 so that the particles fall downward.

5. Boost velocity to go from gently falling snow speed to pelting rain.

You might think it more correct to boost gravity than velocity, but gravity increases velocity over time (as Galileo discovered) and rain begins falling thousands of feet above; however, this is not something you need to replicate, as no one will know the difference.

Figures 13.20a through e The progression to a heavy, wet day (top to bottom).

You do, however, need to do the following:

1. Move the Emitter Y Position to 0 or less so that it sits above frame.

2. Increase the Emitter Size Y to get more depth among those falling particles.

3. Crank up the Particles/sec and Physics Time (under Physics) to get enough particles, full blast from the first frame.

4. If the particles are coming up short at the bottom of frame, increase the Life setting under Particle.

5. Enable motion blur for the layer and comp to get some nice streaky rain (**Figure 13.21**).

From here, you can add Wind and Air Resistance under Physics. If you're creating snow instead of rain, you might want to customize the Particle Type, even referring to your own Custom layer if necessary for snowflakes.

Figure 13.21 In the "good enough" category, two passes of rain, one very near, one far, act together to create a watery deluge. Particular could generate this level of depth with a single field, and the mid-ground rain is missing, but planes are much faster to set up for a fast-moving shot like this. The rain falls mainly on two planes.

Composite Precipitation

What is the color of falling rain? The correct answer to this zen koan-like question is that raindrops and snowflakes are translucent. Their appearance is heavily influenced by the background environment, because they behave like tiny falling lenses. They diffract light, defocusing and lowering the contrast of whatever is behind them, but they themselves also pick up the ambient light.

Therefore, on *The Day After Tomorrow* our crew found success with using the rain or snow element as a track matte for an adjustment layer containing a Fast Blur and a Levels (or Exposure) effect, like a reflective, defocused lens. This type of precipitation changes brightness according to its backlighting, as it should. You may see fit to hold out specific areas and brighten them more, if you see an area where a volumetric light effect might occur.

The final result in Figure 13.19b benefits from a couple of extra touches. The rain is divided into multiple layers, near and far, and motion tracked to match the motion of the car from which we're watching this scene. Particular has the ability to generate parallax without using multiple layers, but I sometimes find this approach gives me more control over the perspective.

Because we're looking out a car window, if we want to call attention to the point of view because the next shot reverses to an actor looking out this window, it's only appropriate that the rain bead up. This is also done with Particular, with Velocity turned off and Custom particles for the droplets.

And because your audience always can tell when you have the details wrong, even if they don't know exactly what's wrong, check out **Figure 13.22** for how the droplet is designed.

Once again, it is attention to detail and creative license that allow you to simulate the complexities of nature. It can be fun and satisfying to transform a scene using the techniques from this chapter, and it can be even more fun and satisfying to design your own based on the same principles: Study how it really works, and notice details others would miss. Your audience will appreciate the difference every time.

The next chapter heats things up with fire, explosions, and other combustibles.

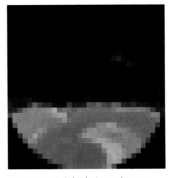

Figure 13.22 It looks jaggy because you don't want particles to be any higher resolution than they need to be, or they take up massive amounts of render time. There are two keys to creating this particle: It uses the adjusted background, inverted, with the CC Lens effect to create the look. Look at raindrops on a window sometime and notice that, as little lenses, they invert their fisheye view of the scene behind them.

14

Pyrotechnics:
Heat, Fire, Explosions

My nature is to be on set, blowing things up.
— Ken Ralston (winner of five Academy
Awards for visual effects)

Pyrotechnics: Heat, Fire, Explosions

It may not be a majority, but many people first become interested in a visual effects career as borderline pyromaniacs or even gun nuts. You have to follow your passion in life, I suppose. Creating a conflagration on the computer isn't quite as much fun as simply blowing stuff up, but it keeps these people off of our streets.

The serious truth is that many types of explosions are still best done through a combination of practical and virtual simulations. There are, however, many cases in which compositing can save a lot of time, expense, and hazard. Blowing stuff up on set is fun, but it involves extensive setup and a not insubstantial amount of danger to the cast and crew. Second chances don't come cheap.

On the other hand, there's often no substitute for the physics of live-action mayhem. I hope it doesn't come as a disappointment to learn that not everything pyrotechnical can be accomplished start to finish in After Effects. Some effects require actual footage of physical or fabricated elements being shot at or blown up, and good reference of such events is immensely beneficial. Practical elements might rely on After Effects to work, but pyrotechnical shots are equally reliant, if not more so, on practical elements.

Firearms

Blanks are dangerous, and real guns deadly. To create a shot with realistic gunfire safely requires

- ▶ A realistic-looking gun prop in the scene
- ▶ Some method to mime or generate firing action on set

- The addition of a muzzle flash, smoke, cartridge, or shell discharge (where appropriate)
- The matching shot showing the result of gunfire: debris, bullet hits, even blood

After Effects can help with all of these to some extent, and some of them completely, relieving you of the need for more expensive or dangerous alternatives.

The Shoot

For the purposes of this discussion let's assume that you begin with a plate shot of an actor re-creating the action of firing a gun, and that the gun that was used on set produces nothing: no muzzle flash, no smoke, no shell. All that's required is some miming by the actor of the recoil, or kick, which is relatively minor with small handguns, and a much bigger deal with a shotgun or fully automatic weapon.

Happily, there's no shortage of reference, as nowhere outside of the NRA is the Second Amendment more cherished than in movies and television. Granted, most such reference is itself staged, but remember, we're going for cinematic reality here, so if it looks right to you, use it as reference.

Figure 14.1 shows something like the minimum amount that needs to be composited to create a realistic shot of a gun being fired (albeit artfully executed in this case). Depending on the gun, smoke or a spent cartridge might also discharge. As important as the look of the frame is the timing; check your favorite reference carefully and you'll find that not much, and certainly not the flash, lingers longer than a single frame.

The actual travel of the bullet out of the barrel is not generally anything to worry about; at roughly one kilometer per second, it moves too fast to be seen amid all the other effects, particularly the blinding muzzle flash.

Muzzle Flash and Smoke

The clearest indication that a gun has gone off is the flash of light around the muzzle, at the end of the barrel. This small, bright explosion of gunpowder actually lasts about $1/48$ second, short enough that when shot live it can fall

NOTES

Stu Maschwitz's book, *The DV Rebel's Guide* (Peachpit Press) is definitive on the subject of creating an action movie, perhaps on a low budget, and likely with the help of After Effects. Included with the cover price, you get a couple of nifty After Effects tools for muzzle flashes and spent shells, and some serious expertise on the subject of making explosive action exciting and real.

Figure 14.1 Much of the good reference for movie gunfire is other movies; you typically want the most dramatic and cinematic look, which is a single frame of muzzle flash and contact lighting on surrounding elements. (Image courtesy of Mars Productions.)

between frames of film (in which case you might need to restore it in order for the action of the scene to be clear). Real guns don't discharge a muzzle flash, as a rule, but movie guns certainly do.

A flash can be painted by hand, cloned in from a practical image, or composited from stock reference. It's not too significant how you generate it, although muzzle flashes have in common with lens flares that they are specific to the device that created them. Someone in your audience is bound to know something about how the muzzle flash of your gun might look, so get reference: certain guns emit a characteristic shape such as a teardrop, cross, or star (**Figure 14.2**).

Figure 14.2 The angle of the shot and the type of gun affect the muzzle flash effect. The first image is from an M16 rifle; the other is from a handgun. (Images courtesy of Artbeats.)

Any such explosion travels in two directions from the end of the barrel: arrayed outward from the firing point and in a straight line out from the barrel. If you don't have source that makes this shape at the correct angle, it's probably simplest to paint it.

The key is to make it look right on one frame; this is a rare case where that's virtually all the audience should see, and where that one frame can be almost completely different from those surrounding it. If it looks blah or only part of the way there, it's too well matched to the surrounding frames. Focus on the one frame until you believe it for explosiveness and dramatic flourish.

Technically speaking some guns, for example rifles, may cause quite a bit of smoke, but most emit little or none at all. If you do make a smoke puff with Turbulent Noise held out by a soft mask, which you certainly could, my advice is to make it evaporate relatively quickly so you don't blow the gag.

Shells and Interactive Light

If the gun in your scene calls for it, that extra little bit of realism can be added with a secondary animation of a shell popping off the top of a semi-automatic. **Figure 14.3** shows how such an element looks being emitted from a real gun and shot with a high-speed shutter.

It's definitely cool to have a detailed-looking shell pop off of the gun, although the truth is that with a lower camera shutter speed, the element will become an unrecognizable two-frame blur anyhow, in which case all you need is a four-point mask of a white (or brass colored) solid.

The bright flash of the muzzle may also cause a brief reflected flash on objects near the gun as well as the subject firing it. Chapter 12 offers the basic methodology: Softly mask a highlight area, or matte the element with its own highlights, then flash it using an adjustment layer containing a Levels effect or a colored solid with a suitable blending mode.

As a general rule, the lower the ambient light and the larger the weapon, the greater the likelihood of interactive lighting. A literal "shot in the dark" would fully illuminate the face of whomever (or whatever) fired it, just for a single frame. It's a great dramatic effect, but one that is very difficult to re-create in post. Firing blanks on set or any other means of getting contact lighting of a flash on set would be invaluable here.

By contrast, or rather by reduced contrast, a daylit scene will heavily dampen the level of interactivity of the light. Instead of a white hot flash, you might more accurately have saturation of orange and yellow in the full muzzle flash element, and the interactive lighting might be minimal. This is where understanding your camera and recording medium can help you gauge the effect of a small aperture hit by a lot of light.

Hits and Squibs

Bullets that ricochet on set are known as squib hits because they typically make use of *squibs*, small explosives with the approximate power of a firecracker that go off during the

Figure 14.3 A shell pops off of the fired gun, but it could just as well be a Shape Layer with motion blur (or check *The DV Rebel's Guide* for a Particle Playground-based setup to create them automatically). (Images courtesy of Artbeats.)

Figure 14.4 This sequence of frames shows a second bullet hitting the cab of the truck, using two elements: the painted bullet hit and the spark element, whose source was shot on black and added via Screen mode. (Images courtesy of markandmatty.com.)

take. Sometimes squibs are actual firecrackers. It is possible to add bullet hits without using explosives on set, but frenetic gunplay will typically demand a mixture of on-set action and post-production enhancement.

Figure 14.4 shows a before-and-after addition of a bullet hit purely in After Effects. Here the bullet does not ricochet but is embedded directly into the solid metal of the truck. In such a case, all you need to do is add the results of the damage on a separate layer at the frame where the bullet hits; you can paint this (it's a few sparks). The element can then be motion tracked to marry it solidly to the background.

At the frame of impact, and continuing a frame or two thereafter, a shooting spark and possibly a bit of smoke (if the target is combustible—not in the case of a steel vehicle) will convey the full violence of the bullets. As with the muzzle flash, this can vary from a single frame to a more fireworks-like shower of sparks tracked in over a few frames (**Figure 14.5**).

A bullet hit explosion can be created via a little miniature effects shoot, using a fire-retardant black background (a flat, black card might do it) and some firecrackers (assuming you can get them). The resulting flash, sparks, and smoke stand out against the black, allowing the element to be composited via a blending mode (such as Add or Screen), a hi-con matte (Chapter 6), or a plug-in such as

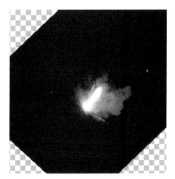

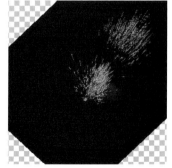

Figure 14.5 A source spark element shot against black can be composited using Add or Screen blending mode—no matte needed. (Images courtesy of markandmatty.com.)

Knoll UnMult. If dangerous explosives aren't your thing, even in a controlled situation, stock footage is available. If debris is also part of the shot, however, the more that can be done practically on set, the better (**Figure 14.6**).

So to recap, a good bullet hit should include

▶ Smoke or sparks at the frame of impact, typically lasting between one and five frames

▶ The physical result of the bullet damage (if any) painted and tracked into the scene

▶ Debris in cases where the target is shatterable or scatterable

Later in this chapter, you'll see how larger explosions have much in common with bullet hits, which are essentially just miniature explosions. In both cases, a bit of practical debris can be crucial to sell the shot.

Energy Effects

There is a whole realm of pyrotechnical effects that are made up of pure energy. At one end of the very bright spectrum is lightning, which occurs in the atmosphere of our own planet daily, on the other end are science fiction weapons that exist only in the mind (not that the U.S. military under Ronald Reagan didn't try).

A lightning simulation and a light saber composite have quite a bit in common, in that they rely on fooling the eye into seeing an element that appears white hot. The funny thing about human vision is that it actually looks for the decay—the not-quite-white-hot areas around the hot core—for indications that an element is brighter than white and hotter than hot.

Core and Decay

In previous editions of this book I half-joked that the recipe for creating a filmic light saber blur was top secret. This time around I'm motivated to spill the (pork and) beans instead of going the quick and easy route, thanks to the Internet superstars of the low-budget light saber,

Figure 14.6 Animating debris is tedious and unrewarding when compared with shooting a BB gun at breakaway objects and hurling debris at the talent. (Images courtesy of The Orphanage.)

Figure 14.7 Spectacular dueling action from Ryan versus Dorkman. (Sequence courtesy of Michael Scott.)

Ryan and Dorkman, who have provided an entire light saber battle on the disc (**Figure 14.7**).

You may find the light saber to be somewhat played out after three decades, but the techniques you need to make a good light saber battle apply to any other energy-driven effect.

The Beam effect (Effect > Generate > Beam) automatically gives you the bare minimum, a core and surrounding glow, and it is 32 bpc and can be built up, but like so many automated solutions it's a compromise; you don't really think they busted out Beam on *Phantom Menace*, do you?

The real thing is created by hand, and it's not really all that much more trouble considering how much more possibility lies in the result. You get more control over the motion and thresholds.

Figures 14.8a through **e** show the basics for a single light saber effect:

1. In the first comp, make the background plate (**Figure 14.8a**) a guide layer (because this is not the final comp) and create a masked white solid. In this case, the position and arcs of the light sabers are all hand rotoscoped (**Figure 14.8b**), as detailed in Chapter 7.

2. Drop (or precomp) this comp into a new comp, apply Fast Blur to the resulting layer (turn on Repeat Edge Pixels), and set the blending mode to Add (or Screen).

3. Duplicate this layer several times, and adjust Fast Blur so that each layer has approximately double the blur of the one above it. With six or seven layers you might have a Blur Radius ranging from 5 on the top level (the core) down to 400 or so.

To automate setup you could even apply this expression text to the duplicate layer's Blurriness setting:

```
thisComp.layer(index-1).effect("Fast Blur")
➥("Blurriness")*2
```

This takes the Blurriness value from the layer above and doubles it so that as you duplicate the layer, each one below the top is twice as soft (**Figure 14.8c**).

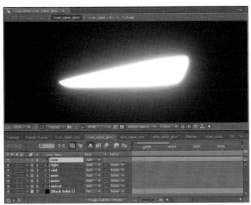

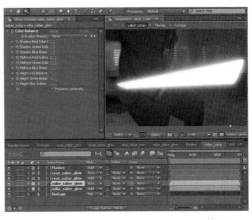

Figures 14.8a through e The initial roto comp is set up with generous padding (a, top left) so that masks can move out of frame without being cut off. The roto itself is shaped to frame the full area of motion blur, where applicable, from the source (b, top right). The glow effect (c, middle left) comes from layering together several copies of the roto, each with different amounts of Feather on the mask. This is then tinted as a single element (d, middle right) and tweaked in Levels (e, bottom) for the proper glow intensity.

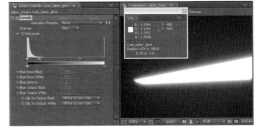

4. Drop this comp into your main composition to combine it with footage and give it color (**Figure 14.8d**). The Ryan versus Dorkman approach uses Color Balance and is composited in 16 bpc; one 32 bpc alternative (becauase Color Balance doesn't work in HDR) is simply to use Levels, adjusting Input White and Gamma on individual red, green, and blue channels; you could also apply Tint and Map White To values brighter than white (**Figure 14.8e**).

That's the fundamental setup; here are some other observations to really sell a scene like this:

- ▶ Motion blur; notice how by rotoscoping the arc of movement and adding the edge threshold you get this for free in the preceding figures.

- ▶ Contact/interactive lighting/glow (**Figure 14.9**).

Figure 14.9 You get a few things for free: contact lighting occurs on the face from the blue glow; it could and should be boosted in low light. Layer order of the sabers doesn't matter when they cross; either way their values are added together.

- ▶ Physical damage/interaction with the environment; the same types of interactions described for bullet hits apply, so add sparks, flares, and other damage to the surrounding environment.

- ▶ Flashes/over-range values (**Figure 14.10**).

Figure 14.10 Flashes occur dozens of times throughout the battle; each one appears to have a unique shape, but they all use the same four-frame flare, and its unique shape comes from being composited with the rest of the scene.

I don't even need to tell you that these techniques are good for more than light sabers; suppose you intend to generate a more natural effect such as lightning. Reference shows this to possess similar qualities (**Figure 14.11**) and the same techniques will sell the effect.

There are a couple of built-in effects that will create lightning in After Effects. With either Lightning or Advanced Lightning, you're not stuck with the rather mediocre look of the effect itself; you can use the same method as with the light saber. Turn off the glow and use the effect to generate a hard white core, and follow the same steps as just described. It's worth the trouble to get beyond the canned look, and it opens all of the possibilities shown here and more.

In some cases you might go beyond these examples and create an element that throws off so much heat and energy that it distorts the environment around it.

Figure 14.11 Actual reference images contain energy effects with realistic thresholding and interaction with the surrounding environment. (Image courtesy of Kevin Miller via Creative Commons license.)

Heat Distortion

Heat distortion, that strange rippling in the air that occurs when hot air meets cooler air, is another one of those effects compositors love. Like a lens flare, it's a highly visible effect that, if properly motivated and adjusted, adds instant realism even if your viewers don't know that hot gas bends light.

Figures 14.12a and **b** show the fabricated results of heat distortion in a close-up of a scene that will also incorporate fire. When your eye sees heat distortion, it understands that something intense is happening, just like with the decay/threshold of bright lights, as described earlier. The mind is drawn to contrast.

What Is Actually Happening

Stare into a swimming pool, and you can see displacement caused by the bending of light as it travels through the water. Rippled waves in the water cause rippled bending of light. There are cases in which our atmosphere behaves like this as well, when ripples are caused in it by the collision of warmer and cooler air, a medium that is not quite as transparent as it seems.

As you know from basic physics, hot air rises and hot particles move faster than cool ones. Air is not a perfectly clear medium but a translucent gas that can act as a lens. This "lens" is typically static and appears flat, but the application of heat causes an abrupt mixture of fast-moving hot

Figures 14.12a and b Heat haze by itself can look a little odd (a) but it adds significantly to the realism of a scene containing a prominent heat source (b).

air particles rising into cooler ambient air. This creates ripples that have the effect of displacing and distorting what is behind the moving air, just like ripples in the pool or ripples in the windows of an old house.

Because this behavior resembles a lens effect, and because the role of air isn't typically taken into account in a 3D render, it can be adequately modeled as a distortion overlaid on whatever sits behind the area of hot air.

How to Re-create It

The basic steps for re-creating heat distortion from an invisible source in After Effects are

1. Create a basic particle animation that simulates the movement and dissipation of hot air particles in the scene.

2. Make two similar but unique passes of this particle animation—one to displace the background vertically, the other to displace it horizontally—and precompose them.

3. Add an adjustment layer containing the Displacement Map effect, which should be set to use the particle animation comp to create the distortion effect. Apply it to the background.

Particle Playground is practically ideal for this purpose because its default settings come close to generating exactly what you need, with the following minor adjustments:

a. Under Cannon, move Position to the source in the frame where the heat haze originates (in this case, the bottom center as the entire layer will be repositioned and reused).

b. Open up Barrel Radius from the default of 0.0 to the width, in pixels, of the source. Higher numbers lead to slower renders.

c. Boost Particles Per Second to something like 200. The larger the Barrel Radius, the more particles are needed.

d. Under Gravity, set Force to 0.0 to prevent the default fountain effect.

NOTES

It can be useful to generate the particles for the displacement map itself in 3D animation software, when the distortion needs to be attached to a 3D animated object, such as a jet engine or rocket exhaust. The distortion is still best created in After Effects using that map.

The default color and scale of the particles is fine for this video resolution example, but you might have to adjust them as well according to your shot. A larger format (in pixels) or a bigger heat source might require bigger, softer particles.

4. Now duplicate the particles layer and set the color of the duplicated layer to pure green. As you'll see below, the Displacement Map effect by default uses the red and green channels for horizontal and vertical displacement. The idea is to vary it so that the particles don't overlap by changing Direction Random Spread and Velocity Random Spread from their defaults.

5. The heat animation is almost complete; it only needs some softening. Add a moderate Fast Blur (**Figure 14.13**).

Figure 14.13 This displacement layer, matted against gray merely for clarity, was created with the included steps and used with the Displacement Map effect to create the effect shown in Figure 14.12.

Now to put the animation to use: Drag it into the main comp, and turn off its visibility. The actual Displacement Map effect is applied either directly to the background plate or preferably to an adjustment layer sitting above all the layers that should be affected by the heat haze. Displacement Map is set by default to use the red channel for horizontal displacement and the green channel for vertical displacement; all you need to do is select the layer containing the red and green particles under the Displacement Map Layer menu.

Heat displacement often dissipates before it reaches the top of the frame. Making particles behave so that their lifespan ends before they reach the top of the frame is accurate, but painstaking. A simpler solution is to add a solid with a black-to-white gradient (created with the Ramp effect) as a luma matte to hold out the adjustment layer containing the displacement effect. You can also use a big, soft mask.

Fire

Within After Effects, fire synthesis (from scratch) is way too hot to handle; there's no tool, built-in or plug-in, to make convincing looking flames. If fire is at all prominent in a shot, it will require elements that come from somewhere else—most likely, shot with a camera, although 3D animators have become increasingly talented at fabricating alternatives here and there.

Creating and Using Fire Elements

Figure 14.14 shows effects plates of fire elements. The big challenge when compositing fire is that it doesn't scale very realistically—a fireplace fire will look like it belongs in the hearth, no matter how you may attempt to scale or retime it.

Fire elements are ideally shot in negative space—against a black background, or at least, at night—so that they can be composited with blending modes and a minimum of rotoscoping. Fire illuminates its surroundings—just something to keep in mind when shooting.

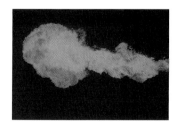  

Figure 14.14 Fire elements are typically shot in negative (black) space or occasionally in a natural setting requiring more careful matting. By adjusting Input Black in Levels, you can control the amount of glow coming off the fire as it is blended via Add mode, lending the scene interactive lighting for free. (Images courtesy of Artbeats.)

This, then, is a case where it can be worth investing in proper elements shot by trained pyrotechnicians (unless that sounds like no fun, but there's more involved with a good fire shoot than a camera rental and a blow torch). In many cases, stock footage companies, such as Artbeats (examples on the book's disc), anticipate your needs. The scale and intensity may be more correct than what you can easily shoot on your own unless you're pals with Mark Pauline.

All Fired Up

Blending modes and linear blending, not mattes, are the key to good looking fire composites. Given a fire element shot against black (for example, the Artbeats_RF001H_ fireExcerpt.mov included on the disc and used for the depicted example), the common newbie mistake is to try to key out the black with an Extract effect, which will lead to a fight between black edges and thin fire.

A first step is to simply lay the fire layer over the background and apply Add mode. To firm up a fire (or flare, or other bright) element you can

▶ Ascertain that Blend Colors Using 1.0 Gamma is enabled in Project Settings.

▶ Apply the Knoll Unmult (this free plug-in, included on your disc, makes all black areas of the image transparent).

▶ Fine-tune the result with a Levels effect, pushing in on Input White and Black (as well as color matching overall).

▶ Add an Exposure effect (with a boosted Exposure setting) to create a raging inferno.

▶ Add interactive lighting for low-lit scenes (next section).

▶ Create displacement above the open flames (as detailed in the previous section).

▶ Add an adjustment layer over the background with a Compound Blur effect, using transparency of the fire and smoke as a blur layer (**Figure 14.15**).

Figures 14.15 The effect of steam (or in other cases, fog) can be re-created with a subtle Compound Blur effect.

NOTES

Compound Blur simply varies the amount of blur according to the brightness of a given pixel in the Blur Layer, up to a given maximum. It's the right thing to use not only for fire and smoke but for fog and mist; heavy particulate in the air acts like little tiny defocused lenses, causing this effect in nature.

Where there's fire there is, of course, smoke, which can at a modest level be created with a Fractal Noise effect as described in the previous chapter, bringing this shot home (**Figure 14.16**).

Figure 14.16 All of the techniques described here build to a result that gives the furniture motivation to jump out the windows.

Light Interacts

Provided that your camera does not rotate too much, a 2D fire layer, or a set of them, offset in 3D space, can read as sufficiently three dimensional. The key to making it interact dimensionally with a scene, particularly a relatively dark one, is often interactive light. As was stated earlier, fire tends to illuminate everything around it with a warm, flickering glow.

As shown in **Figure 14.17**, a fire element may include a certain amount of usable glow. Input White and Input Black in Levels control the extent to which glow is enhanced or suppressed, respectively; you can use these controls to dial it in and out.

Figure 14.17 Input White and Black on the RGB and Red channels of the Levels effect offer control of the natural glow around the element. The better the dynamic range of the source image, the harder you can push this—another case for higher bit depth source.

Note, however, that this glow isn't anything particularly unique or special; you can re-create it either via a heavily blurred duplicate of the source fire or using a masked and heavily feathered orange solid, with perhaps a slight amount of wiggle added to the glow opacity to cause a bit of interactive flickering.

Dimensionality

You can pull off the illusion of fully three-dimensional fire, especially if the camera is moving around in 3D space,

Figure 14.18 Before-and-after sequential stills of a flyover shot. Because of the angle of the aerial camera, the shot required 3D motion tracking, in this case with 2D3's Boujou. (Images courtesy of ABC-TV.)

directly in After Effects. I was frankly surprised at how well this worked back when I created the shot featured in **Figure 14.18**.

As shown, the background plate is an aerial flyby of a forest. Because of the change in altitude and perspective, this shot clearly required 3D tracking (touched upon at the end of Chapter 8). The keys to making this shot look fully dimensional were to break up the source fire elements into discrete chunks and to stagger those in 3D space so that as the plane rose above them, their relationship and parallax changed (**Figure 14.19**).

TIP

For a shot featuring a character or object that reflects firelight, there's no need to go crazy projecting fire onto the subject. In many cases, it is enough to create some flickering in the character's own luminance values, for example by wiggling the Input White value at a low frequency in Levels (Individual Controls).

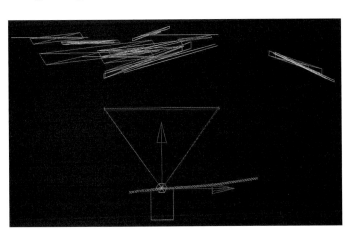

Figure 14.19 A top view of the 3D motion-tracked camera from Figure 14.18 panning past one set of fires (of which the final composition had half a dozen). The pink layers contain fire elements, the gray layers smoke.

It is easy to get away with any individual fire element being 2D in this case. Because fire changes its shape constantly, there is nothing to give away its two dimensionality. Borders of individual fire elements can freely overlap without being distracting, so it doesn't look cut out. The eye sees evidence of parallax between a couple dozen fire elements and does not think to question that any individual one of them looks too flat. The smoke elements were handled in a similar way, organized along overlapping planes. As mentioned in the previous chapter, smoke's translucency aids the illusion that overlapping smoke layers have dimensional depth.

Explosions

The example forest fire shot also contains a large explosion in a clearing. There is not a huge fundamental difference between the methods to composite an explosion and mere fire, except that a convincing explosion might be built up out of more individual elements. It is largely a question of what is exploding.

All explosions are caused by rapidly expanding combustible gases; implosions are caused by rapid contraction. Just by looking at an explosion, viewers can gauge its size and get an idea of what blew up, so you need to design the right explosion for your situation or your result will be too cheesy even for 1980s television sci-fi. How do you do it?

Light and Chunky

Each explosion you will see is unique, but to narrow the discussion, I'll organize all explosions into two basic categories. The easier one to deal with is the gaseous explosion—one made up only of gas and heat. These explosions behave just like fire; in fact, in the shot in **Figure 14.20a** the explosion is fire, a huge ball of it, where something very combustible evidently went up very quickly.

Some shots end up looking fake because they use a gaseous explosion when some chunks of debris are needed. This is a prime reason that exploding miniatures are still in use, shot at high speed (or even, when possible, full-scale explosions, which can be shot at standard speed). The slower moving and bigger the amount of debris, the bigger the apparent explosion.

If your shot calls for a chunky explosion, full of physical debris, and the source lacks them, you need an alternate source. Many 3D programs these days include effective dynamics simulations; if you go that route, be sure to generate a depth map as well because each chunk will be revealed only as it emerges from the fireball. Many other concerns associated with this are beyond the scope of this discussion because they must be solved in other software.

One effect that seems to come close in After Effects is Shatter, but it's hard to recommend this unless it is specifically a pane of glass or other plane that breaks. Shatter isn't bad for a decade-old dynamics simulator, but its primary limitation is a huge one: It can employ only extruded flat polygons to model the chunks. A pane of glass is one of the few physical objects that would shatter into irregular but flat polygons, and Shatter contains built-in controls for specifying the size of the shards in the point of impact. Shatter was also developed prior to the introduction of 3D in After Effects; you can place your imaginary window in perspective space, but not with the help of a camera or 3D controls.

A wide selection of pyrotechnic explosions is also available as stock footage from such companies as Artbeats. In many cases, there is no substitute for footage of a real, physical object being blown to bits (**Figure 14.20b**).

Figure 14.20 Pyrotechnics footage is just the thing when you need a big explosion filled with debris. (Images courtesy of Artbeats.)

In a Blaze of Glory

With good reference and a willingness to take the extra step to marry your shot and effect together, you can create believable footage that would require danger or destruction if taken with a camera. Even when your project has the budget to actually re-create some of the mayhem described in this chapter, you can almost always use After Effects to enhance and build upon what the camera captures. Boom. You might as well go out with a bang.

Index

; key, 46
// (comment designator), 343
– (decrement operator), 322
% (modulo operator), 324
~ (Tilde key), 7
[ ] (brackets), 45
* key, 43
\ (backslash) key, 46
1.0 Gamma toggle, 349, 362, 377–378
2.5D tracking, 251–252
2D compositions, 123
2D layers, 122, 123, 331–333
2D motion blur, 65
2K film plates, 24
3:2 pulldown, 20, 21
3D calculations, 122
3D camera
  mixing 2D effects, 280–281
  scaling 2D layers, 287–288
  smoothing moving, 252–254
  tracking, 250–251, 252, 264
3D Channel Extract effect, 410
3D compositing, 399–403
3D frames, 10
3D layers
  applying 2D layer as decal, 331–333
  fading out, 339–341
  importing 3D models as, 282–284
  rendering and, 122
3D models, 282–284
3D motion blur, 65
3D parallax, 251
3D renders, 10
3D tracking, 263–268
8-bit color mode, 150
8-bit images, 349, 363
8-bit pixels, 363
13.53 film, 365–366
16:9 format, 306
16-bit color mode, 150
16-bit pixels, 363
16-bpc projects, 148, 349

24 fps footage, 20, 21, 305
24 Pa pulldown, 20
29.97 fps footage, 305
32-bit images, 373, 374–378

A

absolute time, 68–69
Adapt Feature on Every Frame option, 243, 245
Adaptive Sample Limit setting, 65
Add Keyframe option, 47
Add mode, 95, 101–103
Add transfer mode, 372
Adjust Tension pointer, 216
adjustment layers, 119–121, 159
Adobe Encore submenu, 11
Adobe Media Encoder, 128–129
Adobe Photoshop
  brushes, 229
  file format, 23
  layers, 22, 23
  PSD files, 23
Advanced tab, 24
.aep extension, xxiii, 15
.aepx extension, xxiii, 131
aerender application, 126
After Effects
  coordinate systems, 328–330
  Help menu, 314
  new features, xxiii–xxiv
  opening multiple versions of, 127–128
  responsiveness of, 26–29
  time manipulation in, 68–75
After Effects pipeline, 8
AfterFX.exe, 128
Aligned toggle, 232
alignment
  Bézier handles, 418
  layers, 104, 233
  pixels, 232
  points, 257, 260

All Panels workspace, 5
Allow Keyframes Between Frames toggle, 54, 58
Alpha Add mode, 98
Alpha Bias control, 195, 196
Alpha Channel view, 194
alpha channels. See also channels
  adjusting settings, 18
  cleaning up, 229
  considerations, xii–xxiii
  density, 96
  described, 80
  frame rate settings, 18–21
  fringing and, 88
  grayscale, 107
  importing and, 18, 89
  misinterpreted, 89
  painting, 229–232
  preferences, 18
  premultiplication and, 87–90
  touching up mattes as, 230
  unlabeled, 89
  viewing matte detail in, 178
  vs. track mattes, 107
Alpha Cleaner, 206–207
Alpha Inverted Matte option, 107
Alpha Matte option, 107
alpha track mattes, 99
Alt key, 9, 26, 47
Always Preview This View toggle, 114
amplitude, 314–315, 332, 343–344
Anchor Point Path option, 61
Anchor Point shortcut, 46
anchor points, 23, 46, 61–62
Angle Control, 332
Angle of View data, 275
angle variable, 341
animated vector masks, 81

animation
 adding decay to, 54
 anchor point, 61
 basic, 48–50
 beat detector, 341–344
 Bézier handles and, 215
 camera, 285–288
 copying/pasting, 57
 deformation, 226–227
 following exact path, 56
 keyframe, 226
 masks, 99, 212, 215, 217
 paths, 52, 56
 presets, 33
 primary vs. secondary, 422
 in real time, 226
 reversing, 54, 61
 scaling, 54, 57
 speed, 50
 stop motion effect, 322–324
 time delays, 316–318
 triggering at markers, 322
animation path, 52
anti-aliasing, 282
aperture, 303, 370, 375
application window, 4–5
applications
 memory management and, 132
 QuickTime and, 358
 text editors, 130, 131, 257
arguments, 254
arithmetic operators, 316
arrays, 326–328, 335, 337–338, 340
arrow keys, 214
Artbeats, xxv
articulated mattes, 213–216
artifacts, 20, 21, 301, 302–305
Ask User dialog, 89
aspect ratio, 302
asterisk (*), 43
attributes, expressions, 315, 318
audio, 16, 314–316
audio levels, 314, 325–327, 341–344
Audio Levels expression, 325, 326, 328

Audio Settings option, 16
audio tracks, 314–316
audio triggers effect, 341–344
"Auto" correctors, 147
Auto Levels effect, 147
Auto Select Graph Type, 50
Auto setting, 24
Automatic Bezier option, 56
auto-orientation, 285–286
Auto-Save command, 15
auto-tracing masks, 81
AV Features tool, 41

B

background renders, 126–129
background swatches, 232
backgrounds
 blue, 176, 184–193, 412
 blurring, 205–206
 color, 30, 176, 203
 gradients, 30–31
 green, 176, 184–193
 holdout mattes for, 187, 197
 matching/creating
  environments, 408–410
 multiplying into edge
  pixels, 87–89
 previews, 30–32
 using with mattes, 177
backlighting, 156, 390–392
backslash (\) key, 46
backups, 12
banding, 150, 349, 360, 377
Beam effect, 336–337
Beam layer, 336–337
beamPos variable, 336
beat detector, 341–344
Best quality, 70, 126
Bézier handles, 51, 93, 213–216, 418
Bézier masks, 93
Bézier shapes, 56, 215
Bézier splines, 256
BG Renderer, 126
Bias settings, 195, 196
bit-depth identifier, 150
bitmap selection channel, 84
bitmapped edges, 84
black and white levels, 138

black levels, 141–142, 165
black pixels, 102
Black Point control, 180
Black Softness control, 180
black-and-white images, 387–388
blacks
 crushed, 147–148
 current displays and, 148
 flashing, 409
 low levels of, 148
blending colors, 377–378
blending frames, 69–70, 118
blending modes
 Add, 101–103
 Alpha Add, 98
 compositing with, 100–106
 described, 82, 100–101
 Difference, 104
 Hard Light, 104
 Hue, Saturation, and
  Brightness, 105
 Light, 104
 Linear, 104
 Linear Dodge, 101
 Luminescent Premultiply, 106
 Multiply, 103
 Overlay, 104
 Screen, 101–103
 Silhouette Alpha, 105
 Stencil Alpha, 105, 190, 391
 Vivid Light, 104
Block Size setting, 74
blown-out whites, 148
blue channel, 180
blue screens, 184–193, 412
blue-screen keys, 184–193
blueScrn_mcu_
 HD.movfootage, 187
blur. *See also* motion blur
 backgrounds, 205–206
 boke, 275, 290–292
 Box Blur, 395
 Compound Blur, 416, 421, 443
 Fast Blur, 371–372, 391, 395
 foregrounds, 205–206
 Gaussian Blur, 395

blur (*continued*)

Lens Blur effect, 294–295

simulating camera blur, 290–292

three-way blur, 395

Blur Before Difference setting, 183

boke blur, 275, 290–292

book, organization of, xii–xxii

Both Channels slider, 315

Boujou, 42, 264

Box Blur, 395

brackets [ ], 45

break statement, 343

Bridge, 9

brightness

adjusting with Add mode, 101–103

adjusting with Brightness control, 139–140

adjusting with Curves, 150–157

adjusting with Levels, 146

adjusting with Screen mode, 101–103

color, 105

foregrounds, 101

gamma adjustments, 142–143

HSB mode, 105

Brightness & Contrast effect, 139–140

Brightness control, 139–140

Brightness mode, 105

Brush Dynamics settings, 230

Brush Tips panel, 229, 230, 232

Brush tool, 229

brush-based tools, 229, 230–232

brushes

adding, 232

adjusting on Brush Tips panel, 229

adjusting size, 231

After Effects vs. Photoshop, 229

clone, 229, 231

defining on the fly, 231

deleting, 232

hardness, 231

Liquify effect, 419–420

preset, 230

renaming, 232

scaling, 231

Build From One Image setting, 74

bullet hits, 431, 434–435, 438

C

cache. *See also* memory

disk, 29–30

RAM, 29–30, 213

camera, 271–308

3D. *See* 3D camera

animating, 285–288

from comp space to layer surface, 336–337

coordinate system, 329

expression controls and, 329

fading as moving away from, 336

fading as turning away from, 339–341

flat representation of, 329

lens blur, 290–295

lens settings, 271–273

mixing 2D/3D effects, 280–281

projection, 288–290

push, 274, 286–288

real camera emulation, 274–280

real camera settings, 273–274

reducing saturation away from, 333–334

simulating camera blur, 290–295

single-node/targeted, 266

stabilizing moving camera, 252–254

storytelling with, 284–290

as tracking tool, 249–251

Unified Camera Tool, 285

virtual compared to real, 271

working with grain, 295–301

camera report, 275–276

Camera Settings dialog, 271

camera shots

reviewing, 37

stabilizing moving shots, 252–254

studying, 37

camera shutter, 64, 65

Caps Lock, 26, 27, 222

CC Light Burst Effect, 331

CC Light Rays effect, 395–396

CC Particle Systems II, 330

central processor unit (CPU), 28

Channel Combiner, 199–200

channels

alpha. *See* alpha channels

bitmap selection, 84

blue, 180

color, 32, 144–145

green, 166, 180, 208

matte, 73

red, 180

transparency, 80

Checkbox Control, 332

child layers, 61, 62–63, 329–331

Choke Matte setting, 190–191

choking, 190–192, 205

chroma sampling, 198

chromatic abberation, 304–305

CIN format, 22

Cinema 4D software, 266

Cineon files, 360–362, 365–366, 378

Cineon log space, 364–367

clean plate, 137, 182

Clip Black setting, 190, 191, 193

Clip controls, 197

Clip Rollback, 297

Clip values, 197

Clip White setting, 190, 191, 193

clipping, 138, 148

clips

animating timing of, 72

cloning from, 233

duration, 69

source, 69, 386

speed, 72

clone brushes, 229, 231
Clone Stamp, 229
clones/cloning, 229, 231, 232–235
clouds, 413–418, 423
Collapse Transformations toggle, 117, 118, 281
collapsed layers, 118, 281
collapsed transforms, 117, 118
Collect Files command, 13–14
Collect Source Files menu, 13
color
    8-bit, 150, 349
    16-bit, 148, 150, 349
    32-bit, 374–378
    background, 30, 203
    balancing, 388, 390
    blending, 377–378
    brightness, 105
    calibration, 350–351
    color-coding layers, 42–43
    converting to black and white, 387–388
    desaturated, 208
    effect on cinematography, 302, 307, 386
    expressed as percentages, 167
    in expressions, 337–338
    foreground, 203
    hue, 105, 157–159, 387
    light, 398–399
    masks, 95, 96, 214
    matching. See color matching
    removing color matting, 90
    RGB, 179–180, 196, 349, 353
    saturation, 105, 157–159, 387–388
    sRGB, 352
    user interface, 129
color channels, 32, 144–145
Color Control, 332
color conversion, 337–338
color correction, 135–174
    applying via adjustment layers, 159
    channels, 144–145

Color Finesse, 159–160
color matching, 144–145
gamma, 142–143
overview, 136–137
three-way color corrector, 160
tools/techniques, 159–160
color depth, 16, 150, 349
Color Finesse, 159–160
Color Key, 179
color keying, 175–209
    best practices, 176–178
    blue-screen, 184–193
    chroma subsampling, 198
    color spills, 207–208
    difference mattes, 182–183
    edge selection, 205–206
    Extract tool for, 179–180
    green-screen, 184–193
    Linear Color Key effect, 180–182
    matte holes, 191, 206–207
    on-set effects, 202–204
    optimizing Keylight, 193–201
    overview, 176
    steps for, 184–188
    tips for creating mattes, 176–178
color management, 347–359
    bypassing, 359
    disabled by default, 348, 351
    display management, 354–357
    enabling, 350–351, 352
    features, 347–350
    input profile, 354–357
    monitor calibration, 350–351
    output profile, 357–358
    output simulation, 354–357
    overview, 346, 347–350
    project working space, 351–353
    QuickTime, 9, 37, 358
Color Management tab, 36
color matching, 161–174
    basic technique, 162–173
    channels for, 144–145

direction, 172–173
dramatic lighting, 167–171
gamma slamming, 173–174
ordinary lighting, 162–166
overview, 161
position, 172–173
scenes with no clear reference, 170–171
color mismatch, 167
Color modes, 105
Color Profile Converter effect, 357
color profiles, 351, 352, 357, 378
color quantization, 349
color range, 100, 208
color sampling, 337–338
Color Settings option, 16
color spaces
    defining, 350
    encoding vs. compositing, 367, 370
    HSLA, 337, 338
    linear, 370, 378
    log, 361–362, 366, 367
    monitor, 361, 373
    RGBA, 337, 338
    toggling between, 374
    YUV, 198, 199–200
color spills, 178, 200, 207–208
color timing, 161, 389–390
color wheels, 160
Colorista plug-in, xxiv, 160, 389
comment designator (//), 343
comments in Timeline, 42–43
Comp Marker Bin, 46
comp markers, 43, 46
Comp Markers option, 43
comp space, 329
Compander effect, 376–377
compositing
    with blending modes, 100–106
    color spaces, 367
    key steps for, xii
    multipass, 399–403
    optical, 100
    overview, 83
compositing formula, 83

Composition panel, 6
Composition section, 34
Composition settings, 119
Composition viewer, 11, 46,
    55, 114
compositions. *See* comps
Compound Blur, 416, 421, 443
Compress-Expand Dynamic
    Range preset, 377
compression
    lossless, 22, 36
    lossy, 22
    LZW, 22, 36
    QuickTime, 36
comps
    2D, 123, 422
    3D, 399–403
    analyzing with Miniflow
        tool, 59
    color-coding, 42–43
    creating, 24
    embedded, 119
    finding in Project panel,
        114–115
    importing PSD files as, 23
    length, 45
    locking, 114
    master, 112, 113, 123
    multiple, 110–119
    naming, 113
    nested, 59, 70–71, 116–119
    numbering, 111
    order, 113
    parenthesized, 118
    placing in Render Queue,
        33
    settings, 14
    subcompositions, 119, 123
    switching to layer surface,
        336–337
    timing, 117
    trimming duration to work
        area, 45
concatenation, 119
Confidence graphs, 355
Confidence settings, 244–245
Consolidate All Footage
    command, 14–15
Constant mode, 231

context-clicking, 11
continue loop, 262–263
Continue Tracking option, 244
contrast
    adjusting with Curves,
        152–157
    adjusting with Input/
        Output levels, 138–142
    adjusting with Levels, 146,
        148
    input/output levels,
        138–142
Contrast value, 139–140
Convert Vertex tool, 93
coordinate systems, 328–330
coplaner 3D layers, 288
Copy Image, xxiv, 469
copying
    animations, 57
    expressions, 313
    keyframes, 57
    masks, 99
    properties, 57
core mattes, 192, 206
Corner Pin effect, 331–333
Corner Pin tracking, 242,
    255–261
Correct Luminance Changes
    setting, 74
Correspondence Points
    (Reshape tool), 222
CPU (central processor unit),
    28
CRT monitor, 148
crushed blacks, 147–148
CRW format, 22
Current Time Indicator, 46,
    57, 60
Curves, 150–157
    adjusting brightness,
        150–157
    adjusting contrast, 152–157
    adjusting gamma, 143, 150,
        152–157
    adjusting gradients, 153
    drawbacks, 150–151
    gamma slamming, 173–174
    S-curve adjustment, 156
    single point adjustments in,
        154, 156–157

uses for, 150
    vs. Levels, 150–151
curves, logarithmic, 366–367
Custom Output Simulation
    dialog, 355–356
Cycle Mask Colors option, 95,
    96, 214
cyclorama, 202

D

Darken mode, 96, 97
day-for-night effect, 388–389
daylight scene, 162–166
Deactivate Live Update toggle,
    26
decay, 54
decay variable, 344
decaying oscillation, 343–344
decimal values, 370
decrement operator (–), 322
decrement/increment method,
    44
Default Spatial Interpolation to
    Linear option, 48
deformation animations,
    226–227
delay variable, 317, 318
deleting
    brushes, 232
    expressions, 313
    items from projects, 14, 15
    keyframes, 60
    points, 93, 217
delta, 197
demos, on DVD, xxiv
density, 96–97
depth, infinite, 413
depth cues, 407, 408, 409
depth map, 410
depth of field, 274, 290–292,
    294
Despill Bias, 189, 196
Despot cleanup tools, 199–200
difference mattes, 182–183
Difference mode, 95, 104, 233
diffraction effect, 416
digital film, 365–367
Directional Blur setting, 67
disk cache, 29–30

displacement map, 440–441

display. *See also* monitors;
screen
black detail and, 148
multiple, 7
resolution, 25
settings, 25–26, 129
setup, 7

Display Style option, 16

dist variable, 334

distortion
heat, 439–442
lens, 275, 276–280
Liquify effect, 419–420
Mesh Warp effect, 418–419
with Reshape, 219–224

dividers, 5

docking zones, 6–7

dot(), 340

dot notation, 315

dot product, 340

double-matte method, 197

downsampling, 24

DPX format, 22, 360–362, 378

Draft quality, 24, 70, 125

drawing
masks, 91–92, 99, 214, 216
points, 216

drop zones, 6

duration
layers, 69
source clips, 69
trimming to Work Area, 45

Duration setting, 231

dust busting, 235

dust removal, 235

DV format, 348, 354

DVCPRO HD format, 198

DVCPRO50 format, 198

DVD, included with book,
xxiv–xxv

dynamic range, 362–364
Cineon files, 360, 365
Compress-Expand Dynamic
Range preset, 377
low, 370, 373
on monitor, 347
overview, 362–363

E

ease(), 334, 336, 341

easeIn(), 335

easeOut(), 335

Easy Ease functions, 50–52

Edge Feather control, 179

edge mattes
creating for edge selection,
205–206
protecting edge detail with,
177

edge multiplication, 87–88, 89

Edge Thin control, 179

edges
bitmapped, 84
feathered, 84, 179
finding, 205
fringing in, 90
refining, 187

Edit Original command, 12

editing
anchor points, 61
Boot.ini file, 132
expressions, 313
masks, 214, 217
preferences, 131
temporal edits, 233

E/EE keyboard shortcuts, 58

effects. *See also* filters; *specific
effects*
accessing in Effects &
Presets panel, 33
animation presets, 33
applying to layers, 33
audio triggers, 341–344
described, 33, 83
energy, 435–439
explosions, 430, 431,
446–447
firearms, 430–435
Glow, 121
heat distortion, 439–442
incompatible, 376–377
in layers, 123
linking to properties,
314–316
resetting, 140
smoke, 103
study of, 37

Effects & Presets panel, 33

Effects Controls panel, 6

effects plug-ins, 33

elements
context-clicking, 11
duplicating, 45
grouping, 111
renaming, 41
rotating, 422–423
showing in layers, 54

else clause, 323

Enable Disk Cache option,
29–30

Enable Motion Blur toggle,
67, 72

Enable OpenGL toggle, 27

encoding color spaces, 366–367

End key, 43, 44

energy effects, 435–439

environment
creating, 408–410
matching, 408

environment reference, 204

Eraser tool, 229

Erodilation plug-in, xxiv, 205,
469

Error Threshold setting, 74

errors
expressions, 11, 313
premultiplication, 90
rendering, 122
rounding, 288
write-errors, 37

Excel, 57

Excel spreadsheets, 57

Expansion property, 227

explosions, 430, 431, 446–447

Exposé feature, 50

exposure, 275, 375–376

Exposure control, 370, 375–376

Expression Controls, 332

Expression menu, 312, 313

expressions, 309–344
attributes, 315, 318
audio triggers effect,
341–344
color in, 337–338
coordinate systems, 328–330
copying, 313
creating, 312–313

expressions *(continued)*
    default, 312
    deleting, 313
    disabling, 313
    editing, 313
    effects tracks parented
        layers, 330–331
    enable/disable toggle, 312,
        313
    errors, 11, 313
    exposing, 313
    fades, 336, 339–341
    Graph Editor toggle, 312
    inserting text, 312
    jittery motion, 324
    keyframes and, 311, 314
    layer index, 316–318
    layer space transforms,
        328–337
    limitations, 311
    linking effects to properties,
        314–316
    links, 314–316
    looping keyframes, 318–320
    markers in, 320–324
    methods, 316
    overview, 310–311
    pasting, 313
    pasting text, 312
    pickwhip, 312, 315, 332
    properties, 315
    reducing layer saturation,
        333–335
    resources for, 344
    Rotation, 318
    text layer formatting and,
        311
    time in, 327–328
    time remapping, 324–328
    using tracking with,
        261–263
    values, 311
    vectors, 340
    wiggle effect, 325–327
EXR format, 22, 374, 376
EXR images, 403
Extensible Markup Language
    (XML), 131–132
extensions, 12

Extract tool, 179–180
Extrapolate Motion option,
    244–245
eyedropper tool, 188

F

fades, 336, 339–341
Fast Blur, 371–372, 391, 395
feathered mattes, 98
feathering
    alpha selections, 84–86
    edges, 84, 179
    masks, 92
feathering effect, 217
.ffx file suffix, xxiv
Field Of View (FOV), 314–315
fields, interlacing, 19–20
file extensions, 12
files
    Cineon, 360–362, 365–366,
        378
    collecting for footage,
        13–14
    floating point, 363, 373, 376
    missing, 12
    naming conventions, 36
    PSD, 23
    QuickTime, 37
    RPF, 403, 410
    source, 11–15
fills, 94
film
    Cineon and, 360
    digital, 365–367
    exposure to light, 367
Film Fix, xxiv
film formats, 306–307
Filtering setting, 74
filters, 386–389
final output, 36, 112
final renders, 46
Find Edges, 205
Find Missing Footage option,
    12
finding items
    comps, 114–115
    effects, 33
    footage, 12
    keyframes, 58

missing items, 12
    presets, 33
    in Project panel, 114–115
    text strings, 12
    unused source, 12
    used source, 12
fire, 442–446. *See also* smoke
firearms, 430–435
First Vertex, 93, 100, 214, 224
flag of Mars, 387
Flame, 70
flares, 275, 392–394
Fleischer, Max, 212
floating panels, 7
floating point files, 363, 373,
    376
floating point TIFF format, 376
Flowchart view, 59, 113
fog, 413–417
folders
    grouping elements with,
        111
    organizing projects with, 14,
        111–112
    source, 112
    watch, 128
footage. *See also* camera shots
    24 fps vs. 29.97 fps, 305
    collecting files for, 13–14
    consolidating, 13–15
    HD. *See* HD footage
    HDTV, 353, 368
    importing into After Effects,
        8–11
    importing still sequences
        for, 19
    importing with
        premultiplied images,
        87–88
    information about, 19
    interpretation of, 17–21,
        87–90
    missing, 11–12
    plate, 24
    raw, 33–36
    reloading, 11–12
    removing unused, 14, 15
    rendering, 33–36
    replacing, 11

searching for, 12
sequences for, 19
source, 11, 14, 17, 22–24, 23, 112
Force Alphabetical Order option, 10
foreground swatches, 232
foregrounds
blurring, 205–206
brightness, 101
color, 203
matching/creating environments, 408–410
mattes with, 177
rotoscoping features in, 187
formats. *See also specific formats*
film, 306–307
non-square pixel, 19, 20–21
raster image, 22
source, 18–19
source footage, 22–24
video, 306–307
virtual cinematography, 305
FOV (Field Of View), 314–315
FOV parameter, 314–315
Fractal Noise effect, 104, 414–416
fractal noise patterns, 104
frame blending, 69–70, 72, 118
Frame Mix mode, 70
frame rates
adjusting, 18–21, 68–69
maintaining, 119
misinterpreted, 18–19
QuickTime, 19
speed and, 305–306
FrameCycler, 37
frames
adding eases to, 50–52
averaging, 69–70
bad, 8, 19
cloned, 232, 233
creating new images from, 69–70
display of, 16, 17
effect of time measurement on, 68–69
filling with layers, 46
freezing, 69, 71

keyframes between, 54
missing, 10
from multiple sequences, 9
navigation, 43–44, 46
overlays, 70
overwriting, 19
playing only frames with markers, 322–324
selecting multiple, 9
skipping, 24–25
snapping to, 54
subsets, 9
Frames Per Second setting, 19
framesToTime(), 343
Free Transform mode, 92
Freeze Frame option, 69, 71, 183
freq variable, 344
frequency parameter, 325–326
fringing, 18, 88, 90, 200
From Current Time option, 30
fromCompToSurface(), 336, 337
Full Screen option, 30
full-screen mode, 7, 30
Furnace plug-ins, 70, 72
fxphd.com site, xxv

G
gamma
1.0 Gamma toggle, 349, 362, 377–378
adjusting with Curves, 143, 150, 152–157
adjusting with Levels, 142–143, 146
described, 143
monitors, 368–369
QuickTime, 348–349, 358
spiking and, 148
video gamma space, 368–369
gamma boost, 143
Gamma control, 142–143
gamma slamming, 173–174
gamut, 353
garbage mattes, 81, 185, 190, 191, 206
Gaussian Blur, 395
gaussRandom(), 328

glints, 393, 394
Global Smoothness setting, 74
Glow effect, 121
gradients
adjusting with Curves, 152, 153, 155
backgrounds, 30–31
banding in, 150
black to white, 138–139
Ramp, 144
grain, 295–301
management of, 295–301
noise as, 299
removal of, 299–300
graininess, 183, 189
Graph Editor, 47–56
animation in, 48–57
Confidence graphs, 244
controlling keyframes in, 47–56
controls, 47–48
copying/pasting animations, 57
Easy Ease functions, 50–52
enabling, 47–48
expressions, 312
Graph Options menu, 50
Graph View, 48–57
Hold keyframes, 55
Show Properties menu, 48
Transform Box, 54
U/UU shortcuts, 58–59
vs. Layer view, 57–58
Graph Options menu, 50
Graph View, 48–57
gray card, 369
gray matching, 162
grayscale alpha channels, 107
grayscale gradient, 138
grayscale ramp, 369
grayscale transparency channel, 146
green channel, 166, 180, 208
green screen keys, 184–193
green screens, 179, 184–193
Gridiron Flow, 14
grids, 30, 31, 265
Grids & Guides preferences, 31
grouping zones, 7

Grow Bounds effect, 118
Guess button, 18, 87, 89
guide layers, 30–31, 119, 121–122
guides, 31
guns, 430–435

H

hack shortcuts, 130–131
halation, 275
halos, 98, 391, 394, 395
Hand tool, 25
handles, Bézier, 51, 93, 213–216, 418
Hard Light mode, 104
HD display, 353
HD footage
    examples, xxv
    multiprocessing and, 24
    pixel aspect ratio and, 21
    resolution, 24
HD format, 276, 306–307
HDR (high dynamic range)
    described, 346
    linear floating-point HDR, 369–378
    linearized working space, 373, 377
    Merge to HDR function, 204, 364
    source, 373–383
HDR Compander, 376–377
HDR images, 204, 363–364
HDR pipeline, 374, 376, 377
HDTV footage, 353, 368
HDTV profile, 353
HDTV standard, 306–307
HDV format, 198, 273
headroom, 148
heat distortion, 439–442
Help menu, 314
hero shots, 161
Hide Layer Controls command, 32
high-contrast mattes, 79, 179–184, 212
highlights
    color matching, 164–166
    gamma slamming and, 173–174

raised gamma, 153
histograms
    Extract tool, 179–180
    gamma adjustments and, 143
    Levels, 138, 145–150
    problem solving with, 148–150
Hold keyframes, 55, 71
Hold option, 56
holdout masks, 201, 259
holdout mattes, 186, 187, 201
Home key, 43, 44
HSB mode, 105
HSLA array, 338
HSLA (hue, saturation, lightness, and alpha) color space, 337, 338
hue, 105, 157–159, 387
hue, saturation, lightness, and alpha (HSLA) color space, 337, 338
Hue mode, 105
Hue/Saturation control, 157–159, 206–208, 387, 388
hue-shift, 207, 208

I

idx variable, 323–324
if statement, 321, 323
Image Lounge, xxiv
image pipeline, 14
image planes, 291–292
image sequences, 8–9
images
    8-bit, 349, 363
    32-bit, 373, 374–378
    black-and-white, 287–388
    downsampling, 24
    EXR, 403
    HDR, 204, 363–364
    importing, 89
    layering over opaque background, 86–87
    morphing, 219–225
    panning around, 61
    plate, 137
    RGB, 179–180
    sharpening, 299, 301
    still, 19

virtual, 83
Import & Replace Usage option, 124
Import dialog, 9, 12
Import option, 124
importing
    3D models, 282–284
    3D tracking data, 263–268
    with alpha channels, 87–88, 89
    alpha channels and, 18
    footage into After Effects, 8–11
    footage with premultiplied images, 87–88
    images, 90
    Maya scenes for 3D tracking, 265–268
    preferences for, 89
    PSD files as compositions, 23
    sequences, 8–10, 119
    source files, 8, 9–10
    still sequences for moving footage, 19
Increment and Save command, 15
increment/decrement method, 44
index attribute, 316–318, 320
infinite depth, 413
Info palette, 37, 164
Info panel, 188
In/Out points, 44, 45, 69, 335
Input Black controls, 138–142
input profile, 354–357
Input White controls, 138–142
Instant HD tool, xxiv
interlaced fields, 19–20
interpolation, 48, 222, 334–335
Interpret Footage dialog, 17–21, 87–90
interpretation rules, 355
Intersect mode, 95
inverse square law, 385
Invert effect, 140
Invert Selection, 45
inverted layers, 45, 96–98
Inverted toggle, 95

J

J key, 60
JavaScript
  arithmetic operators, 316
  arrays, 326–328, 335,
    337–338, 340
  comments, 343
  decrement operator, 322
  described, 314
  if statement, 321, 323
  resources, xxiv
  variables, 317
jitter, 324
JPEG format, 22

K

K key, 60
Keep Colors option, 182
Key Colors setting, 182
Key Correct Pro, xxiv
Key Correct tools, 206–207
keyboard shortcuts. See also
  shortcuts
  brush tools, 231, 232
  context-clicking, 11
  display resolution/size, 25
  E/EE, 58
  J key, 60
  K key, 60
  keyframe navigation, 60
  layers, 45–46
  maximizing screen, 7
  RAM previews, 30
  Timeline, 43–46
  Timeline navigation, 43–44
  transforms, 46–47
  U/UU, 58–59
keyed layers, 189
KeyEd Up script, 131
Keyframe Assistant, 61, 314
keyframe transitions, 56
keyframes
  adding, 47
  animating, 226
  controlling in Graph Editor,
    47–56
  copying/pasting, 57
  deleting, 60
  deselecting, 60
  dropped, 319

effect of time measurement
  on, 68–69
expressions and, 311, 314
finding, 58
between frames, 54
hiding/showing, 32, 60
history of, 213
Hold, 55, 71
linear, 55
looping, 318–320
mask, 98–99, 217, 218
navigation, 45, 60
nudging forward/backward,
  45, 60
offsetting values of, 60–61
Opacity, 222
roving, 56
selecting, 60
selecting multiple, 60
setting, 60
shortcuts, 60
Time Remap, 71, 72
keying. See color keying
Keylight, 188–201
  basic steps, 184–188
  Bias settings, 195, 196
  blue/green screens,
    184–193
  choking, 190–192, 200, 205
  clean-up tools, 197–201
  decision-making
    comparisons, 194
  fringing, 200
  noise suppression, 198–200
  optimizing, 193–201
  Preblur option, 198–200
  Screen Balance, 189, 195,
    196
  Screen Gain, 189, 195
  screen matte generation,
    194–201
  spill suppression in, 200–201
  three-pass method, 190–193
  tips for using, 193–201
  uses for, 184
  vs. Primatte Keyer, 209
Keys tool, 41
Knoll Light Factory, xxiv, 303,
  393

Knoll Light Factory Unmult,
  469
Kodak 5218 profile, 355
Kronos tool, 72, 235

L

Label Defaults command, 42
laptop computers, 43
Layer Controls, 32, 332
layer markers, 43
Layer Markers option, 43
Layer menu, 11
layer space transforms,
  328–337
Layer Switches tool, 41
Layer view, 57–58
layers
  2D, 122, 123, 331–333
  3D. See 3D layers
  adding at specific time, 44
  adding tags to, 42–43
  adding to composition, 45
  adjustment, 119–121, 159
  aligning, 104, 233
  applying motion tracks to,
    218
  applying presets to, 33
  Beam, 336–337
  centering, 46
  child, 61, 62–63, 329–331
  collapsed, 118, 281
  color-coding, 42–43
  context-clicking, 11
  coplaner 3D, 288
  duplicating, 45
  duration, 69
  effects within, 123
  filling frames with, 46
  guide, 30–31, 119, 121–122
  hiding/showing, 42
  index attribute, 316–318
  inverted, 45, 96–98
  keyboard shortcuts for,
    45–46
  keyed, 189
  length, 45
  Live 3D, 23
  locked, 42
  mattes, 42, 98

layers *(continued)*
    moving up/down in stack, 45
    nudging forward/backward in time, 45
    null, 42
    offset, 63
    opacity, 86–87, 325–328
    order of, 44, 104, 108
    parent, 62–63, 329–331
    parenting to single layer, 61
    Photoshop, 22, 23
    pixel, 120
    precomping, 113, 116–117
    properties, 122
    reducing saturation, 333–335
    replacing, 45
    selecting, 45
    Shape, 91, 94, 121
    showing items in, 54
    shy, 42
    soloing, 42
    speed, 48
    splitting, 45
    target, 99
    timing, 117
    transform properties, 46–47
    unlocking, 42
    using as lens filters, 386–389
Layer/Source tool, 41
length(), 334
lens angle, 274
lens artifacts, 301, 302–305
Lens Blur effect, 294–295
lens distortion, 275, 276–280
lens filters, 386–389
Lens Flare effect, 336
lens flares, 302–303, 336, 392–394
lens settings, 271–273
Lenscare, xxiv, 294, 468
lesson files, installing, xxiv
Levels, 137–160
    adjusting gamma with, 142–143, 146
    bracketing Input levels, 147–148
    contrast adjustment with, 138–142

    histograms, 145–150
    overview, 137
    resetting, 140
    vs. Curves, 150–151
Levels (Individual Controls) control, 144
light, 381–403
    adding full-color tint for film, 386–388
    adjusting color with no clear reference, 170–171
    backlighting, 156, 390–392
    CC Light Rays effect, 395–396
    color, 398–399
    color keying and, 203
    color timing effects, 389–390
    day-for-night effect, 388–389
    daylight, 162–166
    diffuse, 203
    dramatic, 167–171
    exposure to film, 367
    flares, 392–394
    glints, 393, 394
    God rays, 394–396
    halos, 98, 391, 394, 395
    hard vs. soft, 383
    hotspots, 384–385
    indirect, 399, 400, 401
    inverse square law, 385
    light wrap, 390–392
    location/quality of, 383
    multipass 3D compositing, 399–403
    neutralizing direction of, 384–385
    ordinary, 162–166
    reflected, 393–394, 399–403
    scattered, 394–396
    shadows and, 383, 384, 396–399
    source/direction of, 382–385
    volumetric, 394–396
Light mode, 104
light sources, 390–399
Lighten mode, 96, 97
Lightning effect, 435, 438–439
linear(), 334–335

linear blending, 349, 373, 377–378
Linear Color Key, 179, 180–182
linear floating-point HDR, 369–378
linear keyers, 179–184
linear keyframes, 55
linear keys, 179–184
Linear mode, 104
Linear option, 56
linear pixels, 370
linearized working space, 101–102, 103, 373, 377
links, 314–316
Liquify effect, 419–420
Live 3D layers, 23, 28
Live Update, 26, 27
LME (Local Motion Estimation) technology, 73
Local Motion Estimation (LME) technology, 73
Local Smoothness setting, 74
Lock icon, 114
Lock Source Time, 233
locking
    comps, 114
    layers, 42
    masks, 96, 214
log color space, 361–362, 366, 367
logarithmic curve, 366–367
loopIn(), 318–319
loopInDuration(), 320
looping
    continue loop, 262–263
    keyframes, 318–320
    previews, 30, 37
    while() loop, 343
loopOut(), 318–319
loopOutDuration(), 320
lossless compression, 22, 36
lossless output, 36
lossy compression, 22
low-loss output, 36
Luma Inverted Matte option, 107
Luma Key, 179–180
Luma Matte option, 107
luma mattes, 107, 180, 183–184
luminance, 179

Luminescent Premultiply mode, 106
LZW compression, 22, 36

M

Mac OS–based systems
  F9 key caution, 50
  forcing a crash, 132
  incompatible formats, 12
  memory and, 132
  rendering and, 126, 128, 130–131
macros, xxiii. *See also* scripts
Magic Bullet Colorista, xxiv, 160, 389, 469
Magic Bullet Looks, 159–160, 469
magnification settings, 24
Make Template option, 36
markers
  comp, 43, 46
  in expressions, 320–324
  layer, 43
  playing only frames with markers, 322–324
  replacing numbers with names, 46
  snapping to, 54
  triggering animation with, 322
Mask Color swatch, 96
Mask Expansion option, 92
Mask Feather property, 92
Mask Interpolation command, 100
mask keyframes, 98–99, 217, 218
Mask Opacity property, 95–96
Mask Path channels, 99
Mask Path keyframes, 99
Mask Path properties, 99
Mask Path stopwatch, 218
mask paths, 92, 93, 99
Mask Shape dialog, 92
Mask Shape tool, 91–92
mask shapes, 91–92, 216, 218
mask tracking, 217, 218, 247–248
mask vertices, 215, 311

masking motion blur, 218–219
masks, 91–100
  adding to images, 95
  animated, 81, 99, 212, 215, 217
  arranging, 91
  auto-tracing, 81
  Bézier, 93
  color, 95, 96, 214
  combining selections, 95–98
  contracting, 92
  copying/pasting, 99–100
  darkening, 96, 97
  deactivating, 95
  density, 96–97
  described, 80, 91
  determining points with First Vertex, 224
  disabling, 91, 95
  drawing, 91–92, 99, 214, 216
  editing, 214, 217
  expanding, 92
  feathering, 92
  garbage matte, 81
  hiding/showing, 32, 96, 214
  holdout, 201, 259
  improving, 201–208
  lightening, 96, 97
  limitations of, 216–219
  locking, 96, 214
  masking motion blur, 218–219
  moving, 99–100
  multiple, 96, 213, 214
  names, 221
  opacity, 95–96
  organizing, 96
  overlapping, 95–98, 213, 214
  overlapping transparency, 96–98
  placing in motion, 98–100
  removing from images, 95
  roto, 187
  scaling, 92
  selections with, 80–81
  setting up to track, 217, 218
  shapes, 91–94, 214, 215, 218
  target, 99, 220, 224
  transparent, 95, 96
  vector, 81

master comps, 112, 113, 123
match moving, 268
Matching Softness setting, 180–181
Matching Tolerance eyedropper, 181
Math.abs(), 326
Math.acos(), 341
Math.cos(), 344
Math.exp(), 344
Math.floor(), 324
Math.Log(), 326, 327
Math.min(), 323
Matte Channel control, 73
matte channels, 73
Matte Choker, 205
Matte Layer control, 73
mattes
  alpha track, 99
  articulated, 213–216
  avoiding holes in, 191, 206–207
  choked, 190–192, 205
  core, 192, 206
  described, 79
  Despot cleanup tools, 199–200
  detecting flaws in, 177, 194
  difference, 182–183
  double, 197
  feathered, 98
  garbage, 81, 185, 190, 191, 206
  for green/blue screens, 184–193
  high-contrast, 79, 179–184
  holdout, 186, 187, 201
  improving, 193
  layers, 42, 98
  luma, 107, 180, 183–184
  problems with, 193–194, 204–208
  protecting edge detail, 177
  refining, 196–201
  screen, 194–201
  sharing, 107
  softening, 198
  tips for, 176–178
  track, 106–108

maxAngle variable, 339, 341
maxOffset variable, 328
Maya 3D scenes, 265–268
Media Encoder, 128–129
MediaCore, 348, 354
memory
    caching, 29–30, 213
    management of, 132
    preferences, 29
Memory & Cache, 29–30
Merge to HDR function, 204, 364
mesh, 226, 227
Mesh Warp effect, 418–419
metadata, 36
methods, expressions, 316
midtones, 162, 166
minAngle variable, 339, 341
Miniflow tool, 59, 113, 114
Minimal workspace, 5
Minimax, 204
mist, 413–417
Mocha X-splines, 256–257, 259
MochaAE, 255–261
modulo operator (%), 324
monitors. *See also* display
    color calibration, 350–351
    CRT, 148
    external broadcast, 351
    Mac vs. PC, 368
    maximizing screen, 7
    multiple, 7
    setup, 7
    video space of, 368–369
morphing, 219–225
morphing tools, 217
motion
    jittery, 324
    placing masks in, 98–100
motion blur, 64–65. *See also* blur
    2D, 65
    3D, 65
    described, 64
    edge multiplication and, 88
    masking, 218–219
    settings, 64–67
    tracking and, 248–249
motion paths
    controlling in viewer, 55
    hiding/showing, 32

motion tracking, 237–268
    2.5D tracking, 251–252
    3D camera, 250–251
    3D tracking, 263–268
    Adapt Feature option, 245
    AE camera as tracking tool, 249–251
    Confidence settings, 244–245
    continue loop, 262–263
    Continue Tracking option, 244
    Corner Pin tracking, 242, 255–261
    essentials, 239–249
    with expressions, 261–263
    Extrapolate option, 244–245
    feature region, 240, 241
    matching motion blur, 248–249
    matching multiple objects, 249–252
    MochaAE, 255–261
    nulls, 245–248
    overview, 238–239
    point tracking, 239–249
    rotation/scale data for, 242–244
    rotoscoping and, 212
    search regions, 240, 241
    setting up to track masks, 218
    smoothing moving camera, 252–254
    stabilizing moving shots, 252–254
    Stop Tracking option, 244
    subpixel motion, 244
    SynthEyes 3D, xxiv, 42, 266–268
    TrackerViz, 217, 218, 247–248
    types of tracks, 241–242
motion tracks
    applying to layers, 218
    averaging, 247
    locking, 245
    mask tracking, 247–248
    offsetting, 245

    relocating, 245
    showing in Timeline, 244
mouse, 11, 25, 214
movies, creating with Output Modules, 35–36
muliprocessing, 132
multidimensional properties, 327
multipass rendering, 399–403
Multiply mode, 103, 372
Multiprocessing option, 28
multiprocessing settings, 28–29

N

naming conventions, 36
navigation
    frames, 43–44, 46
    keyframes, 45, 60
    Timeline shortcuts, 43–44
nearestKey(), 320
negatives, film, 360, 364–365
nesting
    compositions, 59, 70–71, 116–119
    preserving resolution, 119
    time, 118–119
network rendering, 127
New Workspace command, 6
node view, 59
noise
    blurring and, 294–295
    Fractal Noise effect, 104, 414–416
    as grain, 299
    reducing with spill suppression, 201
noise suppression, 198–200
None mode, 95
non-square pixel formats, 19, 20–21
Normality tool, 403
Notepad, 130
NTSC DV format, 198
NTSC format, 305
Nuke, 70
null layers, 42
nulls, 245–248
numbers
    random, 327, 328
    version, 37

numeric keypad, 45
numLayers attribute, 326

O

offset layers, 63
offsetAngle variable, 318
online review, 36
opacity
 fades, 336, 339–341
 layers, 86–87, 325–328
 masks, 95–96
 overlapping, 86
 settings for, 86
Opacity expression, 326, 328, 334
Opacity keyframes, 222
Opacity shortcut, 47
opaque pixels, 106
OpenEXR format, 376
OpenGL options, 27
operators, JavaScript, 316
optical compositing, 100
optical flow, 70
Optics Compensation effect, 278–280
optimizing
 Keylight, 193–201
 output, 36
 pipeline, 109–132
 previews, 123–126
 projects, 129–132
 renders, 123–126
Option key, 25, 26, 47, 63
Options section, 34
orientation, 274, 285–286
Out points. *See* In/Out points
output
 final, 36, 112
 linear floating point and, 378
 lossless, 36
 low-loss, 36
 online review, 36
 optimized, 36
 simulation of, 354–357
 via Render Queue, 33–36
Output Module settings, 35–36, 88, 123–124

Output Modules, 34, 35–36
output profile, 357–358
Over Range preset, 361
overlay grids, 31
Overlay mode, 104

P

Page Up/Page Down keys, 29, 43–44
Paint panel, 229
paint strokes, 212, 230–232
Paint Workspace, 229
painting
 basics, 229–232
 guidelines for, 212
 Photoshop vs. After Effects, 229
 uses for, 212, 229
 vector paint tools, 230
Pan Behind tool, 47, 61–62
panel groups, 4–5, 7
panel tabs, 11
panels, 4–8. *See also specific panels*
Pangrazio, Mike, 44
panning, 61
PAR (Pixel Aspect Ratio), 20–21
parent layers, 62–63, 329–331
Parent tool, 41
parent-child relationships, 61, 62–63
parenthesized comp, 118
parenting layers, 61
Particle Playground, 410
particles, 415, 423, 425–427, 439–440
particulate matter, 406–410
pasting
 animations, 57
 expressions, 313
 keyframes, 57
 masks, 99, 100
 properties, 57
paths
 animating, 52, 56
 mask, 92, 93, 99
 motion. *See* motion paths
pen, stylus, 230

Pen tool, 91, 93, 216
performance, 26–27
Photo-JPEG, 36
Photoshop
 CS4 3D version, 282–284
 file format, 23
 footage, 235
 importing 3D models as 3D layers, 282–284
 layers, 22, 23
 PSD files, 23
Photoshop video, 235
pickwhip, in expressions, 312, 315, 332
pins, 226–227
pipelines
 After Effects, 8
 HDR, 374, 376, 377
 image, 14
 optimizing, 109–132
 render, 122–129
pivot points, 61
Pixel Aspect Ratio (PAR), 20–21
Pixel Corps, xxv
pixel layers, 120
Pixel Motion mode, 70, 72–73
pixels
 8-bit, 363
 16-bit, 363
 black, 102
 Cineon log encoding, 366–367
 dimensions, 117
 fringing, 200
 linear, 370
 multiplying background into edge, 87–89
 non-square formats, 19, 20–21
 opaque, 106
 preserving positions, 232
 semitransparent, 106
 square, 19, 21, 84
 threshold, 84
 tracking motion of, 70
 white, 102
plate footage, 24
plate image, 137

plug-ins
    effects, 33
    on included DVD, xxiv,
       468–469
PNG format, 22
Point Controls, 331–332, 333
point of interest, 285–286
point tracking, 239–249
points
    adding, 93
    adding to masks, 217
    animated masks, 217
    deleting, 93, 217
    drawing, 216
    moving, 93, 214
    rotating, 214
    scaling, 214
    transforming, 214
Position expression, 327
Position property, 61
Position shortcut, 47
post-effect flag parameter, 337
Posterize Time option, 70, 119
Post-Render Actions, 36
precipitation, 423–427
precomping, 113, 114, 116–117
preferences
    described, 45
    display, 129
    general, 129
    grids/guides, 31
    imports, 89
    memory, 29
    previews, 26–27, 30
    projects, 129–132
    restoring to defaults, 129
    setting, 129–132
    text, 130–131
    UI colors, 129
    undo levels, 129
premultiplication, 87–90
Pre-render option, 126
pre-rendering, 123, 124–126
Preserve Constant Vertex
  Count option, 214
Preserve Frame Rate toggle,
  119
Preserve Resolution When
  Nested toggle, 119

Preserve Underlying
  Transparency option,
  105–106
presets
    animation, 33
    brushes, 230
    clones, 233
    keyframe transitions, 56
    settings, 33
Presets folder, 33
preview settings, 30
previews, 24–32
    backgrounds, 30–32
    Draft quality and, 24
    first-pass keys, 186, 187
    looping, 30, 37
    optimizing, 123–126
    preferences, 26–27, 30
    RAM. *See* RAM previews
    speeding up, 24–25
    updating external devices
      for, 30
    video, 30
Primatte Keyer, xxiv, 209
profiles, color, 351, 352, 354,
  378
Project panel, 6, 8, 11, 111,
  114–115
Project Settings dialog, 16–17
projects. *See also* comps
    analyzing, 59
    automatically saving, 15
    backups of, 12
    combining, 13, 14
    considerations, xxiii
    consolidating, 13–15
    copying, 12
    hack shortcuts, 130–131
    moving, 13
    naming conventions, 36
    optimizing, 129–132
    preferences, 129–132
    removing items from, 14, 15
    renaming, 41
    replacing, 124
    reverting to previous, 15
    saving, 15
    settings for, 15–17
    templates, 111–112
    versions, 15, 36, 37

properties. *See also* attributes,
  expressions
    copying/pasting, 57
    layers, 122
    linking effects to, 314–316
    multidimensional, 327
    pre-expression values, 318
    selecting all keyframes for,
      60
    showing in Graph Editor, 48
ProRes 422 format, 198
proxies, 124–126
PSD files, 23. *See also* Adobe
  Photoshop
Pulldown, 20–21
Puppet tools, 225–228
push, 274, 286–288
PV Feather, xxiv, 217, 469
pyrotechnics, 430–435

Q

quality/resolution settings,
  24–26
quantization, 119, 148–150
QuickTime
    challenges, 19, 37
    color management issues, 9,
      37, 358
    frame rates, 19
    gamma, 348–349, 358
    low-loss output, 36
    write-errors, 37
QuickTime files, 37
QuickTime Player, 37

R

rack focus shots, 290–292
Radiance format, 376
`radiansToDegrees()`, 341
radiometrically linear color
  data, 373
rain, 423–427
RAM cache, 29–30, 213. *See also*
  cache; memory
RAM previews
    caching, 29–30, 213
    customizing, 30
    full-screen mode, 30
    keyboard shortcut for, 30

options for, 30
performance, 129
resolution/quality and, 24–25, 24–26
skipping frames, 24–25
specifying output device for, 30
switching to alpha channels, 194
Ramp controls, 146
Ramp effect, 30, 138–139, 146
Ramp gradient, 144
random(), 327, 328
raster image formats, 22
raw footage, 33–36
Raw tracks, 242
rd_MergeProjects.jsx script, 14
Record Options, 226
red, blue, green, and alpha (RGBA) color space, 337, 338
red channel, 180
redefinery, 468
Reduce Project command, 14
ReelSmart Motion Blur plug-in, xxiv, 68
Reference graph, 50
reflected light, 393–394, 399–403
Region of Interest (ROI), 24, 26
Reload Footage command, 12
remapping expressions, 324–328
Remove Color Matting option, 90
Remove Unused Footage command, 14, 15
Render Multiple Frame Simultaneously option, 28
render pipeline, 122–129
Render Queue, 33–36, 119
Render Queue panel, 6
render settings, 34–35
Render Settings dialog, 34–36
Render Settings section, 34–35
rendering
    3D frames, 10
    adjustment layers and, 119–121

Adobe Media Encoder, 128–129
in background, 126–129
final renders, 46
footage, 33–36
guide layers and, 119, 121–122
multipass, 399–403
network renders, 127
optimizing renders, 123–126
post-render options, 123–124
pre-renders, 123, 124–126
proxies, 124–126
raw footage, 33–36
render order, xxii, 108, 122–123
Render Queue, 33–36
settings for, 34–36
showing process of, 123
Watch Folder for, 128
Repeater, 94
Replace Footage option, 11
Reset Levels option, 140
Reshape tool, 219–224
resolution
    Auto setting, 24
    display, 25
    half, 24–25, 35
    HD footage, 24
    keyboard shortcuts, 25
    nesting and, 119
    RAM previews, 24–25
Reveal Composition in Project option, 115
Reveal Expression Errors option, 11
Reveal Layer Source in Project option, 11, 115
Revert command, 15
RGB color, 179–180, 196, 349, 353
RGB histogram, 147
RGB images, 179–180
RGB values, 349, 353, 354
RGBA (red, blue, green, and alpha) color space, 337, 338
rgbToHsl(), 337, 338

rig removal, 234, 235
ROI (Region of Interest), 24, 26
Rosco Ultimatte colors, 195
Rotate tool, 47
rotation
    camera, 285–286
    elements, 422–423
    motion tracking, 242–243
    points, 214
Rotation expression, 318
Rotation property, 318
Rotation shortcut, 47
Rotobezier shapes, 215–216
rotoscoped shapes, 251
rotoscoping, 211–236
    articulated mattes and, 213–216
    automatic, 81
    cloning and, 229, 232–235
    color keying and, 187
    complex shapes, 213
    described, 80, 212
    dust removal, 235
    guidelines for, 212
    history of, 212
    masking motion blur, 218–219
    morphing, 219–225
    Puppet tools, 225–228
    setting up to track masks, 218
    wire removal in, 234–235
    working with Rotobezier shapes, 215–216
roving keyframes, 56
RPF files, 403, 410
rulers, 31–32
Rush Render Queue, 127

S

Safe Margins, 31
sample point parameter, 337
sample radius parameter, 337
sample time parameter, 337
sampleImage(), 337, 338
Samples Per Frame setting, 65
sampleSize variable, 338
sanityCheck.exr file, 374

sanityCheck.tif file, 351, 374
saturation
    color, 105, 157–159,
        387–388
    reducing, 333–335
Saturation mode, 105
saving
    advanced options for, 15
    Auto-Save, 15
    projects, 15
Scale shortcut, 47
scaling
    animation, 54, 57
    brushes, 231
    masks, 92
    motion tracking, 241–242
    nonuniform, 35, 46
    points, 214
    proportionally, 54
    timing, 61
    Transform Box, 54
    values, 54
scene-referred color data, 383
screen. *See also* display
    full-screen mode, 7, 30
    maximizing, 7
Screen Balance control, 189,
    195, 196
Screen Colour eyedropper, 188
Screen Colour setting, 188
Screen Gain control, 189, 195
Screen Grow/Shrink control,
    200
screen matte, 194–201
Screen mode, 101–103
Screen Preblur option,
    198–200
Screen Shrink/Grow value,
    190, 191–192
Screen Softness control, 198
Screen transfer mode, 372
scripts
    background renderers,
        126–127
    hack shortcuts, 130–132
    preferences, 129
    rd_MergeProjects.jsx script,
        14
    resources on DVD, xxiv–xxv

third-party, xxv
scroll wheel, 25
S-curve adjustment, 156
SD (Standard Definition), 21
SDTV NTSC profile, 353, 355
SDTV PAL profile, 353
searches. *See* finding items
seedRandom(), 327
Select Following Keyframes
    option, 60
Select Previous Keyframes
    option, 60
Selection tool, 47, 92, 216, 232
selections, 77–108. *See
    also* blending modes;
    compositing; masks
    alpha channels, 80
    alpha channels/
        premultiplication, 87–90
    bitmap selection channel,
        84
    calculating opacity settings
        for, 86–87
    combining, 83, 95–98
    edge mattes for, 205–206
    feathered alpha, 84–86
    keyframes, 60
    layers, 45
    masks, 80–81
    mattes, 79
    transparency selections
        from effects, 84
    types of, 79–83
semicolon (;) key, 46
Separate Fields setting, 20
Sequence Footage Frames per
    Second option, 119
sequences
    advantages of, 19
    Bridge and, 9
    importing, 8–10, 119
    missing frames, 10
    for moving footage, 19
    multiple, 9
    numbering, 36, 111
    selecting frames from, 9
Set First Vertex command, 100
Set Proxy setting, 124
shadows, 396–399

cast, 396–397, 400
    color keying and, 203
    color matching, 164–165
    contact, 397–398
    techniques for creating,
        396–399
Shake, xxiii, 70, 190
Shape Effects, 94
Shape layers, 91, 94, 121
Shape Path Visibility button, 32
shapes
    Bézier, 56, 215
    complex, 213
    mask, 91–94, 214, 215, 218
    repeatable, 94
    Rotobezier, 215–216
    rotoscoped, 251
    vector, 80
sharpening images, 299, 301
Shatter effect, 447
Shift Channels, 180, 205, 299
Shift key, 46, 47, 58
shortcuts, hack, 130–131. *See
    also* keyboard shortcuts
Shortcuts file, 130
shots. *See* camera shots
Show Animated Properties
    toggle, 48
Show Channel icon, 32
Show Channel pulldown, 144
Show Graph Editor Set toggle,
    48
Show Graph Tool Tips, 53
Show Properties menu, 48
Show Reference Graph option,
    50
Show Rendering in Process
    option, 123
Show Selected Properties
    toggle, 48
Show Transform Box option,
    54
shutter, camera, 64, 65
shutter angle, 274
Shutter Angle setting, 64–67
Shutter Phase setting, 65, 67
shutter speed, 64, 65
shy layers, 42
Shy toggle, 42

Silhouette Alpha mode, 105
Silhouette blending mode, 105
Simple Choker, 190–192, 204
sine wave, 344
Single Frame mode, 231, 232
sky replacement, 410–413
slamming gamma, 173–174
Slider Control, 332
smoke, 413–421. *See also* fire;
    pyrotechnics
        from fire, 442–446
        fractal noise as, 103
        from gun, 431–432
smooth() expression, 253–254
smoothing
        curves, 254
        global, 74
        local, 74
        moving camera, 252–254
Smoothing setting, 73
Smoothness Iterations setting,
    74
Snap button, 54
snapping
        to frames, 54
        to markers, 54
snow, 423, 425, 426–427
Softness option, 183
solo layers, 42
Solo Switches option, 42
sound. *See* audio
source clips, 69, 386
source files, 11–15
        finding, 12
        importing, 8, 9–10
        organizing, 8–11
        replacing, 11–12
        unused, 12, 14, 15
source folders, 112
source footage, 11, 14, 17,
    22–24, 112
source formats, 22–23
Source Frame mode, 72
source materials, 11–12
Source Time Shift, 233
Source tool, 41
Spacebar, 25
spatial offsets, 61–63
Speed graphs, 50

spill correction, 189
spill suppression, 189, 200–201,
    207
splitting layers, 45
spreadsheets, 57
square pixels, 19, 21, 84
squibs, 433–434
sRGB color, 352
sRGB profile, 353
Stabilize tracks, 241, 242, 245
Stamp tool, 229
Standard Definition (SD), 21
Standard workspace, 5–6
Starch tool, 227, 228
Stencil Alpha mode, 105, 190,
    391
Stencil blending mode, 105
still images, 19
stop motion effect, 322–324
Stop Tracking option, 244
stopwatch, 60
Stretch values, 69
strokes
        clone, 232, 234–235
        paint, 212, 230–232
        shapes and, 94
stylus pen, 230
subcompositions, 119, 123
subpixel motion, 244
Subtract mode, 95, 96
Switches Affect Nested Comps
    option, 118
SynthEyes, xxiv, 42, 266–268,
    468

T

tags, adding to layers, 42–43
target layers, 99
target masks, 99, 220, 224
target variable, 338
telecine conversions, 21
Telecine process, 360, 365
templates
        composition settings, 24
        Output Modules, 36
        projects, 111–112
        Render Queue, 36
text editors, 130, 131, 257
text preferences, 130–131

text reminders, 121
TextEdit, 130
TGA format, 22
three-way blur, 395
three-way color corrector, 160,
    389
threshold pixels, 84
TIFF format, 22, 36, 374
Tilde key (~), 7
time. *See also* timing
        absolute, 68–69
        current, 44, 57
        display of, 16
        in expressions, 327–328
        manipulating in Timeline,
            68–75
        nested, 118–119
        random, 327–328
time attribute, 320
time delay, 316–318
Time Indicator, 44
time navigation, 43–44
Time Remap expression, 328
Time Remap feature, 70, 71, 72
Time Remap property,
    323–324, 325
time remapping expressions,
    324–328
Time Sampling section, 34
Time Stretch tool, 41, 69, 70
timecode, 16
Timeline, 39–75
        color-coding layers/
            compositions, 42–43
        column views in, 40–43
        comments added in, 42–43
        described, 40
        keyboard shortcuts, 43–46
        motion blur, 64–65
        navigation keyboard
            shortcuts, 43–44
        spatial offsets, 61–63
        time manipulation in, 68–75
        view options for, 46
        zooming in/out, 46
Timeline panel, 6
Time-Reverse Keyframes
    option, 61
Time-Reverse Layer option, 69

timeToFrames(), 323
Timewarp feature, 72–75, 284
Timewarp setting, 67
time-wiggling effect, 324–327
timing. *See also* time
    color, 389–390
    comps, 117
    considerations, 117
    dimensions, 117
    layers, 117
    scaling, 61
Tint control, 386–388
Title/Action Safe overlays, 31
Toggle Mask button, 32
Tolerance option, 183
Tools panel, 5
track mattes, 106–108
    applying to other track
        mattes, 108, 123
    considerations, 108
    described, 106
    options for, 107
    render order, 108, 123
    transparency and, 183–184
    vs. alpha channels, 107
Tracker Controls panel, 239,
    241, 244
Tracker panel, 241–245
TrackerViz, 217, 218, 247–248
tracking. *See* motion tracking
tracks
    audio, 314–316
    motion. *See* motion tracks
    Raw, 242
    Stabilize, 241
    Transform, 241
Transfer Controls tool, 41
Transform Box, 54, 58
Transform controls, 46–47
Transform effect, 123
Transform menu, 46
Transform tracks, 241
transforms
    collapsed, 117, 118
    keyboard shortcuts, 46–47
    layer space, 328–337
    points, 214
transparency
    masks, 95, 96

overlapping, 96–98
    pixels, 106
    preserving, 105–106
    track mattes and, 183–184
transparency channel, 80
Transparency Grid icon, 30
transparency selections, 84
Trapcode Form, 468
Trapcode Horizon, 469
Trapcode Lux, 396, 469
Trapcode Particular, xxiv, 423,
    468
tree/node view, 59
Triangles, 227
trimming, 45
troubleshooting
    banding, 148–150, 349, 360,
        377
    with histograms, 148–150
    mattes, 193–194
    premultiplication errors, 90
Tuning section, 72, 73
Twixtor, 74

U

überkey, 58
Ultimatte plug-in, 195
undo levels, 129
Unified Camera Tool, 285
unit vectors, 340
Unlock All Layers command,
    42
user interface, 129, 214
User Interface Colors control,
    214
U/UU keyboard shortcuts,
    58–59
UV maps, 400

V

value(), 318
Value Graph, 50
valueAtTime(), 311, 318, 341
Vector Detail setting, 73
vector dot product, 340
vector paint tools, 230, 232
vector shapes, 80
vectors, 73–74, 340

version numbers, 36
versions, project, 15
vertex count, 214, 217
vertices, 100, 311
video formats, 306–307
video gamma space, 368–369
Video Preview settings, 30
video space, 368–373
View menu, 224
View Options command, 32
View panels, 24–32
viewers, 5, 24–32
vignettes, 303–304
virtual camera, 271
virtual cinematography
    "film/video look," 301–307
    formats/aspect ratios for,
        302, 305
    importance of color in, 302,
        307
virtual images, 83
Vivid Light mode, 104

W

Warp plug-in, 469
Warp Layer control, 73
warping tools
    Mesh Warp effect, 418–419
    Reshape, 219–224
Watch Folder option, 128
water
    precipitation, 423–427
    underwater shots, 303
weather conditions, 405–427
    fog/smoke/mist, 413–421
    lightning strikes, 435,
        438–439
    particulate matter in air,
        406–410
    precipitation, 423–427
    sky replacement, 410–413
    snow, 423, 425, 426–427
    wind, 422–423
Weighting setting, 74
while() loop, 343
white levels, 142
white pixels, 102
White Point control, 180
White Softness control, 180

whites
blown-out, 148
color matching, 165–166
wiggle(), 254, 324–327
wiggle effect, 325–327
wind, 422–423
Window menu, 5
windows, working with, 7
Windows systems
incompatible formats, 12
memory and, 132
rendering and, 126, 128,
130–131
wire removal, 234–235
Work Area, 45, 46
workflow
effects/presets, 33
features, xii–xxiii
non-destructive, 8
output with Render Queue,
33–36
streamlining, 8–15

working space
Color Management,
351–353
linearized, 101–102, 103,
373, 377
Workspace menu, 5–6
workspaces, 4–7
world coordinates, 329
world space, 329
Write On option, 231–232

X

X key, 232
XML (Extensible Markup
Language), 131–132
XMP metadata, 36
X-splines, 256–257, 259

Y

Y axis, 286
YUV format, 198, 199–200, 348,
354

Z

Z axis, 288
Z coordinate, 329
Z depth, 67, 251
Z space, 251
ZBornToy plug-in, xxiv, 403,
468
Zoom Blur setting, 67
zoom lenses, 303
zoom settings, 25–26
zooming in/out
methods for, 25–26
with mouse scroll wheel, 46
panels, 7
on Timeline, 46
vs. pushing, 274, 286–288
Zorro Layer Tagger, 42–43

What's on the DVD?

Although this book is designed not to rely on tutorials, many of the techniques described in the text can be further explored via the dozens of projects and accompanying footage and stills included on the disc. Wherever possible, HD (1920×1080) clips are incorporated; other examples use NTSC footage or stills if that is all that's required to get the point across.

Additionally, the DVD includes demos of more than a dozen plug-ins and applications. These demos are similar to the real software for everything but output, allowing you to experiment with your own footage.

▶ **Custom scripts from redefinery**. A number of custom scripts created by Jeff Almasol are included with this edition, including **Lightwrap** and **CameraProjectionSetup,** which duplicate the exact steps described to set those up (Chapters 12 and 9, respectively); the three scripts described in the appendix on the accompanying disc; and two scripts included with previous editions and updated for version CS4: **Duplink,** which creates "instance" objects, and **Merge Projects,** which integrates the structure of an imported project into the master project. More information on these is included as comments in the scripts themselves (which can be opened with any text editor).

▶ **SynthEyes** (*Andersson Technologies*) provides fully automatic, as well as user-controlled, matchmoving for single or batchprocessed shots; it's a stand-alone program that exports to After Effects.

▶ **Lenscare** (*Frischluft*) creates a more natural and beautiful lens blur than the built-in After Effects tools.

▶ **ZbornToy** (*Frischluft*) enhances what you can do with RPF format files in After Effects, including relighting a 3D render that includes a normal map in After Effects.

▶ **Trapcode Particular** (*Red Giant Software*) designs 3D particle systems that simulate air resistance, gravity, and turbulence. It provides a real-time preview, as well as controls that allow you to freeze time and manipulate a camera in the scene.

▶ **Trapcode Form** (*Red Giant Software*) is a cousin to Trapcode Particular and allows you to array particles across a mesh, so that they can hold a three dimensional shape.

- **Trapcode Horizon** (*Red Giant Software*) creates 3D-aware gradients and spherical maps, which is useful to create skies and multi-color gradients for use with a 3D camera.

- **Warp** (*Red Giant Software*) is a natural companion to Mocha for After Effects CS4 and goes far beyond the native After Effects corner pinning tools in both features and image quality.

- **Knoll Light Factory Pro** (*Red Giant Software*) includes such pre-built lighting effects as lens flares, sparkles, glows, and more. It also provides individual lens components so you can create your own custom effects.

- **Knoll Light Factory Unmult** (*Red Giant Software*) is not a demo but a full working version of a plug-in that performs one task: removing all black matting from edges and converting it to transparency.

- **Magic Bullet Colorista** (*Red Giant Software*) adds 3-way Lift/Gamma/Gain color control to After Effects, allowing you to individually style the colors of shadows, mid-tones and highlights.

- **Trapcode Lux** (*Red Giant Software*) simulates light reflection by using After Effects' built-in lights to create visible light that corresponds to your layers' lighting schemes.

- **Magic Bullet Looks** (*Red Giant Software*) is an intuitive, real-world based application that lets you dramatically change the color look of your footage.

- **ReelSmart Motion Blur** (*RE: Vision Effects*) allows you to procedurally generate motion blur for moving elements in a shot which lack it (or lack enough of it). After Effects' built-in motion blur is available only on animated elements.

- **PV Feather** (*RE: Vision Effects*) adds features long missing from After Effects and available in comparable packages such as Shake: the ability to control per-vertex (or per-spline) mask feather.

- **Twixtor** (*RE: Vision Effects*) is an alternative to After Effects' built-in Timewarp effect for optical-flow-based retiming of footage.

- **Erodilation** and **Copy Image** (*ObviousFX*) are not demos but freeware. These plug-ins allow for quick manipulation of matte data and quick production of stills, respectively.

- Also included are dozens of After Effects CS4 project files demonstrating techniques described in the book. These range from simple demonstrations of single concepts to completed shots.

- Live Action effects and location footage is included from Pixel Corps, Kontent Films, and more.